WOMEN AND PROSTITUTION

WOMEN AND PROSTITUTION

A SOCIAL HISTORY

VERN BULLOUGH AND BONNIE BULLOUGH

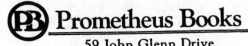

Prometheus Books

59 John Glenn Drive
Amherst, New York 14228-2119

Inquiries should be addressed to
Prometheus Books
59 John Glenn Drive
Amherst, New York 14228–2119
VOICE: 716–691–0133, ext. 210
FAX: 716–.691-0137
WWW.PROMETHEUSBOOKS.COM

Library of Congress Card Catalog No. 86-43207

ISBN 13: 978-0-87975-372-6
ISBN 10: 0-87975-372-2 (pbk. : alk. paper)

Printed in the United States of America on acid-free paper

CONTENTS

ACKNOWLEDGMENTS

This book, we hope, will encourage further investigations into the subject of prostitution, a field that until recently has been neglected or ignored by scholars and scientists. Research for this book was in part supported by the Erickson Educational Foundation. Our attitudes toward the prostitute and prostitution have changed somewhat over the years since we first began writing about it in the late 1950s and early 1960s, and this change has come about in part from our research and in part from our acquaintance with prostitutes themselves. To gather material for our book we have traveled extensively throughout the world and interviewed, observed, and researched wherever we have gone. In the process we built up a major research library dealing with prostitution, part of which is now in the university library at California State University, Northridge, and part in our own personal library. We owe a great debt to librarians in the many countries we have visited. Several typists helped prepare versions of this manuscript including Joy Thornbury, Debra Heisler, Patricia Messinger, and Diane Mann. This edition of the book would not have been possible without the encouragement of Paul Kurtz, Doris Doyle, and Victor Gulotta. Special thanks is also due to Elizabeth Darhansoff for her help in getting permission to reprint it.

INTRODUCTION

This is a book about prostitution. It is being reprinted at a time when there is increasing interest in the topic not only by law enforcement and government officials but also by feminists and the general public. What is needed and what this book does is to give an overall picture of prostitution in various eras and in different cultural settings. This is necessary not only as a foundation for ongoing studies but also for the development of public policies.

The need for better understanding by public authorities cannot be overemphasized, since most attempts to deal with prostitution seem to be based more on wishful thinking than on any solid data. Police, for example, point to court decisions which they claim have made it almost impossible to control prostitution effectively, but there is no evidence that prostitution was better controlled before such court decisions were made. Usually the police are only reacting to media pressure, since periodically the media rediscovers prostitution and, instead of trying to analyze or understand it, uses it as a symbol of all the problems associated with urban blight. The New York City media in the 1970s lamented that prostitutes had caused the decline of Times Square, while in Los Angeles, prostitutes were said to regard Hollywood as a hooker's paradise. Any person who knew these areas at first-hand, however, would have to regard prostitution as a symptom of the decline of a particular section of the city rather than as a cause of the decline. In fact, as economic conditions in these areas improved and police enforcement of existing laws was stepped up, the prostitutes went on to other areas, where the same cycle will be repeated.

Boston officials attempted to deal with prostitution by segregating it in "vice" areas, a new version of the old tolerated red-light districts, so common in this country at the turn of the century. In a sense, this system is based upon the European system, which some people erroneously call the legalization of prostitution. Germany, the Netherlands, and several other European countries have regulated prostitution; *reglementation* is the technical term. In such areas, prostitutes undergo health exams and are usually confined to certain houses or districts.

The closest approach to this in the United States is the system established by Nevada. Nevada, however, does not allow such a system in the two counties in which Las Vegas and Reno are located. Instead it is a small town affair, and most Nevada small towns have fewer people than can be found in one city block or a large urban apartment building. Cities in Nevada are also far apart, more than 50 miles, with few signs of civilization in between. Even in the small towns, the houses of prostitution are often isolated, and some of them are mere trailer colonies or motels isolated and far removed from the center of the small Nevada towns. Obviously, what is adopted in rural Nevada would not necessarily work in metropolitan Chicago.

What the segregated plan does is concentrate vice and petty crime, putting tremendous demands upon police departments. Crime has to be kept down or customers will not enter the area reserved for prostitution, and police have to use a disproportionate share of their resources to enforce the law. But the law-enforcement problems are not confined to the designated districts. Police have to be organized to arrest prostitutes not practicing in designated districts. What ultimately seems to be the case is that reglementation does not save police time or energy but creates greater problems for police.

The same case can be made against reglementation and sexually transmitted diseases. Though reglementation, at least as practiced in Europe and Nevada, involves medical inspection of the prostitute, this has never proved to be a very effective way of eliminating such diseases. Far more effective was the policy adopted by the U.S. Armed Forces during World War II, requiring the medical inspection of male clients. One reason this is more effective is that the symptoms are usually more obvious in the male. Moreover, even if a prostitute could be certified as free from the disease at any one time, she could be infected by her next client. Though the prostitute often does a visual survey of her customer, to detect gross cases of infection, and she usually douches after intercourse, such procedures will not prevent passing on infections. It is an effective commentary on the double standard in this country that there has not been more pressure exerted to have the customers of prostitutes inspected or tested.

Reglementation also raises the problem of labeling women as prostitutes. Though in a sense this might be done in nonregulated areas by arrest records for solicitation, registration is a more formal procedure and implies a choice which might or might not be real. It is important to emphasize that prostitution in American society, for the most part, is neither a lifetime occupation nor a full-time one. Why the woman should be stigmatized by such registration while her male customer is not is difficult to answer. Though we might justify such action by indicating that antique dealers, restaurant operators, and a whole host of other occupations are licensed and registered, none of these occupations have the stigma attached to them that prostitution does.

When should a person be registered as a prostitute? Officially, in those countries which have registration, there is a minimum age. But what happens to an underage promiscuous girl who is consistently picked up by police for practicing prostitution without being registered? Should she be forced to register at 13 or 16, or wait until she is 18 or whatever other age that is set? What happens in the period between the beginning of her paid sexual acts and the time of the official registration? These and similar questions addressed in this book are not satisfactorily answered by reglementation, which poses as many problems as it allegedly solves.

In the 1970s, the police in Salt Lake City started arresting customers of prostitutes. In other cities, the names of men found consorting with prostitutes when prostitutes are arrested have been published in the local paper. Neither of these actions have proved particularly effective either. For police to arrest customers of prostitutes, policewomen have to act as prostitutes, and somehow without openingly encouraging a proposition manage to be propositioned and offered money. Though many men have been arrested in such cases, judges in many jurisdictions have been reluctant to convict because of the difficulty in determining whether entrapment is involved. Arrests can only be made after prices are mentioned, but male customers become fairly sophisticated in asking about prices and if a customer does bring it up, he can argue after his arrest that he was only joking, bantering with the woman as it were. Because of the difficulty in obtaining convictions with such tactics and the hostility that both women police officers and male judges display toward such tactics, there has been difficulty in getting convictions. Perhaps for this reason newspapers in some areas took to publishing names of male customers; but, after a few threats of libel suits, many newspapers have been reluctant to continue such practices.

The problems encountered in trying these solutions (and others that are dealt with in the book) only emphasize the importance of recognizing that prostitution is not simply an issue for our time. Its existence today is not a necessary correlative of an alleged decline in moral standards or the new sexual permissiveness. Rather, prostitution is the institutionalized marketplace for the sale of sex, and though the marketplace of today differs from that of the past, and the European marketplace is different from that in Japan or Nigeria, the sex marketplace has shown a remarkable persistence in different times and cultures.

This book assumes that before we as a society can come to terms with prostitution, before we can decide what we want to do about it as a society, we have to look at the historical, cultural, psychological, sociological, and economic factors that relate to it. When we have done so, it should appear obvious that there is no one answer to the social questions raised by prostitution. Since prostitution has appeared in various guises and since what has been defined in one society as prostitution might not be so defined in another, it ought not be a surprise that even in the United States today there is considerable ambiguity about what constitutes prostitution. Several state penal codes, for example, define prostitution as the hiring out of one's body for sexual intercourse. Other states fail to stipulate that money has to be exchanged, defining prostitution only as the giving or receiving of the body for indiscriminate sexual intercourse. Sexual intercourse, per se, however, is not always necessary, and one dictionary defines prostitution as the "offering of the body to indicate lewdness for hire,"[1] a definition so broad that the girl who sells kisses at a church fundraiser could be labeled a prostitute, since what constitutes lewdness is just as unclear as what constitutes prostitution.

An even more ambiguous case is that of the sexual surrogate used by some sex therapists to help their patients overcome impotence or frigidity. These surrogates, some of whom have organized into a professional association, see their mission as helping patients achieve a more satisfactory sex life. This includes not only offering theoretical analyses of sexual dysfunction but also engaging in intercourse with their clients if it is a necessary part of the teaching-learning process. In other words, they perform sex for hire. A similar function has often been served by prostitutes in the past. Does the participation of surrogates under the sponsorship of a physician or psychologist make them paraprofessionals rather than prostitutes?

Traditionally prostitution has been defined in terms of females, but such a definition excludes the large number of male prostitutes. For this reason Havelock Ellis, a pioneer in the scientific investigation of sex, defined a prostitute as "a person who makes it a profession to gratify the lust of various persons of the opposite or the same sex."[2] This definition has the advantage of including both sexes but leaves unanswered the question as to when prostitution becomes a profession. Does a person who sells his or her body for lustful purposes a single time become a prostitute, or is he or she so labeled after ten times or after a hundred times? Saint Jerome, one of the early Christian Church Fathers, thought that a prostitute was a woman who served the urge of many, although he never bothered to define what he meant by "many," and he ignored homosexual prostitution.

Other churchmen concerned with the ambiguity inherent in Jerome's definition attempted to be more specific, but this only added to the confusion. One held that a woman could be called a prostitute if she served from forty to sixty different men, while a medieval canon lawyer, Johannes Teutonicus, suggested that to be called a prostitute a woman must have had sex with a minimum of 23,000.[3] Johannes did not take this figure altogether seriously, for elsewhere he suggests that sixty or possibly even as few as forty lovers qualified a woman as a prostitute. Another legal commentator, Thomas of Chobham, argued that a woman who was secretly promiscuous or who engaged only in long-term liaisons (although perhaps with a number of men) should not be classed as a harlot.[4] While Accursius, a contemporary, held that accepting money or other consideration was not an essential element in prostitution, even though that was normative practice.[5] In short there is a long tradition of disagreement on what makes a person a prostitute.

As far as police records are concerned, a prostitute is a person who has been charged, arrested, or convicted of prostitution, but this ignores some of the more successful prostitutes who have never been arrested. In some European countries where there is a state regulation of prostitution, a prostitute is an inscribed person, that is, a person who has been registered as a prostitute and who has no means of support other than prostitution. Parent-Duchâtelet, a nineteenth-century pioneer in the investigation of prostitution, restricted the term to those cases where "several mercenary acts of immorality have been legally established, when the woman involved is publicly notorious, when she has been caught in the act by other witnesses than her accuser or the police agent."[6] His definition excluded vast numbers of men and women classed as prostitutes by others but who were never arrested or brought to the police's attention.

Most definitions of prostitution include phrases about promiscuity, multiplicity of sexual partners, continuous sexual offenses, payment, and an element of notoriety, but no one of these factors is enough to establish a person as a prostitute. The girl who participates in premarital intercourse with her lover, even though she might have a succession of lovers, is not usually considered a prostitute, nor is the married woman who indulges in extramarital relations with her lover or lovers. The economic aspects of prostitution make sense in modern American society, where standards of value are expressed in monetary terms, but in other cultures this standard might not be relevant. At least one writer has remarked that in this respect there is only a small distinction between many wives and prostitutes, namely, that the wife has the patience to wait for her price, while the prostitute is compelled to seek her material reward almost immediately.

Many a girl has achieved a reputation as a prostitute or promiscuous person by innocently, or perhaps not so innocently, acting in such a way as to lead people to think she was promiscuous. Is the woman who enjoys the publicity of being seen with important people and who goes out with them for money but who does not engage in sex a prostitute? Even when the factors of promiscuity—the multiplicity of sexual partners, payment, and notoriety—are combined, there still might be doubt as to whether the person is a prostitute. Many would-be actresses, for example, have found that they were expected to engage in sex with producers and others, and for this they were occasionally rewarded with bit parts. As some went from casting couch to casting couch, their reputations, at least within the industry, became notorious, but only a few could really be classed as prostitutes, and a few even became noted actresses. At various times in the past, of course, *actress* and *prostitute* were more or less synonymous.

Some investigators into prostitution have argued that one of the keys to determining whether a person is or is not a prostitute is the emotional involvement and the pleasure gained. Probably most prostitutes are emotionally uninvolved with their clients and get little pleasure themselves, but this is not always the case. Unfortunately, in the past at least, many married women did not obtain sexual satisfaction from intercourse with their husbands,[7] and were actually repulsed by the sexual act, but we would not call these women prostitutes. Much nineteenth-century medical opinion asserted that God had created women indifferent to sex, and only out of need for babies or from fear that their husbands would desert them for professional prostitutes (i.e., women with a distorted sexual sense) did good women waive their own repugnance of sex and submit to the ardent embraces of the male. So great was the repugnance of "good" women to sex that their husbands were forced to perform the biological function of impregnation in as expeditious a way as possible, thus never really giving the woman a chance to respond with anything but indifference.[8] It was widely believed that sexual activities were to be limited to procreation because the loss of male semen was so debilitating to the male that it was for this reason that the human female had been created with an indifference to sex. Even today some married women feel they are performing a pleasureless duty in order to gratify the men who support them—and this, by some definition, could be classified as an act of prostitution.

Is a mistress a prostitute? Obviously in most cases there is a mercenary relationship, and not infrequently over a period of time a woman passes from one lover to another, but whether she can be classified as a prostitute probably ultimately depends on the nature of her relationship with her lover. Simply because an act lacks the moral sanction of society does not make it prostitution, but it is this very intangible factor that makes it so difficult to determine whether a mistress should be classed as a prostitute.

Many people have struggled to set forth definitions of prostitution to include all possible forms. Perhaps the most comprehensive definition was that offered by Iwan Bloch at the beginning of the twentieth century, and it is worth repeating to demonstrate the complexity of the problem. Bloch held that prostitution was a distinct form of extramarital sexual activity characterized by being more or less promiscuous, was seldom without reward, and was a form of professional commercialism for the purpose either of intercourse or of other forms of sexual activities and allurement, resulting in due time in the formation of a special type.[9] This wide-ranging definition allowed Bloch to include the procurer or pimp as well as the prostitute, since he (or she) engaged in activity associated with the commercialism of sex and its allurement. His definition would include both male and female prostitutes, and is broad enough to include the mistress, since she is a recognizable type and engaged in sex or allurement for the rewards attached to it.

Bloch's definition is the one generally used in this book. But any definition presents problems since different societies have different standards. It is the social evaluation and legal determination of a society that give prostitution a special status. Since this book is a history, there has been an attempt to look both at what present-day society would stigmatize as prostitution and at what a particular society and period in the past regarded it to be. Some sexual activities that only occasionally have been classed as prostitution have been included in order to make the study as comprehensive as possible and to indicate the wide range of behavior that has been labeled prostitution.

Any book attempting to deal with prostitution in a comprehensive way has a problem of organization. For this book, since one of the authors is a historian, we have chosen to be chronological, but in the process we have tried to look at the economic, social, psychological, religious, and other variables present at any given time. Investigating prostitution presents problems for the researcher regardless of the period or culture examined. Much of what we know about prostitution is based on written records; and, though these records might reflect personal observations or even detailed research, the authors have almost always been men. This means that a masculine bias, conscious or unconscious, is virtually omnipresent. These records also reflect a class bias, since they are usually either written for or by the upper classes. The upper-class woman often was more protected sexually than her lower-class sister. Upper-class women, for example, were believed to adulterate their blood by intercourse with males of the lesser classes, whereas for women of the lower classes to have intercourse with upper-class men was historically considered a great honor. Such an attitude was an inevitable result of masculine bias that regarded begetting (a male function) and conceiving (a female function) as different: The woman could only debase her class in such a relationship; the man, on the contrary, could bestow his princely virtue on any lower-class woman with whom he cohabited.[10] Such biases must of necessity distort the true picture of prostitution in almost any society.

Though this study occasionally includes references to male prostitutes, it is essentially a study of women and their sexual relationships with men. As such, it supplements some of the other studies we have made about women and about sex. Since usually it is the male who seeks and claims and the female who consents and submits, any study of prostitution has to come to terms with the role and place of the woman in society. Several aspects of the woman's role seem to predominate in any cross-cultural examination of prostitution. One of these is the belief that women were property. In many societies women were regarded as a male possession, belonging to their fathers, husbands, sons, or brothers. Any damage to property, including the loss of female chastity or adultery, was a punishable crime. Often a woman so "dishonored" had no alternative except prostitution. On the other hand, the male suffered under no such disabilities, and was much freer to engage in sexual activities. The result was a double standard that inevitably led to the establishment of a class of women, prostitutes, free from the restrictions of proper women, and with whom other men could have sex. (Traditionally the existence of such a class of women has been justified as a societal protection against adultery, rape, or other forms of disapproved sex behavior.) Good women, however, had no such outlet.

One of the reasons for this double standard is that the woman who wanted to engage in sex on an equal basis with men in the past faced the ever present possibility of pregnancy. Though contraceptives have been used throughout history, most were not effective, and the women who had become pregnant outside of marriage in many societies either had to attempt abortion or suffer through the pregnancy and resulting stigma. The men who got them pregnant were more difficult to identify, and though forced marriages existed in many societies, usually it was the woman who bore the onus of violating societal taboos. Even if an unmarried woman did not become pregnant through her sexual activities, her hymen was damaged and this made her less valuable as a prospective bride. Today in many parts of the world, brides are still inspected by their mothers-in-law-to-be, and to protect themselves against any suspicions about their virginity, young women often take the precaution of having the vaginal introitus (vaginal opening) sewn together several months before the examination is to take place. Neither pregnancy nor hymen loss affects the male who engages in sex; hence the male has always been freer than the female to engage in sexual activity. Prostitutes were a tolerated form of sexual outlet for males before and during marriage.

Since women in the past have often been confined to the home and limited in the type of occupations they could pursue, those women who were turned down for marriage because they were not virgins, or were for some other reason without homes or husbands or supporting male relatives, were often forced to turn to prostitution in order to support themselves. Society has tolerated this rather than face the issue of alternative employment for women. Probably most women had little say about prostitution themselves. In societies in which slavery was widespread, many women were designated as prostitutes. Women classified as prostitutes were ostracized from the company of proper women. However, a woman might achieve status in society if she became mistress or companion to a powerful man, and since such a mistress was in an influential position and her family could benefit from her influence, many well-to-do families were willing to see their daughters become mistresses of kings or powerful princes.

One other factor is important in understanding prostitution in the past, and that is prostitution as a form of contraception. Women who did not want more pregnancies ignored or encouraged the extracurricular sexual activities of their husbands and lovers. They were victims of the belief that men had greater sexual drives than women. Today as women gain control over their own bodies through the use of contraceptives and are more willing to assert their own sexuality, that form of support for prostitution will decrease. Moreover, as women attain economic equality, the foundation for prostitution is undermined, something we believe is now taking place in the United States. We see a lessening of the double standard, an increase in the "kept" man, a male who is economically supported by a female who wants his sexual services. The acceptance of this change, especially among the youthful counterculture, is worth a particular note.

Prostitution's antiquity is evidenced by the hoary expression "the oldest profession," although it is probably no older than the occupations of priest, nurse, or medicine man. Despite its antiquity, it was more or less neglected by the serious scholar until the past few years—this in spite of the fact that prostitution has been a major social institution, closely tied to the status of women, the spread of venereal disease, the birth rate, and any number of social, political, and cultural matters. Much of this lack of interest was due to Western society's dualism about sexual activity, condemned but also tolerated. It was as if society would prefer that the problems associated with prostitution be ignored: If we do not discuss them, they do not exist. Scholars unfortunately adopted the societal attitudes, and as a result those who studied stigmatized behavior were stigmatized by other scholars and researchers. This meant that much of the writing about prostitution was of the level of what might be called the "men's" magazine—juicy, semi-pornographic, and not particularly accurate. Much of this has changed in the past decade, due in large part to the growing interest of women scholars. Monograph studies have appeared on various historical periods and cultures, and they have been reviewed in scholarly journals. Some of these have been incorporated in this study, but many have appeared too late to be part of this study. Much of the recent findings, however, has been anticipated, and these studies fill in the details. We hope that this study will continue to serve as a foundation for others and that as the studies mount we can better understand prostitution itself.

1 ORIGINS OF PROSTITUTION

When did prostitution begin? Investigators of animal behavior have reported prostitution among some of the higher primates, but other investigators have disagreed.

The controversy stems from the fact that female primates (as well as younger males) have been observed offering their sexual services—"presentation" is the technical term—in return for food or to avoid attack. Whether or not these behaviors can be described as prostitution depends on definition. If prostitution is taken to mean a stigmatized form of behavior, then this activity cannot be regarded as prostitution but rather a pattern behavior that is biologically justified, an indication of friendship and submission.[1] If prostitution is a term used to describe such activity without the onus of stigmatizing it, then prostitution is older than men and women themselves.

A similar debate continues about the existence of prostitution in early human society. Here the question is tied in with theories about the origins of society, circumstances about which we can be sure of little but about which there is considerable speculation. Much of the speculation stems from the nineteenth century when the Western intellectual community began to realize that the biblical account of creation ignored millions or billions of years. Encouraged by the research and theories of the geologist Charles Lyell and of the biologist Charles Darwin, as well as others, scholars began to challenge the Judeo-Christian account of the beginnings of mankind and the place of women in early society. Two early theoreticians who wrote on the subject were Sir Henry Maine and J. J. Bachofen, both of whose works appeared in 1861. Maine held that the patriarchal system of authority was the original and universal system of social organization. The family was the original unit, and the male parent held supreme authority in the household. From the family, authority was extended to clans, from clans to tribes, and so until the nation state had resulted. Almost always men had ruled; temporarily there might have been a matriarchy, but this was an unstable and degrading form of organization that only lasted briefly.[2] In short, Maine believed that the subordination of women was a law of nature, inevitable by the very nature of civilization. Prostitution existed in patriarchal society, but outside the family system, since no proper family head would allow any of his wives or daughters to engage in such activities.

Bachofen agreed that patriarchy was a superior kind of organization to matriarchy, but he did not feel it was the original or universal system of social organization. Instead, patriarchy had been an advance up the evolutionary scale. Originally society had existed in a state of sexual promiscuity with no stable family life, and in such a state women, "defenseless against abuses by men" and exhausted by male "lusts," felt the need for regulated conditions and purer ethics. Since mothers were the only parents the younger generation knew with certainty, women were able to seize upon this fact to lay the foundation of a rule by women— gynecocracy. Men accepted these new female constraints unwillingly, but in return for giving up the right to take any woman he wanted, a man obtained a woman's surrender of herself for a limited period to one man. In this evolution of society, according to Bachofen, women were aided by religious beliefs, since mankind at this stage in its development was wholly dominated by faith. It was the woman, with her profound sense of the divine presence obtained through her ability to bear children, who capitalized on man's reverence for nature, and though physically weaker, asserted her strength over the male as the repository of the first revelation. Eventually, however, men usurped power, subjugated their women, and only then was society able to advance further on the evolutionary scale. This was because women ruled only when society remained close to nature, but when intelligence was essential, men were needed to rule.[3] With men in control, prostitution was an inevitable result.

With the opposing theories of Maine and Bachofen as a base, nineteenth-century scholars set to work to try to find out whether matriarchy or patriarchy was the earliest form of organization. Much of the fuel for the controversy was furnished by the American ethnologist Lewis N. Morgan, who believed he had observed the transition from a system based on *jus maternum* (mother right) to *jus paternum* (father right) among the Iroquois Indians. From his observations Morgan evolved a system of sex and family law for primitive peoples in which society progresses from the complete promiscuity of the primitive horde into the organized hunter tribes in which sex was strictly regulated. At this stage the mother, since the father was unknown, remained the decisive factor in all questions of family relationship and inheritance. It was only when production developed enough for two human beings, man and woman, to maintain themselves economically by stock breeding and agriculture that the family split off and became a monogamous unit. In effect monogamy went hand in hand with the evolution of private property, and since economically the male was the more active and physically the stronger, the woman fell under his domination, sexually and otherwise. The natural superiority of woman, Morgan asserted—natural because she was more closely connected with offspring—was succeeded by the unnatural primacy of man. Man held the primacy on the basis of his physical strength.[4] Prostitution resulted from this inequality.

Probably the nineteenth-century arguments over whether society was matriarchal or patriarchal would have remained a question for debate among specialists[5] if they had not become entangled with larger issues. The Marxists, for example, made use of Bachofen and Morgan to buttress their own theoretical assumptions about the original nature of society. The most influential Marxist theoretician in this respect was Friedrich Engels, the collaborator and friend of Karl Marx. Engels held that the passage from matriarchy to patriarchy marked not only the great historical defeat of the feminine sex but also the development of private property. In the Stone Age, when land belonged in common to all members of the clan, the rudimentary character of the primitive spade and the limited possibilities of agriculture meant that women's strength was adequate for gardening. Though the two sexes in essence constituted separate classes, there was an equal division of tasks, with no one task more important than another. The men hunted and fished while the women remained at home doing the essential domestic tasks. With the discovery of copper, tin, bronze, and eventually iron, and with the appearance of the plow, agriculture and other economic activity became so important that more intensive labor was required. To accomplish this, man turned to the labor of other men, whom he often reduced to slavery. Private property appeared, and as man became the master of slaves, he became the proprietor of women. Mother right was overthrown quite simply by decreeing that the male offspring remain with their family while the female take up residence with her husband.[6] The male thereby took command of the home, the "woman was degraded and reduced to servitude," became a slave of the male lust, and "a mere instrument for the production of children."[7] Man in his newfound sovereignty indulged himself in all kinds of sexual activity simply because woman was subjugated, and the only revenge the female had was through infidelity. Adultery, according to Engels, was endemic in societies that emphasized private property, and so was prostitution. Engels wrote that *hetaerism,* that is, sexual intercourse between men and unmarried women outside marriage but coexistent with monogamous marriage, derived

directly from group marriage, from the ceremonial surrender by which
women purchased the right of chastity. Surrender for money was at first
a religious act; it took place in the temple of the goddess of love, and
the money originally went into the temple treasury. The temple slaves of
Anaitis in Armenia and of Aphrodite in Corinth, like the sacred danc-
ing-girls attached to the temples of India . . . were the first prostitutes.
Originally the duty of every woman, this surrender was later performed
by those priestesses alone as representatives of all other women. Among
other peoples hetaerism derives from the sexual freedom allowed to girls
before marriage—again, therefore, a relic of group marriage, but handed
down in a different way. With the rise of the inequality of property—already at the upper stage of barbarism, therefore—wage-labor appears
sporadically side by side with slave labor, and at the same time, as its
necessary correlate, the professional prostitution of free women side by
side with the forced surrender of the slave. Thus the heritage which
group marriage has bequeathed to civilization is double-edged, just as
everything civilization brings forth is double-edged, double-tongued, divided against itself, contradictory: here monogamy, there hetaerism,
with its most extreme form, prostitution. For hetaerism is as much a social institution as any other; it continues the old sexual freedom—to the
advantage of men. Actually not merely tolerated, but gaily practiced, by
the ruling classes particularly, it is condemned in words. But in reality
this condemnation never falls on the men concerned, but only on the
women; they are despised and outcast, in order that the unconditional
supremacy of men over the female sex may be once more proclaimed as
a fundamental law of society.[8]

Associated in Engels' theorizing was the belief that a change in the
economic system would bring about an elimination of prostitution.

We are now approaching a social revolution in which the economic
foundations of monogamy as they have existed hitherto will disappear
just as surely as those of its complement—prostitution. Monogamy
arose from the concentration of wealth in the hands of a single individual—a man—and from the need to bequeath this wealth to the children of that man and of no other. For this purpose, the monogamy of
the woman did not in any way interfere with open or concealed polygamy on the part of the man. But by transforming by far the greater
portion, at any rate, of permanent, heritable wealth—the means of production—into social property, the coming social revolution will reduce
to a minimum all this anxiety about bequeathing and inheriting . . .
with the transformation of the means of production into social property
there will disappear also wage-labor, the proletariat, and therefore the
necessity for a certain— statistically calculable—number of women to
surrender themselves for money. Prostitution disappears; monogamy,
instead of collapsing, at last becomes a reality for men.[9]

As August Bebel, a disciple of Engels, emphasized, the problem of women could be reduced to their capacity to labor, and it was the resistance of the "capitalistic" paternalism that prevented the female from fully developing her personality. Bebel criticized the "bourgeois emancipationists" for failing to recognize that the "woman question," as he called it, could not be solved until the "social question," the economic reorganization, was solved.[10] For him prostitution was a social institution of the capitalist world, "the same as the police, standing armies, the Church, and wage-mastership."[11] Inevitably women could be free, and prostitution eliminated, if the capitalistic nature of society itself changed. The result of such beliefs has been the rather naive assertion by some that prostitution does not exist in truly socialist countries. Such a claim has been advanced in the past by some supporters of the Soviet Union, China, Cuba, and other areas where rhetoric sometimes has outrun reality. Though no one would deny the economic exploitation of prostitution, the explanation for prostitution and the solution are much more complicated than it seemed to some of the early socialist thinkers.

Not all advocates of matriarchal theory are Marxists. The most important twentieth-century study emphasizing both promiscuity and mother right was Robert Briffault's *The Mothers;* Briffault believed that mother right was the source of all social organization and that male influence had been entirely irrelevant in the dawn of culture. Kinship, political organization, the beginnings of law, economic life, magic, and religion were created and completely dominated by women until men had seized power.[12] Since the character that marked the religious ritual of women in early society applied equally to all magical operations, sex and prostitution became closely interlinked. In those societies that worshipped male gods, the high priestess or the queen was believed to be married to the god. Because she had a divine paramour she gained magical and oracular powers, but in return she was forbidden from marrying mere mortals. This, in Briffault's words, did not mean that she was debarred from sexual commerce; on the contrary priestesses were allowed to gratify their passions with any man who took their fancy. Only when the power of the sacred king became highly developed did virgin priestesses appear. Goddesses, on the other hand, never had priest husbands, and when men served them they did so by renouncing their sex, assimilating themselves to women's ways, dressing as women, and often even emasculating themselves. These goddesses were also served by priestesses who were sacred prostitutes, and it was on them that the rites of fruitfulness fell. By having intercourse with males they were imitating the female principle of nature.[13] Secular prostitution, according to Briffault, was a direct descendant of these sacred prostitutes, and this was why organized prostitution still retained religious terms such as "abbeys" to refer to brothels, and prostitutes themselves have often been given protection by special gods or saints. Since it was a fundamental function of the prostitute priestess to engage in coitus with any man who presented himself in order to promote the fertility of nature, it became a fundamental rule of prostitution that the prostitute could not refuse any man who proffered the appointed price.[14]

The most notable opponent of the theories of Briffault was Edward Westermarck, who held that monogamous marriage was a primeval institution rooted in the individual family; that the matriarchate was not a universal stage in human development; that group marriage never existed, much less promiscuity; and that the whole problem had to be approached using biology and psychology as well as a more critical application of the ethnological evidence.[15] Though Westermarck recognized the existence of religious prostitution, he did not believe it was a survival of a period of communal marriage. Nor was religious prostitution necessarily an attempt to symbolize the union of the Mother Goddess with her mate. Rather there were several possible explanations. Some peoples probably practiced religious prostitution because they believed female sexuality posed dangers to the male, particularly the new bridegroom; others because such an act would guarantee the easy delivery of a child; others because sexual intercourse with a holy person was believed beneficial, and others practiced it as an act of friendship or a token of goodwill. Regardless of the reasons, it was not due to any holdover from a period of sexual anarchy or communism.[15]

Adopting more or less the same theme was Ernest Crawley. He regarded sexual communism, mother right, and the total eclipse of the male sex as imaginary fantasies constructed against all evidence.

> It may be confidently assumed that individual marriage has been, as far as we can trace it back, the regular type of union of man and woman. The promiscuity theory really belongs to the mythological stage of human intelligence, and is on a par with many savage myths concerning the origin of marriage, and the like. These are interesting but of no scientific value. They are cases of mental actualization of apparently potential states which were really impossible except as abnormal occurrences.[17]

Crawley, however, believed that men were fearful of women due to "physiological thought" rather than primitive fear of matriarchy or its consequences. By physiological thought, he meant the concentration of the female on physiological functions, particularly nutrition and sex. Theodore Besterman, who revised and enlarged Crawley's original work, held that the antagonism between the sexes was so great that man had continuously attempted to protect himself against women, and the result was a collective emotion of sexual solidarity in both men and women.[18] This led to misunderstanding, and one of the grounds for fear of the female was the belief that human qualities regarded as weakening to masculinity could be transmitted by contact. Inevitably males who believed strongly in female inferiority would attempt to dominate women in order to lessen the dangers of contact. This fear of the female was ever present during sexual intercourse and was accentuated in times of female sexual crisis such as menstruation or childbirth, and inevitably there were elaborate precautions taken in order to avoid the weakening effect of the female.[19] Women were necessary to have children, but their position in marriage was strictly controlled, and men further asserted their domination by sanctioning prostitution. Proper women were excluded from official society, and their place was taken by those women outside the bounds usually imposed on women, i.e., the prostitute.[20]

As anthropologists have improved their methodology their theoretical assumptions have become more cautious: they have become increasingly reluctant to speak of the existence of matriarchy and in general would deny the existence of societies where women have been dominant. Many societies identified as matriarchies in the past could better be called *matrilineal,* that is, societies tracing descent through the female; or *matrilocal,* societies in which the husband lives with the wife's people, but neither type of society is particularly matriarchal since ultimate authority was vested in the male. Present empirical evidence suggests that males almost universally have been the dominant decision makers.

In the presence of so much speculation and so little fact, all we can now say about prostitution's origins is that it probably existed from very early in human development; that it has economic, sociological, psychological, and religious overtones that are tied with the man-woman relationship; and that neither matriarchal nor patriarchal assumptions about the nature of society fully explain it.

Psychoanalytic theorists approached the question from a different angle. Many of them seized upon the ideas of Sigmund Freud, who wrote that "civilization has been built up, under the pressure of the struggle for existence, by sacrifices in gratification of the primitive impulses, and that it is to a great extent forever being re-created, as each individual, successively joining the community, repeats the sacrifice of his instinctive pleasures for the common good. The sexual are amongst the most important of the instinctive forces thus utilized: they are in this way sublimated, that is to say, their energy is turned aside from its sexual goal and diverted towards other ends, no longer sexual and socially more viable."[21]

Freud never developed this thesis as an explanation for prostitution. Rather he adopted the concept of the split between the tender and sexual components of the sexual impulse. Some men preferred prostitutes, he reasoned, because they could only achieve sexual satisfaction with a woman they regarded as inferior and whom they did not love. Thus the prostitute served as an example of a "bad" woman in order to enable the male more readily to believe in the existence of a "good" woman. Even if prostitution had not been stigmatized by society, such individuals would have had to stigmatize their sex companion as bad in order to reinforce their feelings of disgust.[22]

Carl G. Jung, at one time a disciple and later a rival of Freud, went further, tying in prostitution with the collection of symbols or archetypes in the unconscious associated with the concept of the Great Mother.[23] The symbol mother aroused attitudes ranging from archetypes of the compassionate mother on the one hand to the devouring witch on the other. These symbols were not so much a historical entity associated with matriarchy but a psychological reality whose fateful power was still alive in the psychic depths of present-day people. Thus it was easy for images of the Great Mother to become distorted, secularized, and sexualized. In fact, the association of certain types of women with prostitution could be regarded as an archaic remnant of the mother complex in the male.[24]

Taking Freud's idea that it was essential for civilization to sacrifice the gratification of primitive impulses, J. E. Unwin took off in another direction. He argued that the cultural conditions of any society were dependent on the amount of physical and social energy extant in a society, and this in turn was dependent on the amount of sexuality. Creative societies, in his mind, could exist only when sexual outlets were highly restricted and compulsory continence the norm. No society, he wrote, could "display productive social energy unless a new generation inherits a social system under which sexual opportunity" was reduced to a minimum. If such a system could be established and preserved, a "richer and yet richer tradition" would be created and refined. Unwin held that historically the only way sexual opportunity had been kept at a minimum was through "absolute monogamy," where the husband had absolute control over his wife and children, even to the point of making them legal nonentities. Therefore, women inevitably made demands for changes, usually achieving a gradual relaxation of female prenuptial continence. The resultant weakening of monogamy produced a weakening of society until compulsory continence could be reestablished. Though Unwin was not particularly happy with the subordination of women in absolute monogamy, he believed a double standard was permissible in order to keep sexual opportunity to a minimum.[25] In short, prostitution was necessary for civilization to advance, although it, too, had to be strictly controlled.

The global theories about the origin of prostitution are valuable for understanding how deeply ingrained prostitution has been in our society. They are no more nor less valid than John Locke's theory of the Social Contract or the Biblical account of creation. The only way we can determine the beginnings of prostitution would be to look at paleolithic societies, an impossible task. Failing this, looking at contemporary or near contemporary primitives raises the difficulty of the very nature of such societies. Contemporary primitives, even if not the recipients of Western material culture, are highly developed. Primitive civilization itself is the product of a long evolution and usually represents a highly integrated society. In other words, the practices of modern primitives are not the practices of the cave men. Accepting this as a truism, there are also other difficulties, not the least of which is the fact that many of the early observers themselves were products of various theories. Havelock Ellis, for example, did not believe that prostitution was possible until civilization had appeared, and though some rudimentary forms of prostitution might be evident in primitive groups, they were temporary and were not usually stigmatized by the societies in question.[26] This is much too dogmatic a statement to accept, although Ellis is more often right than wrong. Part of the difficulty is that Ellis believed that societies passed through stages from savagery to barbarism to civilization, and his statement conformed to his assumptions.

Until fairly recently, most of the information about primitive societies was gained from reports of Western observers who had occasion to live or work among such people. These observers were not trained ethnographers but rather missionaries, trappers, prospectors, teachers, businessmen of one kind or another, and their reports consciously or unconsciously reflected their bias. In recent decades an increasing number of reports have been compiled by professional anthropologists, but often the societies they have reported on have been greatly influenced by outsiders before the observers appeared. Anthropologists are increasingly conscious of the influence of the observer on the peoples observed. Most now make allowances for this, but the difficulty is that few pristine societies existed even in the recent past that had not had contact with outsiders. Contact with Western culture has usually had some influence on primitive societies, so it is possible that prostitution, or at least some forms of it, might have been introduced by Western visitors.[27] Western travelers or observers, however, cannot introduce social features, customs, standards, and conceptions that do not exist in Western society, and therefore where such customs or institutions exist, it seems safe to regard them as indigenous to the society. Based on this assumption, it seems clear that prostitution existed in some primitive societies, and although Western intervention might well have changed or altered the original forms, they still bear resemblance to what existed before.

The difficulty with examining such customs is that since each society is different, observers conditioned by their experiences in one society might not observe prostitution, or if they had, they might misunderstand it. The late Prince Peter of Greece, for example, in his Tibetan studies, reported that there were no prostitutes there. He recognized that the Tibetans could not have been entirely ignorant of the existence of such an institution since they believed that tobacco was a plant grown with the aid of the menstrual flow of a prostitute, but he did not see any prostitutes and concluded that the Tibetans must have gotten their concept of prostitution from outside Tibet.[28] Other observers, however, contradicted Prince Peter and reported that prostitution was rampant. Prostitutes commonly accompanied the caravans, they were present in large numbers around most army garrisons, and it was a common custom for Tibetan men to utilize the services of prostitutes as an act of bravado, either to boast about to their friends or as a means of indicating that they were rich.[29] One observer even compiled a price list.[30] In sum, the good prince either did not know what to look for or was blind to what was going on.

Part of the difficulty is that prostitution does not necessarily take Western forms. In Ugra (Outer Mongolia) prostitutes were regarded as temporary wives. Merchants and lamas took prostitutes as companions on short journeys, and when these were paid and discharged, they sought others to take their place.[31] Though this is prostitution by some definitions, it was not defined as such by the society. Among some of the American Indian tribes it was customary for a man to be accompanied by a woman when he went on an extended hunting expedition in order to satisfy both his material and sexual needs. The woman received a liberal share of the profits for her services and the arrangement terminated at the end of the hunt.[32] In other Indian tribes women were purchased to serve as sexual partners for the night, week, month, or season. Most of these temporary liaisons were not regarded as marriages unless children resulted. Often the same elaborate negotiations were carried out for the short-term marriages as for the long-term ones.[33] Among the Navajo, girls who refused to marry had the right to establish a house of their own where they were able to welcome male visitors. Such women could move from settlement to settlement seeking out bedmates, responsible to no one but themselves.[34] A similar group of traveling women existed among the Papago, and the Pima songs describe the sexual attractiveness of such women.[35] The Creeks recruited their traveling women from women who had been cast aside by their husbands.[36] To most of these peoples, however, such practices were not prostitution since even temporary cohabitation could be classed as a marriage relationship, unless the woman involved was the wife of another man.[37]

Another reason for the difficulty in determining whether prostitution existed or not is the confusion between promiscuity and prostitution. Tarahumara Indian women became somewhat promiscuous during various fiestas, but their status as prostitutes is doubtful since they refused payment for their services. The refusal of money was not on any moral grounds but because they believed that if they accepted money for their sexual services they would become sick and could not be cured; on the other hand, if they refused payment they still might become sick, but they would be cured.[38] A clearer instance of prostitution existed among the Sierra Tarascans, who had an arrangement similar to that of the modern call girl. Certain elderly women in each village knew, or were expected to know, the names of women who would consent to have intercourse with a man for money. Interested males went to the house of these village madams, and they in turn sent messengers to fetch the girls to come and serve the waiting customers. Sometimes the girls were the daughters of the madams, but often girls from other families came to the houses, more or less secretly. Young bachelors were the primary patrons of such houses, but a large number of clients came from those men whose wives were pregnant. The payment was split between the old woman and her young assistants, although it was customary for the prostitute to receive the bulk of the fee.[39]

Some tribes considered it perfectly acceptable for a married woman to have an additional lover, provided he was a kinsman. Among the Tlinget, a tribe in Alaska, the husband could do nothing in these circumstances but share his wife with the other man; to add insult to injury, the lover often lived in the same house with him. There was no marriage ceremony involved in these love relationships, but the man carrying on an affair was not permitted to marry another woman so long as his lover desired to keep him. The custom was strictly limited to women of high rank and was justified as a means of keeping the idle women of the rich satisfied and at home[40]—a remedy that most American husbands would probably be loath to adopt.

Prostitution in our society—at least in the immediate past—has been associated with loose sexual morals, and often there is a failure to make a distinction between adolescent promiscuity and prostitution. Probably we should not classify as prostitution promiscuous sexual behavior in those societies that do not put a premium on virginity and where intercourse outside of marriage is permissible. For example, many peoples from a wide range of cultures have utilized trial marriage to prove fertility, and marriage was not considered possible until the woman became pregnant. When this happened, the man had to marry the woman or sever connections completely. If the arrangement did not work out, both partners started over again with a new would-be spouse. Such practices still exist in parts of South America,[41] and undoubtedly elsewhere. There are many other examples of related customs that some Western observers erroneously regard as prostitution. Many primitive peoples looked upon a certain amount of premarital sexual experiences for both sexes as natural; in fact, in some societies it was essential that a girl not be a virgin before she was married. The idea of a woman remaining a lifelong virgin has been regarded by some as not only unhealthy but impossible. One primitive informant told an observer that if there really was a woman of thirty who had never been sexually initiated the woman would probably grab the nearest man or boy she saw and drag him to the ground on top of her to remedy the difficulty. Continence for boys also has been regarded as actually dangerous and looked upon as reason enough for a man to "lose his brains" and "go crazy."[42] Some writers have classed the hospitality tradition of the Eskimos as prostitution since it was long a custom for a host to offer a woman, usually his wife, to a visitor.[43] In return for her sexual favors the guest was expected to give a small gift. Though this may be prostitution in the Western sense, it is not according to the Eskimo culture, even if the woman hid from her husband the extra gifts she occasionally received.[44]

There are some relationships, however, which primitive societies themselves looked upon as prostitution. Among the Nupe peoples of Africa, the public marketplace of the daylight hours changed its character at night to become a marketplace of love and sex. The women who remained late were not dressed for ordinary market work but instead wore their most beautiful dresses of light-colored and embroidered cloth and bangles, bracelets, and rings; their eyes were painted and their fingers and hands were hennaed. Technically they were selling not themselves but Kolanuts, an article that only men could buy—and the buyer took the woman along with the nut he purchased. Each female seller was usually surrounded by men with whom she gossiped and joked, and then after a whispered appointment, a man would leave followed by his feminine companion (and her Kolanut) for the night.[45]

In some African societies when a woman wanted to leave her huband she merely moved on to another village and set up as a free woman, i.e., a prostitute. When a woman of the upper Volta River area entered a new village she asked for hospitality and the word rapidly spread around that a "free" woman was visiting the village. Interested men contacted her or her sponsor in order to seek sexual pleasure from her. Her presence brought about a veritable festival, and little work was accomplished until things settled down. If her husband still desired her he was supposed to hunt her down and bargain with the village chief for her return, and reimburse the village for the money spent on his wife if she decided to return to his house. If the woman did not want to return, she fled to another village where the process was repeated until either the husband or the wife gave up.[46]

In some societies certain women who chose not to marry were designated as public women; that is, they welcomed the sexual attention of the men in the village.[47] In Buganda, a woman who had refused to enter into any permanent relationship with a particular man put herself under the protection of the chief; she was then free to have any number of temporary husbands. Such women were regarded as desirable by the men in almost any village because they were looked upon as the "pulsating" center of activity.[48] At times girls turned to prostitution in order to escape from the control of their parents.[49] In still other societies, girls, who for one reason or another were not married at the customary age, were allowed to become temporary prostitutes in order that they could be initiated into marriage. Usually they were paid for their sexual services.[50] Some tribes utilized prostitutes, usually widows or older unmarried girls, to initiate young men into the mysteries of sexual intercourse.[51] In the past it was not unusual for women in some societies to be forced into prostitution. In some of the polygamous Congo societies, for example, a husband could force his wives either to sell or give their services to passing strangers,[52] while among the Nkundu it was common practice for the polygamist male to prostitute at least some of his wives;[53] in fact, some men apparently chose new wives because they would bring high prices as prostitutes.[54] There were numerous other variations, including homosexual prostitution.[55]

Primitive societies do not furnish any easy answer about the development of prostitution. Many of the practices of near contemporary primitives would be regarded as prostitution by most Americans, but the primitives regard them as something else, as short-term marriages or temporary cohabitations. When children result from such liaisons, however, these temporary marriages become somewhat more binding. The American divorce, when children are involved, would be regarded by many of these primitive peoples as prostitution, and in fact would have been so regarded by many nineteenth-century English and Americans. One generalization that appears obvious to us is that in those societies in which female promiscuity is tolerated there is much less sexual activity that can be classified as prostitution.

Prostitution is obviously tied to the religious outlook and philosophical assumptions about sexual intercourse, female virginity, and female adultery. In those societies where female virginity is prized and the female adulteress punished, there is probably a greater likelihood of institutionalized prostitution. Prostitution is also related to marriage patterns, and if marriage is difficult and highly prized among women, there will probably be a greater incidence of prostitution. Incidentally, despite considerable speculation to the contrary, the existence of a polygamous society does not in itself cut down the incidence of prostitution since it leaves large numbers of males without legal sexual partners. Prostitution did not develop in all societies at the same time, and does not exist in all societies today, at least in an institutionalized form. The fact that some societies lack institutionalized prostitution, and that sexual standards, at least as applied to prostitution and promiscuity, vary widely indicates that each society attempts to solve its sexual needs in idiosyncratic ways. Prostitution does not appear to be a necessary stage in any societal development, but is dependent upon factors, some of which could be eliminated in today's society.[56]

In sum, prostitution is very much a matter of definition. Certain factors, nonetheless, appear essential to the existence of prostitution, specifically a moral code that frowns on certain promiscuous practices by females yet tolerates a different standard for males, and at the same time rewards those women, either by money or other means, who either choose or are forced to violate the societal code. Prostitution might be publicly condemned, but until society deals with conditions that encourage prostitution, condemnation will only serve as a rhetorical exercise and fail to deal with the real issues. Unfortunately, in Western society we have employed much rhetoric and done very little to deal with basic problems.

2 THE ANCIENT NEAR EAST: SACRED AND PROFANE

The peoples of the ancient Near East, the area today comprising the land belt stretching from Egypt to Iraq, are regarded as the founders of Western civilization. Attitudes formed in these areas were incorporated into later Greek, Roman, and Christian cultures. It was here also that writing was invented, a fact that makes it possible to examine recorded material for attitudes about prostitution for the early periods. Probably the oldest of the civilizations in the area was that which originated in the Tigris-Euphrates valley, an area sometimes referred to as Mesopotamia, sometimes as Babylonia. The earliest builders of this civilization were the Sumerians, and they were succeeded by the Akkadians, the Amorites, the Assyrians, the Neo-Babylonians, and other peoples who adopted and modified the epics, tales, love poems, annals, and laws of the early Sumerians.

Whether women once had a higher status in the area is debatable, but by the time the Sumerian theology was organized into the form in which it has come down to us, women were clearly regarded as inferior beings and the most powerful gods were all male. The main female goddess, Inanna (later known as Ishtar), the goddess of fertility, was also associated with promiscuity and prostitution, and when she descended to earth she was accompanied by courtesans and prostitutes. Throughout the history of the area she remained an unmarried and erotic figure whose lovers were legion. She was identified with the planet Venus, the morning and evening star, able to arouse the amorous instinct in all males.[1]

Associated with her cult worship were prostitutes whose power and influence were early indicated in the Gilgamesh epic, one of the great classics of Babylonian literature and one of the earliest recorded poems. According to the story recounted in the epic, Gilgamesh was oppressing the city of Erech, taking sons from their fathers and maidens from their lovers. So great was his harassment that the people finally complained to the gods, who created a rival, Enkidu, out of mud, to deal with him.

Enkidu was described in the poem as a wild man who knew neither people nor country, and ignorant of the ways of man. Gilgamesh, fearful of defeat by such a wild creature, tried to weaken him. To do this he sent forth a temple prostitute to ensnare him, ordering her to strip off her garments, and lay open her comeliness, so that Enkidu, attracted by her, would come close and then engage in intercourse. Once Enkidu had intercourse he would lose his innocence, and then and only then could he be handled by Gilgamesh. The prostitute did as she was told; she

> untied her loin-cloth and opened her legs,
> and he took possession of her comeliness:
> She used not restraint but accepted his ardour,
> She put aside her robe and he lay upon her.
> She used on him, the savage, a woman's wiles,
> His passion responded to her.
> For six days and seven nights Enkidu approached and coupled with
>   the prostitute.
> After he was sated with her charms,
> He set his face toward his game.
> [But] when the gazelles saw him, Enkidu, they ran away;
> The game of the steppe fled from his presence.
> Enkidu tried to hasten [after them, but] his body was [as if it were]
>   bound.
> His knees failed him who tried to run after his game.
> Enkidu had become weak, his speed was not as before.
> But he had intelligence, wide was his understanding.

Eventually when he did find Gilgamesh the two engaged in combat and though Enkidu was defeated, he and Gilgamesh ultimately became fast friends.[2] The legend not only suggests that women were creatures designed to snare men, but that they weakened the male, a theme that appears often in Western culture. In the Gilgamesh story, however, it was not just any woman who was able to entrap a man, but a special woman, a prostitute.

Further information is found on the subject of prostitution in the surviving law codes of the Mesopotamian valley. Formal law codes have survived from Ur-Nammu of the Third Dynasty of Ur (c. 2050 B.C.) and Lipit Ishtar if Isin (c. 1870 B.C.). Neither of these codes, however, is preserved completely, and their importance to the historian lies mostly in the influence they apparently had on later law. In the Semitic dialect the first law code to survive is that from the town of Eshnunna, dating from about 1800 B.C., and the best known is that of Hammurabi (c. 1700 B.C.). There is also a surviving set of laws from about 1100 B.C.

These codes give us some insight into the subject of prostitution, and offer some verification of the assumption that prostitution is closely related to attitudes about women and marriage. A survey of the laws emphasizes that the purpose of marriage was procreation, not companionship. Marriage was usually monogamous, but a woman who was unable to bear children could be divorced or supplanted by a concubine. The wife's first duty was to raise her children, and the woman who gave birth to children, particularly to sons, was accorded special protection. The man who divorced the mother of his sons or took another wife was committing a culpable act. The value set on a woman's childbearing responsibilities was emphasized by the penalties imposed on anyone injuring a woman sufficiently to cause a miscarriage, and also in the statutes against abortion.

A woman, however, was basically the property of a male, whether husband, father, brother, or son, and though she had rights of her own, including control of her dowry and other property rights, her freedom was limited, at least as compared to the male. Adultery, for example, was a trespass against a husband's property, and the woman who so injured her husband could be punished by him. A husband had freedom to fornicate, but a free woman, whether married or unmarried, was inviolable and guarded. A man who so much as gave employment to a married woman not closely related to him could be in difficulty with her husband, father, brother, or son. The punishments given to those who had intercourse with unmarried free women emphasized the fact that women were considered property. If the offender had a wife, she was taken from him and given to the father of the woman he had engaged in sex with; the father could then sell the wife into prostitution. The only punishment the offender himself received was being compelled to marry the girl who was his victim. If he had no wife to exchange, he had to pay a sum of money to the girl's father as well as marry the girl, although the father might accept money and refuse to give his daughter in marriage. In any case, the payment was for damaging property, lessening the value of the girl, and the wife of the offender suffered more than the offender. If a man could prove by oath that an unmarried girl had given herself to him, he was not compelled to surrender his own wife, although he still had to pay a sum of money for the damage he had caused. Even when a woman was raped, she often became a double victim. If a married woman was seized by a man in a public place and attempted to defend herself, she was regarded as innocent even if she was violated. If, however, she acted in a provocative manner she was guilty and a man who raped her could not be convicted for damaging her value unless it could be shown that he had knowledge of her married state beforehand.[3]

Obviously the lot of a free woman was carefully circumscribed, while

the free man had more freedom both in his public and personal life.
Generally it appears that the stricter the provisions of family law, the
greater the need for a free zone in which men could satisfy their sexual
desires without incurring obligations; and therefore prostitution flour-
ished.[4] Since free women were so carefully protected and off limits, men
provided for their sexual needs by turning to other women. Among these
other women were the slaves, and a female slave was under obligation to
give her owner not only her labor but also herself, without any counter
obligation on his part. He could use her for his sexual satisfaction or turn
her over to prostitution. Even if she became a more or less official concubine and had children by him, she still remained a slave liable to be
sold. The only limits to sexual expression by a slave were those imposed
by the owners. Women, as well as men, could own slaves and if a woman
herself bought a female slave either as a servant for herself or as a
concubine for her husband, the slave remained the property of the
woman, not the husband. There were also temple slaves who were not
confined to the temple but worked in the towns and hired out to private
employers. Their legal status was harsher than that of ordinary slaves
since they had no hope of adoption, while their children became the
property of gods.

The economic dependence of the female on the male is emphasized
by the special provisions allowing a woman to remarry even though she
had not been divorced and her husband was still alive. This was permitted
in cases where a woman's husband had been taken captive and he had not
left enough for her to eat. She was free to live with another man as his
wife until her husband returned. Any children she had by the temporary
husband, however, remained with him. If the absence of her husband was
malicious, motivated by a "hatred of king and country," he had no further
claim on his wife if she took a second husband. The economic necessity
of such arrangements is indicated by the fact that the only occupations
mentioned for women in the various law codes are priestess, tavern
worker, and prostitute. Probably the women winesellers and "ale-wives"
who made up the category of tavern workers were also a kind of prostitute. Since few women could have become priestesses, prostitution often
was the only alternative for a woman who could not find a temporary
husband or who was not accepted back into her family.

In general, priestesses were women who had been dedicated to the
gods. They were expected to remain virgins until at least after the meno-
pause, when in some cases they were allowed to take a husband. The
conduct of the woman priest was rigidly circumscribed and a priestess
who went to a tavern could be put to death. In addition to these virgin
priestesses, there was a second group of women associated with the temple,

the *qadishtu* or *qadiltu*, who probably in some cases were also called *kulmashitu*.[5] These were temple prostitutes. Some of the temple prostitutes reenacted the annual rebirth of vegetation by engaging in intercourse with either the rulers of the various city-states or a priest.[6] Within the temple at Babylon, there was a special room set aside for the god Marduk (or Baal as he was sometimes called) to have sexual intercourse. This room was located in the topmost tower and had a large couch that was occupied at night by a woman specially chosen to serve the sexual needs of the god. The Greek historian Herodotus, who wrote in the fifth century B.C., reported that the people told him the god came every night to have intercourse with the woman but that he himself did not believe it.[7] Once a woman had shared her bed with a god, or his human personification, she was debarred from ever sharing her bed with a mere mortal man. Similar practices are reported to have existed elsewhere in the ancient Near East and continued to exist until the Emperor Constantine, the first Christian ruler of the Roman Empire, abolished the practice in the fourth century A.D.[8]

Another type of temple sexual activity was also recorded by Herodotus. He stated that every woman went to the temple of Mylitta (Ishtar) in Babylon at least once during her lifetime to have intercourse with a stranger. The women came from all walks of life, but once they had taken their seats they were not allowed to leave until a stranger had thrown a silver coin on their laps and repeated the words, "I summon you in the name of the goddess Mylitta." The coin could be of any size or denomination but the woman had no right to refuse it. After she had completed the sexual act, but not before, she was free to return to her normal duties. According to Herodotus, the women who were not immediately "picked up" by a stranger had to remain at the temple until they were; he added that some of the less beautiful had to wait as long as three or four years before they could leave.[9]

Modern historians are not in agreement about the existence of the custom described by Herodotus. Those who do accept it are not agreed on the causes. Some believe that it was a holdover of the belief that intercourse with a virgin was dangerous but the dangers could be lessened by delegating this task to strangers; others think it was the result of an ancient taboo against shedding blood; still others feel that it was part of the necessary preliminary physical preparation for marriage. Herodotus himself stated it was a religious act, a sacrifice to the god or a fertility offering of the first fruits.[10] Whether such an action, regardless of the reasons for it, can be classed as prostitution, is dependent on how prostitution is defined. The Babylonians themselves did not regard it as prostitution. Though there is a question of how much reliance to put on

Herodotus, in this case there are far too many other references in the surviving literature to dismiss such practices as myths. Documents referring to it exist not only in Babylonia, but come from Phrygia, Phoenicia, Syria, Lydia, Cyprus, Egypt, Israel, and Greece. In addition to the prostitute priestess, and women offering themselves to strangers, there were also many slave prostitutes (both male and female) attached to the temple whose income from prostitution reverted to the temple.

So strong were the religious associations of prostitution that even regular Babylonian prostitutes maintained an illusion of serving the gods by dedicating themselves to the services of their patron Ishtar. Some lived in a special house, the *Gagum,* under the supervision of the priestess-madam who managed the house. There were at least three categories of prostitutes, the Kizrete (or *Kizritu*), the Senhate (*Ukhatu*), and the Harimate (*Kharimtu*), this last group being the most notorious and the lowest in status. Men were warned against marrying the Harimates not only because they had possessed so many men but because they would not even give succor to a man in distress, would testify before a judge against any man, would not respect a husband, would bring low any house into which they came, and in general would bring unhappiness and depression to any men who married them.[11] It would seem that after receiving such warnings men would stay clear of any entanglements with such women, but they did not. Prostitutes were also attached to the wine or ale shops, which sometimes were run by women. Some of the women workers there might have been dancing girls or had other special talents.

The presence of a large number of female slaves was also conducive to prostitution, and documents dating from the seventh century B.C. indicate that some of the more well-to-do citizens of Babylonia derived substantial income through prostituting their female slaves. One such individual, Nabu-Aki-Iddin, established his female slaves in a brothel where he took seventy-five percent of their income.[12] Some of the poorer village people also sold their daughters into prostitution,[13] perhaps because they were unable to afford the necessary dowry.

It is possible that prostitutes were utilized by some Babylonian males as sex therapists. The basis for such a statement comes from a collection of documents grouped under the Sumerian term SA.ZI.GA., literally the "rising of the heart," which is generally translated as meaning sexual potency. Since the incantations are ostensibly recited by a woman who addresses a man, and the purpose of the incantation is a stimulation to make love, it is quite possible that these were associated with prostitution. While she was reciting the incantation, the woman would rub the penis of her client with a special mixture of *puru*-oil, an oil usually used for anointing the body. This special mixture was mixed with pulverized magnetic iron ore, perhaps to provide additional friction.[14] Males suffering from impotency went for the treatment, and could then demonstrate their cure on their partner.

Since modern methods of birth control were unknown, it would seem obvious that many of the prostitutes had children, although over the long period many of them might have become sterile through gonorrhea. The prostitutes probably kept their children sometimes, but many were adopted by the more respectable families. These children were desirable because the Babylonians believed that the dead would be utterly miserable in the afterlife unless there were survivors to look after them. Consequently, childless couples and other individuals, such as eunuchs, resorted to the adoption of the children of prostitutes in order to secure family continuity. The Hammurabic Code has a whole section dealing with adoption,[15] and such practices continued throughout most of Babylonian history.[16]

Although prostitution was recognized and accepted in Babylonia, the prostitute, at least the secular one, was considered an outcast. Assyrian law, which was similar to Babylonian, Akkadian, and other Near Eastern laws, required the prostitute to walk in the street with a bare head as a sign of her calling. Since the respectable woman wore both a veil and a head covering and the slave woman covered her head even though she went unveiled,[17] the implication was that the prostitute was considered to be lower than the slave. There were similiar laws regarding prostitution among the Hittites, a powerful people centered in Asia Minor. The Hittite Code recognized two different types of prostitutes, free and slave; there was no punishment for any free man who picked them up in order to spend the night.[18] There were also male prostitutes who engaged in sex with other men.

The peoples of the Mesopotamian valley looked on prostitution as a necessary operating principle of the universe,[19] as a necessary fact of life, and it obviously fitted well with the masculine assumptions of the Babylonian writers and theologians. Women in the area, regardless of particular peoples who were dominant, were property, and as such had special status. Female virginity and chastity was prized as a valuable commodity. At the same time there was a double standard for males, and the way the contradictions between female virtue and male promiscuity were resolved was by prostitution, the establishment of a special class of women outside the category of decent and respectable women. Among the prostitutes there was a hierarchical ranking; at the lowest level were the temple and other slaves who turned over their income to the temple or their masters. Somewhat higher were the tavern women and the women established in houses of prostitutino. Higher yet were the concubines and courtesans, who perhaps had special talents for entertaining their male companions. At the top were the temple prostitutes, the mistresses of the gods, although the whole question of sacred prostitution is a difficult one to generalize about, and many questions about the practice in Babylonia remain unclear. Excluding the sacred prostitutes, it seems that prostitutes were a special group of women with special status, cut off from proper society, and therefore associated with a loss of status. But in compensation for this loss, prostitutes were somewhat freer of the restrictions put on other women.

The double standard practiced in the Tigris-Euphrates valley can also be observed in ancient Egypt, another great center of civilization in the ancient Near East. Obviously there were changes in ideas and customs over the 2,500 years or more of Pharaonic Egypt, but these changes, at least as far as prostitution is concerned, are difficult to document, and all it is possible to do is generalize, using data from several periods in Egyptian history. In all periods monogamy was the rule for common people; girls married young, probably at 12 or 13, and their husbands were not much older, perhaps 15 or 16, although among the upper classes marriage for men might not take place until 20. Probably sexual relations took place from the time males felt the urge, since slave girl prostitutes were available and there was no particular emphasis on male premarital chastity. Maidservants belonged to their owner, and even adultery for the male was not considered a sin. Many of the more powerful figures had harems,[20] and concubinage was widespread.[21] Ramses II (thirteenth century B.C.) had five or six great wives (and over 100 children) and Ramses III (twelfth century) fell victim to a harem conspiracy. The word for harem was synonymous with the word for prison, and some Pharaohs had several harems, located in different places throughout their kingdoms. In the New Kingdom they were great institutions supported by rents and taxes. In the harems the queens and their maidservants engaged in weaving on a large scale. Apparently many nobles and kings wanted to take some of their sexual companions with them into the next world, and tombs of the Nile Valley have often been found to contain small figurines of women emphasizing the more alluring physical endowments of the females. It is possible these "dancing dolls," as they have been called, are fertility symbols, but they apparently had much more erotic meaning as well and have been taken to be representations of favored concubines or prostitutes not only from Egypt but from outside Egypt, since many of them have the Nubian characteristics of the Negro slave girls from the Upper Nile.[22]

The average Egyptian, however, was generally monogamous and the usual family unit was a husband, wife, and children. The laws made a clear distinction between a bachelor with a concubine and a married man. Adultery by a woman was cause for divorce and could mean burning at the stake, but a man could divorce his wife for many reasons, provided he paid compensation. If a couple was unable to have children, they could jointly acquire a young female slave and if she bore the husband children they could be legitimized by emancipation at his death.

Lifelong celibacy was apparently discouraged for both sexes, although during the reign of the Libyan, Ethiopian, and Saite kings of the first millennium B.C. there were divine wives or votaries of Amon, who were to remain chaste. Before this period, during the last part of the New Kingdom at the end of the second millennium B.C., some queens were at the same time the wife of the Pharaoh, the mother of his children, and the wife of the god Amon for purposes of ritual. By the time of the Twenty-first Dynasty it had been decreed that a virgin daughter of a king should be specially consecrated as the wife of the god. Married only to the god, the Divine Wife offered his cult a mildly erotic element since she was supposed to charm the god with her beauty and the music of her sistrums. Sitting on the knee of his statue she would put her arms around his neck in order to arouse him. She had a house specially endowed with services, lands, and all the formal attributes of the male Pharaoh although her power was spiritual and not particularly political. Still, each new ruler took care to see that a female member of his family became the presumptive heiress of the reigning Divine Wife. The court of the Divine Wife also included a harem of Amon's concubines, who were supposed to be virgins like herself, and who became the adoptive mothers of their successors.

Biologically women were regarded as a vessel for a man's seed, and the Egyptians considered the male element as the key to reproduction. They also, however, recognized the sexual enticements of the female, and the male recordkeepers were both fearful and admiring of this. Though Egyptian sources do not include the type of law codes that existed in the Tigris-Euphrates valley, some indication of the ambiguous view of women appears in the popular folktales. Two folktales dating from the Middle and New Kingdom periods deal with women committing adultery, and emphasize the double standard. In the first story, the woman is burned to death; in the second, her husband kills her and throws her corpse to the hounds. In these as well as other stories, women are pictured as sexual creatures, willing to betray their husbands and to use any form of trickery to get the men who physically attract them into bed. Gaston Maspero, the nineteenth-century editor of a collection of these stories, believed that such stories proved that the morals of the ancient Egyptian women were lax.[23] This and similar statements probably helped create legends about

the promiscuous Egyptian women. There is, however, another alternative
explanation that can also be documented from other sources, namely,
that these tales represent male wish-fulfillment much as the stories in
male magazines do today. In fact, the Egyptian woman is usually portrayed in art as the faithful, caring wife. Motherhood was her revered
function. Failure to have children was a terrible and lamentable situation,
and mothers and children are depicted at all periods in Egyptian tombs
and pictures.

Probably as in Babylonia, women's sexual role was highly restricted,
confined to two basic alternatives: the good woman, the wife, mother, or
virginal priestess; and the bad woman, the erotic, sexually enticing prostitute or mistress. Both exist in the literature, and prostitution was apparently widespread. In the so-called erotic papyrus of Turin, the adventures of an inexperienced man in a brothel are described in such great
detail that the work has remained unpublished because scholars in the
past regarded it as obscene. Though the males recognized the erotic nature
of the "bad" woman, they were also fearful of her, and there were dangers
that her sexuality would enable her to dominate. Since sexual aggressiveness was regarded as a way of dominating others,[24] one way the prostitute
could be kept in place was by assigning her to a position outside of
society. Even then there was danger. In one story, the courtesan, Tbubui,
was so attractive that her lover, Satni, turned over his money, power, and
children to her, and fell under her wicked influence.[25]

Still men were attracted to women, and since the role of the proper
wife was restricted, the prostitute often became the symbol of sexuality.
Young men especially turned to the prostitute, and they were warned
about going to beer halls:

> Thou sittest in the house and the girls encircle thee . . . thou sittest in
> front of the wench and art besprinkled with oil; thy garland of ishet-
> penu hangeth about thy neck and thou drummest on thy paunch. Thou
> doest reel, and [then] fallest upon thy belly.[26]

A "wise" man warned his reader to beware of the prostitute.

> Beware of a strange woman, one that is not known in the city. Wink not
> at her . . . have no carnal knowledge of her . . . [She is] a deep water
> whose twisting men know not. A woman that is far from her husband,
> "I am fair," she saith to thee every day, when she hath no witnesses.[27]

Instead, man would be best advised to ignore the prostitute and the
strange woman. Instead he should establish a household, marry, and love
his wife at home.

Fill her belly, clothe her back; unguent is the remedy for her limbs. Gladden her heart, so long as she lives; she is a goodly field for her lord. But hold her back from getting the mastery. [Remember that] her eye is her stormwind, and her vulva and her mouth are her strength.[28]

There was no denying that women were attractive and there was nothing "sweeter" than an hour spent with a lovely woman who says:

For I am with you, and you lift up my heart—for is there not embracing and fondling when you visit me and we give ourselves up to delights? If you wish to caress my things, then I will offer you my breast also—it won't thrust you away! Would you leave because you are hungry?—are you such a man of your belly?

Would you leave because you need something to wear?—I have a chestful of fine linen.

I go down into the water to be with you, and come up again to see you with a red fish lying so fine and splendid within my fingers [i.e. a penis]; and I place it upon my breast— Oh, brother! look and see![29]

Yet sex is dangerous and men are warned against approaching women other than their wives because "men are made fools by their gleaming limbs of carnelian. A trifle, a little, the likeness of a dream, and death comes as the end of knowing her."[30]

As in Babylonia there were probably slave prostitutes attached to temples although probably not on the same scale. An inscription of the Pharaoh Ramses III stated that he had captured many prisoners, and carried them away, "the males to thy store house; their women, to be subject of thy temples."[31] There is other evidence also indicating the existence of prostitution around the temple,[32] although much of the evidence for "sacred" prostitution comes from Greek writers, particularly Herodotus, and to a lesser extent Strabo,[33] and how far this can be applied to an earlier period is not at all clear.

Compared to women in the Tigris-Euphrates valley, Egyptian women had considerable freedom. Though most appeared only rarely in public life, a few did manage to hold important positions. There are records of a woman director of a dining hall, a manageress of a wig workshop, the headmistress of a group of singers, the supervisor of a house of weavers, a mistress of a royal harem, and a superintendent of a house. We know of at least one woman scribe who belonged to the household of a Thirteenth Dynasty queen, and it is possible that some queens and princesses knew how to write. Women also served as musicians and dancers outside the temple as well as inside, although most accounts of the secular dancers indicate they might have been a class of prostitute. Secular dancers, for example, dressed in diaphanous robes in order to show off their figures, and even at times left off the robes and danced wearing only anklets, bracelets, and rings. Even ordinary women occasionally were able to assert their sexuality, and at special religious festivals some of the prohibitions under which women lived were discarded and some women during such fetes went so far as to deliberately expose themselves to the males.[34]

Several women achieved legendary fame as prostitutes, although most of the information we have about famous prostitutes comes from the Greek writers, and belongs to mythology rather than history. One of the most famous of legendary prostitutes was the daughter of Cheops. According to Herodotus, Cheops found himself short of funds to build his pyramid, and in a desperate attempt to earn more he sent his daughter into the brothels with instructions to turn her fees over to him. His daughter did not mind prostituting herself but felt that the memory of her efforts should be preserved. In order to ensure a monument for herself, she required all her customers to bring a stone in addition to her fee. From these stones she built herself a pyramid that measured over 150 feet (an obviously apocryphal story about the scope of her prostitution).[35]

Herodotus also recounted a legendary story about the daughter of Ramses, who had been forced into prostitution by her father. Ramses had built a special vault for his vast treasures of silver and other valuables. The builder during the construction had inserted a special stone in the wall that could be removed from outside, and he planned to enter the treasure-house and take a share of the king's silver through this means. Before he could do so, he died but he passed on the information about the secret passage to his two sons, who used it to relieve the king of part of his treasure. Ramses, noticing the loss, set traps to capture the thieves. During their next raid one of the brothers was trapped, and in order to prevent recognition of the imprisoned brother, the other brother cut off his head and took it with him when he escaped. In a desperate attempt to find the thief, Ramses ordered his daughter into the brothels. There, instead of charging a fee, she would ask her prospective customers to tell her the cleverest and wickedest things that they had done in their life. The girl eventually found the man who had entered her father's tomb, but he was prepared for her and managed to escape. Later, Ramses issued a public pardon to the thief in order that the ex-thief might become the husband of his prostitute daughter.[36]

Still another legendary Egyptian courtesan was Rhodopis, who allegedly had been brought to Egypt from Greece as a slave. After her freedom she remained in Egypt practicing her profession and amassing a large fortune. In one version of the story Rhodopis is said to have built a pyramid for herself as a monument to her conquests, but another version has her giving a tenth part of her possessions to the temple at Delphi in Greece, where it was used to purchase roasting spits for the god.[37] There are many other famous Egyptian courtesans, especially at the Greek-Egyptian city of Naucratis, but though Herodotus mentions some of these he does not go into great detail.[38] If sex were one of the few weapons that women could use to get along in a man's world, it appears obvious that some Egyptian women were prepared to use it to advance themselves. Though the tales of Herodotus fall in the realm of mythology, they represent the ability of Egyptian courtesans to get ahead, and from other sources we know that even average women were not bashful in matters of love. In various poems and letters that have survived women pressed their suits directly.[39] Perhaps the most successful, and most tragic in this respect, was Cleopatra, who apparently gave birth to an illegiti-mate son of Julius Caesar, and somewhat later became the beloved of Marc Antony. At Antony's death she tried unsuccessfully to negotiate an alliance with Octavian, better known as Augustus. Perhaps she would have been successful in this last effort as well, but the difficulty with using sex as a base for advancement is that it grows less effective with age, and even Cleopatra, one of the most successful women ever in her ability to capitalize on her sex, found that out.

The people of the ancient Near East about whom we know the most are the Jews. Scriptures furnish us a great deal of information. Prostitu-tion is frequently mentioned in the Bible and prostitutes held a regulated status in the Jewish Scriptures. Though there are occasional injunctions against it, the normal practice was to accept prostitution as a fact of life without any moral condemnation, in much the same way it was accepted throughout the Near East. Moses did issue injunctions against fathers prostituting their daughters,[40] but at the same time the law allowed a father to sell his daughter as a concubine.[41] Priests, descendants of Aaron, were prohibited from marrying harlots or divorced women, and the death penalty of burning was decreed for the daughter of a priest who became a harlot,[42] but other Israelites could still marry prostitutes, and their daughters were not killed if they chose that profession.

Probably the hostility to the association of prostitution with any priestly family was an attempt of the Jews to stamp out sacred prostitu-tion, which they associated with idol worship and paganism. Sacred pros-titution, where the prostitute herself was regarded as a priestess or a sacred person, was practiced by many of the neighboring peoples in the area, and occasionally crept into Judaism itself. The sons of Eli, for example, are said to have employed their priestly office in the rite of sacred prostitution, by lying with the "women that did service at the door" of the tabernacle of the congregation.[43] The author of the First Book of Samuel ascribed the defeat of Israel by the Philistines, the capture of the ark of the Law, and the death of Eli and his sons to this action. Later Rehoboam, son of Solomon, is said to have introduced the practice into the Temple of Jerusalem under the influence of his Ammonite mother.[44] Though there were attempts to eradicate it, Biblical sources indicated it continued to exist until the reign of King Josiah.[45] The Hebrew term for sacred prostitute was *kedeshah* (for the female) and *kadesh* (for the male), and the author of Deuteronomy emphasized that there should be no *kedeshah* among the daughters of Israel, nor *kadesh* among the sons of Israel.[46]

Apparently, after the reign of Josiah this kind of sacred prostitution disappeared in Israel, but a second kind of temple prostitution, whereby women donated income earned from prostitution to the Temple, continued to exist. It is believed that this type of prostitution was involved in the account of Judah and Tamar and that Judah mistook his daughter-in-law for a temple prostitute. In Genesis, Tamar was the daughter-in-law of Judah and the wife of Er, Judah's eldest son. When Er was killed, she was married to Judah's next son, Onan, in accordance with the levirate custom. Onan, however, did not want to fulfill his brotherly duty of getting Tamar pregnant, and for his refusal God struck him dead. Judah, perhaps fearful that Tamar was an evil influence, refused to marry her to Shelah, his remaining son. Instead he sent her back to her father's house in widow's garments, disgraced and unhappy because she remained childless. Determined to continue the seed of her husband's family, Tamar cast aside her widow's garment, and disguising herself as a heavily veiled prostitute, stationed herself at the side of the road that she knew Judah would have to pass on his way to shear his sheep. Judah took the road, saw her, and thinking she was a temple prostitute, became enamored of her, and bargained for her sexual services. She obliged, but since he had no money with him she kept his signet, bracelets, and staff as a pledge. Later Judah sent a friend with a young kid, her fee, to redeem the pledge, but the prostitute was no longer at her regular waiting place. When he learned that he could not pay the woman, Judah was very much afraid of being publicly shamed, an indication that recourse to a temple prostitute was regarded as an honorable business transaction; it was only dishonorable not to pay her. Though Judah felt no guilt about his act, he reacted differently when he heard stories that his daughter-in-law was pregnant and had been prostituting herself. He immediately ordered her to be brought forth in order to be burned to death, the punishment for adultery.

Tamar came, showed Judah his own signet, bracelets, and staff, and forced him to admit that she had been more righteous than he because he had not given her his third son as a husband.[47] How widespread such prostitution was is not clear from the sources nor is it clear when it originated. It might have originated centuries before the Jews entered Palestine or it might have been adopted by them from their Canaanite neighbors. Whatever the source, there soon came to be stringent prohibitions against bringing either a prostitute or money for the hiring of a prostitute into the house of the Lord.[48]

Apparently some types of prostitution were also associated with some of the pagan festivals that continued to exist in Israel, although there is no record of such sex orgies on uniquely Jewish holidays. From the sources, however, it seems that many Jews joined the pagans in celebrating their festivals, and in fact it has been claimed that it was the sexual implications of the pagan festivals both that proved so fascinating to the Jews and that led to the extreme intolerance of the Biblical commentators toward the original inhabitants of Canaan.[49]

Whether or not religious prostitution was alien to Judasim is perhaps debatable, but this is not the case with secular prostitution, which probably was as widespread among the Jews as among the other peoples of the ancient Near East. The Hebrew term for prostitute was *zonah,* technically the "faithless one." Louis Epstein felt the term dated from remote antiquity among the Hebrews, when many had metronymic wives, that is, wives who stayed with their families and were only occasionally visited by their husbands. In addition to these metronymic marriages, the man probably also had a patronymic wife at home who was part of his household and was entirely under his control. Since the metronymic wife was not subject to her husband's domination, she could send him away when she was dissatisfied with him, and take on another. As the custom of having a metronymic wife receded into the past, the term *zonah* came more and more to refer to prostitute, an indication of the difficulty of fitting a metronymic wife in the regular family framework.[50] Also called *zonah* were women innkeepers, and this emphasizes the very early association of prostitution with hotels and inns, and thus suggests the origin of the word. Since the natural location of an inn was near the gate of the city, it seems clear that brothels were also near the exterior of the city, although they were probably segregated from the other hotels. The antiquity of segregating such houses appears in the Biblical story of Rahab the harlot. It was to her house, near the walls of Jericho, that emissaries of Joshua went.[51] When Jericho fell into the hands of Joshua and his followers, she was able to continue her profession,[52] and for her services the lives of her parents, brothers, and sisters were also spared.

In addition to the prostitutes in the brothels, there were also street-walkers who were somewhat lower on the social scale. It is possible that such women had their origin in the temple prostitute women who dedicated their gain from prostitution to the Temple, but if so, they soon became secularized, attracting attention by singing. The prophet Isaiah, for example, referred to the song of the harlot:

> Take a harp,
> Go about the city,
> Thou harlot long forgotten;
> Make sweet melody,
> Sing many songs,
> That you mayest be remembered.[53]

There are numerous other Biblical references to prostitution, most of them indicating acceptance of the prostitute as a fact of life. Jephthah was the son of Gilead and a harlot, and although he was prevented from inheriting because his mother was not his father's legal wife, he was not taunted because his mother was a prostitute.[54] Samson the Nazarite, that is, a man dedicated to God while still in his mother's womb, was reported to have visited the prostitutes in Gaza,[55] and this was accepted as a more or less normal thing to do. Prostitutes could even appeal to the king for judgments, and one such quarrel between two harlots who each claimed the same child as her own was settled by Solomon, who demonstrated his legendary wisdom and determined the true mother.[56] It is possible, however, that the quarrel was not between two prostitutes but between two metronymic wives.[57] Prostitutes could be seen everywhere in ancient Palestine: passing along the city street where they sang and played the harp,[58] sitting at important intersections,[59] watching from the doorsteps of their houses where they provocatively called to passersby,[60] or parading in colorful attire throughout the city.[61] Houses of prostitution were a permanent feature of city life,[62] were identified by displaying a red emblem, and attracted a host of onlookers as well as customers.[63] Though prostitutes are often characterized as being brazen, full of arrogance, riotous and rebellious, or honeyed and seductive,[64] they are not necessarily regarded as evil persons. Perhaps the attitude is best expressed in the apocryphal Book of Tobit, in which the young man is warned to beware of whores and whoredom[65] in much the same manner as a banker father might advise his college-age son to avoid speculation and invest in gilt-edged securities. Probably similar attitudes existed in other parts of the Near East, but the documentation is not so detailed.

Regardless of the toleration toward prostitution, it seems clear that parents whose daughters turned to prostitution were disgraced. The daughter of a priest who turned to prostitution was to be put to death by burning,[66] and even the daughter of an ordinary man was in trouble if she proved not to be a virgin on her marriage. Deuteronomic legislation stated that if the "tokens" of virginity were not found in her, "they shall bring out the damsel to the door of her father's house, and the men of her city shall stone her with stones that she die; because she hath wrought a wanton deed in Israel, to play the *harlot* in her father's house; so shalt thou put away the evil from the midst of thee."[67]

Once a woman was a prostitute, free from the influence of her male relatives, no such punishment was forthcoming. Then the prostitute was accepted as a necessary fact of life. One of the most detailed descriptions of the ways of the harlot is found in the Book of Proverbs.

> In the twilight, in the evening, in the black and dark night:
> And behold, there met him a woman with the attire of a harlot, and subtil of heart.
> (She is loud and stubborn; her feet abide not in her house: Now is she without, now in the streets, and lieth in wait at every corner.) So she caught him, and kissed him, and with an impudent face said unto him, I have peace offerings with me; this day have I paid my vows.
> Therefore came I forth to meet thee, diligently to see thy face, and I have found thee.
> I have decked my bed with coverings of tapestry, with carved works, with fine linen of Egypt.
> I have perfumed my bed with myrrh, aloes, and cinnamon.
> Come, let us take our fill of love until the morning: let us solace ourselves with loves.
> For the good man is not at home, he is gone a long journey:
> He hath taken a bag of money with him, and will come at the day appointed.
> With her much fair speech she caused him to yield, with the flattering of her lips she forced him.
> He goeth after her straightway, as an ox goeth to the slaughter, or as a fool to the correction of the stocks:
> Till a dart strike through his liver; as a bird hasteth to the snare, and knoweth not that it is for his life.[68]

Although both men and women were urged to observe premarital chastity, Jewish law never prohibited sexual relations between unmarried persons. Still there was a double standard. Virginity in a bride was especially prized, although the seduction or rape of a virgin was not so much a moral crime as a crime against some other man's property. For the lost virginity, the family could demand compensation or force her ravisher to take her in marriage. Children resulting from premarital activities or even from prostitution were regarded as legitimate. The Biblical references to bastards are restricted to offspring of unions that were regarded as impermissible in marriage, such as incestuous or adulterous relations, or relations between a member of a priestly caste and a divorcée.[69]

Polygamy was widespread among the Biblical patriarchs, but a married woman who had intercourse with another man was an adulteress. Gideon, the Israelite judge, had enough wives to bear him seventy sons.[70] Other polygamists included Jair, Ibzan, Abdon, David, Solomon, and Rehoboam, although it is sometimes difficult to separate wives from concubines since Abraham, Jacob, Gideon, Saul, David, and Solomon all had concubines. A concubine could be the slave girl of a man's wife, as was the case of Hagar and Sarah or Bilhah and Rachel, and several others, but a man could also buy a concubine for himself or take one captured in war. A woman's status in society was dependent to a large extent on her fruitfulness, and the inability to bear children was a cause of disgrace. The childless Sarah, for example, was despised by her handmaid Hagar, and Sarah was beside herself when Hagar gave Abraham a son. Inevitably, married women were far more restricted in their sexual relations than men, and the adultery of a married woman could result in the death penalty,[71] while a married man suffered no such punishment.

Complicating this double standard was the fact that women were recognized as sexual creatures, the good wife as well as the prostitute. It was Potiphar's wife who tried to seduce Joseph;[72] Rachel and Leah engaged in bargaining for sexual rights to their husband, Jacob;[73] Delilah was the cause of Samson's downfall;[74] and even when a woman was peacefully taking a sunbath her sexuality showed through, as the innocent Bathsheba found when she attracted the attention of David.[75] The straying of Solomon, the "beloved of God," was due to women, since his "wives turned away his heart after other gods: and his heart was not perfect with the Lord his God, as was the heart of David his father."[76] The term Jezebel, the name of the wife of Ahab, has become a pejorative term in English because the Biblical writers state that she led her husband to worship the pagan god, Baal.[77] Inevitably a man had to be ever watchful and it was not his fault if he strayed. In Proverbs, the most conspicuous and vividly developed theme is the importance of avoiding "strange women," or any woman other than one's wife. Proverbs also characteristically present the erring woman as more guilty than the man, and though he might be weak she is the one who has sinister designs. A poor credulous man would follow a woman just as an ox goes to the slaughter.[78] In this Adam himself had served as an example.

Though some of the Biblical prophets made efforts to stamp out harlotry, it was tolerated as a lesser of two evils. Women had to be protected both from themselves and from men, and the way to do so was to tolerate prostitution. In this way Jewish girls could enter their nuptials in purity and innocence, while the sexual activities of unmarried males could be allowed. Though Jewish tradition attempted to raise the level of morality among males, it recognized the difficulties, and under the circumstances prostitution was an accepted outlet. It was a necessity but it should not be glamorized, only recognized by law and carefully regulated. There were limits: Jews were warned not to establish prostitutes in their temples, in part because this was a heathen ceremony; and any prostitution with overtones of paganism was looked upon with horror. Periodically we find accounts of the destruction of the sacred groves around the temples that served as centers for prostitution, and the worship of Baal was closely related in the minds of the Biblical prophets with temple prostitution.[79] Though monogamy was generally the rule, the rich often had concubines, a few had harems, and polygamy also existed.

This encouraged a tolerant attitude toward prostitution since such practices cut down on the availability of women as wives. Though the family with a prostitute daughter was often considered a disgrace, it is not always clear why women became prostitutes. Undoubtedly many had no choice; they were either slaves or widows or orphans without any livelihood. Some were disowned by their families or had families who could not support them. When this happened, prostitution was one of the few ways in which they could earn a living. How many women entered into prostitution willingly either as full- or part-time professionals is difficult to say. For those who did, the condemnation of the harlot was so severe that it took special courage to defy such social and moral forces.

The various peoples of the Near East, in spite of their differences, held basic attitudes in common that had an effect on prostitution. Marriage was increasingly regarded as an economic transaction and the woman herself represented a kind of property. The richer man emphasized his prosperity by establishing harems, taking concubines, or engaging in polygamy. Since a wife was property there were also special premiums attached to her virginity; a lack of virtue lowered a girl's bride price or in some cases disqualified her for marriage. The emphasis on female virtue was not matched by a similar premium on male virtue, perhaps because this was more difficult to ascertain. Women who became prostitutes lost their standing among the proper women who were wives or mothers, but gained some freedom from the restrictions imposed on other women. Often prostitution was the only alternative occupation available to women who lacked a husband.

All the peoples made a distinction between the sexual privileges of the male and those of the female by putting limits on female promiscuity. In all these societies, prostitution became one way of meeting the demands imposed by a double standard, and by a shortage of women. In many societies the women who turned to prostitution did so originally in the name of religion, and engaged in it only occasionally, but increasingly this form of prostitution was secularized. As money increased and urbanization grew, what might have been an occasional occupation for some women, such as innkeepers or tavern operators, became a full-time speciality trade. Women who entered such a field must have suffered great ostracism from their families, since promiscuity was regarded as essentially a male prerogative. Women were prized as mothers, but mothers were not regarded as particularly desirable sex companions. Since the male believed that he was the main force in procreation, it was important that his wife be kept pure for his seed. No such restrictions were put on his sexual pleasure, while the good woman found her sex life very restricted.

3 THE GREEKS: PORNOGRAPHY AND FEARS ABOUT SEX

Pornography is derived from Greek words meaning "the writing of prostitutes." By extension any description of the life, manners, and action of prostitutes or their patrons constituted pornography, a form of literature invented by the Greeks. Though much of the literature concerning prostitution is no longer extant, references to it can be found in the works of Lucian, Alciphron, Athenaeus, Demosthenes, and others. Although many of the stories seemed designed to excite and titillate, and are more fiction than reality (for example, the account of Egyptian courtesans by Herodotus), there are still enough hard kernels of information to reconstruct some basic account of prostitution and its place in Greek culture.

An indication of the passionate interest of the Greeks in prostitution is the variety of terms they developed to describe the prostitute as well as the allied personnel involved, such as the brothelkeeper or procurer. Generally the term *pornoi* (perhaps best translated by the English word *whore*) was used for the lowest class of prostitutes, or as a term of denigration when applied to others. The euphemism *hetaira,* literally meaning comrade or companion, was the preferred term for the higher-class courtesans. In between there were many other terms, including such expressions as the chopper-up, the bridge woman, the parish worker, the public woman, the runner, the shut-in, the she-wolf, the dice, the foal, the kneading trough, the ground thumper, the bedroom article, and so on.[1]

Probably the main reason for the plethora of references to prostitution was that Greek civilization was so male-oriented. Prostitutes were probably not any more plentiful in Greek society than in many other societies, but the only women most Greeks had contact with in a social sense were prostitutes. The fascination of the Greeks with them is found in extant literature. Proper women did not take part in public life but were confined to home and children. To the men of the time it was inappropriate for a non-prostitute to make a public display of herself, to attract attention. Proper women did not accompany their husbands as guests in other houses, and if their husbands had dinner guests, wives were excluded from eating with them. Women did have some legal rights: we know that they took part in making wills, in some family councils, and that they had organizations of their own. But generally women were almost entirely dependent on their male relatives, husbands, fathers, brothers, or sons. A proper woman was cut off from the public world almost entirely, and this enforced retirement from the outside world might have contributed toward making the Greek wife somewhat uninteresting; at least the portrayal of them in most of Greek literature is not particularly attractive.

The civic necessity for female virginity ensured that girls would be married very young, probably at fourteen, though there were some Athenian writers who thought the age should be eighteen or twenty as it was said to be in Sparta. The husband on the other hand was usually much older when he married, and a sixteen- to twenty-year age difference was not uncommon. The chief purpose of women was childbearing, particularly of sons, and children were regarded as essential in the Greek world. It was woman as mother who was most praised in the Greek world; otherwise women were not to be seen or heard. The women who seemed to break through these stereotypes most effectively were the courtesans and prostitutes. For a woman to enter male society, even at the level of an unequal, she had to lose her status as a proper woman.[2]

Prostitution was accepted as a natural way of life, so much so that many states levied a tax on its practitioners. Tradition ascribes the beginning of the tax in Athens to the famed constitution-giver Solon, who filled the brothels with female slaves, taxed the proceeds, and built a temple to Aphrodite with the income. The women who worked in these houses were the lowest of the law, lacking status even among other prostitutes. They awaited their customers clad only in thin dresses of diaphanous material, or sometimes even without any clothing at all, so that the customer could pick out the type and shape that pleased him most. Their cost was next to nothing, only an obol (or a penny and a half).[3] Though there was probably a difference of fees among the brothels, the competition was such that one brothel was not much different from another. The customer paid a small fee to enter the brothel, and usually gave the girl or girls a small additional present. Most of the Greek states regulated the fees, kept track of them in order to collect the prostitute tax, and sent out a "whore collector" to see that it was paid. A special official supervised the brothels; it was his duty to see that public decency prevailed in the houses and to decide the various disputes that might arise.[4]

Slightly above the *pornoi* in the hierarchy of the prostitutes were the streetwalkers, who did not wait for their customers in the brothel but sought them out in the streets, in taverns, or similar places. Often these seem to have been older women, perhaps ex-hetairae, who had fallen on bad times. Some might well have been local residents who had turned to the streets, and others were servants (slaves?) of hotels and taverns who were there to serve the customers. A surviving erotic poem gives an example of chance pickups by a streetwalker.

He:	Good evening.	She:	Good evening.
He:	What may your name be?	She:	And yours?
He:	Don't be so inquisitive all at once.	She:	Well don't you?
He:	Are you engaged?	She:	To anyone that likes me.
He:	Will you come to supper tonight?	She:	If you like.
He:	Very well. How much shall it be?	She:	Don't give me anything in advance.
He:	That is strange.	She:	Give me what you think right after sleeping with me.
He:	That is quite fair. Where do you live? I will send.	She:	I will tell you.
He:	And when will you come?	She:	Anytime you like.
He:	I would like now.	She:	Then go in front.

At times the streetwalker did not make the arrangements herself but rather had them made for her by her maid or assistant, who followed a few steps behind. Another erotic poem gives an example of this.

He:	Good day, my dear.	She:	Good day.
He:	Who is she who is walking in front of you?	She:	What is that to you?
He:	I have a reason for asking.	She:	My mistress.
He:	May I hope?	She:	What do you want?
He:	A night.	She:	What have you for her?
He:	Gold.	She:	Then take her at once.
He:	So much (showing the amount).	She:	You can't.

Some of the more blatant advertised their presence by painting or engraving words or phrases on their shoes; one shoe is preserved that has the phrase "Follow me" etched into it so that when the prostitute walked her message was imprinted on the ground.[7] The Greek writer Asclepiades wrote that he once met a prostitute named Hermione, who wore a flowered girdle that had words reading "Love me always, but do not be jealous if others do as you do" embroidered on it.[8]

Many of the streetwalkers were older women who perhaps lacked the stamina to remain in a brothel; at least some of the evidence indicated that they relied on cosmetics to make them more attractive or to make them appear younger than they were. Some did not bother to go out at all but stationed themselves at open windows, beckoning to prospective customers on the street. If a client appeared interested, a go-between, usually the maid of the prostitute, collected the fee and led the man to the designated place of assignation, which was often so poorly lighted that it was difficult to see the actual features of the prostitute.[9] Streetwalkers perhaps inevitably were allowed to engage in more deception of their customers than the more regulated women in the brothels. Greek inns were also centers of prostitution, and it was not uncommon for them to have girls available to satisfy the varied desires of the weary but not yet sleepy traveler. Theophrastus, for example, classed brothels and inns in the same category,[10] whereas Plato remarked on the poor reputation of innkeepers.[11] The geographer Strabo reported that an earthquake that destroyed a Phrygian village inn had also killed a great number of prostitutes.[12] Some hotels apparently established living merchandise counters for their customers, although occasionally travelers brought their own feminine companionship with them.[13]

A step above the streetwalker were the flute and cithara players, dancers, acrobats, and other female entertainers, who supplemented their earnings with prostitution. Flute players, *auletrides,* were often sold at high prices at slave auctions and apparently their sexual abilities were a factor in increasing their price. This was true of dancers as well. It was not unusual for female dancers to bare their thighs during a dance in order to better show their charms,[14] and several of the surviving vase paintings show them in provocative poses. Dancers and musicians often performed in such diaphanous clothes that they gave the illusion of wearing nothing, and to further encourage amorous advances they often sang phallic songs.[15] The girls who danced for King Antigonus of Macedonia at a reception he gave for an embassy from Arcadia did so in such a provocative manner that the Arcadian ambassadors rushed upon the girls and literally raped them on the spot.[16] Another flute player-dancer was so provocative in her performance that an aged pacifist philosopher started fighting over her.[17] Many of the female professionals boasted of the reaction that they provoked.

Some of the dancing girls became rich. Their homes along with those of the hetairae were among the showplaces of ancient Alexandria.[18] One of the most famous was Lamia, who entertained and served King Ptolemy of Egypt, and then after his death, when she herself was forty, became the mistress of King Demetrius of Macedonia. Plutarch reported that she was called Lamia, vampire or bloodsucker, because of her depravity. Though this remark can be dismissed as that of a hostile witness, her power was said to be so great that Demetrius levied a special tax on Athens just in order to buy her soap. Nevertheless the Athenians became enamored of her, nicknamed her the city taker, built a temple in her honor, and deified her under the name of Venus Lamia.[19]

At the top of the prostitute's social ladder were the hetairae, women who enjoyed a position unequaled by any other of their sex. The hetairae knew how to fascinate the most distinguished male personalities of the time—generals, statesmen, men of letters, artists, and others, and how to keep the affection of such men over a period of time. They were among the best educated of Greek women and, at least in the minds and hearts of the males, had considerable unofficial social status, although officially they lacked status. Statues of several of these women were set up in temples or other public buildings, often close to those of meritorious generals and statesmen. Almost every important male personality had some contact with them.

The chief center of the hetairae was the city of Corinth, but they were spread throughout the Greek world. Corinth gave them special honor in the celebration of the festivals of the goddess Aphrodite because allegedly they had, through their prayers, helped save Corinth from the Persians. Legend has it that the Corinthians had a plaque set up bearing the name of the hetairae who had "united in devout prayer to the heavenly Cyprian goddess," since their brave championing of the Corinthian cause had encouraged the divine Aphrodite to use her powers to support the Greeks.[20] Some have equated the hetairae with religious prostitution, but if this argument has merit, it is clear that they were not sacred prostitutes but temple prostitutes, that is, women who gave part of their income to the temple of Aphrodite. Temples of Aphrodite were located at several places in the Greek world, but none matched the riches at Corinth. Some indication of the reason for this is given by the geographer Strabo, who reported that the Corinthian temple had more than a thousand prostitutes dedicated to the goddess. This number probably included hetairae as well as slaves who were owned by the temple. These proved to be a great attraction for sailors and other travelers, and one of the reasons Corinth was such a rich city was that thousands of strangers came there to visit the girls.[21] Prostitutes were given to the temple of Aphrodite in much the same way that a person might now donate a candle or offer a prayer. Xenophon of Corinth, who won the pentathalon and stadium (the 220-yard dash) in the Olympic games of 464 B.C., made a vow that if he won he would dedicate a hundred girls to the service of the temple.[22] Other temples of Aphrodite might also have had slave prostitutes.[23]

Aphrodite was the goddess of love and she not only bestowed the enjoyment of love, but in fact this enjoyment for others was given only with her permission. If a girl earned her dowry by prostitution in the service of Aphrodite, marriage could be promoted at the same time that an act of piety was performed. If the girls prostituted themselves for money, part of which they donated to the temple treasury, this too could be an act of piety since it was a thanks offering to the goddess for female beauty, maturity, and fruitfulness. It would be a mistake, however, to look on the hetairae as priestesses of Aphrodite; instead they were women who looked to her as patroness. The true religious prostitutes, the *hieroduli* of the ancient Near East, were not entirely unknown in the Greek world, but were outnumbered by their lay sisters. The hetairae undoubtedly attempted to established some connection with Aphrodite since by so doing they could dignify their sexual activities with an overlay of religion. Thus they were not only devoted to gaining a living and satisfying sensual desires, but fulfilling a religious obligation as well.

The attempt of the hetairae to become something more than a simple sexual mate for the male perhaps accounts for the difference in status between them and lesser prostitutes. The poet Pindar dedicated a hymn to them that begins, "O girls, guest-loving servants of persuasion in wealthy Corinth, who so piously send up the golden tears of fresh incense, and in spirit direct your flight to Aphrodite, the heavenly mother of Love, who from above grants you sweet forgiveness, O girls, who so blamelessly cull the fruit of tender youth in the joys of love."[24]

To be a high-class hetaira required special training or experience. Correct dress and the proper application of cosmetics played an important part in this,[25] as did an understanding of the needs and desires of the male. The more the cortesans knew, the more they could charge their customers. Inevitably their prices were high, and there was a common saying that not every man could afford to go to Corinth. The hetairae were also expected to be good conversationalists, and all of this implies a kind of schooling that could pass the knowledge down from generation to generation. Aspasia, the beloved of Pericles, perhaps conducted such a school but this is open to question. Probably at first the instruction was irregular, then as the hetairae became institutionalized some sort of oral catechism might have come into being, and eventually would have been written down. No such manuals have actually survived, but both Greeks and Latin writers hint that there was a certain core of common knowledge among the better-class prostitute. The Latin sources will be discussed later; in Greek, the best source of information on the education of courtesans is in Lucian's *Dialogues of Courtesans*. In one of the dialogues the widow Crobyle is attempting to persuade her fatherless daughter, Corinna, to become a professional prostitute, a not too difficult task since the girl has been well paid for her first efforts in this direction. Crobyle, however, has high ambitions for her daughter, and she wants her not to be an ordinary prostitute but a hetaira, a woman who always dresses correctly, is well behaved, and is much admired by men because she never tricks them or attempts to marry them. The most desirable prostitute is described as one who is careful to avoid drunkenness and overeating since this weakens her ability to get men under her power. Crobyle also takes care to caution her daughter that handsome men are not necessarily the best customers since they too often want to pay only with their person. The mother states that if her daughter follows her advice she can become one of the greatest of courtesans.[26]

Inevitably the prostitute attracted the attention of the Greek writers, and though none of the comedies by such writers as Eubulus, Perecrates, Diocles, Alexis, or Menander have survived, there is still a vast literature about the legendary courtesans. One of the most well-known was Thaïs, the mistress of Alexander the Great, who accompanied him on his campaigns. Supposedly at her suggestion, Alexander burned the Persian royal palace. After his death, Thaïs became queen of Egypt through her marriage to Ptolemy.[27] Lamia of Athens, previously mentioned, allegedly rebuilt the ruined picture gallery of the Sicyonians from her earnings.[28] Cottina dedicated a bronze statue of a cow at Sparta,[29] and many other such monuments are recorded.[30]

The literature is especially filled with their wit and their ability to use all sorts of double-entendres in their conversation.[31] A dramatist admirer of the prostitute Gnathaena remarked on the delicious chill of the wine that she served him. She replied that she had used his plays to cool it with. Another admirer sent her a small bottle of wine with the remark that it was sixteen years old too, and she replied that for "its years" it was "very small."[32] At least two famous prostitutes were named Laïs, both of them celebrated in various anecdotes and epigrams. Laïs the elder was a native of Corinth, who lived at the time of the Peloponnesian War. She was equally famous for her beauty and her greed. Laïs the younger was a native of Sicily, whose friends and lovers included painters, orators, and philosophers. She was supposedly killed by some women who were jealous of her beauty.

In the following stories no effort has been made to distinguish one

Laïs from another if only because the stories are not always clear. The philosopher Diogenes, who spent much of his time hunting for an honest man, was much attracted to Laïs, as was the rhetorician Aristippus. When Aristippus was reproached for spending so much money on Laïs while Diogenes allegedly enjoyed her favors for nothing, he reportedly replied: "I am generous to Laïs in order that I may enjoy her; not in order to prevent another from enjoying her as well."[33] On the other hand, Laïs gave of herself free to Diogenes in order, she said, to have a philosopher at her feet. The two men also quarreled over her. Diogenes allegedly reproached Aristippus for being intimate with a whore and Aristippus in turn asked Diogenes if he did not think it absurd to put up at a house where others had lived before. When Diogenes replied that he had no objections, Aristippus then asked him if he objected to boarding a ship on which others had traveled before him. Again Diogenes answered in the negative. Aristippus concluded that he could then see no reason why Diogenes should object if one lived with a woman whom others also had possessed.[34]

The great sculptor Myron, in his old age, persuaded Laïs to pose for him but she walked out on him when he proposed she share his bed. Myron, not to be put off, had his beard cut off, put a gold chain around his neck, bought a new scarlet robe with a golden girdle, rouged his cheeks, perfumed himself, and approached her again. After hearing the pleas of the "new" Myron, Laïs again sent him away stating that she could not give to him what she had refused to his father the day before. The Greeks at her death supposedly honored her with a tomb to commemorate her reputation as the greatest conquerer they had ever known.[35]

The woman considered the most beautiful, the most famous, and the most dangerous courtesan in Athens was Phryne. Once when Phryne was on trial in Athens, her defender, Hyperides, seeing little hope in the merits of her case, suddenly tore off her clothes to disclose the beauty of her breasts. The judges were so taken with awe at her beauty that they failed to find her guilty.[36] Allegedly Phryne had a very beautiful body but her modesty was such that she was reluctant to put herself on display. Even at festivals she refused to remove her clothes although once at a festival of Poseidon she walked clothed into the sea, where she removed her clothing so that the god Poseidon alone could see her.[37] Phryne consented to be the model for the famous sculptor Praxiteles only because she wanted some sort of permanent memento of herself. Allegedly she also offered to rebuild the ruined walls of Thebes if the Thebans would agree to put the inscription "Destroyed by Alexander, rebuilt by Phryne" on them.[38]

Much less legendary, and therefore also more tragic, was Aspasia, the mistress of Pericles, the leader of Athens in the fifth century B.C.

Pericles was so enamored of Aspasia that he divorced his wife in order to live with her, even though she could never be considered a legitimate wife. For her alliance with Pericles she was attacked by the poets and comic writers, as well as by the virtuous women, who had been willing to tolerate her as mistress but not as a respectable matron. All kinds of rumors floated around about her. It was said she procured free women for the immoral purposes of her husband, that she maintained a regular brothel, that she dominated Pericles, and some even maintained that the Peloponnesian War had been caused by her efforts to recover two of her harlots who had been stolen by the Megarians.[39] She was publicly insulted at the theater, attacked in the street, and as a final act of revenge, she was accused of treasonable impiety. Pericles, his power already in decline, appeared as her advocate but his legendary eloquence failed him. All he could do was to put his arms around her and burst into tears. In the end this proved to be the most effective defense since, in spite of popular prejudice, Aspasia was acquitted and restored to society. After the death of Pericles in 429 B.C., Aspasia became the mistress of Lysicles, another popular leader, and old animosities gradually died. She lived to see her son by Pericles legitimatized by the Athenians.[40]

There were many other legendary hetairae. Included in any list would be Klepsydra (hourglass), so called because she accepted and dismissed her lovers by the hourglass. Thargelia, a Milesian prostitute, accompanied the Persian Xerxes on his invasion of Greece and helped his cause by sending back reports on the Greek military leaders whom she met in the course of her profession. Danaë and Leontis allegedly taught Epicurus the philosophy of pleasure, and Themistonoe practiced her art until she had lost her last tooth and the last lock of her hair. Theoris and Archippe served as mistresses to Sophocles, and Archaenassa served Plato in a like capacity. Pythionike rose to become queen of Babylon, and after her death, Glycera, another prostitute, succeeded to the same honor. Theodota was the disciple and companion of Socrates. Gnathaena taught her daughter Gnathaenion to follow in her footsteps but encouraged her to hold out for a price of one thousand drachmas for her services. Niko also taught her daughter Pythias to adopt her profession.[41]

The literature also includes a great amount of information about the mercenary character of the hetairae. Euphro, Laïs (both), and Boidion are said to have turned three merchant seamen out after having robbed them of everything but their ships, with the result that they were poorer than if they had been shipwrecked. Philumena, the courtesan, reportedly told her friend Criton not to send her any more letters but instead fifty gold pieces since these would mean more than any letter.[42] Europa was satisfied with a drachma for a visit, but Gnathaena, as indicated, wanted a thousand for her daughter. Probably both prices represent extremes and the regular price was somewhere in between. The hetairae had to charge high prices since they had their position to maintain: they gave expensive dedicatory gifts to the gods, their homes had to be comfortable for their guests, their beds soft, their clothes expensive, and their beauty carefully maintained.

A few prostitutes were also known for their intellectual ability. The more educated hetairae knew the current literature of Greece as well as the traditional literature of the past; they attended lectures, and were able to amuse their more distinguished patrons with their conversation. Some of them, notably Thaïs and Aspasia, were celebrated as philosophical disputants and were famous for their literary style, although none was recognized as equal to the male masters. Aspasia had a school for young women at which she herself taught.[43] Hipparchia, the mistress of the cynic Crates, and a philosopher in her own right, often engaged in a fierce interchange with rivals.[44]

Still the hetairae were vulnerable creatures in a man's world. Many ultimately were deserted by their lovers. Bacchis, a famous prostitute, had been presented very early in her career with a necklace of enormous value. Later in her career she fell in love with the orator Hyperides and became his mistress. Hyperides, however, was rather fickle and when one of his loves demanded that he give her the necklace of Bacchis as a fee, he did so. The news quickly reached Bacchis, but the only thing she could do was to demonstrate how little Hyperides meant to her by becoming a friend to his new girl.[45]

The stories go on, but there is a sameness about them. Obviously the prostitute deeply impressed the Greek male and held an important place in Greek society. It is possible to hypothesize from the Greek example that when the personality of the wife and mother are submerged, the prostitute emerges. The Greeks emphasized two opposite images of woman to correspond with her two different functions. In one, women were wives and mothers. This role was clearly distinguished from the sexual woman, the companion, whose beauty was cultivated and adorned with all the arts of elegance and cosmetics, and whose mind was attuned to the aesthetic and intellectual interests of the male. The mother was the cloistered housekeeper, the breeder of legal heirs, her mind was forcibly stunted, her adornment was forbidden by law, and her value and virtue were determined by the strict observation of the marriage vows.[46] As Demosthenes so rightly put it, the Greeks had "hetairae for delight, concubines for the daily needs of the body, and wives in order to beget legitimate children and have faithful housekeepers."[47] He could have added that there were prostitutes everywhere for those who could not afford concubines or who tired of them.

But why, if women were so denigrated, did the Greeks turn to prostitutes? One explanation of this phenomenon suggests that since the Greek home was the domain of the Greek women it appears obvious that the child, male or female, was under strong female control. Perhaps women got their revenge on the adult male by subordinating the child male. Later as an adult, the male with such a strong feeling of inferiority vis-á-vis the female tried to convince himself that women were of no account, but feared that the reverse was true since women played so dominating a role in his formative years. The adult male might try to denigrate his wife by staying out of the house, by turning to a prostitute, or even by participating in homosexuality, all of which the Greeks did. This explanation is essentially based on the psychoanalytic theories of Karen Horney, but there is not enough evidence in the Greek records to prove it.[48] All we can say with certainty is that the theory is interesting and it might be valid, but surely there are a number of other factors involved about which we know little.

Quite clearly Greece, as pictured in the extant literature, was a male-oriented society emphasizing the double standard that inevitably sanctioned prostitution. There is, however, another side of the Greek character that had considerable influence on later attitudes, namely the growing tradition that taught that sex was bad if not evil. Though such a tradition had little direct influence on the "pornography" we have mentioned above, it had increasing influence on Western religious and philosophic assumptions, and thus ultimately on Western culture as a whole. The sources of these countercurrents lie deep in Greek mythology and religion, and from there they worked themselves into Greek philosophic thought. Traces of these ideas can be found in the Greek Orphic religion, that religion centered on the person of the poet-musician Orpheus, who in legend journeyed to Hades to rescue his beloved Eurydice. The cardinal tenet of the Orphic religion, as reconstructed by modern scholars, is the belief in the possibility of attaining immortality.[49] To do so required purity, not only in ritual matters, but as a way of life. The Orphics taught that the soul was undergoing punishment for sin, and that the body was an enclosure or prison in which the soul was incarcerated.[50] In Orphic theology man was believed to have a twofold nature: good and evil. To realize eventual divinity, man had to cherish and cultivate the divine, the spiritual, and purge the evil element in his nature, the material one. Life was regarded as a conflict between an essentially "higher" and a basically "lower" nature, one equated with the mind and the other with the body. Since sex was a function of the body, and therefore material, it potentially was evil.

Amplifying these ideas was Pythagoras, a semi-legendary philosopher, magician, and scientist who lived in the sixteenth century B.C. Pythagoras taught that the universe itself was divisible into two opposing principles, one of which he described as Unlimited, the other as Limit. The opposition of Limit to the Unlimited was reflected in the opposition of light to darkness, odd to even, one to many, right and left, male and female, resting and moving, straight and curved, good and bad, square and oblong, better and worse. Male, Limit, light, odd, and so forth were right, whereas female, Unlimited, darkness, even, were wrong.[51] The soul was a higher principle imprisoned in the mortal body, a body governed by evil passions. Thus men should not be the slaves of their own bodies; they should always attempt to escape the domination of the flesh. Sexual intercourse and consummation was regarded by the Pythagoreans as the prime pandering to indwelling Furies, and every passion, as well as every symbol associated with it, had to be repudiated. Prostitution was frowned upon as an indication of man's inability to control his evil materialistic urges.

The most influential figure in this growing hostility to sex was Plato (427–347 B.C.), who rejected the cultic aspects of religion but elevated the philosophical ideals. He postulated two universal principles, Ideas and Matter, and he equated these with the intelligible and the sensible world. Ideas were eternal and immutable, present always and everywhere, absolute, separate, self-existent, without beginning or end. Matter, or the material world of sensible objects, was only an imperfect imitation of the idea. The soul, an immaterial agent, was superior in nature to the body, and in fact was hindered by the body in its performance of the higher, psychic functions of human life. Sex and love were also conceived in dualistic terms, the sacred and the profane, the one occupied with the mind and character of the beloved, the other with the body. It was only through the higher love, the non-physical, that true happiness could be found.[52]

Plato compared the types of love to a charioteer driving two winged steeds, one of which (true love) was a thoroughbred, gentle and eager to pull its driver upward into the presence of the ideal, the other (physical love) vicious and refractory, forever bolting in pursuit of physical satisfaction. True love lay in training the unruly steed to run in harmony with the thoroughbred, and the successful charioteer would thus be borne away from the world of material senses to the vision of absolute loveliness that alone was true love.[53] In effect, the true state of goodness was one devoid of physical activity, and prostitution thus was always a reminder of the failure of mankind to reach such a state. Other Greeks emphasized that mankind could not be truly happy by virtue of the physical pleasures of their bodies, but only by virtue of right living and fullness of understanding.

Also influential were some of the Greek schools of philosophy, especially the Epicureans and the Stoics. The Epicurean school, founded by Epicurus in the fourth century B.C., was rather hostile to sex. Epicurus himself held that "sexual intercourse never benefited any man," and argued that the pleasant life could not result from the product of "sexual intercourse with women."[54] Zeno (340–265 B.C.), the founder of Stoicism, admired the ascetic life of Greeks like Diogenes, but recognized that man lived in a material environment. Thus, though he and his followers did not condemn sex and reproduction, they felt that both must be carefully regulated and controlled, and any immoderation in bodily activities was irrational.[55] The Stoic watchwords were nature, virtue, decorum, freedom from excess, and though prostitution might be tolerated, it was better if men confined themselves to sex within marriage.[56]

Many of these ideas were later amplified by Roman writers as well as by Greeks who lived during the period of Roman hegemony. Inevitably Western culture begins to express mixed feelings about prostitution, recognizing the existence of the prostitute, but expressing hostility to the institution. In the Greek period, such hostility was probably confined to a small minority of the population. But the idea spread, and in the Roman period were incorporated into Christianity, becoming the dominant values of Western culture. The Greeks, who in a sense were the inventors of pornography, were also the creators of a new fear relating to sexuality. Inevitably this fear affected the role and status of the prostitute. The double standard still existed; women were considered property, and most of the Greek males gloried in their sexuality, but an increasing number, if Plato and others are any example, began to experience pangs of guilt about too much sexuality. Might not the pornographers' proclamations of love of sexuality and admiration for the successful prostitute be cover-ups of their own anxieties?

4 THE ROMANS: AMBIVALENCE

The Greeks held conflicting views of sex and the Romans ambivalent views about prostitution. Though Latin culture was deeply influenced by Greek thinking, and many of the Greek "pornographic" writings about prostitutes were compiled in the Roman period, the Romans did little to romanticize prostitution and the practitioners themselves were neither honored nor revered. Prostitution was a trade, a necessary one for which there was great demand, but the women who practiced it were clearly low-status creatures. In fact, it was probably the main way a woman without inherited wealth or a husband could earn a living, and a standard Latin term for prostitute, *meretrix,* means "she who earns," as if to imply that this was the only thing a woman could do. Other terms include *scorta* (whore), *lupa* (she-wolf), and the word we use, *prostitute.*

The stories about prostitutes in Latin literature differ in tone from those in Greek literature. The *Elegies* of Propertius, a Latin love poet of the first century B.C., is an example. At first Propertius idealizes Cynthia, a woman who does not fully reciprocate his love. Later he expresses his disillusionment, a disillusionment that leads him to put women into one of two categories: the devoted wife and mother who dedicates her life and energies to her family; and the woman who takes as much from the male as she can get. The first type is represented by an epitaph he wrote for the tomb of a noble Roman lady,[1] and the second by a lecture he has a procuress give to a prospective courtesan. The procuress warns the girl never to be loyal to any man but to lie and deceive whenever and however she can; she was to forget modesty, and always pretend that she had other lovers, since a man's interest would increase if he could be kept jealous and in suspense. The girl should turn to her own advantage every action of a man. Even if he became furious enough to pull her hair, the wise woman would use such behavior to get more money from him. If a man became impossible, a woman could always tell him that this was the day of Isis or some other festal day sacred to her that prevented her from engaging in sexual intercourse. The way to riches through sex was to be cautious and never open one's door at the first knock in the middle of the night. Instead, the wise woman should view her prospective visitors secretly, and only if he were rich would he be allowed entrance. At other times, however, a woman should not restrict herself to the rich but keep in mind that the poor can also pay well on occasion. Even slaves, provided they had a lot of money in their pocket, could be accepted as temporary lovers.[2]

Similar advice appears in the writings of Ovid. In the *Amores* a procuress is unhappy that her young female charge seems to be more interested in love than money, but manages to console herself that the cause is not yet lost because the young man is rich as well as handsome. She tells the young woman that the successful courtesan should drain the lover of all his money as soon as possible since her beauty will not last forever, and a woman has to make it pay while it lasts. To this end the girl encourages her lover with words and gestures to increase his hopes of getting what he wants, but she is never to give in until payment is received. If the young lover does not pay, the procuress advises the girl to be ill, to cry, to swear, in short, to utilize every possible stratagem to obtain something material for herself, her sister, and her mother. She is encouraged to keep her lover always jealous and is reminded that if he does not give her material things she is to borrow from him and not pay him back. If the young girl learns her lessons thoroughly, she is always grateful to the old procuress.[3]

Prostitutes were not officially taxed until the principate of Gaius Caligula in the first century A.D., when they were required to give the sum that in any day they received from a single client.[4] Before the tax was established, prostitutes (or at least lewd women) were often called upon for special contributions, and during the Samnite Wars of the fourth century B.C. they gave enough money to erect a temple to Venus.[5] Though prostitutes were at first not associated with temples, as the Roman power spread throughout the Middle East and new religions were imported into Rome, many of the oriental divinities had prostitutes attached to their temples.[6]

Besides the temple prostitutes, there were several other kinds of prostitutes. Most worked in brothels, the so-called *lupanaria,* or as streetwalkers, but in neither case were the working conditions healthy or desirable. The lupanaria, also called *fornices,* were located close to the wall of Rome, and prostitutes could be found on the Sacred Via, in the Subura, outside the walls in the Esquiline-Viminal district, on the Caelian and in the Circus Maximus.[7] The brothels were such evil-smelling places that the visitor often took away some of the stench with him.[8] In each brothel there were a number of rooms or chambers *(cellae),*[9] above which was written the name of the girl who worked there.[10] Occasionally the lowest price she would take was also posted. Each room had a bed or a cover thrown on the floor, and a lamp.[11] The girls received their fees in advance, probably in order to be assured of getting their price. The lupanaria were closed during much of the day, and were not opened until late in the afternoon, supposedly in order that the young men might not be enticed away from their work or exercises. At the brothels the girls often stood or sat where they could be seen by passers-by; hence the Latin word *prostitute,* meaning "to set forth in public" or to be exposed for sale, which has entered the English language. When a girl had a customer in her cell she shut the door and hung a ticket on it bearing the word *occupata* (engaged).[12] Though the doors were closed they were normally not locked unless specifically requested by the customer.[13] The remains of the lupanaria are still standing, especially in Pompeii, where the cell walls in Insula 12, No. 18, are covered with pornographic paintings and inscriptions.[14] In the later Empire there were as many as forty-five brothels in Rome under official supervision. In Pompeii there were at least seven (one run in connection with a hairdressing establishment).[15]

Many of the brothels in Rome were located near the Circus Maximus,[16] which has been taken by some to indicate a significant correlation between the sadism and cruelty taking place in the arena and the sexual excitement of some of the onlookers, which the prostitute could easily satisfy.[17] A much simpler explanation is that the brothels were located near places where crowds were likely to gather, and the circus in this case was a natural location, since horse racing as well as sadistic events were held there. The proprietor of the brothel was known as a *leno* or *lena* depending on his or her sex; the term can be translated into pimp, panderer, procurer or procuress, bawd, seductress, go-between, and so on. There were at least two kinds of brothels, one that catered to the independent prostitutes who paid rent to the proprietor, and another that was staffed with slaves or freed women to whom the *leno* or *lena* paid a small sum.[18] The prices charged by the prostitutes varied, but the standard price in the brothels was figured in terms of an *as,* a copper coin worth less than a penny, and they had to take all customers.[19] At Pompeii the prices varied from two *asses* to eighteen, but many prostitutes elsewhere charged an *as* or even half or quarter of an *as.* Prostitutes were often known by the price they charged.[20]

Probably most of the girls in the brothels of Rome were slaves, many of them from countries like Syria or Egypt.[21] Slave girls were bought and sold by brothelkeepers at auctions. Seneca the Elder wrote in some detail about the sale of such a girl and described how she was forced to expose herself naked to prospective purchasers in order that they could examine all parts of her body intimately.[22] Martial has an epigram about an old prostitute whom the auctioneer kissed repeatedly in order to persuade everyone that she was clean. His efforts proved counterproductive since the only bid made for the woman was withdrawn after he began pawing her.[23]

In the demand for prostitutes, neither the auctioneer nor the brothel-keepers were concerned about the backgrounds of the girls involved; many of them were not wartime captives but kidnapped girls in which there apparently was a flourishing traffic. It was not until the time of Emperor Hadrian in the second century that there were attempts to deal with this.[24] Very little is known about the actual working conditions of the slave prostitutes, but their lives must have been short. Plautus had a male slave in one of his comedies complain that he would prefer to pass his days in a stone quarry fastened to an iron weight than serve as a slave to a brothel-keeper. Since stone quarrying was one of the lowest types of slave labor, prostitution, by comparison, must have been particularly unattractive, for prostitutes had to accept all clients who had the price.[25] Few women would have entered the lower echelons of prostitution willingly.

Apart from the brothel prostitutes, there were also women who picked up additional income through selling sex but who were not necessarily required to list themselves as prostitutes. In this group were women employed by low-class hotels *(tabernae cauponiae);* women employed by establishments run close to or in cooperation with the public baths; women in bakeries and inns, where women might be employed to entertain certain customers.[26] A wit left a relief at Aesernia in Campania dealing with his difficulties over a hotel bill:

> Erected in his lifetime by C. Calidus Eroticus to himself and Fannia Voluptas. Innkeeper, my bill, please. You have got down: a pint of wine, 1 as; bread, 1 as; food, 2 asses. Agreed. Girl, 8 asses. Agreed. Hay for mule, 2 asses. That mule is going to make me bankrupt.[27]

Among the part-time prostitutes were the streetwalkers known also as "night moths," "grave-watchers," "strollers," or even "two asses" (because that was their price), who practiced their profession at street corners, in baths, in the obscure byways of the city, near some of the temples, and even apparently on gravestones and in tombs.[28] Also unregistered were the actresses, harp players, barmaids, and others who had jobs but used their beds to supplement their incomes.[29]

Usually the lower-class prostitute was pictured as insatiable, a vicious kind of woman, who took perverse delight in corrupting children and others. This portrayal probably allowed the Romans to close their eyes to the real abuses that the prostitute suffered. Petronius in his *Satyricon* had the prostitute Quartilla state that she could never remember "being a virgin." "When I was a little girl, I played ducks and drakes with the little boys; as I got bigger, I applied myself to bigger boys, until I reached my present age—when I think the proverb arose, she'll bear the bull that bore the calf."[30] Quartilla allegedly took delight in seducing children and when she observed the child Giton, she laughingly said that tomorrow "this will make a fine antipasto for my lechery. But today's entree stuffed me so full, I couldn't swallow even this little tidbit now." Instead she found a little girl to introduce Giton into the "joys" of sex, put the two children in a separate room, and peeked through a slit in the panel to watch them at play.[31] In the minds of many Romans, prostitutes were sex-mad women who would do anything for their own pleasure. Petronius and Juvenal indicate that many had a taste for bestiality, and Apuleius, who fictionally was turned into a donkey, describes an act of bestiality he engaged in with a woman.[32]

At the top of the prostitute pyramid were the courtesans, some of whom served long periods as mistresses. Several such women were immortalized in literature: Catulus wrote of his Lesbia, Ovid his Corinna, and Propertius his Cynthia. Other famous courtesans were Lydia, Chloe, Delia, and Neaerea. The experienced courtesans were said to be so witty, so charming, so gay, and so exciting that the Roman male could be content and would need not go hunting wives and daughters of the citizens.[33] Though the dedicated male regarded the seduction of a female as among his greatest accomplishments, it was dangerous to prey on wives and daughters of the citizens. Even to hint at such a thing was dangerous, and Ovid was banished from Rome in A.D. 8 partly because of his book *Ars Amoris* [Art of Love] and partly because of his influence upon Julia, the daughter of Emperor Augustus, whose profligacy gravely angered her father.

Though the upper-class courtesan excited the imagination of the poets, her position in society was nowhere near as glamorous as it had been in Greece. The Romans traditionally were more family centered, with the position of wife and mother receiving more attention. The greatest tragedy a courtesan could suffer was to fall in love with the man who kept her but who might throw her out at any moment. Hence the advice of the procuress in Propertius and Ovid about keeping the man uncertain. Generally courtesans kept to the background in Rome, and even when they became mistresses to famous men they remained more or less colorless individuals. The dictator Sulla had several mistresses, most notably Sempronia, the wife of a consul and mother of one of Caesar's murderers.

Cicero enjoyed the companionship of Cytheris. Other philosophers also had their mistresses. Cato the Censor, the self-appointed guardian of Roman public morals, however, made do with a slave girl and was greatly surprised to find that his son and daughter-in-law were irritated by the fact that he had engaged in sex with a slave while his wife was still alive. To Cato this was simply a matter of male prerogative, not of morals. Many mistresses must have come from the slave class, and when a contemporary of Cato's, Scipio Africanus, died, his bereaved widow enfranchised his favorite slave girl and even found a freed man to marry her.

Marriage in Rome usually took place along class lines, and certain cross-class marriages were forbidden. Inevitably there were a great many relationshps that were not legally classed as marriages but also fell short of prostitution. Concubinage was particularly popular with soldiers, who were forbidden to marry during their twenty-year term of enlistment, although many turned to prostitutes for sexual relief, reluctant to become deeply involved even with a concubine. Concubines were often taken on by powerful people, who chose this way of getting feminine companionship rather than enter into second marriages. The Emperors Vespasian, Marcus Aurelius, and Antoninus Pius all took concubines after their wives died. Marcus Aurelius said he did so because he did not wish his children to suffer from a stepmother, although he himself wrote that he always tried to avoid contact with his grandfather's concubine. Earlier Caesar, Augustus, and Tiberius had mistresses. Commodus, at the end of the second century, rid himself of his wife, but rather than negotiating another marriage took a concubine. The Emperor Constantine was the son of his father's concubine, Helena. No question was raised about his legitimacy, perhaps because his father's mother was also a concubine of Constantine's grandfather. The Emperor Gordian set some sort of record with his twenty-two concubines, each of whom bore him three or four children.[34] Probably few married men kept a concubine, since this implied a much too formal arrangement. Even keeping a mistress was an expensive proposition, and Plautus wrote about a young man who sold his father's property in order to free and set up a slave girl whom he loved.[35] Rome was a land of double standards, however, and noble women were never as free to engage in such relationships. A Roman woman who wanted to free a slave in order to marry him was forbidden to do so unless she herself had recently been freed and her prospective husband had been a slave with her. The Emperor Septimus Severus prohibited such alliances altogether.[36]

Generally the courtesan, mistress, or concubine remained in the background, and none reached the level of political or intellectual influence of their Greek sisters. The most famous of Roman courtesans was a semi-legendary figure known as Flora, whose memory is also confused with Flora, goddess of the flowering or blossoming plants. According to tradition, Flora, who had acquired great wealth in her calling, left a large sum of money on her death around 240 B.C., the interest on which was to be used annually to celebrate the festival dedicated to the goddess after whom she was named. How much of the legend is fact is debatable, but the Floralia (perhaps with Greek influence) included pantomimes in which prostitutes appeared nude on the stage to perform lascivious dances, and to mimic the customs and manners of the day.[37] The Romans, however, were always somewhat uneasy about such celebrations, and when Cato the Younger found them offensive,[38] they became more sober.[39] Some of the more famous courtesans approached concubinage by hiring out for the year rather than the hour or day.[40]

The Romans never exalted the courtesan to the extent the Greeks had; the woman occupied a different position in Roman society. The Roman wife was not as sheltered from the world as her Greek counterpart, and, in fact, the proper Roman woman could play an important role in commercial and political affairs. She often accompanied her husband on outings and was involved in social life much more than the Greek woman. It was probably this that worked against the development of hetairae since a man's own wife could offer him the female intellectual stimulation he wanted. This meant that the Roman male who went to a prostitute or patronized the courtesans or who took a mistress did not do so for intellectual or social reasons; more clearly the reasons were sexual, and this implied low status for the prostitute. It perhaps also implied greater guilt feelings for the man.

The loss of status associated with prostitution is emphasized by the fact that no woman whose husband, father, or grandfather was, or had been, a Roman knight, could be licensed as a prostitute.[41] Women of this class who ignored the prohibition were probably originally let off with a fine, but at times they were actually banished.[42] Moreover, the men who engaged in sex with such women were liable to charges of unnatural vice (*stuprum*) or of adultery.[43] Professional prostitutes were forbidden to approach the temple of Juno since it was believed they would pollute it if they came too close.[44] Prostitutes (as well as adulteresses) were also required to wear a short toga-like gown, similar to the garb of men, in order that they be distinguished from proper matrons,[45] an indication that the Roman matron herself, unlike her Greek counterpart, had considerable freedom to appear in the streets and public places. Usually the prostitutes wore much brighter colors than the ordinary women and many peroxided their hair to give them a more distinctive appearance. Gradually, however, some of the dress restrictions were relaxed and for a time some of the more popular courtesans became the fashion leaders of Rome. The result was a new series of legislative efforts to restrict prostitutes. The Emperor Domitian ruled at the end of the first century A.D. that prostitutes could no longer use litters for transportation and he also attempted to prevent them from receiving inheritances and legacies.[46] Roman citizens were also prevented from marrying slaves who had been prostitutes, although they could marry free women who had been or were prostitutes. No senator, however, could marry a woman who had earned her living with her body or was descended from any woman who had done so.[47] Slave prostitutes who gained their freedom were not eligible for citizenship although a brothelkeeper, provided he paid a tax,[48] was eligible.[49]

Policing of the prostitutes was in the hands of the *aediles,* and they were supposed to visit the brothels periodically in order to make certain that all was in order, as well as to collect the various fees and taxes levied on the prostitutes. Occasionally aediles tried to take advantage of their official position, but if caught, they were subject to persecution. In one case where an aedile had been knocked unconscious by a prostitute after he had tried to force his way into her house, he took the case to court. The woman was acquitted on the grounds that the aedile had no right to enter her house unless he was on official business. Since the aedile was not wearing the symbols of his office at the time of the altercation, the judges ruled that the woman had every right to protect her property.[50]

Just as the prostitutes themselves were ranked into a pyramidal hierarchy, so were the customers. Many of the brothels catered to men of the lowest economic class, particularly slaves. Probably many male slaves had no other sexual contact with females. Soldiers also furnished a large class of clientele. Travelers often turned to prostitutes, as the existence of prostitutes in inns and hotels would indicate. The Romans also apparently used the prostitute as a means of controlling the sexual activities of the young men. Since female chastity was prized, and marriage for males was often delayed, prostitution became a sanctioned way of keeping sex drives under control. Moralists such as Cicero and Cato condoned prostitution as a necessary institution designed to protect and preserve marriage. Cato, for example, is reported to have given his blessing to a young man seen leaving a brothel, since his visit to such a place ensured that he would not be tempted to tamper with "other men's wives."[51] Young men, however, should visit a prostitute only occasionally, and when Cato saw the same young man repeatedly coming out of the same brothel he is said to have remarked: "I praised you then, since I assumed you came here now and again, not that you lived here."[52] Cicero maintained that male continence was an ideal, but it was difficult to maintain since it was a Roman custom to visit prostitutes.[53] Few Roman writers assaulted prostitution although Dio Chrysostom strongly disapproved of brothels.[54]

The prostitute's existence also allowed the love poets to express hostility toward women with greater freedom than if they were writing about women as wives and mothers. The Clodia of Catullus, the Nemesis of Tibullus, and the Cynthia of Propertius could all be berated for their faults with impunity. And from the difficulties the poets had with their mistresses they could generalize about women and conclude that love (and women) inevitably brought misery to man.[55] The philosophical poet Lucretius agreed that love made one miserable, but he proposed a solution, namely the eradication of love. The first sign of love had to be forcibly lanced with a quick incision; the best way to free a male from the course of the disease was to destroy the romantic idealization of the beloved. In effect Catullus, Tibullus, and Propertius did just this by denying that a woman even in love had any right to assert control over a man. Lucretius went further. Though he admitted there was always a possibility that a mistress might be faultless, a man could best free himself from the dangers of love by reflecting that physically one woman was like every other woman, and by continually reminding himself of this, a man would prevent any woman from gaining sway over him.[56]

Perhaps for this reason Latin literature is more or less devoid of the joyous celebration of the courtesan. Instead, writers emphasize the evil of women who succumbed to what they might have called the "baser" sexual instincts. Valeria Messalina, the third wife of Emperor Claudius, might be taken as an example of this. Contemporary Roman literature paints her with an evil brush. As soon as her position as empress was secure she allegedly took to visiting the brothels in order to partake in the pleasures of venal love. The satirist Juvenal reported that as soon as Claudius fell asleep, Messalina put on a night coat, concealed her dark hair under a light-colored wig, slipped out of the palace, and sought her cell in a foul-smelling brothel where she worked under the name of Lycisca. Here she delighted in gilding her nipples and exposing herself to all passersby. Only when the brothel closed did she leave her cell to sneak back to the palace.[57] Messalina allegedly carried on her activities rather flagrantly, even bringing a youthful lover, Gaius Silius, into the royal palace to entertain her during the day. Eventually Claudius caught on and had her put to death—not for her sexual activities, however, but because she was planning a revolt. The story may be no more true than those told about the famous Greek courtesans; the important thing is the difference in tone between the Greeks and the Romans.

Undoubtedly one of the reasons the Romans were so ambiguous about prostitutes and prostitution is that they had created for themselves a past that had never existed. They believed they were a straitlaced, family-oriented people, who always upheld virtue. This is most obvious in the writings of such historians as Livy (d. A.D. 17), who deliberately set out to record the great achievements of the Romans, the sovereigns of the world, and to teach future generations by examples of the noble conduct and virtues of their ancestors. He wrote:

> I hope everyone will pay keen attention to the moral life of earlier times, to the personalities and principles of the men responsible at home and in the field for the foundation and growth of the empire, and will appreciate the subsequent decline in discipline and in moral standards, the collapse and disintegration of morality down to the present day. For we have now reached a point where our degeneracy is intolerable—and so are the measures by which alone it can be reformed.[58]

Livy, his contemporaries, and his imitators distorted the history of the past in order to emphasize the evils of their own day and in an unsuccessful effort to call people back to the good old days when the virtues of courage, obedience, simplicity, *gravitas* (dignity and seriousness), and *pietas* (loyal respectful feelings toward the established moral order) were dominant. Livy's hortatory but inaccurate retelling of early history was designed to indoctrinate readers in the manner of Parson Weems, who rewrote the story of George Washington and the cherry tree as fiction with a moral.

Roman tradition emphasized the family, but the emphasis was on a power structure, not on biology or intimacy. The head of the family was the *pater familias,* the patriarch with absolute life and death power over his wife, his sons and daughters, his son's wives and children, his slaves, and property. In effect, women in the family were little more than another piece of property, and inevitably when men regard women as their special property there is a double standard. Women are important as mothers and as such are to be safeguarded and protected, kept free from sexual temptation.

Although the Romans never denied the biological mothering role of the female, the social role of motherhood was more ambiguous. The only female involved in a socializing role in the lives of Romulus and Remus, the founders of Rome, was a *lupa,* a term that came to mean either prostitute or she-wolf. The fact that the Romans interpreted it to mean wolf mother rather than human mother is significant, and monuments of a wolf suckling two children have existed in Rome since as early as 296 B.C. Still Romulus and Remus recognized that only human females could give birth to human infants, and after they founded their city, they and their male gang took steps to solve the problem in a way indicating their belief that women were property. They invited a group of neighboring Sabines to a banquet, and in the middle of the banquet seized the women and killed or drove off the men. Before the Sabine men could mount a rescue effort the Sabine women were pregnant by their Roman husbands, and according to Roman mythology, they intervened to separate the combatants on the grounds that they had lost one set of husbands and did not want to lose another.[59] But while the Romans might steal other men's wives, once they had their own she had to be above suspicion. The importance of wifely virtue appears in the legendary story of the Rape of Lucretia by the historian Livy. Livy impressed on his readers the devotion of Lucretia for her husband Collatinus, and how saddened she was that he had to leave her to go to war. At the front Collatinus and several of his companions engaged in a discussion about the women they had left behind and what they were doing. Some of the men were rather cynical about their wives' activities, but Collatinus assured his companions that his wife would be hard at work anxiously awaiting his return. Few believed him, bets were made, and to prove him wrong several men, including Collatinus and the son of the Etruscan king of Rome, Sextus Tarquinius, rode back to check on their wives. They first looked in on the wife of Tarquinius, who was at a splendid banquet celebrating the absence of her husband. They then proceeded to the house of Collatinus, where Lucretia was found spinning away, anxiously awaiting her husband's return, alone except for her servants. Sextus paid off the wager, but attracted by Lucretia, he decided to pay her a visit himself. Lucretia, who recognized him as a kinsman of her husband, welcomed him to the house, as was the custom. In the dead of night he entered her chamber with a drawn sword, demanding that she sleep with him. When she refused, he threatened not only to kill her but a male slave as well and leave both bodies naked in the bedroom in order to prove to the world that he had caught her in the act of adultery. Lucretia yielded to his wishes since as a male kinsman he had the right to kill an adulterous female relative. When Sextus rode off the next morning, Lucretia quickly summoned her husband as well as her father, reported to them what had happened, apologized for betraying them, and then stabbed herself to death, requesting as she died that they avenge her dishonor. Her body was carried to the Roman forum, where the account of her virtuous death so inflamed the Romans against the family of the king that they began a rebellion which eventually established the Roman Republic.[60] The implications of this story for prostitution are obvious. Female chastity must be preserved at all costs, and prostitution was a way of helping keep the male sex drive under control.

Also influential in forming attitudes about prostitution were the

Roman marriage customs. Marriage was usually arranged, and it was duty, not love, that brought two young people together. Marriageable age for girls was from thirteen to nineteen, after which they were considered spinsters.[61] The men were usually older then the women, sometimes much older. The fact that people had so little choice in mates probably contributed to the idea that love or sexual pleasure could be found outside marriage. The Roman male, however, expected his wife to be faithful since she was a kind of property, and he did not wish to leave his property to another man's child. This in no way prevented the male from seeking outside sexual contacts for himself. He did have to be careful not to commit adultery, since this was harmful to another man's property, but other than that there were few limitations.

Roman women, however, remained much freer than the Greek women, and their influence was a factor in causing prostitution to be looked down upon, since inevitably women regarded female prostitution differently. Prostitution was something the Romans tolerated but did not respect or admire. The writers Tacitus and Suetonius portray various figures visiting brothels but they usually use this device to indicate disapproval. Still, the Romans were never concerned enough about prostitution to try to remove the factors contributing to it. Roman soldiers could have been permitted to marry, for example, but this would have raised other problems about military training and defense that the Romans preferred to avoid. It was long the Roman custom for even high administrative officials to leave their wives at home, and when there were attempts to change this policy it ran into great opposition.[62] Female slaves in great numbers were an open invitation for their owners to put them to work as prostitutes; slavery was a way of life to the Romans. The list could go on. Though the Romans had ambivalent feelings, most men apparently visited some prostitutes sometime in their lives. Prostitution was not easy for the Romans to control, particularly in the large megalopolis of Rome. There are indications that criminal elements were associated with the brothels,[63] as one stigmatized group found support from another. Unfortunately the sources do not give us enough information to elaborate on this aspect of prostitution, which in modern times has been a great problem.

There is still another dynamic among the attitudes toward prostitution, a dynamic already visible in the Greek world but one that gained impetus in the Roman period, namely, the attempt to paint all sexuality as dangerous and evil. The first-century Stoic teacher Musonius Rufus taught that sexual intercourse should be permitted only for procreation; intercourse for pleasure, even within the limits of marriage, was reprehensible.[64] Seneca, the first-century A.D. Stoic rhetorician and statesman stated:

A wise man ought to love his wife with judgment, not affection. Let him control his impulse and not be borne headlong into copulation. Nothing is fouler than to love a wife like an adulteress. Certainly those who say that they united themselves to wives to produce children for the sake of the state and the human race ought, at any rate, to imitate the beasts, and when their wife's belly swells not destroy the offspring. Let them show themselves to their wives not as lovers, but as husbands.[65]

It is difficult to determine just how great an influence these philosophical concepts had on everyday attitudes. For the most part they seemed to appeal to the intellectuals, not to the masses, but they exercised at least some influence on the poets, the essayists, and others, and ultimately helped give intellectual backing for the condemnation of prostitutes. Such hostile sex ideas were not yet institutionalized in Roman law or religion, but this took place increasingly with the emergence of Christianity. An indication of the influence of such ideas on the intellectual community appears in Celsus's *De Medicina*. He wrote in the first century A.D. that sexual

intercourse neither should be avidly desired, nor should it be feared very much. Rarely performed, it revives the bodies, performed frequently it weakens. However, since nature, and not number, should be considered in frequency with consideration of age and the body, sexual union is recognized as not harmful when it is followed by neither apathy nor pain.[66]

Celsus, moreover, was not alone in the medical community. Soranus of Ephesus, one of the most famous of Roman physicians of the second century A.D., argued that "permanent virginity" could be healthful and that intercourse was harmful in itself.[67]

In trying to direct public opinion in certain channels, the philosophical and theological writers found it easier to concentrate on some aspects more than others, and they emphasized the good of sex within marriage, condemning it outside of marriage. Inevitably prostitution was frowned upon, although the double standard still permitted it to exist. The obvious solution was to eliminate the double standard, and this was attempted by a number of religious writers in the Roman period. Among the most notable was Philo, an Alexandrian Jew born in the last quarter of the first century B.C., who described sex for pleasure as being "like pigs or goats in quest of enjoyment."[68] The only justification for sexual activity was procreation, and this was the sole reason that people should engage in sex.[69] Platonic and Pythagorean thought was particularly influential in Alexandria, and out of this came a neo-Pythagoreanism and neo-Platonism that incorporated the science and religion of the time into a unified body. The culmination of such thought is personified by Plotinus, who lived and wrote during the third century A.D., first in Alexandria and then in Rome. He taught that the goal of life was to merge with the universal spirit into a kind of indescribable immortal ecstasy. This required long and careful training to accomplish.[70] The first step was to gain perfection in the practice of ordinary social and practical virtues. Though the body and its needs were not to be despised and suppressed, the body must be disciplined in such a way that the body's needs did not distract the soul from the contemplation of higher things.[71] The core of human virtue lay in detachment from worldly things, a sort of indifference that would put an individual out of reach of the caresses and stings of material life. Then having attained this "apathy" from the material, the soul was free to turn its attention on the intelligible world, to identify with the path toward Divine Reason in which alone truth lay.[72] By implication it was necessary to become indifferent to sex. This indifference becomes clearer in the writings of Porphyry, a pupil of Plotinus, who condemned any kind of pleasure as sinful, most particularly sexual intercourse under any condition.[73]

Obviously many "respectable" people utilized the service of prostitutes, but the Romans increasingly glossed over this fact, and if mentioned, it was usually regarded merely as a weakness. Women were important in Roman society, held greater direct power than in Greek society, and had considerably more freedom, but there was still a double standard. Female virtue was the ideal, and though the male could not quite reach this ideal because of his biological inheritance, it too was desirable. In the meantime, prostitution was tolerated because to move against it would require a reorganization of Roman society. Though equity demanded the same continence by the husband as he expected of his wife, the Romans hesitated to go that far. The courtesan, however, was. not romanticized. Instead, the Romans looked down on prostitution as a necessary evil, and the prostitute herself as a low-status person; it was this attitude, adopted and modified by Christianity, that survived into the medieval period and into much of the modern world.

5 CHRISTIANITY, ISLAM, AND SEXUAL MORALITY

Christianity, like any great cultural force, was built on existing foundations. It incorporated not only parts of the Jewish religious tradition but also many pagan attitudes and ideals, although both were modified and changed.

Traditionally, Christianity has been regarded as a religion of love and charity, but it is equally a religion of asceticism and renunciation, and quite early in Christian history asceticism was equated with sexual celibacy. At times the sexual aspects of holiness have seemed to eclipse all other issues. Saint Athanasius, an early Church Father, for example, went so far as to claim that the appreciation of virginity and of chastity was the supreme revelation and blessing brought into the world by Jesus.[1] Christianity adopted almost intact the sex-hostile attitudes of the neo-Pythagoteans and neo-Platonists, and did so with such vigor that sexual continence became both a chief virtue and a chief doctrine of the Christian faith, the first and indispensable condition of righteousness.[2] Tertullian, another Church Father, argued that a stain on one's chastity was even more dreadful "than any punishment or any death."[3] Some of the early Christians, like Origen, were so fearful of sex that they castrated themselves in order to avoid temptation,[4] or at least sought out surgeons to perform such operations.[5] If such attitudes were followed to their logical conclusions it would seem that in the ideal Christian society prostitution would be utterly condemned, stamped out, and removed, if not from the face of the earth, then at least from the presence of all good Christians. Though this might well have been the ambition of a few, such an ideal was never fully accepted and certainly was never achieved. Rather, the Christians adopted the ambivalent attitudes of the Romans toward prostitution, but mixed these with considerable compassion toward the prositute herself.

A significant factor in this development is the importance of Mary Magdalene in Christian thought. A onetime harlot, Mary Magdalene became the great example of converted sinner in the New Testament. The Gospels tell us very little of the background of Mary before she met Jesus, except that she had been "a woman of the city, which was sinner."[6] She could have been a comparatively insignificant streetwalker or an important hetaira, or she might have used prostitution as a sideline since some philologists derive the Greek word Magdalene not from a place, Magdala, but from a word meaning "hairdresser." Since so little information is actually known about her past, legends developed that gave her an interesting history. A typical one dating from the ninth century portrayed Mary as the widow of a rich landowner in Magdala, who had squandered her inheritance on frivolous pleasures, and gradually sunk into prostitution. Regardless of details Mary is always portrayed as a prostitute.

This is important because in Christian tradition Mary Magdalene is, next to Mary, mother of Jesus, the most significant female figure. It was Mary Magdalene who first discovered that the grave of Jesus was empty. She was also the first witness to the reappearance of Jesus. Perhaps because of her influence, the Gospel writers are careful to portray prostitutes as poor and exploited women, more to be pitied than condemned. This portrayal is evident in the dispute of Jesus with the Pharisees, where he is reported to have said that harlots would enter the kingdom of God before they did.[7] Obviously this did not mean that prostitutes would achieve eternal bliss if they persisted in their sinful ways, but only that the case of prostitutes was not as hopeless as that of the Pharisees, since "fallen women" could be taught and converted and were capable of repentance and improvement.

The legend of Mary Magdalene also emphasizes the difficulty of a woman making her way in the world alone without male guidance, and this appears in Christian attitudes toward prostitution as well. Jesus, however, did not condone prostitution itself, and in his Sermon on the Mount he stated that "every one that looketh on a woman to lust after her hath committed adultery with her already in his heart,"[8] a clear condemnation of lustful thinking that can also be taken as a dununciation of prostitution, since prostitution, at least in Christianity, is associated with lust. Yet he also spoke out when the people were willing to stone the adulteress, saying, "He that is without sin among you, let him first cast a stone at her."[9] Biblical specialists usually emphasize that Jesus himself, at least as far as his extant teachings demonstrate, did not proclaim a new code of sexual relationships but rather built on the attitudes of his own time. In fact, the radical change in sex morality associated with Christianity appears not in any of Jesus' utterances but rather in the writings attributed to Saint Paul, particularly in the First Epistle to the Corinthians.[10]

Paul first attributes too much to sex, and then attempts to curb it.

He denied that sex was merely a detached and peripheral venereal function involving little more than an exercise of the genital organs. Instead he
emphasized that it was an act which engaged and expressed the whole
personality in such a way as to constitute a unique mode of self-disclosure
and self-commitment.[11] As such, sex was dangerous, and celibacy for him
became the ideal,[12] an ideal based perhaps on a literal interpretation of the
praise of Jesus for those who had "made themselves eunuchs for the
kingdom of heaven's sake."[13] Marriage was only a reluctant concession to
human frailty since God had not called all to celibacy.[14] Those who chose
marriage, however, were forbidden to defraud one another of the coitus,
which was their due, and were reminded that they conceded to each other
the power over their bodies.[15] In fact, in the Epistle to the Ephesians,
which probably represents the thinking of Saint Paul, wedlock is regarded
as "the great mystery" by which Christ's union with the Church is signi-
fied.[16] Saint Paul could not quite affirm the naturalism of marriage inherent in Judaism, nor could he quite condemn it as some of the more
ascetic religious teachers of his time were doing. Instead he chose a sort of
middle way, approving continence for those who had the ability to be
continent but warning others that it was better to marry than to burn,[17]
although what he meant by burning is not clear. In retrospect, Saint Paul
appears to be a misogynist, somewhat fearful of women, but recognizing
marriage might also be the way of God. Not so the author of the Apoca-
lypse, who saw the great procession of the redeemed as a company of
144,000 virgin males who had not been defiled by women.[18] This emphasizes the androcentric orientation of the Biblical writers, and reaffirms one
of the underpinnings of prostitution, namely the belief that women were
created for the benefit of the male.[19] Moreover, the philandering male
could not help himself since in the view of Saint Paul and others, it was
woman who had beguiled man into transgression,[20] and woman, the
weaker vessel, who was the potential temptress, although why the stronger
male was so weak is never quite clear.

    As the Christian Church grew and expanded, the ambiguous attitude
of the New Testament writers about sex, as well as about other subjects,
resulted in heated controversies. Some of the Christian communities refused to baptize those who were married,[21] while others saw nothing
wrong with either marriage or sex within marriage, and some groups had
such strong antinomian strains that they taught that no human act could
be considered sinful to those who were true believers.[22] The extremes at
both ends ultimately were classed as heresies, but even in the middle there
was considerable contradiction. In order to resolve these differences
learned Christians appealed to the Scriptures; they amplified, rationalized,
and explained them, thus formulating the basic dogma of the Christian

Church. These writers collectively are known as the patristics, the Fathers of the Church, and among them are Saint Augustine, Saint Jerome, Saint Basil, Saint Athanasius, Saint Ambrose, Saint Gregory, and scores of others not so well known. Since the Church Fathers disagreed among themselves, the conflicts were eventually resolved by Church Councils, an institution that became fully developed only after Christianity was legalized in the fourth century.

Defining sexual dogma was difficult because of the contradictions in the Bible and the different backgrounds of the converts to Christianity. Significant segments of the intellectual Christian community attempted to define Christianity in terms of their own neo-Platonic or neo-Pythagorean backgrounds, others in terms of the more early Jewish traditions. Personal life-styles also accounted for some differences. Saint Paul was a bachelor, and Saint Peter was married. Most of the Church Fathers were bachelors, and so strong was the emphasis on celibacy that even those, such as Tertullian, who were married tended to denigrate marriage. The biases of various individuals are important because such questions as premarital sexual intercourse were not even discussed in the New Testament, and there soon developed conflicting opinions regarding polygamy, digamy (the remarrying of persons who had been widowed), rape, and adultery. About the only thing the Church Fathers agreed on was a double standard, a different standard for women then men. Mosaic law, for example, demanded sexual purity from the bride but not expressly from the bridegroom. In fact, a man was entitled to return his bride to her father if on the bridal night he found that she did not come to bed a virgin. Christians, however, as a rule were opposed to divorce and classed such actions as a divorce. This raised several difficulties, since it is not clear that this would have prevented a husband from putting aside a bride who had lost her virginity, or a wife who had committed adultery. It probably did, though, prevent the woman involved in such actions from marrying again. Another difficulty that Christians had to face was the polygamous tradition among God's chosen prophets. The Church Fathers were forced to deal with such questions in order to arrive at Christian definitions.

Generally the Christians tended to impose a stricter sex morality than that of the Old Testament. Much of the patristic literature on sexual topics seems to be devoted to a vindication of celibacy against marriage, and of widowhood against digamy. To maintain and justify this doctrine demanded considerable theological and dialectical adroitness since all agreed that the Scriptures indicated marriage had been instituted and blessed by God. To justify the new Christian emphasis on celibacy, the patristics emphasized that though marriage might be good, celibacy was better. Thus it was not a question of a good succeeding a bad but of a better replacing a good. By distinguishing between the good and the better, the Fathers attempted to uphold the superiority of the virgin state without quite denouncing marriage as an evil. Nevertheless, they tended to regard matrimony as a concession to the inordinate sexual desires of fallen humanity. This attitude resulted in an attempt to impose a rule of abstinence from coitus upon bishops, presbyters, deacons, and others employed in the service of the altar, and within a hundred years the concept was well established in theory if not in practice, although it did not become a matter of required discipline until the thirteenth century. In the Eastern Christian community (generally in the Orthodox churches) marriage for clergy was allowed still later, but with restrictions.

Perhaps the most remarkable manifestation of sexual asceticism in the early Church was the phenomenon known as *syneisaktism* (also *agapetae*), or spiritual marriage. This was a practice whereby a male and female (or several couples) shared the same house, the same room, even the same bed, yet conducted themselves under conditions of strict continence as brother and sister.[23] In theory this would show that the devoted could withstand temptation at the closest quarters, but in practice the flesh proved weaker than the mind. By the fourth century Church Councils were condemning the custom and even took actions against those clergy who refused to part with their virgins.[24] As part of the same movement the more devout attempted to show their indifference to sexual temptation by visiting prostitutes and houses of prostitution. Inevitably stories about such activities became encrusted with legend and helped reaffirm the Magdalene image of prostitution.

Two themes seem to predominate. Either the male is able to remain indifferent to the prostitute's charms or else he is able to convert her. Saint Jerome, for example, told the story of a young Christian who was being punished for his Christian beliefs by being put in the midst of a lovely garden and beguiled by a beautiful courtesan. Fearful that he would not be able to withstand her blandishments, he preserved his vows by biting out his tongue and spitting it in her face.[25] The more usual story, however, is of dedicated missionaries who pretend to be prospective customers of prostitutes in order to convert them. When they found prostitutes willing to leave their life, the young men then exchanged garments with them so the new convert could leave immediately.[26] It was perhaps from such a venture that a courtesan was able to accuse Saint Gregory Thaumaturgus of having been her lover but of refusing to pay her the sum that he had promised. Rather than argue with the woman, Saint Gregory paid her what she asked but his innocence was almost immediately demonstrated when the prostitute became possessed by a demon.[27]

One story dealing with a holy man and a prostitute is that told about the hermit Abraham and his niece Saint Mary the Harlot. According to the account of Saint Ephraem of Edessa, the ascetic hermit Abraham found himself the guardian and protector of his seven-year-old niece, Mary. Unwilling to give up his ascetic holy life but conscious of his family responsiblities, he attempted to solve his dilemma by adding a room to his desert cell in which the young girl could live and in which he could observe her through a windowlike opening. The young Mary quickly adapted to her cell and spent her time learning passages of Holy Scriptures, praying, and in fact imitating her uncle in all his ascetic ways. Her reputation for holiness grew as she matured into a beautiful woman. Watching the young Mary develop was a young monk who had at first visited Abraham but increasingly began to pay attention to the devout young woman. Enamored of Mary, he set out on a campaign to entrap her, and the innocent Mary, ever anxious to help a troubled soul, finally consented to leave her cell and pray with him. When she came to her senses, she found that she was no longer a virgin. Weighed down with the anguish of betrayal, she felt she could no longer face her saintly uncle, and as a fallen woman the only place for her was a brothel in the city.

Abraham at first did not notice that his niece was missing since he thought she was in a period of deep meditation, but eventually when he realized it, he began to ask his infrequent visitors if they knew of her whereabouts. After two years of questioning, he learned she had become a prostitute in Alexandria and immediately resolved to go see her. Casting aside his ascetic garments, he dressed himself in military garb, took a gold piece that a devoted disciple had given him, and went there. Finding Mary, he bargained with her, and followed her to her house. Though Mary at first failed to recognize her uncle, when she began to kiss and fondle him a certain ascetic smell came to her, and she tearfully recalled the good old days when she had been a devoted hermit with her uncle. To cheer her up, her uncle, still unrecognized, ordered a supper for the two, thereby breaking his fast (in his fifty years of ascetic retirement he had never tasted bread). After the dinner, Abraham went with Mary to her cell, where he finally revealed his true identity, pleaded with her to come back with him, and assured her that God would accept her atonement if she did penance. Mary was so overwhelmed that she returned with him to the desert. Her prayers became legendary as she performed miracles, and crowds flocked to her to be healed of their sicknesses.[28] So great was her miraculous ability that on her death she was recognized as a saint.

This story, like that of Mary Magdalene, emphasizes the good in the prostitute, and also gives some evidence of the helplessness that women who had lost their virginity might feel. The dedication of the converted prostitute is also emphasized by still a third Mary, Saint Mary the

Egyptian, who achieved sainthood even though she had spent seventeen years of her life as a harlot in Alexandria. On her conversion she isolated herself for another seventeen years in order to purge herself of her sins, and during this whole second period she miraculously lived only on three loaves of bread and wild herbs. So holy had her repentance made her that when she made the sign of the cross, the monk Zosimus was able to walk on water. When she died, her body was placed in a lion's cave, but allegedly the lion left the cave so that her body would remain undisturbed.[29]

Saint Afra, Saint Pelagia, Saint Thaïs, and Saint Theodota had also at one time or another in their lives been prostitutes. Saint Afra, after her conversion, was one of the Christians caught up in the Diocletian persecutions at the end of the third century. So devout had she become that when she was ordered to sacrifice to the pagan idols she refused. Though taunted by her persecutors for her past as a prostitute, she remained steadfast to her new faith and died a martyr. Her nude exposed body was rescued by her mother and three of her former companions in prostitution, Digna, Eunomia, and Eutropia, whom she had converted, and they too suffered martyrdom for their part in this act.[30] Saint Pelagia, a hetaira of the grand tradition in Antioch, was so beautiful that even the saintly Bishop Nonnus, a most ascetic monk, was moved to remark on her beauty, much to his own discomforture. Pelagia heard Nonnus preach and was converted by him. He acted as her patron for her baptism. After she was baptized, Pelagia left the city disguised as a man, dressed in the tunic and cloak of the blessed Nonnus, which she had borrowed without asking. She went to Jerusalem, where she became known as the eunuch monk Pelagius, admired throughout the holy land for his ascetic habits and holiness. It was not until after her death that her secret was revealed and she took her place among the female rather than the male saints.[31]

Saint Thaïs was a former Christian turned prostitute, one of the many famous hetairae to bear the name Thaïs.[32] She was reconverted to Christianity by a holy abbot who had deliberately gone to her chambers, after paying a fee, in order to convert her. To do repentance for her sins, she had herself walled up in a cell in a convent in which there was only a small opening through which she received a little bread and water. After some three years she was thoroughly cleansed of her sins. Saint Theodota, another former prostitute, became such a sincere convert that she refused to recant even after torture had been inflicted on her. She too became a Christian martyr.[33] The early Christian stories about the famous courtesans are as plentiful as those told by the Greeks, but the Christian stories had a moral, the conversion of the lost and forsaken, and their ultimate salvation.

Prostitution was defined by the patristic writers in terms of promiscuity and not in terms of accepting payment. Saint Jerome, for example, defined a whore as a woman who was available for the lust of many men.[34] Since by definition any promiscuous woman was a prostitute, any woman who had intercourse with more than one man regardless of the reason could be regarded as a prostitute. There were some exceptions, however, and the Church Fathers created a special category for concubines. A concubine, for example, could be baptized if she had been faithful to her master and reared their children, but baptism could be administered only after the children were grown.

By far the most influential of the Church Fathers on the subject of prostitution was Saint Augustine (354-439). Before he converted to Christianity, Saint Augustine had belonged to the Manichaean sect, a rival religion that posed a major threat to Christianity in the fourth century. The Manichaeans were so hostile to sex that they regarded procreation as the defiling birth of the divine substance. Following the Greek dualistic tradition, the Manichaeans emphasized the evil of material things, particularly sex, and emphasized the value of spiritual over material things. The true Manichaean was to remain celibate, observe strict vegetarianism, avoid engaging in trade, and never kill any living creature. Since this ideal life-style required great dedication, the Manichaeans did not expect all potential believers to adopt such standards immediately, but rather to try to attain the ideal through dedication over the years. Only the group known as the Elect followed the principles rigidly; below the Elect were the Auditors, those who as yet could not control their material desires but attempted to do so and in the meantime supported the Elect. Saint Augustine was an adherent of the group for some eleven years, but never reached the Elect stage largely because of his difficulties with sex. During all the period of his auditorship he kept a mistress (whose name we do not know), who gave birth to a son, Adeoatus. Though Augustine believed it was essential for him to renounce his sexuality, he was loath to surrender the sensual pleasures associated with it. He later reported that his constant prayer at this time was "Give me chastity—but not yet."[35] During his years as a Manichaean his mother, Saint Monica, kept pressuring him to become a Christian and to get married. Finally to please her, he sent his mistress away (along with his son Adeoatus) and picked out a girl to be his bride. Unable to control his sexual urges during the interval between the departure of his mistress and his marriage, he took another mistress.[36] At this point, tormented by his sexuality, increasingly disenchanted with Manichaeanism, he underwent conversion to Christianity and swore to be celibate the rest of his life.

In light of his background, it is easy to understand why Saint Augustine dwelt so extensively on the sexuality of mankind. Though he had rejected Manichaeanism, his writings still conveyed the idea that sexual intercourse was the greatest threat to spiritual freedom. "I know nothing that brings the manly mind down from the heights more than a woman's caresses and that joining of bodies without which one cannot have a wife."[37] He could not quite reject marriage outright since it clearly had Biblical sanction, but he was offended and embarrassed by the act of coitus. He rationalized his dilemma by equating original sin with concupiscence (the unbidden motion of the genitals) and venereal emotion. Coitus in theory was good, since it was of God, but every concrete act of coitus performed by man was intrinsically evil, so that every child could be said literally to have been conceived from the sin of its parents.[38] Marriage was designed to moderate venereal desire by diverting it to the task of procreation, the only justifiable purpose of sex. Procreation then was the only purpose of marriage, and if intercourse was employed for other purposes, there was no difference between the *copula carnalis* of the man and wife and the *copula fornicatoria,* or physical union with a prostitute. Both were equally sinful. It was probably this attitude that allowed Augustine to tolerate prostitution. In his mind there was nothing more sordid, more void of modesty, more full of shame than prostitutes, brothels, and other evils of this kind, yet if they were to be removed from human affairs, everything would be polluted with lust.[39] Lust in his mind was equal to the actual act. From this the Church Fathers concluded that though prostitutes were to be excluded from the Church as long as they continued their profession,[40] prostitution itself was to be tolerated as a necessary evil. Saint Augustine believed that if prostitutes were not available, established patterns of sexual relationships would be endangered. Thus, it was better to tolerate prostitution, with all its associated evils, than to risk the perils that would follow the elimination of harlots from society. There was always hope that prostitutes could be converted as were their predecessors, but in the meantime they served a useful purpose.

Since prostitution was equated with female promiscuity, the effect of such attitudes was to institutionalize the traditional double standard within Christianity, namely, that what was permissible for a man was not permissible for a woman, and that it was not the male's fault if he strayed, but it was the female's if she—or he—did. Further evidence of this double standard appears in Saint Basil of Caesarea, who argued that though both partners in the marriage contract were to observe their vows about sexual morality, if the husband strayed it was the duty of the wife to take him back. Conversely, if a wife engaged in extramarital sex relations the husband should consider the circumstances, but it was not an absolute necessity that he take her back. Basil felt somewhat uneasy about this double standard but justified it on the ground that this was the custom.[41]

In sum, Christianity turned out to be a male-centered, sex-negative religion with strong misogynistic tendencies and suspicion of female sexuality. By looking with disfavor on women who expressed sexual feelings, yet tolerating sexual promiscuity in males, Christianity gave a religious and institutional base for prostitution; prostitution in fact became the price of social purity. Christian writers emphasized the degradation of prostitution, and for that matter of all sexual activities, but also accepted the fact that, through Christian charity, the prostitute herself might mend her ways. Prostitution was to be accepted until men could live up to the high ideals of Christianity. What started out as a questionably charitable impulse soon became institutionalized, and prostitution continued to flourish in the Christian medieval period with the reluctant toleration of the Church. Since the Church Fathers were male, and many of them became conscious of the physical desires of their bodies when in the presence of women, misogyny became engrained in Christianity. Marriage and motherhood were recognized, but married women and mothers were not as virtuous as the women who denied their sex. The ideal woman was the virgin, particularly one who appeared sexless, detached from the world, preoccupied with spiritual things, all the things a prostitute was not.

The fact that Christianity, with its open and avowed hostility toward sexual intercourse, tolerated prostitution as a necessary evil indicates how deeply the subordination of women and the double standard are set in Western culture. Though Christians attempted to ameliorate some of the conditions of the prostitute, they never challenged traditional attitudes enough to grant sexual equality or to regard women, except for the virginal unmarried woman, as other than part of the family unit. Women gained status as wife and mother, not as individuals, and though Christianity developed the convent to deal with the dedicated virgin, it never came to terms with female sexuality.

The Christian interpretation of the Jewish and classical heritage was not the only version that has survived. Drawing from some of the same elements, as well as from other forces, is the religion of Islam, founded by the prophet Muhammad in the seventh century of the Christian era. Like Christianity, Islam regards the Jewish Scriptures as a sacred book, and the Koran, the Bible of Islam, includes many of the characters from the Old as well as the New Testament. Greek ideas and attitudes as well as Roman administrative concepts were important influences. Part of the explanation for this is that Islam found many of its converts among people with Christian and Jewish backgrounds, both within the boundaries of the old Roman Empire and without.

A woman, according to the Koran, was to be under the control of her nearest male kinsman—father, brothers, or husband—whose right over her was regarded in the same way as a man's right over any other property.[42] In Islamic tradition the wife's honor was in the hands of her husband, whose business it was to make certain that it was not violated. She was "his woman to be guarded," and if he failed in his duty it was not his wife's fault if she strayed. There were no legal sanctions to enforce observance of the wife's subjection to her husband, but within a tribe this was accepted as the normal and honorable way of life. If a man from another tribe seduced a married woman, he committed no unlawful or dishonorable act; poets in fact constantly boasted of their stolen loves.[43] Seducers, however, were subject to the vengeance of the outraged husband or his kinsmen. The woman's kinsmen were especially quick to resent an accusation of adultery because it gave the husband grounds for repudiating the wife. In short, Islam, like Christianity and Judaism, was very much a male-centered religion, and as such found it not too difficult to justify prostitution. Islam was, however, much more sexually positive than Christianity.

This attitude toward sexuality was expressed by the prophet Muhammad himself. Though the marital status of Jesus is not specifically mentioned, and Paul is known to have been celibate, Muhammad was polygamous, and happily so. Inevitably Islam accepts sex much more casually and openly than does Christianity. Sexual intercourse is regarded by Moslems in general as one of the great pleasures of the world, common to rich and poor alike, to men as well as women. This attitude was reflected by the late King Ibn-Saud of Saudi Arabia, who stated that the most wonderful experience of his life, and which above all things made life worth living, was to "put his lips to the woman's lips, his body on her body, and his feet on her feet."[44]

To have sexual intercourse with one's spouse was a good religious deed. Individuals should not counteract sexual desires, but if necessary stimulate them; hence, various devices, such as special diets and aphrodisiacs, were used. Christianity recognized marriage as acceptable for those who could not live the celibate life; Islam accepted polygamy for those who could not be monogamous. Women were recognized as sexual companions for the male, and a pious male Moslem could praise Allah for having created woman in all her beauty, for having formed her body with all the charms that awakened desire, for having made her hair so silky, and for having made the precious curves of her breast. Again, as in Christian and Judaic literature, these are male descriptions of the female and there are no similar female descriptions of the male.

Polygamy had not been instituted among the Arabs by Muhammad, but rather the Prophet had attempted to reform an existing institution by limiting the number of legal wives, by giving every wife a legal personality and legal rights that had to be respected, and by making every man legally responsible for his conduct toward every woman. Within the Islamic world, whether monogamy or polygamy has prevailed in a particular country or time has been less a matter of faith than a result of social, sexual, and economic factors. Muhammad himself married at least fourteen times, but all except one of his wives had been widows before they married him. Thus in a sense many of his marriages can be regarded as political alignments or as a means of supporting women who had no other protector. Muhammad was conscious of the abuses inherent in polygamy, and the Koran has usually been interpreted to limit the number of wives to four,[45] although the Scriptures are not clear-cut, and several early Islamic rulers had more than four spouses. There was no limit, however, on the number of concubines although men were cautioned that they were not to have any married woman as a concubine unless she was a captive.[46]

In spite of the toleration of polygamy, it was probably only the well-to-do who engaged in polygamy on any scale. Among the most powerful chiefs and rulers, the number of wives and concubines became a status symbol. In such instances, the harem, the forbidden area or woman's quarters, housed large numbers of women and in fact much of the history of Islam may be understood in terms of harem politics.[47] Such politics were perhaps inevitable, since the only way a woman in a large harem could gain and hold power was through her son, and many women spent much of their lives in intrigue to have or advance sons. Part of the difficulty of their lot was that women in Islam led secluded lives, excluded from masculine society, confined to the house or to the women's quarters. Whenever they ventured outside their home they wore a veil and outer garment that disguised their appearance. In the individual home, where at least the wife could deal with her husband on a one-to-one basis, such seclusion might have been tolerable, but in the larger households, where there were several wives, numerous concubines, and large numbers of female slaves the harem was more or less a prison. In some of the great princely harems where hundreds of women were shut up, the lot of a woman would have been boring and not particularly happy. Complicating the matter was the fact that the masters of harems were not usually fiery young lovers, but more often elderly men for whom the harem was a social necessity, and a duty, rather than a source of sexual pleasures.

With a plentitude of wives or concubines, there was no need for a man to be a great lover or even an adequate one. Usually the master of the harem had a favorite or favorites and only occasionally took another as sexual mate. The rest of the women were condemned to an unwilling celibacy, unwilling because there was no religious sanction for it, and made worse by the fact that technically they were wives and concubines, off limits to all other males. Reaction to continued neglect varied with individual women, but many undoubtedly retaliated by trying to deceive their neglectful husbands. Traditionally, Western observers have regarded the harems as centers of lesbianism, and many probably were, although not all servants of the harem were eunuchs. If a woman watched her opportunities, she might be able to have sex with a male, hopefully become pregnant, and pass her son (not a daughter) off as the son of her master. The risks were great, but the stakes were high.

The battle of wits between the harem women and their husband or master is one of the major themes of Arabic and Islamic literature. It is, for example, the narrative thread on which A Thousand and One Nights is based. King Shahriah, to whom Scheherazade told the stories, had become so suspicious of women that he refused to trust any, even his wife, and for three years he had executed each of his wives after the bridal night. Supposedly Shahriah had good grounds for his suspicion of women since he had surprised his brother's wife in the arms of a slave, then observed his own wife engaging in sexual acrobatics in the confines of the harem. He had even seen the mistress of a powerful genie prostitute herself with every male she could find. From this he concluded that the only way a male could avoid being deceived was to execute the woman after having engaged in sex with her. This he had done until he married Scheherazade, the beautiful and intelligent daughter of the grand vizier. Scheherazade knew what was in store for her but succeeded in outwitting her jealous husband by telling unfinished stories after lovemaking for some one thousand and one nights, at the end of which she had convinced her husband that at least one woman could be faithful.[48]

It was perhaps as an antidote to polygamy that divorce in Islam was made easy for men.[49] The available supply of women could thus be recirculated to more men. In Islamic tradition a husband can divorce his wife without any misbehavior on her part or without assigning any cause. In fact, repudiation of a wife by any husband, whether he is free or slave, willing or acting under compulsion, jesting or serious, is legal, provided the man is of sound mind when he does so. Technically, all a husband has to do is repudiate his wife three times, saying, "Thou art divorced, thou art divorced, thou art divorced," or similar phrases. A refusal of a husband to have intercourse with his wife for over four months also is regarded as divorce, although the woman has some protection if before her marriage she drew up a contract that dealt with such situations. A divorced man could remarry his divorced wife, but if he divorced her a third time she had to have been married and divorced by another man before she could remarry her first husband. Though it is possible for a woman to divorce her husband, the grounds for her divorce are very limited,[50] and usually have to be agreed on in advance of the marriage contract. In the over-whelming majority of cases the decision to separate is made by the husband.

Though divorce was one way of recirculating marriage partners, Islam also provided another way in the *mut'a,* an old Arabic custom of temporary marriage. Muhammad declared that such relations were not a crime as long as they were done by mutual agreement.[51] Though technically a marriage in many ways, *mut'a* was a kind of legalized prostitution since the system lent itself to so many abuses that even today many orthodox Moslems regard such marriages as a "union of pleasure." Contracts could be made for a fraction of a day, or for a year, or for even longer periods. During the period of the contract the male partner was bound to support the woman, usually by paying a fixed sum, but the woman had no claim to a financial settlement on the expiration of the period. If *mut'a* can be considered a form of prostitution, it had the advantage over other forms of prostitution of recognizing the children of such unions as legitimate, with a right to share in the inheritance of their father even though the woman herself had no legal claim to anything more than the gift stipulated in the contract.[52]

Perhaps because it was so easy for the *mut'a* relations to be abused, *mut'a* has been the subject of much study and comment by the writers of Islamic legal schools. It is said to have been prohibited by the caliph Omar (A.D. 634-644) on the grounds that it was no different from fornication, but the practice continued in spite of such prohibitions. It was most widely practiced among the Shiite Moslems, who today are dominant in Iran. A seventeenth-century visitor to Persia remarked that the men of Iran took courtesans for periods of hours, nights, weeks, or longer. A young and fair woman could be hired for 450 livres a year and such contracts were binding on both parties. If a man attempted to end the relationship before the contract expired, he had to pay the woman anyway. When such long contracts ended, a woman was not to hire herself out to any other man before undergoing a period of purification of forty days. *Mut'a* companions were specially favored by men who spent considerable time away from their homes and families. Women who accompanied them on their journeys were paid specific sums, negotiated before the journey began.[53] Even among the Sunni Moslems, where *mut'a* is somewhat frowned on, it is practiced, although no terminal dates are put in the marriage contract in order to avoid prosecution. Instead, the terminal date is agreed to orally by both parties, becoming a regular marriage contract but one that ends in an amicable divorce.[54] Even today in many of the Islamic countries, certain women enter into temporary marriages of one night in return for financial considerations. Most refuse to make a contract for less than one night, because to do so would, at least in their minds, make them the same as prostitutes.[55]

Concubinage is also recognized in Islam. There are some restrictions in the Koran as to what women were eligible to be concubines: they had to be Moslems, Jews, or Christians, and could not already be married unless they had been captured. Certain other kinds of relations were forbidden, both in the case of concubines or of wives: a man could not have intercourse with two sisters, for example, nor with his own mother, daughter, sister, aunts, nieces, mothers-in-law, stepdaughters, foster mothers, foster sisters.[56] Female slaves were also fair game for their masters, although if such a woman bore a child of her master the slave was to be given her freedom on his death. Some masters tried to get around this by disputing the paternity of the child, but Islamic lawyers usually felt that if a master had intercourse with a slave, he had no right to dispute paternity.[57] This was true even though he engaged in coitus interruptus, a form of birth control permissible in the case of slaves and concubines. Though a man could sell his concubines and his female slaves to other men, he could not force them to prostitute themselves for his gain "if they would preserve their chastity."[58]

In spite of this, some men did prostitute their slaves and concubines as evident from a *hadith,* that is, a report of the Prophet Muhammad's actions or sayings not found in the Koran, to the effect that the wages gained from prostitution of a slave girl were not to be enjoyed by her owner.[59] In the Koran itself there are at least two references to prostitution. An early *sura* (chapter) required four witnesses against women accused of prostituting themselves and those found guilty were to be locked up in their houses until death or until new legislation was provided.[60] The new legislation was probably that mentioned in a later *sura,* which imposed a punishment of a hundred strokes on those women convicted of adultery on the testimony of four male witnesses. There were safeguards, however, and if the women were falsely accused, those bringing the false accusations were themselves punished with eighty strokes.[61] The effect of requiring four witnesses, all of whom had to be male, was to give the prostitute more or less free reign if she exercised any kind of caution.

Prior to Muhammad, there was no prohibition against prostitution except that the male always had to keep in mind that fornication with any woman who was not his wife could be regarded as an injury to the rights of the property of a fellow tribesman.[62] Islam itself was not quite so tolerant, and chastity in the Koran is represented as one of the marks of the believer, distinguishing him (or her) from the unbeliever.[63] Inevitably there was considerable hostility to prostitution although Islam, like Christianity, usually tolerated it. To banish it outright would have required a radical reorganization of societal values. In a society where polygamy was widespread and where there probably was a shortage of available wives, prostitution became an acceptable form of sex relief for many males. Prostitutes (other than the temporary wives), however, were an outcast group excluded from fellowship with women (and men) of their own clan, confined to special houses, or found at special markets and fairs, or walking the streets in the larger areas. Houses of prostitution were apparently marked by a flag that was hung at the door. In spite of hostility, a few prostitutes became famous. One of the most famous was a certain Kharqa of Mecca, who considered herself one of the "pilgrimage rites." To emphasize her calling and distinguish herself from the "good" women, Kharqa would unveil only before strangers, but if she was in the presence of any man she knew she kept her face discreetly covered.[64] Kharqa to the contrary, the prostitute was looked down on, and to be called the son of a whore was derogatory, indicating great contempt.[65] Still, literature abounds with stories about prostitutes, panderers, and procuresses. Prostitutes were tolerated, in spite of hostility, because they served a need. For any Moslem male to seduce an innocent woman or girl was to commit a dishonorable act, whereas to consort with prostitutes was merely regarded as a form of contemptible conduct. Islamic moralists and lawyers, like their Christian counterparts, justified the existence of prostitution as necessary to ensure the safety of the "good" women in the "decent" homes and harems. In fact, in a polygamous society, in spite of the ease of divorce, prostitution became an important way of assuring that all males who wanted heterosexual contacts would have a female available. To eliminate prostitution the Moslems would have had to eliminate a double standard that tolerated promiscuity for the male but punished it in a woman.

Further encouraging prostitution was the erotic portraiture of women in Arabic and Islamic literature. It should be noted that the emphasis of the poet was usually on woman as object rather than on the emotional experience shared. Women were drawn as erotic creatures, continually giving trouble to men. Muhammad, conscious of this, advised women

> always to lower their gaze and be modest, and to display as their adornment only that which is apparent, and to draw their veils over their bosoms, and not to reveal their adornments save to their own husbands or fathers or husband's fathers, or their sons or their husband's sons, or their brothers or their brothers' sons or sisters' sons, or their women, or their slaves, or male attendants who lack vigour, or children who know naught of women's nakedness. And let them not stamp their feet so as to reveal what they hide of their adornment.[66]

To avoid being aroused, men were advised never to look at the body of a strange woman but only her face, hands, or feet.[67] In fact, the whole body of a free woman was regarded as pudendal, and no part of her was to be seen by anyone except her husband or close kin—for her own protection. Vis, the heroine of an Islamic romance, was made to confess by her male author:

> In women desire is stronger than modesty and wisdom. Among created beings woman is imperfect, and in consequence capricious and of ill repute, hazarding this world and the next for the sake of a moment's desire, losing all reason when her desire is fulfilled.[68]

Since women were excluded from male company for the most part, a special class of women developed to entertain men. These high-priced courtesans were in demand in the court, and by the rich nobles. When the Duke of Holstein entered the Persian provincial capital of Qazvin in 1637, he was met by

> fifteen young women, well mounted, very richly clothed in many kinds of velvet with a base of gold, wearing necklaces of great pearls, ear pendants, and many rings. They had their faces bare, contrary to the custom of honest women in Persia. Thus we soon knew, both by their resolute mien and by what we were told, that these were the principal courtesans of the town, come out to meet us and entertain us with their music.[69]

The whole Islamic denigration of women encouraged the growth of a special class of women whose mission in life was to entertain the male, and in spite of official religious hostility, they continued to exist. Probably they were more ubiquitious in Islamic than in Christian society because Islam never emphasized celibacy as a virtue, although chastity within marriage for males was respected.

What kind of women became prostitutes in Islamic countries where the prostitute was such a disgrace to her family? Probably many were orphans without relatives, others were imported from outside areas to serve as prostitutes, or were daughters of prostitutes who had grown up in the trade. All three classes of women would be without male relatives, or else would have managed to escape from their clutches. This was important because in many parts of the Islamic world the prostitute herself was in personal danger from her family for disgracing them.[70] Many prostitutes might have been slaves, or concubines, or even former wives tossed aside by their husbands and lovers, far from their tribal homes and with no way of earning a living. This was often the case in urban areas where the tribal ties were never particularly strong and where most prostitutes were located.[71] Not all Islamic tribes sought retribution on the woman who became a prostitute, and certain oases and tribal groups had a reputation for "loose women." Many devoted Moslems, in spite of the Koranic prohibitions, sought out these areas.[72]

In some of the larger cities such as Cairo and Baghdad there was an attempt to deal with the problems of urban living by appointing inspectors of public morals, the Muhtasib. They made certain that people attended prayers at the proper times, inspected the produce in the markets as to quality, and among other things patrolled the streets to prevent unrelated men and women from walking together, inspected the public bath to make certain there was no nakedness and that men did not mix with "foreign" women, and solicited information on sexual immorality.[73] These officials could usually give punishment directly, thus avoiding the legal wrangling associated with charges of immorality or prostitution in the courts. They could whip offenders, or parade an accused person through the streets, to bring about public disgrace. The purpose of the office was to intimidate people and make certain that the moral precepts of Islam were observed. Obviously, with dedicated, efficient Muhtasibs on the job, prostitution did not flourish, but some officials tolerated both prostitution and dancing girls.[74] Probably the effect of such officials overall was to make prostitution not too obvious.

Though Islam was much more willing to accept human sexuality than Christianity, it was no less ambivalent about prostitution, resulting partly from the double standard of morality and the subordinate status of women in society. Women were far more limited in their public activities in the Islamic world than they were in the Christian world, which helped encourage prostitution. The prostitute could engage in a great many more activities than a "good woman" could, but she was also exposed to general hostility. Men of the upper social and literary groups who sometimes glamorized the prostitute in the West had no need to do so because they could easily obtain divorces, or wives, or take on concubines, or *mut'a*. These latter unions possessed the advantage of giving the children of such liaisons some semblance of legitimacy. At the same time they increased the likelihood of prostitution. Polygamy and concubinage, for example, tended to draw off numbers of eligible women from the marriage market. Thus, for large numbers of men, prostitution was the only heterosexual alternative. The possibilities of divorce tended to lessen some of the inequalities of polygamy, but in a society that regarded sex as a positive good, there was little wrong from the male point of view in visiting a prostitute. Moreover, in a society where the role of women was so rigidly restricted, the prostitute offered an exciting interlude. Society's contradictory hostility to the prostitute rested on her alluring violation of what a good woman should be. Punishment for her could be harsh. Islamic authorities, however, compounded their hypocrisy with self-serving toleration, much as did their Western counterparts, and often viewed the prostitute's activities with a blind eye.

6 INDIA AND CHINA: OTHER VIEWS

The sexual freedom of the indigenous inhabitants of the Indian sub-continent was a matter of considerable surprise and great abhorrence to the Aryan immigrants who first came in contact with them. If the classic Vedic texts are to be believed, both male and female were allowed great freedom in their sexual activities; unrestricted sexual activity was toler-ated, and various festivals, tournaments, and athletic contests permitted intermingling of the sexes and encouraged more intimate contacts.[1] If a woman became pregnant as a result of her sexual activities, she usually entered into agreement with her partner to marry, but if the negotiations fell through, the child was exposed and the parties were free to go their own way.

In certain parts of ancient India the marriage bond was unknown as such, and the women in such areas had the privilege of having sexual intercourse with anyone they pleased without restrictions. According to the *Mahabharata,* one of the classic epics of Hinduism, marriage had been instituted only because the sage Svetaketu, one of the legendary authors of a treatise on sexual techniques, had seen his own mother being led away from his father by another man. Therefore, when Svetaketu later obtained power he ordained that such customs stop, and tried to force women to be faithful to one man.[2] Classical Greek writers who either visited India or repeated what they had heard about India reported the existence of remark-able sexual freedom—although by the time they were writing, women had lost much of their individual sexual freedom and were more subject to males. For example, the Greek historian and geographer Strabo, who wrote in the first century A.D., described how some of the male citizens of Taxilia who had unmarried daughters took them forth to the marketplace with trumpets blowing and drums playing, and then when a crowd had assembled, exposed the girl from the rear and then from the front, and if she pleased a man who also was acceptable to her, terms were drawn up, and the couple were married.[3]

Customs varied from region to region in India, and the problem of the historian in dealing with prostitution in the subcontinent is the bewildering variety of conflicting schools of philosophy or systems of theology. Moreover, Hinduism, the traditional religion of India, and probably the oldest of the existing mass religions in the world today, has no particular individual whom it regards as its chief founder or guide, and thus possesses many permutations and interpretations. Like Judaism, Hinduism has given birth to other world religions, the most influential of which are Buddhism and Jainism, but within India Hinduism is still the dominant religion. It has survived in part because of its tolerance, finding a place for various thoughts at every level of life. Although Hinduism has not attempted to impose its special rituals, philosophy, or beliefs upon others, it has had an all-pervasive influence on the peoples with whom it has come in contact. Like the ancient Hebrew, the Hindu thought primarily in religious terms, so that almost all the extant literature of ancient India is in some way connected with religion. This gives Hinduism a rich store of scriptures to draw from, but because they were written at different times to serve different needs, they also often express different and contradictory attitudes.

Despite these contradictions there is a certain unity to Hinduism based on common scriptures, common deities, common ideals, common beliefs, and common practices. For any historical study of prostitution, the scriptures give the greatest amount of information. The earliest scriptures and the most important are the Vedas, the record of eternal truths of the great sages. The rest of the religious writings are supplemental to these, and in fact derive their authority from the Vedas. Besides the Vedas, Indian scriptures include the epics, the sacred romances, the codes of law, the manuals of philosophy, and various sectarian scriptures. Hindu religion is also divided into several stages of development that can be connected to political events in India's history. Probably the most important was the Aryan invasion that began sometime in the second millennium B.C. and gradually spread throughout India. The Aryans, an Indo-European language group, not a racial group, were related to other Indo-European groups such as the Greeks, who were spreading westward at the same time. It was in part this Aryan conquest that either led to the emergence of or strengthened the incipient castes in India, since the new conquerors subjected the indigenous inhabitants to their rule. It also had important effects on the status of women, and the role of prostitution.

Hindu scriptures express conflicting thoughts about the female. Women are portrayed both as a delight and a torment to man, a reflection perhaps of the dualism in Indian thought that wavers between burning sensuality and stark renunciation. Nowhere in any religion has woman as loving wife and tender mother been more extolled or appreciated.[4] The epics continually sing of honoring women since to honor women gladdens the heart of the gods; where women are not honored, all other religious deeds are barren.[5] The *Ramayana,* one of the great epics of Hinduism, states that at first all beings were alike in stature, sex, speech, and so on, but then the Maker made a distinction, took the best from all beings, and from this shaped woman. Good women cannot be soiled or spoiled, and like the pearl, can be found in the most sordid of environments.[6]

Other passages, however, express the opposite view, painting woman as the sum and substance of all that is evil. When the divine wise man Narada attempted to find the cause of evil in the world, he found that women were its roots. Women lacked the moral bonds of men; even when they found husbands who were rich and worthy of them they were likely to throw themselves into the arms of bad men as soon as they had a chance. If a woman did remain faithful, it was only because she did not have a chance to stray, or that no other man could be found willing to woo her. Women were regarded as envious of youth, envious of other women who were sought after by men, and continually in need of love. Women were death, the wind, the underworld, the ever-burning entrance to hell, the knife edge, the snake, the fire; she was each of these and she was all of them. Though there were good women, the glorious ones, the mothers of the world, they were more than balanced by the evil ones, who loved no man with whom they united.[7]

By the time the scriptures were composed, Hindu society was extremely male oriented. The son was preferred to the daughter since the son was the hope of the family while the daughter was only a source of trouble. Being born female was regarded as a penalty for sins committed in previous incarnations. The denigration of women was probably attributable to the family's burden in seeing that she was well married. Marriage was essential for a woman since she could not stand alone in Hinduism; her duty was to assist her husband and family in performing certain religious rituals. Marriage was not only a necessity but a religious sacrament, arranged for by the father. Daughters were dependent for both support and protection on their fathers; if the father died his role was taken over by a girl's brothers. Brotherless maidens were believed to be exposed to such danger that their value as brides went down. Even after her marriage a woman always had to have a man to lean on since females were unable to protect themselves against temptation. The absolute necessity of acquiring a husband led to earlier and earlier marriages; the great age discrepancy often present between brides and bridegrooms further lowered women's status until they had little independence in religion or law. Even their deaths were often determined for them by the institution of suttee.[8]

As one modern Hindu woman lamented, the only place a woman could be free of a man was "in hell."[9]

Women, however, were recognized as enjoying sex. Virginity had no special cult; and while lifelong celibacy was permitted for men (but never enjoined as a permanent ideal), it was discouraged for women. Even the ascetic looked on celibacy as a temporary discipline, a self-restraint as a means to the acquisition of magical powers. The power of sex, however, was never denied and sexual symbolism was omnipresent in Indian religion: in sculptural portrayals of the gods, in myths about the lives of the gods, and in songs and dances. This pervasive sexuality proved shocking and unsettling to Western observers. James Mill in his *History of British India* in 1817 stated:

> A religion which subjects to the eyes of its votaries the grossest images of sensual pleasure, and renders even the emblems of generation objects of worship, which ascribes to the supreme God an immense train of obscene acts; which has them engraved on the sacred cars, portrayed in the temples and presented to the people as objects of adoration, which pays worship to the Yoni [female organ], and the Lingam [male organ], cannot be regarded as favourable to chastity.[10]

An early Christian missionary was somewhat more violent:

> The Bible must supplant the narratives of their false divinities; their temples, covered now with sculptures and paintings which crimson the face of modesty even to glance at, must be demolished; the vile *lingam* must be levelled to the ground.[11]

Erotic representations of the gods are still widespread thoughout India, and have been much commented on and photographed.[12] The reasons given for the existence of such sculpture are almost as varied as those who have written about it. Some have said that the sexual scenes represent the oneness of god, others that they are representations of supreme bliss, while still others believe they are deliberate temptations put there to be overcome by the devout. They have been called innocent depictions of human activity in the same way as other sculptures show scenes of dancing, fighting, praying, and so forth. Some have written that they are intended as protection against the evil eye, and some that they were designed to force grosser-minded people to pay attention to their religious duties. A few authorities have stated that they served as a source of sexual information for the young and ignorant while still others regard them as straightforward representations of ritualistic orgies or Yogic postures. Regardless of the reason, Hinduism accepted sex, and rejoiced in it.

Contrary to Islam, which emphasized that the sex act was primarily for the enjoyment of the male, Hinduism depicted the female as the more sexual of the two partners. Several popular folk tales deal with males turned into females, who, in spite of the loss of status, the seclusion, and the helplessness suffered as women, ultimately chose to remain female because the joy of sex was so much greater. One of the stories recounts the adventures of a king named Bhangasvana, who had first fathered a hundred sons, and then after being transformed into a female by the powerful god Indra, gave birth to a hundred sons. After a horrifying series of adventures, Indra took pity on her and gave her a choice of remaining a woman or becoming a man again. She chose to remain a woman because the

> woman has in union with the man always the greater joy, that is why . . .
> I choose to be a woman. I feel greater pleasure in love as a woman,
> that is the truth, best among the gods. I am content with existence
> as a woman.[13]

There is an old Indian proverb which states that woman's power in eating is twice as great as that of man's, her cunning or bashfulness four times as great, her decision or boldness six times as great, and her impetuosity or delight in love eight times as great.[14] Without the possibilities of sexual pleasures a woman would ache and pine away. Love filled her whole being, made her steadfast and faithful, and as it grew even deeper, it strongly mingled with the altruistic. Increasingly, however, Hinduism emphasized that for women the greatest joys of love could be found only in the bonds of marriage, and it was only in wedlock that the full depth of the glowing colors and innermost perfumes were revealed. Though mythically a state of promiscuity had existed, the blind seer Dirghatamas had ordained that woman was to have only one husband as long as she lived, and then further handicapped her by stating that if he died, she was not to remarry. If a woman had sex with a man other than her husband, she lost her caste, as did an unmarried woman who prostituted herself. As limitations were put on female sexuality, the only alternatives were to be a chaste, devoted wife or a prostitute, and prostitution already was common in the Vedic period.[15] It was even sanctioned. Dirghatamas, for example, stipulated that when sexual intercourse did take place between women and men who were not their husbands, women were to be paid for their services.[16]

Marriage was so important to a girl that at times formal marriage ceremonies were performed over the corpses of girls who had not been married. This necessity for girls to partake in the sacrament of marriage led devout Hindu parents frenziedly to concentrate on gaining husbands for their daughters, and inevitably the marriage age moved downward. In the Vedic period, when the emphasis on marriage had not been so great, girls usually were married at fifteen or sixteen years of age. By A.D. 500-1000, many of the writers urged marriage before the age of ten, the age at which it was believed girls reached puberty. Certain factions argued for even younger marriages so that five- and six-year-old brides were not unknown. Early marriages helped the parents secure for their daughter a guardian in case the father died and the mother immolated herself (suttee).[17] As younger marriages came more and more into vogue, the chance for a woman to be independent decreased, her educational accomplishment went down, and increasingly she was restricted to the home. Though some girls in cultured and rich families were given an education, increasingly it was the outcast woman who acquired some independence; and as in Greek society when women were subordinated, men turned to prostitutes and hetairae.

These hetairae had a peculiar position in India. As women who had sacrificed what was regarded as an honorable status for a woman, they were held in low esteem by society; on the other hand, as custodians of the fine arts, arts that had ceased to be cultivated by respectable women, they were admired and respected. As in Greece, hetairae were often employed as tutors for the daughters of the rich in order that they too might learn something about the arts, although here also the increasing emphasis on marriages weakened this movement in Indian society. Famous capitals had courts of courtesans, headed by a chief courtesan formally installed in her position with considerable pomp and ceremony.

Researchers have uncovered some three hundred and thirty synonyms for the word *prostitute* in Sanskrit, covering hierarchies of the profession in all its abundant variety. The list includes divine woman, temple girl, royal concubine, society courtesan, streetwalker, and brothel prostitute. The prostitute is spoken of as a pleasure woman and a joy girl and is referred to by dozens of epithets such as melon-breasted, mountain-bosomed, hip-shaker, rolling-buttocked, lotus-scented, and fish-fragranced. Persons also classed as old husbandless women and eunuchs were traditionally regarded as procuresses or procurers, while the wives of actors, dancers, singers, washermen, dyers, and others were usually regarded as being the same as harlots.

The highest class of prostitute was the *devadasi* (slave of the god), dedicated to the service of the deity in a Hindu temple. Several of the Puranas, legendary tales of the ancient times compiled between the sixth and sixteenth centuries A.D., include materials about temple prostitution. The *Padma Purana,* for example, recommends the purchase of girls for dedication to the temples, and the *Bhavishya Purana* states that a special heaven is reserved for those men who dedicate *devadasis* to the solar temple. When the custom originated is a matter of some debate, although it seems clear that the custom was fairly widespread by the third century. It was not unusual for some of the devout to give their daughters for temple service to secure spiritual blessings. Huien-Tsang, who visited India in the seventh century, referred to the hordes of dancing girls at the sun temple at Multan. The nominal purpose of the women was to provide vocal and instrumental music for the religious service, as well as to perform ceremonial ablutions at the temple. Most of them were not well paid and soon took up prostitution as a sideline; in fact they became so associated with prostitution that many were specifically purchased by temples for the income that they could earn. The famous temple of Samanatha had some five hundred dancing girls attached to it in order to provide music for the god twenty-four hours a day, as well as earthly respite for the male worshippers. When King Rajaraja built the Tanjore temple in the tenth century, he provided it with some four hundred dancing girls.[18]

If the firstborn of a family happened to be a girl, she was often dedicated to the temple as a *devadasi* in hope of getting a son through this gift to the god. Others presented their daughters to the temple in fulfillment of a vow, others simply to get rid of them. Abbé Dubois, an eighteenth-century observer, described the recruiting methods used by priests during a festival devoted to the god Vishnu. While the image of the god was borne through the streets, the priests who were associated with the temple went about in the crowd, selecting the most beautiful women they could find, demanding

> them of their husbands or parents in the name of Venkatesvara [Vishnu] for whose service, it is asserted they are destined. Those husbands who have not lost all common sense, understanding or at least suspecting that a god of stone has no need for wives, indignantly refuse to deliver up theirs, and bluntly speak their mind to the hypocritical rogues. The latter, far from being disconcerted, proceed to apply to others who are delighted at the honour conferred upon them . . . . It is thus that the seraglio of Tirupati is recruited. When the god takes it into his head that some of his wives are beginning to grow old or are no longer pleasing him, he signifies through the priests his intention of divorcing them. A mark is branded on their thighs or breasts with a red-hot iron, representing the god . . . and they receive a certificate showing that they have faithfully served a certain number of years as legitimate wives of the god, and are therefore recommended to the charitable public.[19]

Usually the temple prostitute was not recruited as an adult but entered service as a child of seven or so. In order to conform to a woman's need for marriage, she was often "married" to the deity and a marriage badge was tied around her neck. Gods were not the only marriage partners. One class of dancing girl (*patar*) was married to a pipal tree, and another to inanimate objects such as daggers or swords. Krishna was looked on as their personal god and Siva as their guardian. After their formal marriage ceremony the girl was usually ritually deflowered by the temple priest or had her hymen punctured by being made to sit astride a stone *lingam*. Sometimes, however, a privileged customer or patron was permitted the rite of defloration.

Once accepted, the girls were trained by the temple priests in dancing and the erotic arts, and served as temple prostitutes available to the public; their earnings were kept by the priests and any children born to them became attendants at the temples. Their duties included those of a general temple servant, keeping the temple clean, fanning the idol with a palm leaf or yak tail, carrying the sacred lights, dancing and singing before the idol of the god and the public.[20] Each shrine had its own name for its women. In some areas they were known as *murali*, others called them *jogavin, bhanvini, jogti, naikini,* and so on, and in English they generally came to be called Nautch girls or dancing girls.[21] Though many Hindu reformers condemned the use of dancing girls in the temple on the grounds that they lowered the spiritual and moral atmosphere of the religious rituals and interfered with honest pilgrims in performing their religious duties, they continued to exist. The shrines of south India were particularly notorious for the temple women, and several large temples such as those at Madura, Conjeeveram, and Tanjore were worked like brothels.

The great difference between the religious or temple prostitute and the secular prostitute was that the temple prostitute was dedicated to the god; the temple prostitute differed from the high-class courtesan in that she performed in public whereas the hetairae danced in private. The high-class courtesans were proficient in all the arts that attract men. They were accomplished singers and dancers, and were free to go about as they pleased. Vatsyayana, the great authority on Indian eroticism, who wrote in the fifth century A.D., devoted a whole section to them, laying down the rules of the trade. Courtesans, he stated, obtained both sexual pleasure and their own maintenance by having intercourse with men. Even if a courtesan failed to receive pleasure, she was to pretend she did, since men had confidence in women who apparently loved them. The successful courtesan was to be possessed of beauty and amiability, with good physical features. She should have a liking for good qualities in people as well as love of wealth, and she should take delight in sexual union. Though he recognized that others had given many reasons for women resorting to prostitution (love, fear, money, pleasure, enmity, curiosity, sorrow, celebrity, compassion, shame, and so on), he believed there were only three basic reasons: desire of wealth, freedom from misfortune, and love. Occasionally a courtesan would live a long period with the same man, almost as if she were his wife, and when this happened Vatsyayana urged her to behave like a chaste woman. At other times, however, the courtesan was to try to get money out of her lovers either by direct means or by artifices. When a man failed to offer enough money, the prostitute was to borrow money from him for purchasing clothes, ornaments, perfumes; ingratiate herself by praising his intelligence; beg money to make gifts for festivals; pretend that her jewels had been stolen or that her property been destroyed by fire; contract debts for his sake; and a whole series of similar devices. He also advised a courtesan on how to get rid of an unwanted lover by censuring his disagreeable habits and vices, talking on subjects with which he was not acquainted, failing to show admiration for his learning, praising men who he felt were superior to him, expressing dissatisfaction with his love technique, urging sex on him when he was fatigued, and responding passively when he was ardent, interrupting him in the middle of his stories, and making asides to others about him. In his words:

> The duty of a courtesan consists in forming connections with suitable men after due and full consideration, and attaching the person with whom she is united to herself; in obtaining wealth from the person who is attached to her; and then dismissing him after she has taken away all his possessions.[22]

He classified prostitutes into nine groups. The common harlots, mostly slaves, who were cheap as spittoons (*khumbas*) and hence were known as *khumbhadasi*. They gave themselves up to all and sundry for a small fee and had neither beauty nor accomplishment. Above them in status was the female attendant, or *paricharika*, the daughter or ward of an elderly courtesan; she worked in a brothel but had a special relation with one or more men with whom she was bound in contract. A third category was the *kulata*, or secret prostitute who, though married, earned an income on her own. Similar to her was the *sairini*, or free woman, who was also married but had the permission of her husband to engage in prostitution. Still another category included the dancers and actresses who made up the better class of common courtesan in medieval India. They ostensibly earned their living by acting or dancing but never refused a good offer for their favors. The *silpakarika*, or artisan's wife, drawn from the *sudra* caste, the caste created to serve others, furnished another group of prostitutes. Often wives of artisans worked in the households of higher castes where they were regarded as fair game by the men of such households. Separate from any of these was the *prakashavinashta,* or runaway wife, who eloped with a paramour and lived with him as a concubine. The *rupajibi,* or lovely body seller, was a courtesan noted for her flawless body proportions. The highest type was the *ganika,* or super courtesan, who in addition to a desirable body possessed dancing and musical skills, as well as literary ones.[23]

Each writer, however, had a different classification of prostitutes. The *Mahabharata* broke them down into five categories. The *rajavecya,* or royal courtesan, who catered to the needs of the kings; *nagari,* or city prostitute; the *guptavecya,* or secret prostitute; who came from a good family and practiced the trade secretly; the *devayecya,* or temple prostitute; and the *brahmavecya* (or *tirthaga*), the prostitute of the bathing place.[24]

Several Indian erotic manuals have prostitutes as central characters. Damodaragupta, an eighth-century minister to the king of the Kashmir, wrote the *Kuttani mata* [Lessons of a Bawd], in which an elderly professional prostitute instructed a young novice on how to attract lovers and gold.[25] Kshemendra in the eleventh century wrote the *Samaya-matrika* [Harlot's Breviary], which portrayed with considerable realism the life of a courtesan. In his judgment the successful courtesan had

> the allurement of toilet and jewelry upon her side, and the gracious harmony of gesture and attitude to plead for her. Her cause is urged by a balm of insinuating perfumes upon her tended body, by careful coquetry, and intellectual grace. She lives by the sciences of matching conversation and of matching colors, by the flash of fortune and the flash of luxury; so that we honour and adore her. She is rich in every resource at her full flowering, each natural attraction and unnatural wile is hers; she bears the lights of well-being and joy upon her face through all her multitude of arduous pleasures.

This was the male view of the prostitute. He also tried to describe the profession from the prostitute's point of view; he said the prostitute should be always cautious and watchful because there were dangerous

> crevasses where a black race of serpents lie on watch; there rutting elephants abide; these caves are the resort of lions . . . thus that old, experienced bawds speak of us men, when, in the thickets of the pleasure houses they warn poor girls against the ferocity of exploitation.[26]

The more ambitious and successful prostitutes employed agents and others to gain them the necessary access to fashionable society where they could find the better-paying clients. Some had pimps, who not only shared the income but demanded sexual satisfaction as well. Particularly notorious both as pimps and procurers were petty police officers, clerks in law courts, astrologers, florists, perfumers, barmen, barbers, and others who had access to the rich and powerful. It was expected that a prostitute would welcome a pimp since it was believed important that she have a lover to whom she was attached without any pecuniary motive, although never was her personal predilection toward a lover allowed to stand in her way of duty or profit.[27]

Prostitution, obviously, was accepted as a way of life in both ancient and medieval India. It was one of the few occupations open to women. Public women were distinguished from other women by their red apparel, and this identification served to notify potential customers and warned respectable women to avoid their company. They accompanied the army, went on hunting parties, and were prominent in all the Indian cities where they usually gathered at the public well or frequented other well-traveled areas. Travelers were often welcomed by being entertained by beautiful sensual prostitutes who performed the dances that were noted for miraculously reinvigorating males. When the god Krishna was sent on a mission, the king gave orders that his sons and grandsons should meet him in a splendid chariot accompanied by fair prostitutes who were to prepare the welcome on foot. Ordinary politeness required that when persons of distinction made a formal visit they be accompanied by a bevy of hetairae.[28] A courtesan had to be present with the king in certain state ceremonies, and when he sat on the throne she held the royal umbrella.

One of the most complete of ancient discussions of the prostitute in public life is that by Kautilya (who lived sometime between 290 B.C. and A.D. 300), whose treatise on government, the *Arthasatra,* was rediscovered in 1905. In ideology a predecessor of Machiavelli, Kautilya advocates a rather ruthless and cynical manipulation of power and explains how royal ordinances could override every law. Included in his work is much discussion of public morals. For him prostitution was a well-established institution, approved and organized by the state. He described an official superintendent of prostitutes, known as the *ganikadhyaksa,* who had the power to grant the status of courtesan to a deserving prostitute based on her beauty, youth, and artistic ability. Obviously this class of prostitute held a high rank. She could draw a state grant of 1,000 *panas* for her establishment, and if it was large, it was overseen by a special deputy, *pratiganika,* appointed by the chief superintendent. In case of the courtesan's death or desertion, her establishment descended to her sister or daughter, whose duty it was to run it. Sometimes her mother could also run it, but in default of these successors, the establishment reverted to the crown. Prostitutes were classed in three grades, and according to their grade drew a salary of 1,000, 2,000, or 3,000 *panas*. The highest class attended the king upon public affairs, the middle group catered to the royal wives at official ceremonies, and the lowest catered to the king's private needs.

When the army went to war, women accompanied the troops, and the food and beverage for the troops were made by such women, who in battle were supposed to stand by urging the men to fight. Some of the prostitutes were born into prostitution as children of other prostitutes, some were purchased from their parents, some were captured in warfare, and some became prostitutes as punishment for adultery. Usually a prostitute of the higher class had a choice in the selection of her sexual partners. The chief exception: a king might force a companion on her. Prostitutes were entitled to own property, and in addition to the money she received from the state, she was entitled to ornaments, fees, profits, and slave women. As prostitutes became older, they were made matrons to guide the younger prostitutes, or were attached to one of the king's storehouses or kitchens.

The brothel was regarded as a den of criminal activity; some crimes were committed against the prostitute, some were committed by her against her customer, and others were planned there to take place elsewhere. It was perhaps for this reason that the prostitutes were regarded as good informers for the police. In addition to the prostitutes under the control of the superintendent of courtesans, there were women who indulged in unregulated liaison, the type of occasional prostitute mentioned earlier in this chapter, as well as the market whore. Regardless of how closely regulated the prostitute was, however, Kautilya felt that prostitutes had certain rights. A contract between a prostitute and her paramour was a legitimate contract, and the prostitute was to be protected from violence, and in return was to give some of her income to the state. He also felt that the state had to make adequate provisions for the training of those women who entertained men by teaching them singing, playing musical instruments, and other fine arts, in order that they be most effective in their work.[29]

From other sources it appears that the prostitute was most usually a member of the lower castes; if she had been born into one of the upper castes she suffered a loss of status by entering the profession. Generally the law was ambiguous about their status, but public women usually received humane treatment; often the state regulated their activities and for this the officials took the equivalent of two days' earnings from each prostitute every month as tax. In the fifteenth and sixteenth centuries the tax imposed on prostitutes in the kingdom of Vijayanagar paid for the upkeep of the entire police force of 12,000 men.[30] Even when the prostitute ran afoul of the law there was some effort to protect her. For example, a prostitute's ornamentation could not be confiscated even though the rest of her property might be; Indian jurists thought her ornamentation was essential for her practice. The law also intervened in her contract disputes with customers. Traditionally, if a prostitute was hired by a man and then refused to accompany him, she was to be fined an amount equivalent to double her fee. If she promised herself to one man, yet went with another, she had to pay the injured customer not only double the amount he had paid but also a fine to the royal treasury. If there was a dispute between a prostitute and her customer, the case was decided by the chief courtesan of the city in consultation with the litigants.[31] Most people considered the incidental meeting with a prostitute a favorable omen, and conversely the accidental meeting with a widow was a bad omen.[32]

It was recognized, however, that a married man who visited a prostitute might be insulting his wife, and a chaste wife was allowed to correct her wayward husband who visited prostitutes by abusing him or beating him within the limits of the law. Generally when a man was visiting a prostitute, he was to avoid the company of respectable women. If accidentally there occurred a meeting of courtesans and respectable ladies, the prostitutes were supposed to be careful of their language and manners. The most that the Hindu rulers hoped to do was to keep prostitution under control, either by direct state interference or indirect control.[33]

Monogamy was the general rule in Indian society, although polygamy was occasionally practiced by the rich. In part, polygamy was encouraged by the need to have children to continue the prescribed oblations for one's ancestors. Wives were encouraged to urge their husbands to take second wives if they had proved barren or failed to provide a son. There were some protections built into polygamy for the women, at least in theory, since ten years was supposed to elapse before a wife could be considered officially barren. Second wives were also not to be taken without the permission of the first, although historically women had little say about the second marriage and their only real means of rebellion was to leave their husband's households.[34] Women who left their husbands often ended as prostitutes without family to fall back on.

Early Hindu thinkers were fairly lenient toward women who had strayed, since women were the weaker vessels. In the Vedic period, women who had committed adultery or prostituted themselves were allowed to take part in religious services, provided they confessed their error; in later periods, a double standard similar to that of Christianity and Islam developed. As the standards became stricter, a single lapse into promiscuity was considered fatal for the women, but even the most promiscuous husband was to be revered by a dutiful wife.[35] There was little or no stigma attached to the male who used the services of a prostitute, although the Brahmin who did so was considered polluted and had to cleanse himself.[36] Though Hinduism must be classed as a sex-positive religion, it failed to recognize an alternative life for women other than marriage, and became more and more hostile to wives or daughters who engaged in sex outside marriage. Inevitably there were large numbers of prostitutes. In fact, women were supposed to be so committed to marriage and their husbands that suttee, self-immolation of the widow on her husband's funeral pyre, was advocated as an ideal, and often practiced. Many women who failed to perform suttee found themselves forced into prostitution in order to support themselves.[37] Hinduism had started with a higher status for women than any of the other world religions, but because of conquests by foreigners, the growing rigidity of the caste system, and because of the increasing emphasis on marriage for women, women became more and more subordinated to the male. Prostitution was one of the few outlets that a woman had and many women entered willingly.

More influential than Hinduism outside India was Buddhism, a religion founded by an Indian prince, Gautama Sakyamuni, during the fifth century B.C. Though Buddhism eventually declined in much of India, it spread throughout the Far East, where Buddhist ideas still remain influential. A brief discussion of the Indian background to Buddhism serves as an effective introduction to Chinese sexual and prostitutional ideas. The teachings of the Buddha are complicated by the fact that his life is shrouded in legend, and there are different interpretations of both his life and teachings preserved in Pali (an ancient Indian literary language), Sanskrit, Chinese, and Tibetan, languages in the areas where Buddhism later became influential.

According to some traditions, even the Buddha himself did not deem it inappropriate to accept the luncheon invitation of the famous courtesan Ambapalli. The chief courtesan in northern Bihar, Ambapalli was noted for her beauty, accomplishments, and wealth. Other tales about prostitutes appear in the popular Buddhist mythology. One of the stories in the *Jatakasm,* a collection of stories about the Buddha in his previous incarnations, tells how the dedication of a young courtesan to her contract was so strict that she almost starved to death. The young woman had accepted 3,000 rupees from a young man for an evening of pleasure, but before the young man could enjoy his evening he was called away. The young courtesan, unwilling to spend her fee because she had not fulfilled her contract, and unable to engage in sex with other men until it was completed, barely survived the three years' wait for the return of her customer. So strict was she in observing her contract that she would not even accept a betal leaf from another man for fear it would compromise her position.[38]

This story obviously reflects the Hindu tradition of the dutiful prostitute, but more important in influencing other cultures were the Hindu concepts of *karma* and rebirth. *Karma,* literally "the deed or act," is based on the belief that every act produces a result or fruit, and this fruit can be either good or evil. For Buddha, *karma* involved not only the deed but the intention behind the deed, and the intention was more important than the deed. When a living being died, the *karma* that had accumulated determined the nature of his next rebirth, which would be either as a diety, a man, an animal, a hungry ghost, or as a resident of hell. This belief led to a kind of ascetic dedication, and in most schools of Buddhism the monastic community was regarded as providing the best possible condition for the pursuit of the religious ideals preached by Buddha. However, one school, Tantric Buddhism, had quite strong sexual overtones. Tantrism included a highly specialized sexual mysticism, which taught that complete unity with the deity could be achieved by a meditative process based on coitus reservatus, whereby the adept tried to effect a kind of mystic marriage between the male elements and female elements present in all, and the man forced his semen not into the waiting vagina but, by withholding orgasm and practicing breath control, directed it upward to his brain.[39]

Each person, male or female, included elements of the opposite sex in his body. The *lalana,* the female element, ran along the left side of the spinal cord and represented female creative energy, mother, ova, the vowel series, and corresponded to the moon; in the final sublimation it was the void, the gnosis, or spiritual truth. *Rasana,* the male element, ran along the right side of the spinal cord, and represented the male creative energy, father, semen, the consonant series, and corresponded to the sun. In the final sublimation it was compassion and practical truth. As long as dualism existed in men and women, each was caught in the chain of rebirths separated from the deity. In order to overcome this dualism the practitioner must join in imagined or real sexual embrace with a partner of the opposite sex. The male concentrated on the *bodhicitta,* which resided in germinal form in the nerve center around his navel. The female energy acquired from the woman stimulated the *bodhicitta* of the man, blended with his activated but unspent semen to form a new, more powerful essence called *bindu.* This could only be done by concentrating since *bindu* was derived from the essence of the five elements, earth, water, fire, air, and ether, the same elements that formed the human embryo, and the formation of *bindu* in the male was similar to conception

in the uterus. Instead of resulting in conception, however, the concentra
tion of the *bodhicitta* allowed the *bindu* to break through the separation
of the *lalana* and *rasana,* opening up a new nerve channel, proceeding
upward until it reached the brain. During its upward course the *bindu*
blended the five elements into one homogeneous effulgence, the male
and female elements also merged, and the final identification of the practitioner with the deity and with the void was completed, and the partners
gained the state of eternal bliss, *Nirvana.*[40]

Tantric Buddhists believe that man is sunk in ignorance although
a divine spark, his Buddha-nature, remains within him. For redemption
from his prison of ignorance he needs to arouse this divine spark, something he can accomplish only by esoteric concentration and consecration.
The decisive stage is the formation of the *bindu*, effectuated through
the stimulus received from the woman partner. Some texts imply that
the female is only an image invoked by concentrated meditation and
that union therefore is only spiritual, but the majority of texts imply
that she must be a real woman, stating rather plainly that Buddha-hood
abides in the female organ. Some imply that this woman should be the
initiate's wife, but others argue that she could be any woman the man
chooses. Obviously if this last interpretation has any validity, it would
provide a religious sanction for prostitution. Such an interpretation gains
validity from the extreme idealism inherent in Tantrism, namely, the belief
that the external world has no objective basis and all phenomena are merely
illusory appearances created by the mind. If such a view is carried to its
logical conclusion, then action by itself can be neither moral nor immoral.
Instead, the motive behind the action is all-important, and any action taken
that can lead to salvation can be justified regardless of the effects of the
act. The *bodhisattva* under such conditions could not be judged by ordinary moral standards. As soon as the initiate knew the truth, that is,
when the world appeared as a dream without any reality, there was no
restriction on his actions. A stanza in an early Tantric work states that
the initiate could freely immolate animals, utter falsehoods without ceremony, take things that do not belong to him, and even commit adultery.[41]

Tantrism existed not only in Buddhism but in Hinduism too. It was
in its Buddhist form that it was imported into China, and later into
Japan. It exists today in its Hindu form primarily in Nepal and Tibet,[42]
but it is to China that the remainder of this chapter is devoted. Before
entering into a discussion of Chinese sexual techniques, and the place
of prostitution in Chinese society, it is important to look at the position
of women in general. In the earliest periods of Chinese history, prior to
1100 B.C., women were apparently held in higher esteem than they were later.

Evidence for this assertion appears in an examination of family organization and of Chinese sexual concepts. Some of the earliest surviving texts, for example, describe women as the initiator of sex, with the male as a mere student. In spite of changes, this seems to hold true as well for much later periods. As in the other societies discussed in this book, the woman was most revered as mother, an incidence of which is the Shang graphic character for *woman,* with its emphasis on the large breasts of the pregnant woman.[43] Women were also associated with the color red, which among other things stood for sexual potency, creative power, and happiness; white, on the other hand, was the color associated with the male, the color of death, impotency, and negative influences. The symbol for family was also closely linked with woman and birth.

As in India and the West, religious tradition had a great deal to do with ideas about sex and ultimately with prostitution. The indigenous religion of China underwent a radical reformation from 570 to 420 B.C. through the efforts of three great reformers, Confucius, Lao-tze, and Mo Ti (or Tzu). Each of these men founded a school of thought that was elaborated on by disciples, eventually emerging into the religious philosophical movements of Confucianism and Taoism. Contemporary with these Chinese reformers was the Indian reformer Buddha, whose teachings began to permeate China shortly after his death (c. 483 B.C.?) but which did not arrive in force until the first centuries of the Christian era. Within India, as indicated, Buddhism was gradually absorbed into Hinduism, but in China, modified by Chinese disciples, it found new force and vigor, becoming less Indian and more Chinese, and it probably carried with it some of the Tantric beliefs. It should be emphasized, however, that though Confucianism, Taoism, and Buddhism became formal religions of the Chinese, preceding, combining, and overshadowing them was a nebulous Chinese religion that predated them. Because of the combination and interaction among these religious beliefs it is hard to draw lines since, apart from the professional Buddhists and Taoists, the people at large did not identify themselves exclusively as Confucianists, Taoists, or Buddhists. Authorities have refused to classify Confucianism as a religion but rather regard it as a philosophy, even though it has been more or less the state cult since the second century B.C. The state cult, however, meant little more than the official sanction and participation in the worship of heaven, ancestors, Confucius, and so on, and was in fact more political than religious. Ethical ideas over the years probably have been more Confucian than anything else, although these have not been uninfluenced by Taoism and Buddhism. The average Chinese was eclectic, taking what he considered helpful from each school of religious thought; even when he attended Buddhist or Taoist temples he was not unconscious of other deities in the general pantheon of the gods.

Confucius wrote little, or else little that he wrote has survived, about women. He stated that women, like people of lowly station, were difficult to deal with and if "you become close to them, they turn noncompliant, if you keep them at a distance, they turn resentful."[44] Disciples and interpreters of Confucius, however, worked out a more detailed concept of woman: she was absolutely and unconditionally inferior to man, and she simply did not count.[45] The first and foremost duty of woman was to serve and obey her husband and her parents, to look after the household, and to bear healthy male children. The biological functions of being female were emphasized; psychological considerations were given only secondary importance. Female chastity was regarded as a requisite for the orderly family life as well as for the undisturbed continuation of the lineage. The emphasis on the need for women to observe both pre- and postmarital chastity verged on cultism, and to prevent the least temptation or contamination, the Confucianists advocated the complete separation of the sexes. This was carried to such extremes that the husband and wife were not supposed to hang their garments in the same closet. The ideal woman was the one who concentrated all her efforts on her household tasks. Participation in outside affairs was regarded as the root of all evil.[46]

The Taoists had a different view of woman. They reasoned that the greater part of man-made activities had served only to estrange man from nature, giving rise to an unnatural and artificial human society with its family, its state, its rites and ceremonials, its arbitrary differentiation between good and bad. As a remedy for these artificialities they advocated a return to man's pristine simplicity, to a golden age where people would live long and happily, where there would be no good or bad, where everyone would live in perfect harmony with nature. Woman was venerated by the Taoists because she was considered to be closer than man to the primordial forces of nature, and because it was in her womb that new life was created and fostered. It was woman who possessed the indispensable elements for achieving the elixir of life.[47]

These seemingly contradictory attitudes were reconciled in Chinese society by following the Confucian ideal regarding the social position of the two sexes, but their sexual relations were governed by Taoist ideology. Outside the bedchamber the wife was usually little more than an essential but emotionally negligible member of the household; inside the bedroom she was the guardian of the mysteries of life and of sex. It was as mother, especially of sons, that the Chinese woman achieved her glory, and many a Chinese literary figure commemorated the dedication of his mother. In her old age the mother was served by the wives of her sons as well as the sons themselves, and her position was so powerful that even an emperor hesitated to question the authority of his mother.[48]

Buddhism differed both from Taoism and Confucianism in holding women equal to men, at least in theory. Buddhist texts introduced into China mentioned Buddha's position on women, but as Buddhism was adapted to Chinese needs these teachings were glossed over. The censorship or modification of Buddhism in this respect made it more palatable to Confucian sensibilities, and though later there were more accurate translations, there were also drastic revisions and expurgations.[49] In time, the subordination of women became the ideal.

Writers from all backgrounds emphasized that women as wives and mothers were to spend their lives running their homes and bringing children into the world. Women were discouraged from devoting much of their time to education or to perfecting themselves in the arts. Most of those who did turned to prostitution. Before her marriage, the girl's fate was identified with that of her father; after marriage with that of her husband; and after his death, with that of her son. Marriage was the most important thing in life. Even in this the girl had no say since it was arranged by the family. She could even be sold into prostitution if her father decided.

The childless widow in China was somewhat better off than in India since she was allowed to adopt a male child if she could, and at times was also allowed to remarry. Under Buddhism, widows were also allowed to become nuns. In spite of these advantages, the childless widow usually was a creature to be pitied.[50]

The Chinese, at least the males, were a sex-positive society, although they became somewhat ambiguous about women's sexual activity. Sex was conceived as symbolic of the functions of the universe. Like many Greeks, the Chinese saw the world in dualistic terms, but they emphasized the inherent unity of the opposing forces rather than the conflict so apparent in the West. Man was a microcosmos functioning in the same way as the macrocosmos, with the sexual union of male and female symbolic of the interaction of heaven and earth. As in Western thought, heaven was regarded as masculine and earth feminine, but the comparison was carried further. Clouds were the vaginal secretions, or the lining of the womb necessary for allowing the heavenly sperm, i.e., the rain, into the earth womb, and it was from the union of these two forces that all life came.

Various terms appear to have been used to describe these dualistic cosmic forces, but by the sixth century B.C., the words *yin* and *yang* had come to dominate. *Yang* was heaven, sun, male; *yin* was earth, moon, female. In the *I Ching,* the oldest of the Chinese classics, the hexagram symbolizing sexual union is a combination of the trigram *k'an* (water,

clouds, or woman) on top and the trigram *li* (fire, light, or man) on the
bottom.

When written in this way it meant that everything was in its proper place,
emphasizing the combination of perfect harmony of man and woman.[51]

Primarily the purpose of the sexual act was to bring about conception, especially of sons, to continue the family, but the sexual act was also
vital in strengthening the male's vitality by allowing him to absorb essence
from the woman. At birth an individual was filled with the principle of
primordial *yang* and *yin*, and though both would grow and increase as
the individual matured, the *yang* would reach a peak and begin to wane,
just as the sun does as it travels from the winter solstice to the summer
solstice and then back again. Death is caused by the imbalance of *yin* and
yang, so that as a man's *yang* begins to decline he has to take positive
steps to maintain it. The purpose of the ancient Chinese sexual techniques,
which were part of Taoist alchemy as well as Tantric Buddhism, was to
increase the amount of life-giving seminal essence (*ching*) by sexual stimulus and at the same time avoid possible loss. If the *yang* force in man
was continually fed by the *yin* force from women, it would not only be
conducive to health but to longevity. It was therefore essential that every
time a couple engaged in intercourse the woman reached orgasm so the
man could draw from her *yin* essence, and the more *yin* essence he
himself received without giving out his precious male substance the greater
his strength would grow. Thus the ideal was to practice coitus reservatus
except when there was an attempt to impregnate. By keeping his penis in
the female vagina but avoiding orgasm, the male semen was preserved
and made its way to the brain. Since the male usually was unable to
practice coitus reservatus without training, he could achieve the same

result by exerting pressure on the urethra between the scrotum and the anus at the moment of orgasm, thus diverting the seminal secretion to the brain. Though we now know that the seminal secretion not ejaculated enters the bladder where it is later voided with excreted urine, the Taoists did not understand modern physiology, and they believed that it could be made to ascend and rejuvenate or revivify the upper parts of the body.[52]

To explain the secrets of intercourse there were a number of manuals collectively called *fang chung,* literally "inside the bedchamber," or sometimes *fang-chung-shu,* the "art of the bedchamber." The earliest listing of such works occurs in the Han dynasty (206 B.C.–A.D. 220), but the only extant material is a brief explanatory note:

> The Art of the Bedchamber constitutes the climax of human emotions, it emcompasses the Supreme Way (Tao). Therefore the Saint Kings of antiquity regulated man's outer pleasures in order to restrain his inner passions and made detailed rules for sexual intercourse. An old record says: 'The Ancients created sexual pleasure thereby to regulate all human affairs." If one regulates his sexual pleasure he will feel at peace and attain a high age. If, on the other hand, one abandons himself to its pleasure disregarding the rules set forth in the above mentioned treatises one will fall ill and harm one's very life.[53]

Other works were composed during the Sui dynasty (A.D. 590–618), but the only ones that have been preserved to any extent are found in Japanese translations made in the late tenth century.[54]

How far back into Chinese history these sex practices go is perhaps debatable, but fairly early in recorded history there were special court ladies who regulated and supervised the sexual relations of the king with his wives, making certain that the king cohabitated with them on the correct calendar days and with the frequency established by the rites for each rank. The general rule was that women of the lower ranks should be visited frequently and before those of higher rank, although the man was to try to avoid orgasm. With the queen the king has intercourse only once a month, at the time when his potency was at its greatest because his *yang* had been built up by visits to women of lesser rank. A person with strong *yang* then would be able to beget strong and intelligent heirs to the throne, as well as live a long life.[55]

Chinese society was polygamous. Besides his principal wife, a man was entitled to several secondary wives as well as concubines, although a man's auxiliary wives were to be subordinate to his first wife.[56] The number of wives and concubines as well as special companions depended on the wealth and position of the master and varied from period to period in Chinese history. During the Chou dynasty (c. 1120–222 B.C.)

there was believed to be a magical number of female partners essential to nourish and invigorate the king. Each king was to have one queen, three consorts, nine wives of the second rank, twenty-seven wives of the third rank, and eighty-one concubines. These numbers were fixed by a system in which odd numbers stood for the positive forces of nature, male and male potency, while the even numbers were passive, a sign of the female and of female fertility. Three, the first odd number, had special potency, while nine, three times three, stood for superabundant potency. Multiplying nine by three led to twenty-seven, and twenty-seven by three to eighty-one, hence the number of required female partners.[57] Probably some of the Chinese men were willing to go beyond even these numbers, but if they did they turned to courtesans, prostitutes, and dancing girls; the ordinary king was much too exhausted to think beyond the one hundred and twenty-one women he had to keep sexually satisfied. Many high officials, however, kept troupes of trained dancing girls and girl musicians who performed at official banquets and drinking bouts and served the guests in other ways.

Since the higher public officials had numerous sexual contacts, the same privileges could not be denied lesser citizens. According to Chinese tradition, commercial brothels were started in the seventh century B.C. by the statesman-philosopher Kuang Chung as a means for increasing the state's income. Though there is some doubt as to whether Kuang Chung actually established the principle of licensing prostitutes, prostitution very early was set apart in special areas of the town. Prostitution itself was said to have been originated by a woman, Hung Yai, and was closely connected with the arts. In fact the same symbol, *chi,* is used to describe a prostitute and art, and by implication the earliest prostitutes were probably specialized singing and dancing girls. Organized brothels at first were known as *ch'ang-chia,* or *ch'ang-lou,* houses of singing girls, but later they became known as *ch'ing-lou,* houses of green bowers, because of their green lacquered woodwork. Fairly early also special houses staffed by *ying-chi,* or camp girls, were established to serve the army.[58]

Prostitution was a recognized fact of Chinese culture, and the Chinese courtesan achieved a position equal to that of the hetairae in ancient Greece. Though the Chinese emphasized virtue in wives, there was no corresponding emphasis on chastity in males, and in fact the whole alchemical theory encouraged sexual activity. During the T'ang dynasty (A.D. 618–907) the palace grounds even had a special brothel quarter, called the "northern quarter," in which girls from the most accomplished courtesan to the most illiterate prostitute lived. Many of the girls in the quarter were purchased from poor families, others were victims of kidnapping, still others entered the profession voluntarily. Once within the quarter the women were registered and housed in different areas according to rank and received special training under an adopted "mother." They could leave the quarter only with special guests or for special holidays.[59] Probably the concept behind the quarter was similar to that described by Kautilya in India, where the state took a direct interest in seeing that the women who did become prostitutes were well qualified; ultimately many became wives.

In a society in which most women had no real chance to acquire an education, where formal contact between men and women was frowned on, it became the function of the courtesan to entertain a man and be his friend. By losing her status as a good and proper woman, she gained a special status as a prostitute. The rules and regulations governing the relationship between a courtesan and her admirer were carefully established so that the lover knew in advance exactly what proportion of his income he would hand over to her. The prostitute was an indispensable part of the elegant life. Every prominent official, writer, artist, or merchant customarily left his wife at home when he traveled; instead he was accompanied by dancing girls or other women skilled in making men feel at ease. These girls enlivened parties with their songs, dances, and conversation, although after footbinding became more prominent, dancing became less important. Social relationships as well as business deals were always conducted outside the home, in restaurants, temples, and brothels; these gatherings formed such an integral part of official and business routine that providing prostitutes on such occasions was a matter of good taste and custom. The greater the demand for the separation of the sexes, the greater the demand for prostitutes as entertainers at private and public parties.[60] Often men turned to the same prostitute for companionship, and it was not unusual to purchase a concubine from a house of prostitution. Some of these concubines even became official wives.

Courtesans with literary, musical, or dancing ability were much in demand as companions, and many poems attributed to courtesans have been preserved. Two courtesans seem to have been women of genuine talent, Yü Hsüan-chi and Hsüeh T'ao. Hsüan-chi lived in the ninth century A.D., and her story might well be similar to those of other courtesans. She was born of a poor family and grew into a beautiful girl with a natural talent for song and dance and a strong desire to get ahead in the world. Leaving home, she became acquainted with a group of students who taught her much about literature as well as life in general. Her poetical efforts were encouraged by the students, who also gave her money to live on, thus eliminating the necessity to register as a prostitute. Eventually one of the students took her as his concubine. After he had passed his examinations, he took her back to his hometown to meet his wife, but the two women continually quarreled. Hsüan-chi refused to give up the man she loved until he eventually tired of her and turned her away.

Disillusioned with love, she turned to religion, becoming a Taoist nun. The reputation of a nun in China, whether Taoist or Buddhist, however, was somewhat different from that in the West because of the Chinese suspicion of unmarried women. Convents were not only reserved for the pious but were open to widows and divorced women as well as those who wanted to live a somewhat freer life than the Chinese custom normally allowed women to do. To further complicate matters, convent authorities often made good incomes by supplying food and wine to male guests who visited nuns. Moreover, since nuns were not required to register as prostitutes, they did not have to pay the state tax.

While a nun Hsüan-chi became interested in a young poet. She left the convent to travel across the country with him and when once again she found herself on her own she established a special "house" for students, scholars, and officials. Like most prostitutes, she had difficulty adjusting to aging; as she grew older and her popularity declined, she lost most of her influential patrons, fell into financial difficulties, and found herself in trouble with the law. She was convicted, probably unjustly, of having beaten a maidservant to death and was executed. One of her poems, lamenting the absence of her lover, concludes:

> Separated from you,
> What can I offer?
> Only this one poem,
> Stained with bright tears.[61]

Hsüeh T'ao, who lived a century before Yü, provides a study in contrast. She came from a well-established family. Her father was a government official who saw to it that she received a literary education that allowed her to develop her poetical talents. Tradition has it that very early in her training her father had requested she write a short poem dealing with a tree. Her couplet:

> The boughs meet the birds alighting from north and south,
> The leaves move with every coming gust of wind

greatly distressed her father since he felt that it demonstrated she had a lascivious nature. Before he died, her father fell into financial difficulties, and the young T'ao was left with little money. She immediately registered as a prostitute and soon found herself much in demand for both her wit and her beauty. Several prominent writers encouraged her to write poetry. One amorous general provided for her in his will, thus enabling her to retire to a large villa, where she devoted herself to literary and artistic pursuits. She died at an advanced age, the recognized queen of fashion in her part of the country.[62]

Both Hsüan-chi and T'ao had been ambitious women from economically deprived backgrounds, although T'ao's family originally had been wealthy. Their economic need probably was a major factor in their becoming prostitutes. Many literary figures wrote about prostitution, and there are several stories about prostitution that have survived. Pô Hsing-chien in the ninth century wrote about the Lady of Ch-ien-kuo, who after taking large sums of money from a rich lover, causing him to be disgraced, felt such great love and compassion for him that she used her fortune to advance his career.[63] Many poets felt great love for their mistresses. Wu-ti, a Han dynasty emperor of the first century B.C., wrote a poem of mourning when his mistress died:

> The sound of her silk skirt has stopped.
> On the marble pavement dust grows.
> Her empty room is cold and still.
> Fallen leaves are piled against the doors.
> Longing for that lovely lady
> How can I bring my aching heart to rest?[64]

He was so grief-stricken that he sent for wizards from all parts of China requesting that he be put in communication with her spirit, and according to tradition one did manage to project her shape on a curtain, although the emperor was not quite sure that it was she.

In order to better control them, prostitutes were organized into trade associations. In return for the taxes the brothelkeepers and prostitutes paid the government, they were given the same sort of protection received by any other commercial enterprise in ancient China. There were undoubtedly amateur prostitutes who did not register, such as Yü Hsüan-chi, but the authorities discouraged that since evasion prevented the government from collecting taxes or keeping a watchful eye. Many of the brothelkeepers maintained armed guards who also gave the independent prostitutes considerable trouble. It is possible that Hsüan-chi might not have been a recognized professional. Classification of prostitutes was primarily on the basis of their accomplishments. Those who simply relied on the fact that they were female constituted the lowest class, although there were exceptions. The lower-class prostitute had to live with her co-workers in one apartment strictly supervised by the management. Those skilled in music or dancing or who had literary talents formed a higher class. Most of the higher-status prostitutes had a bedroom and sitting room of their own, and within certain limits, could pick and choose their suitors. Brothelkeepers, in fact, sometimes encouraged their more popular residents to be reticent about granting their favors since this tended to increase the fees they could ask. Moreover, once a courtesan became famous, the chance of her being bought by a wealthy patron increased; this was both to her advantage and that of the brothelkeeper who owned her. Occasionally women purchased their own freedom, as did the Lady of Ch-ien-kuo in the story by Po Hsing-chien mentioned above. Self-purchase was infrequent since prostitutes were notorious for not saving their income.

Since the more talented courtesans demanded high prices, their customers were restricted to upper-class patrons, and in many cases actual sexual intercourse was only a secondary purpose for their visitors. Most men from these upper classes had several wives and concubines who were more than willing to satisfy their sexual needs. Many men ignored their wives and their concubines in favor of a courtesan, since both wives and concubines were often taken for political reasons. Even when wives and concubines proved sexually satisfying, these men might still visit brothels, if only to escape the sexual demands of their own harems. Even those who had no sexual reason might visit a brothel because this was where political, military, and commercial enterprises were decided, and for these tasks feminine companionship was considered essential. Men who visited courtesans were in effect complying with an established social custom. Undoubtedly many prominent people became intimate with a specified courtesan although she was not always obliged to engage in sex with them.[65]

The more famous a courtesan became, the less she had to engage in sex with her customers, since she could demand a rather long period of courtship before consenting to bestow her sexual favors. The courtship experience was probably exciting to many of the men involved, who usually did not have to go through such activities, but a courtesan could not be too demanding since a rich and powerful patron could have his way without too much interference from the authorities.[66] To be successful, a courtesan had to toe a thin line between success and failure, and those who were most successful utilized the same kind of dedication and energy that the male did in the political, military, or commercial fields. She was always handicapped, however, because a prostitute, no matter how high she climbed, was still a prostitute, and not all aspects of prostitution were conducted at a high intellectual and literary level. She was a woman in a man's world. Moreover, the highest prices were not necessarily paid to the skilled courtesan but to young virgins, who were very much in demand.

In the lower-class brothels, the life of a prostitute was not particularly pleasant. In some the inmates were women criminals condemned to serve as government prostitutes as part of their punishment. Others were female relatives of criminals, whose punishment included a clause that all their close relatives become slaves, and in such cases prostitution was the usual fate of their female relatives. Women prisoners of war often ended up as prostitutes, while others were simply slaves. The women in such houses belonged to lower castes, and their status was defined by law. They were subject to many social disabilities, including the prohibition against marrying outside their caste. Their association with criminals and lower-caste people, however, was only one reason for their low standing in the ranks of prostitutes; another important factor was that they lacked the artistic accomplishments of their more successful sisters. Many women, of both the upper and lower castes of prostitution, had been sold into it by their parents, guardians, or even in many cases, kidnappers. Since they had been purchased by the brothelowners, they could become free only if they were redeemed by a devoted lover or if they bought their own freedom.[67] Prostitutes of the lower castes served the lower-status customers, soldiers, sailors, lower-status civil servants, and the poorer citizens. Women from these brothels were often recruited by the government to travel with the army, and prostitutes were hired out on a monthly basis at a regular salary, much of which went to the brothelowner. Unfortunately, very little is known about this lower-class prostitute because Chinese writers until recently more or less ignored the subject, and information can be gained only indirectly through stories and poems which usually concentrated on the upper-class prostitute.

In the thirteenth century the writer Chou Mi distinguished three classes of prostitutes: the common prostitute (already discussed), the prostitute in the winehouses, and the courtesan. The prostitutes in winehouses served in the winehouses that were operated both by the government and private operators. The women had an amazing capacity for wine, and were accustomed to drinking great quantities at banquets, at least until the Ming and Ching dynasties, when consumption of alcohol was regarded a disgrace. Government winehouses served wine and light appetizers to government employees, and it was difficult for others to gain admittance. Beautifully dressed prostitutes, probably the pick of the lower-status houses, acted as waitresses and companions in these. The private winehouses were the early Chinese equivalent of restaurants and hotels, and provided both female company and beds for their customers. The prostitutes employed as waitresses were to restrict their sexual services to the regular customers. The highest-class brothels were those of the singing girls, the courtesans, women skilled in poetry, art, dancing, and singing. The women in these upper-class houses were often written about, and they formed an integral part of the Chinese social and literary scene. This higher class of prostitute dominated women's roles on the stage, set fashions, were the female literary lights, the skilled artists and musicians. Though all three classes of prostitutes served as recruiting grounds for concubines (and occasionally wives), the wealthy and important especially sought their companions from the courtesan class.[68] In fact, one of the differences between the Chinese prostitute and those of other cultures is that many of the Chinese prostitutes did marry or were elevated to the status of mistress to a distinguished and wealthy person.[69]

Actual statistics as to the number of Chinese prostitutes are difficult to estimate but they must have been fairly numerous. Marco Polo, the Western traveler of the thirteenth century, reported that the capital city of Peking had over 20,000 women earning a living through prostitution,[70] and Hang-chau (Hangchow) had so many he felt he was unable to estimate the number.[71] Though Polo's estimate might be exaggerated, there is little doubt that prostitution played an important part in Chinese life during the ancient and medieval period. The secluded, if not subdued, status of the official wife encouraged the use of other women, especially courtesans. Marriages were not made for love but were usually aranged, and were for the purpose of perpetuating family lines, not for romantic attachment. The religious tradition of China did not discourage sex but rather emphasized its necessity for both men and women, but most particularly for the male. China, like most of the other cultures we have examined, had a double standard in that pre- and extramarital relations were encouraged for men and not for women, but Chinese literature includes many stories of ex-courtesans who made good wives, for, unlike those in other cultures, prostitutes could marry. Women were often offered as tribute to seal agreements, and the royal harem was full of women who had been received as tribute. Prominent families also presented beautiful daughters to the emperor in order to obtain imperial favors, and palace agents went on special recruiting expeditions to bring home talented women. In the larger harems meticulous bookkeeping was kept on the date and hour of every successful sexual union as well as notes dealing with the physiognomy of each woman. In the eighth century every woman with whom an emperor slept received a stamp on her arm with the appropriate legend "wind and moon [sexual intercourse] are forever new." This stamp, which was indelible, enabled the emperor to keep a trace on those with whom he had gone to bed.[72]

Taoist ideas on sex encouraged prostitution, while Confucian and Buddhist teachings at least tolerated it. The Confucianists generally stressed eugenics and offspring, whereas the Taoists stressed the sexual discipline necessary for prolonging life and obtaining the elixir of immortality. Even the Confucianists, however, encouraged regular participation in the sex act until a man reached his sixtieth birthday. At that age a man was supposed to limit his sexual activities in order to nurture his waning strength. If a man lived to be seventy, however, he was encouraged to be more active on the grounds that it was only through intercourse that the aging man could supplement his failing vital power.[73]

Obviously, the key factor in the past in deciding the role that the prostitute and prostitution would play in society was religious teaching. In spite of hostility to prostitution, Judaism, Christianity, and Islam tolerated the prostitute. Though the three religions were not in agreement as to the nature and purpose of human sexuality, all three tended to encourage a double standard of sexual morality that in the long run gave institutional support to prostitution. The religions of India and China also tolerated prostitution, and some encouraged it, but increasingly they adopted the double standard as well. The key to religious attitudes is that religious teachings have almost always been recorded by men, and it is the male attitude toward the female as a creature who should be subordinate that dominates religious ideas about prostitution. The "loose" woman had a potential for being a dangerous woman, and had to be controlled. Though men often turned to prostitutes for sex, they generally tried to keep their wives, mothers, sisters, and daughters under control. Since female promiscuity usually could be demonstrated by the presence or lack of a hymen, virginity, because it demonstrated "sexual purity," was highly prized except in parts of India. Here mothers themselves often punctured the hymen of their daughters by inserting their finger and carefully manipulating and enlarging the vaginal orifice of their infant daughters. The lack of a hymen might demonstrate that a woman was not a virgin, but it was not the only indication used to keep women in their place. Since it is the biological nature of women to become pregnant, premarital or extramarital intercourse was more likely to be detected in a woman than in a man. As long as the double standard existed and was tolerated by religious teachings, prostitution also had to be tolerated. Otherwise the burden of guarding one's female relatives would have proven impossible.

7   MEDIEVAL EUROPE

Complex as it is, the medieval period is far more important in understanding modern Western attitudes and institutions than the Greek or Roman period. Its complexity requires a discussion to include several separate cultural groupings, the Greek-speaking Byzantine Empire, the declining remnants of the Roman Empire in the West, and the growing influence of new peoples, Germans, Slavs, Magyars, Vikings, and others. The theme unifying these peoples is their eventual Christianization. But Christianity in the Byzantine East is not necessarily the same as in the Roman Catholic West, and within these large groupings, the German Christian differs from the Irish, who in turn differs from the Italian despite the great efforts to pull them all together. Since the Byzantine East is the most powerful of the early medieval groupings, we have to examine how prostitution was regarded there before we begin to examine the West.

The Byzantine East

One of the most important contributions of the early medieval period to the development of modern Western civilization was the codification of Roman law. The most comprehensive of such collections was the *Corpus Juris Civilis,* a body of civil laws compiled under the direction of the Emperor Justinian in the sixth century A.D. Earlier collections, however, had been made by the Emperor Theodosius in 438, and by the various rulers of the Ostrogoths, Visigoths, Burgundians, and other German groups who had made their way into the declining Roman Empire in the fourth, fifth, and sixth centuries. It was in these codes that the legal basis for prostitution in Christian Europe was established, since, by the time the law was codified, Christianity had become the official religion of the state. The lawyers, judges, and legal scholars who compiled such collections could do little more than continue the ambivalence expressed by the Church Fathers, eliminating only some of the excesses and dangers that they associated with prostitution. Such a trend appears in the Code issued by the Christian Emperor Theodosius, which deprived fathers and mothers of their legal right to compel their daughters or slaves to prostitute themselves.[1] The code also took steps to abolish the prostitute tax,[2] thus giving the state less of a financial interest in prostitution. although the tax was not formally abolished until the reign of Anastasius I at the end of the fifth century. Under the Emperior Justinian in the sixth century, prostitution was still officially tolerated,[3] but there was a concerted effort to curtail the abuses of organized prostitution by banishing procuresses and brothelkeepers from Constantinople, the capital of the Byzantine Empire.[4] The Justinian legislation also institutionalized the patristic distinction between concubines and prostitutes by classifying the former as an informal type of marriage since the concubine and her lover were bound to each other, not simply by lust and sexual attraction but also by "marital affection."[5] Similar trends appear throughout the Middle Ages.

Motivated by a concern for the poor and helpless who became entrapped in prostitution, Theodora (the wife of the Emperor Justinian) opened a convent named Metanoia (Repentance) for former prostitutes. She became concerned when she realized that procurers visited villages and country towns, persuading hard-pressed parents to sell their daughters, promising that if they did so the girls would be given shoes, clothes, and other necessities. Most girls sold by their parents to such salesmen ended up in Constantinople, where they were confined to miserable dens of prostitution, slaving for the benefit of their masters.[6] To help women escape from such conditions, Theodora converted a neglected palace on the Euxine Sea across from Constantinople into a home for them, and endowed it with a plentiful income. In her lifetime there were more than five hundred women relocated there.[7]

It is possible that Theodora was motivated by something more than Christian concern in assisting prostitutes, since according to tradition, Theodora herself had once been a prostitute. The chief source for information about her early life is the *Anecdota*—"not given out"—of the historian Procopius, who had also composed a more or less official history of Justinian's reign. The *Anecdota*, or *Secret History*, was, therefore, according to Procopius, the information he could not put in the official history. Since Procopius was opposed to all that he felt Theodora represented, his secret history demonstrates an extreme hatred for the woman. How true a portrait it is gives us a matter of scholarly debate, but it is worth noting that in his effort to blacken her reputation he portrayed her as an ex-prostitute, an indication of the low esteem that the prostitute must have had in the Byzantine Empire. Procopius stated that when Theodora's father, one of the keepers of wild beasts in the Hippodrome, died, he left his widow and three young daughters without any means of support. The widow almost immediately married the man whom she expected to succeed her late husband in his job, a more or less accepted practice, but through internal intrigues he failed to be appointed. Undaunted, the resourceful woman sent her daughters into the arena to appeal to the crowd, and the opposing faction, moved by the little girls, appointed their stepfather as an animal keeper. After this first public success, the stage seemed indicated, and the mother encouraged her daughters to become actresses, a profession almost synonymous with prostitution.

Theodora eventually became one of the most famous actresses of the day although Procopius also disparages her acting ability. According to him she was inadequate as a flute or harp player, and she danced poorly, although he conceded she was a good mimic. Theodora, nevertheless, was a favorite of the male audiences since she raised her skirts, showed her legs, and was a virtuoso in what later came to be known as the burlesque routine. At the height of her career she left Constantinople to become the mistress of a provincial governor, but after quarreling with him and his wife, she was forced to earn her way back to Constantinople by selling her body (at least according to Procopius). When she reached Constantinople she left the stage to become a wool spinner, and it was in this capacity that she came to the attention of Justinian. Justinian fell in love with her, but because of the objections of his aunt, the Empress Euphemia, he hesitated to marry her. There was also the possibility that in marrying her he would have violated the old Roman law prohibiting senators from marrying prostitutes. While Justinian was attempting to deal with these obstacles, Theodora became his mistress, and finally on the death of his aunt, she became his wife, a marriage made possible through a change in the law regarding ex-prostitutes made by his Uncle Justin.[8] When Justin died, Justinian became emperor and Theodora empress.[9] Historians usually find the Procopius story fascinating but tend to discount much of it.

Theodora was not the only ex-prostitute who might have overcome her past in the Byzantine Empire. Procopius also recounted the adventures of Antonina, wife of Belisarius, Justinian's trusted general. According to Procopius, Antonina, the daughter of a prostitute actress, had embarked on the same career as her mother and had several illegitimate children before she became the wife of Belisarius.[10] Since Procopius hated Antonina as much as he did Theodora, the story is equally suspect. Not so suspect, however, is the portrayal of his attitude toward the theater, which by this time was regarded as a haunt for prostitutes. Unlike the Greek period when men had often enacted the female roles, the Byzantine theater used women to portray themselves, and pantomimes, farces, lewd singing, and dances in which troups of chorus girls appeared with little or no clothes were the standard features; many of the Church Fathers, shocked at such antics, denounced the theater as the center of iniquity. *Actress* and *prostitute* became synonymous terms, and all persons engaged in the theatrical profession were thought to be vile and disreputable. In fact, one of the streets near the theaters in Constantinople was called the street of harlots. Until the law was changed for Justinian, the Byzantine aristocracy had been forbidden to marry an actress or any woman engaged in a similar type of work. The new reforms, in keeping with the Christian tradition, always left open the possibility that actresses could reform, but only if they left the stage. If the ex-actress prostitute showed any sign of returning to the stage after her reformation, she could be forcibly restrained from so doing and in any case her chastity was carefully guarded until old age made assault upon it unlikely.[11]

Not all prostitutes were actresses. Many were located in the *xenones,* hostels for strangers, foreigners, and travelers. The primary function of such institutions was to provide food and shelter for country people, visitors, and pilgrims coming to the capital or some other city, whether on private business or for religious purposes. Traveling was not an easy undertaking in either the ancient or medieval world, and it was especially difficult for poor people. To offer succor to those who needed to travel, *xenones* were established as a sort of charitable hostel. Obviously many guests and visitors, as well as administrators, were of questionable morality and intentions; since the *xenones* offered hospitality to all people, there was always the danger that they would become houses of prostitution, or a center of more serious criminal activity.[12] There were also ordinary houses of prostitution that did not masquerade under any other guise, and these are mentioned periodically in the course of Byzantine history. The Emperor Leo VI, the Wise (886-917), for example, expelled the inmates of a house of prostitution and turned it into a home for the aged.[13] Another house of prostitution was transformed first into a convent and then into a kind of reformatory for fallen women of the aristocratic class.[14]

Periodically the Byzantine emperors tried to eliminate some of the worst abuses of prostitution and also gain forgiveness for their own sins by establishing refuges for prostitutes. Emperor Michael IV (1034—1041), for example, founded such a house. A historian of the time, Michael Psellus, described it thus:

Scattered all over the city was a vast multitude of harlots, and without attempting to turn them from their trade by argument—that class of woman is deaf anyway to all advice that would save them—without even trying to curb their activities by force, lest he should earn the reputation of violence, he built in the Queen of Cities a place of refuge to house them, an edifice of enormous size and very great beauty. Then, in the stentorian notes of the public herald, he issued a proclamation: all women who trafficked in their beauty, provided they were willing to renounce their trade and live in luxury, were to find sanctuary in this building: they were to change their own clothes for the habit of nuns, and all fear of poverty would be banished from their lives for ever, "for all things unsown, without labour of hands, would spring forth for their use." [Homer, *Odyssey,* IX, 108—109]. Thereupon a great swarm of prostitutes descended upon this refuge, relying on the emperor's proclamation, and changed both their garments and their manner of life, a youthful band enrolled in the service of God, as soldiers of virtue.[15]

Obviously prostitution was widespread in the Byzantine Empire,[16] and, though prostitution itself was condemned, the prostitute was not. Many of the civil disabilities and stigmas that had afflicted her in Rome were removed, and there was always the hope that she would be redeemed. Many devoted Christians, besides emperors, worked to encourage prostitutes to repent, and to restore them to proper life. Though economic conditions often led girls into prostitution, and the double standard provided a market for the prostitute, it was always hoped that the prostitute herself would abandon her sinful work. To this end she was permitted to marry, and as an alternative, there were a number of refuge houses established to help her.

Western Europe in the Early Middle Ages

As indicated in the discussion of the Byzantine, or Eastern Roman, Empire, Roman law and Roman tradition continued to exist, although with a strong overlay of Greek concepts. In the West, however, political unity had broken down, and in place of the Roman powers there appeared various Germanic "nations." Only gradually did the West achieve the sophistication of the East. City life, so characteristic of the old Mediterranean civilization, was in a period of decline in the West. In part the decline was caused by economic conditions, conditions that had led the Roman emperors to transfer the imperial capital from Rome to Constantinople; another factor in the decline was the incoming Germans, who were rurally oriented, hostile to city life, and suspicious of much of it.

Rome continued to function as a Western capital for a time, but gradually the government offices were transferred to other cities, first to Milan, and eventually to Ravenna, which remained an outpost of the Byzantine Empire for centuries. In the West, Roman ideas and concepts took on a German imprint, and though Christianity was the dominant intellectual force, Latin Christianity grew apart from the Byzantine and other Christian groups.

The nature of prostitution in rural areas was different because the clients were fewer and the extremes between the rich courtesan and the poor prostitute were narrow, almost nonexistent. Traditionally, the Germans had looked askance at any evidence of feminine sexual promiscuity. German custom gave the husband the right to execute a wife along with her lover if she was caught in an adulterous relationship. Males were obliged to keep a watchful eye on the virtue of their female relatives and dependents. Female chastity had property value and women were, to put it simply, the property of their menfolk, always under the protection of some male: father, brother, son, or near male relative.

The laws of one of the Germanic groups, the Alemanni, provided that if a man deprived a free woman of all that she wore above the waist, he had to pay a penalty of six *solidi*. If he stripped her entirely, the fine was doubled, and if he raped her, he had to pay 40 *solidi*.[17] Women were valuable and had to be protected. The laws of the Ripuarian Franks, another Germanic group, set the penalty for killing a free woman between the age of puberty and her fortieth year at 600 *solidi*, while the death of a young girl cost 200. Some indication of the severity of these penalities is indicated by the fact that 600 *solidi* was regarded as the equivalent of 300 cattle or 50 male horses, and was such a drain that payments often extended over three generations.[18]

With such attitudes about female virtue, prostitution at first was largely an affront to male relatives, who were therefore free to deal with a prostitute relative as they wished. But as the Germans moved from a pastoral economy to an agricultural one, private punishment of such activities posed a threat to long-range peace and order. In this situation, various secular German rulers began to assert themselves by making prostitution a public crime, a crime committed against the mores of society. There were limitations, however, and only gradually did changes occur. For example, the abduction of a woman was a private crime (it was against the individual), but if a woman was raped, this act could be considered a public crime. Officials were set up to deal with such crimes and failure to take action was subject to punishment. A country judge, for example, who through negligence or bribery permitted a prostitute to ply her trade was not only fined thirty *solidi* but was also sentenced to one hundred lashes.[19] Penalties were also provided for prostitutes. Women who lived in illegal liaisons or lived immoral lives were to be flogged. Prostitutes in the Visigothic kingdom in Spain who continued to practice their art were to receive 300 lashes, the highest number of lashes for any crime in the Visigothic code.[20] Prostitutes also often had their hair cut off, and if they then continued, they could be sold into slavery. Since not all the male guardians of female virtue felt compelled to revenge their female relatives who were engaged in prostitution, the law also stipulated that those who allowed a woman to become a prostitute or who lived off the earnings of a prostitute could be punished with a hundred lashes as well.[21]

Because the punishment for prostitution was so severe, accusing a woman unjustly of prostitution was also a punishable offense. In the Lombard code, a person found guilty of making an unfounded charge had to pay twenty *solidi*. If he persisted in his charges, and could not prove them, he had to fight a duel with a relative of the suspected woman. Only if he proved to be the winner was the charge accepted as proved. If he was defeated, she was adjudged innocent and he had to pay an amount equal to her *wergeld* (her monetary worth to her family) for defaming her character.[22] Similar punishments were given to men who unjustly cut a woman's hair, the allegation being that women who had their hair cut were prostitutes.[23] It is possible that one of the punishments for women convicted of crimes, or whose husbands were convicted of crimes, was for them to become public prostitutes, although the laws are somewhat ambiguous on this.[24]

Among the Franks, eventually the dominant Germanic group in the West, women were highly restricted in their activities. No woman could marry without the consent of her parents; if she had children they inherited her status, slave if she was slave, free if she was free. Polygamy was widespread, as was concubinage and prostitution. Though the Franks were converted to Christianity, their religious beliefs at first did not interfere with their sexual activity. For several centuries after their conversion the more important Frankish nobles maintained a separate women's quarter in their castles, similar to a Moslem harem, where they housed wives, servants, and mistresses.[25] Several early Frankish kings set themselves up as leaders in sexual license. King Charibert, for example, deserted his wife for two sisters, one a nun, who acted conjointly as his mistresses; King Dagobert had three wives at one time, and King Guntram had children by several different women.[26] Though Frankish males were free to be promiscuous, no such license was extended to females, and women were punished severely for any adulterous activity. Since Frankish society was essentially rural, houses of prostitution were uncommon, but there were still many part-time prostitutes, and some of the "nuns" in convents apparently supplemented their income by providing illicit sexual relations.[27]

Charlemagne, the eighth-century ruler and the greatest of the Frankish kings, kept alive the sexual tradition of his forebears. In addition to his various wives, he had a bevy of mistresses, although only a few of them are known by name. Unlike the earlier Frankish kings, however, Charlemagne did not insist on a rigid double standard, at least for his daughters. Charlemagne had prohibited his daughters from marrying supposedly because he loved them too much. In actuality it was to prevent their husbands from becoming too strong a political force in his kingdom. If he denied his daughters legitimate husbands, however, he did not deny them lovers, provided they remained discreet about their affairs. One of the biographers of Charlemagne tells how one of the ruler's daughters was visited by her lover and when the two awoke the next morning they found that snow had fallen during the night. Fearful of being seen together, and yet fearful that if the man left alone he would leave telltale tracks, the daughter carried her lover out of the palace on her back so that only her footprints could be seen.[28] The escapade was viewed rather tolerantly by Charlemagne himself but his toleration did not extend to the common prostitutes. He attempted to impose strict punishments on those women.[28] His son, Louis the Pious, was far stricter in his own sexual practices, and in fact one of his first acts was to cast out his father's mistresses and force his sisters to be more discreet in their sexual activity. Neither Charlemagne nor Louis, however, was able to abolish prostitution.

Western Christian Attitudes

Increasingly, however, the German tribes in the West adopted Christian attitudes toward prostitution and left the question of sexual morality in the hands of the clergy, missionaries, monks, and nuns. Several methods were used to inculcate the austere standards of sexual behavior inherent in Christian ideology, and there were various types of discipline for those who violated the teachings. One of these was confession. In the earliest phases of Christianity, offending Christians often made public confession before an assembled congregation, and in case of graver offenses such confession was accompanied by a period of exclusion from its fellowship. There was considerable debate among early Christians about just what sins were so unforgivable that the guilty could never be restored to full fellowship. Some groups of Christians, for example, wanted to expel fornicators and adulterers entirely, but Christian charity won out, and by the third century fornication was regarded as a forgivable sin. As Christianity spread, the public confession was replaced by a private and secret rite involving confession to and absolution by a priestly confessor, who prescribed acts of penance that were mainly or wholly private. To guide the confessor priest in determining the seriousness of a sin as well as the penance required, penitential books were written. These books are one of our chief sources for medieval concepts about many sexual activities. Often the penitential books are quite detailed since it was believed essential to determine the intent and the specific nature of the sin before a penalty could be set, and a hierarchy of sexual sins developed. Very early in Christian Church history, illicit sexual activities, including fornication, incest, adultery, masturbation, anal intercourse, and prostitution, were regarded as capital sins. Later the number of major sins was expanded to seven (sometimes eight), but the sexual sins always remained high on the list. In one of the early lists of sins, sometimes attributed to Saint Patrick, illicit sex activities were classed with murder and idolatry and the offenders were to do penance for a year, besides receiving punishment from secular authorities. A Christian woman who committed adultery was to be excommunicated. A man who had a prostitute wife was permitted to put her away, and to remarry, even though remarriage was forbidden in the early Christian Church.[30] If a married man had intercourse with a female slave, the female slave was to be sold and the guilty male was forbidden to have intercourse with his wife for a full year. If, however, a man had children by the slave he was to set her free and could not sell her. If a wife engaged in fornication or prostitution, and then repented of it, her husband was supposed to take her back.[31] Penalties varied from one penitential guide to another and from period to period, but in general the penitential writers were more hostile to women who engaged in premarital or extramarital fornication than to men,[32] and prostitution was more heavily condemned than simple fornication.[33]

Prostitution, however, proved an increasingly complex topic to the medieval churchmen. What was the difference between a prostitute and a concubine? When did a woman become a prostitute? How did simple fornication differ from prostitution? These and other topics were discussed by medieval lawyers who attempted to interpret Roman law in terms of Christian morality and to find a logical way out of the difficulties involved in such a complex subject. Obviously a dedicated Christian had to disapprove of prostitution: it was morally offensive, theologically repugnant, and ought to be suppressed. Yet following Saint Augustine they found it necessary to tolerate prostitution because without it, established patterns of societal and sexual relationships would be endangered.

The medieval canon lawyers looked on intercourse as part of the natural law, but were inculcated with the belief that sexual desire could and did usually lead to sin. Sexual desire, moreover, probably had a diabolical origin since it was a product of original sin and man's subsequent fallen state. As followers of Saint Augustine they believed that the only legitimate outlet for sexual desire was to be found in marriage, but many believed that even in marriage sexual pleasure was sinful. Sex outside marriage was clearly wrong and intercourse with a prostitute compounded the wrong, involving the bad use of an evil thing.

Complicating the medieval lawyers' view of prostitution was the fact that most of them were clerics who strongly believed that the sexuality of women differed from that of men. Women had not been created in the image of God, as man was, but out of a rib of man to serve as his companion and helpmate. The chastity of women, particularly young women, therefore was always suspect since women were always ready for sexual intercourse. It was a woman who led Adam astray in the Garden of Eden. The canon lawyer Henry of Susa (Hostiensis) was so suspicious of the sexuality of women that he said if a priest rode with one girl in front of him and one girl behind, he could never be sure that the girl in back remained a virgin on the trip, only the one in front who was always under his watchful eye.[34]

Since women were considered so susceptible to sexual temptations, great care had to be taken to confine their sexual activities within a properly structured marriage relationship, and husbands had a moral obligation to keep their wives sexually satisfied lest they be tempted to stray to other beds.[35] Still, women often yielded to their sexual desires, even through innocence, because they were too trusting or too ignorant; in any case, they were usually fickle and inconstant. In spite of this, women were expected to observe a more austere standard of sexual conduct than were men. Modesty was woman's glory, and by implication a woman who was sexually desirous and ardent, who did not blush at sex, was at heart a whore, though she need not legally be classsified as a prostitute as long as she remained faithful to her husband.[36] Even within the marriage relationship, however, a woman was not to use the sexual wiles of a prostitute, and a matron who dressed like one was legally classed as one by the canonists. Males obviously proved weak in the presence of such rampant female sexuality, and it was believed that even casual conversation with members of the opposite sex could lead to sexual intimacy. Since this was the case, the medieval lawyers were not so concerned with punishing the prostitute. She was, after all, simply acting in accord with her sexual character. Instead, the major punishment, they felt, should be inflicted on those who made a profit from her, the pimps, procurers, and brothelkeepers, and even those who regularly used her services. This is the idea expressed in the Byzantine legislation.

Though the medieval canonists saw that a woman might turn to prostitution because of economic necessity, this was not regarded as a mitigating circumstance. No matter how hungry she might be, no matter how desperate her situation, no woman was justified in turning to prostitution to earn a living. This in spite of the fact that poverty and desperation were occasionally looked upon as mitigating circumstances for theft or murder. Also rejected as a mitigating factor was a natural craving for sexual gratification. In fact, the more pleasure a prostitute derived from her sexual encounters, the more serious her offense was regarded. The only mitigating situation for the medieval lawyer was that in which a girl had been forced into prostitution by her parents or someone who had legal control over her actions. In such a situation the prostitute herself was not accountable for her action; those who forced her into a life of sin bore the guilt.[37]

As in Roman times, the prostitute had little social status. In fact, her status was so low that she was not even required to obey the law since she was beneath the law's contempt.[38] She was so base that she was canonically barred from accusing others of crime, was forbidden to inherit property, and if charges were brought against her, she was not allowed to answer in person but had to employ a representative to respond to them. Still, the money she received for her actions belonged to her and her rights to it were legally valid. She was on much shakier grounds, however, if she had not received money from a customer but only a promise to pay; then there was no way she could collect from an unwilling customer.

It was not only the medieval lawyers who accepted prostitution while condemning it. Medieval theologians, including the greatest and most famous of them, Saint Thomas Aquinas, agreed that though fornication was sinful, prostitution could not be entirely disallowed. He compared it to a sewer in the palace; if the sewer was removed, the palace would be filled with pollution; similarly if prostitution was removed the world would be filled with "sodomy" and other crimes. Though the money paid to a prostitute was used for an unlawful purpose, the giving itself was not unlawful and the woman was entitled to keep what she had received.[39]

Ecclesiastical punishments for prostitution generally proved ineffective, in part at least because the ecclesiastical authorities themselves were not entirely free of the taint of prostitution. Edward Gibbon, in one of the more famous passages of his *Decline and Fall of the Roman Empire,* described the influence of two sisters who were prostitutes, Marozia and Theodora in Rome in the ninth and tenth centuries. Gibbon wrote that the bastard son, the grandson, and the great-grandson of the prostitute Marozia were seated in the chair of Saint Peter, and that during the reign of one of these descendants, John XII, the

Lateran palace was turned into a school for prostitution; and that his rape of virgins and widows had deterred the female pilgrims from visiting the tomb of St. Peter, lest, in the devout act, they should be violated by his successor.[40]

Gibbon might be overly harsh in his condemnation of the popes of this period, but it is indubitable that prostitution was widespread in the Middle Ages. Urbanization, fairs and carnivals, and the gathering together of large numbers of men without women promoted it. The prostitute went where the customers were, even on religious expeditions such as crusades and pilgrimages. During the First Crusade, for example, prostitutes were very much in evidence and driven out of the crusaders' camps as early as 1097.[41] On some of the pilgrimages women "pilgrims" are said to have supported themselves by selling sex in towns on the route.[42] On both crusades and pilgrimages prostitutes sometimes traveled disguised as men, and even the saintly King of France, Louis IX, could not prevent prostitutes from establishing themselves near the royal tent on the crusades he led.[43]

So ubiquitous were the prostitutes on the crusades that the canon lawyer Hostiensis posed a tantalizing question about a crusading harlot. He wondered how the Church courts should deal if a whore took the cross, i.e., took vows to go on the crusade. Obviously such a woman could recruit numerous men and the men would clearly bolster the defensive forces of the Holy Land, a thing much needed. Would this greater good brought about by the prostitute outweigh the dangers of a prostitute taking the cross? After some discussion he concluded that it would not, because the motivation of her followers was not likely to be spiritual. He also opposed allowing the harlot to redeem her vow by making a financial offering for the defense of the Holy Places, and in effect concluded that it would be best if prostitutes stayed clear of the crusades.[44]

This was probably a heartfelt wish of many ecclesiastical writers, who undoubtedly desired prostitution to disappear. It did not, however, and Christian charity demanded the prostitute be forgiven. This was the moral emphasized by Hroswitha (c. 932-1002), a nun at the abbey of Gandersheim. In her play about Thaïs, a prostitute saint, she has the character Paphnutius worring about Thaïs, whose beauty was wonderful but whose impurity was horrible. Thaïs was not "satisfied to ruin herself with a small band of lovers"; she also sought "to allure all men through her marvellous beauty, and drag them down with her." Her efforts in this respect proved successful and citizens of great substance and virtue lay their wealth at her feet. Dismayed at this, Paphnutius resolved to rescue Thaïs from the wicked life, and he went to see her in the disguise of a lover. After gaining admission to her house, Paphnutius engaged in a dialogue about Christian salvation with her, converted her, and took her to a convent where she lived in a small cell the rest of her life. Though Thaïs grieved that she had to attend to all the needs of her body in the cell and there was not one "clean sweet spot" in which she could call on God, she lived there for three years before she died and the angels led her to paradise.[45] So popular legend continued to emphasize the salvation of the prostitutes.

Prostitution and the State

In light of the Church's difficulty in dealing with prostitution, it is not difficult to understand why prostitution prospered in medieval Europe. Omnipresent in the developing cities, the prostitutes of Paris, in particular, had a reputation for boldness. According to tradition, they were so numerous they had organized into a guild with Mary Magdalene as their patron saint. Though the tradition is suspect, there was a chapel dedicated to Saint Mary the Egyptian (the prostitute mentioned in an earlier chapter). Allegedly, the chapel also had a window depicting the saint about to embark in a boat with her skirt pulled up to her thighs, with an inscription reading: "How the saint offered the body to the boatman to pay for her passage."[46]

As Europe grew more sophisticated and rulers more powerful, ecclesiastical discipline was reinforced by secular laws. One king, Louis IX of France, attempted to regulate it. It was said that Louis IX became involved when a Parisian prostitute sat next to the queen of France in Church, and the queen, as was her custom, bestowed a kiss on her. When the identity of the woman reached the ears of the king, he decided that the only way to prevent future incidents was to outlaw prostitution throughout his kingdom. Though the incident might well be apocryphal, there is no doubt that Louis in 1254 decreed that all prostitutes, as well as all persons making a living from prostitution, be regarded as outlaws, that is, denied protection of the king's law, and that all their personal goods, clothing, furs, tunics, and linen chemises, be seized.[47] The first effect of the ordinance was to eliminate all open signs of prostitution in Paris, but difficulties soon began to appear, and complaints began to reach the king that it was difficult to protect honest wives and virtuous daughters from lecherous attacks. As the difficulties in enforcement mounted, the king turned from outlawing prostitutes to attempting to regulate them.

Prostitutes were forbidden from living in certain parts of Paris, prohibited from wearing certain types of jewelry or fine cloth dresses, and placed under the supervision of a police-type magistrate, whose popular title was *roi des ribauds,* king of the bawds, beggars, and vagabonds. This official had the power to arrest and confine prostitutes who infringed the law by their dress, domicile, or behavior. Though the regulations seemed to be effective in dealing with some of the abuses associated with prostitution, Louis, the only king of France to be officially recognized as a saint, worried about tolerating such evil, and there was an attempt to return to the spirit of his early ordinance. Other matters occupied the king's mind, and so in his instructions to his son and successor, Philip, he requested that the stain of prostitution be removed from France. Philip, dutifully following his father's request, declared prostitution a legal misdemeanor and brought a formidable array of penalties to bear against the offending women and their accomplices. The program was soon abandoned, and secular officials were put in charge of regulating it. Each municipality was given the right to control prostitution.[48]

Even before the French had turned to regulation, other medieval rulers had begun to experiment with ways of dealing with prostitution. The Holy Roman emperor, Frederick Barbarossa, as early as 1158 had attempted to eliminate the prostitutes traveling with his army then in Italy, by punishing both the prostitute and her customer. According to *Lex Pacis Castrensis* soldiers caught fornicating with prostitutes were to be severely punished, while the women themselves were to have their noses cut off.[49] This became a standard punishment for prostitutes involved with the law, although there were only occasional other efforts to punish their customers. Apparently the justification behind slitting or cutting off a woman's nose was the belief that this would make her less attractive. Mutilation as punishment was not unusual in the Middle Ages, but a man was usually punished in a way to curtail his efficiency, such as cutting off his fingers or pulling out an eye. Apparently Frederick's legislation was not particularly effective and it was not repeated. Instead, the example of Alfonso IX of Castile (1188–1230) was followed. His regulations about prostitution are among the earliest in Europe. In a section of the code issued under his name he concentrated on those who profited from prostitutes. These belonged to five categories: those who trafficked in prostitutes; landlords who let their premises to whores; men or women who kept brothels; husbands who prostituted their wives; and pimps who solicited or recruited women. Those involved in selling prostitutes were to be exiled from the kingdom; landlords who rented rooms to prostitutes were to have their houses impounded and also pay a fine; brothelkeepers had to free the women found in their brothels (an implication that the prostitutes in such houses might have been slaves) and find them husbands or else suffer the possibility of execution; husbands who prostituted their wives were to be executed; and pimps were to be flogged for a first offense, and if they persisted were to be sent to the galleys as convicts. Women who supported pimps were to be publicly whipped and have the clothes they wore destroyed.[50]

One of the reasons the medieval authorities increasingly turned to regulation was that brothels were always potential centers of public disturbance and often served as a cover for criminal activity. Some cities attempted to meet the problem by banning prostitution within their walls as did Leicester and Cambridge in England, while others, like the city of Sandwich, attempted to confine it to certain specified areas and persons. The city of Bristol, for example, classed prostitutes with lepers and would allow neither group within the city walls. What worked for a smaller city did not necessarily work for a larger one. London for a time attempted to exclude prostitutes from the city, and in fact established a section just outside the city wall, but when this proved unsatisfactory, it restricted prostitution to certain streets within the city. Brothels found outside the stipulated districts had their doors and windows removed; if the women still refused to leave their illegal brothels, the beadle of London had authority to dismantle the whole house. Though prostitution might be tolerated as a necessary evil, almost universally officials were hostile to those who lived off it. A male procurer discovered inside the city of London was ordered tonsured, shaved, and exhibited in the pillory for a first offense; a second offense resulted in imprisonment, and a third, expulsion from the city. A woman procurer on her first offense had her hair cut "round her head" (the same as tonsure) and was exhibited in the stocks; the penalties for subsequent offenses followed those for the male. With such harsh punishments many of those associated with prostitution attempted to cloak their activities with some respectable trade or profession. In the process of so doing, many trades became tainted with the shame associated with prostitution. This was particularly true of barbers and bathkeepers. As a result the city required that the premises of stewkeepers (bathhouse keepers) be periodically examined to see that they kept out prostitutes, and there were regular monthly inspections of the premises of all barber surgeons for the same reason.[51]

The most favored way of dealing with prostitution in the later Middle Ages was to confine prostitutes to certain districts and/or require them to dress in certain ways. In Bristol, England, the hoods of prostitutes had to be made with a striped fur, different from the type worn by respectable women. Though prostitutes could not be denied entrance into other sections of a town, they were closely watched to make certain that they did not enter any house with a customer other than brothels in the designated area. The city of London, for example, specifically forbade prostitutes from "parading" anywhere except in certain regulated districts, and those women who violated the law were subject to eventual expulsion from the city.[52] In Paris, most prostitutes lived in a section of the town known as the Clapier,[53] a name perpetuated in the slang term *clap* describing the venereal disease gonorrhea, which then and now is associated with prostitution. Since the prostitute was so confined in her activity, only rarely was she a streetwalker. Rather, she lived in a brothel, and if she did entice customers outside the brothel, her activities were confined to special quarters. Prostitutes had to live in these quarters, wear clothes specified for them—armbands or other attire—dye their hair, or in other ways distinguish themselves from respectable society matrons.[54]

Prostitutes proved difficult to control and Jacques de Vitry, writing in the first quarter of the thirteenth century, gives a vivid description of the Parisian prostitutes of his day who he said were everywhere in the city, soliciting even passing clerics to sample their delights. To those males who passed them by without greeting they cried out, "Sodomite," to embarrass them. De Vitry reported that a brothel and a scholars' hall often occupied the same premises; while the master was delivering his lectures in an upper room, the prostitutes were exercising their trade below. Occasionally, he claimed, the arguments between the prostitutes and their pimps rose to mingle with the disputations of the scholars. The proximity in a sense was logical since obviously one of the groups most likely to patronize the prostitutes were the students, this in spite of the fact that they were technically classed as clerics in the eyes of the law, in large part because of their ability to read Latin. Jacques de Vitry described the Parisian students as more dissolute than the regular population, since unlike the general public they "counted fornication no sin."[55] Paris was not alone in having students who consorted with prostitutes. One of the jobs assigned to the university chancellor at Cambridge (as well as elsewhere) was to deal with prostitutes.[56]

In Toulouse, the profits from the town brothel were divided between the city and the university. The town bordello was housed in a building known as the Grande Abbaye, and the prostitutes quartered there had to wear a kind of uniform of white scarf and ribbons. Apparently they did not like the uniform and when Charles VI of France visited the city in the fourteenth century the prostitutes presented a petition to him requesting the right to dispense this mark of their profession.[57] The king granted their request, so upsetting the "decent" citizens of the town that whenever a prostitute was recognized she was insulted, harassed, and even assaulted. In retaliation for such treatment the prostitutes barricaded the doors of their brothel, which caused a drop in the city income. To resolve the conflict, the king placed the prostitutes under his special protection, but rather than solving the difficulty, this only further enraged the citizens, who forced the prostitutes to move to another quarter of town. Their new quarters, however, were not nearly as grand as their old, but this was remedied when the university, in order to gain the land on which the brothel was located, agreed to build a new château as the town brothel.[58]

Students were not the only ecclesiastical figures involved with prostitutes. In fact, the ambivalence expressed toward prostitution by the Christian Church often led to strange bedfellows, with even convents acting or being accused of acting as houses of prostitution. Though such charges have a kind of pro-forma tone to them, and in most cases are probably exaggerated, there undoubtedly was some basis in fact for such charges, as indicated by the whole nomenclature of the convent adopted by the brothel. Brothels were frequently called convents; madams were known as abbesses or mother superiors, and the prostitutes as sisters. Often the charges against convents were made by revered figures. Saint Brigitta of Sweden in the fourteenth century, for example, stated that convents left their doors open at night in order that males, both clergy and laity, could be admitted, and this occurred to such a great extent that the "convents resembled brothels rather than hallowed convents."[59] A report to Pope Gregory XII stated that several nunneries were so full of corruption that the nuns fornicated with prelates, monks, and lay brethren and gave birth to numerous illegitimate children.[60] The French ecclesiastic, Jean Gerson, charged that his investigation of convents had uncovered many cloisters that were similar to "brothels of harlots."[61] Though monasteries, since they were inhabited by males, were more difficult to classify as brothels, charges were made that monks were going with "loose women secretly and openly," wasting church "money on vicious pleasures," and bringing women even into the monastery itself.[62]

Once the states accepted the necessity for regulating prostitution, it was not difficult to rationalize that the state should get some renumeration for its efforts. In effect, attitudes toward prostitution in this respect had gone almost full circle from the attempts of Justinian to remove the prostitute tax, to the attempt of Saint Louis to abolish it, to regulation, and finally to using brothels as a source of revenue. Some cities even set up official brothels.

The regulations for brothels survived in several score medieval cities. One of the most controversial sets of regulations comes from the city of Avignon, where a public house of ill fame (i.e., established by the state) was set up under the official patronage of Queen Joanna, ruler of Naples and of Provence, in 1347. Though there is some doubt about their authenticity, the regulations are only slightly different from other surviving statutes. The ordinance stipulated that a public brothel be set up in order to keep the prostitutes off the streets. If the prostitutes left the brothel for any reason they had to wear a red knot on their left shoulder. Any prostitute failing to live in the brothel or refusing to wear the red knot was to be led through the city with drums playing, a red knot hanging at her shoulder so all could recognize her, and be publicly whipped. If she persisted in her offenses, she was to be turned out of the city. The brothel was erected near the Convent of the Augustin Friars near Bridge Street, and it was stipulated that the door always be kept locked so that no person could gain admittance without permission of the abbess or governess chosen by the city fathers each year. Those men admitted to the brothel were to be warned that if they created disturbances or frightened the women or violated the house rules in any way they would be turned over to the beadles of the city for punishment. The aspect of regulation that has aroused the most controversy is one stipulating that the abbess and a surgeon examine the prostitutes every Saturday to see if they had any illness and to determine whether they were pregnant. A prostitute found pregnant was to be given special care in order that there not be a spontaneous abortion. The brothel was to be closed on Good Friday, Holy Saturday, and Easter Sunday, and if customers were allowed in by the abbess at such times she was to be publicly whipped and dismissed from her job. The abbess was also to see to it that Jews were not admitted into the brothel and if any Jew was found to be a customer he was to be whipped.[63] The brothel continued to function after Joanna sold the town to Pope Clement VI. The only difference then was that it operated under papal sponsorship. The old laws were enforced, and a Jew was publicly whipped for entering the brothel in 1498.

The reference to Jews in houses of prostitution points to the rather complex nature of prostitution and the influence Christianity had on regulating it. The medieval Church saw a danger to Christianity in sexual intimacies between Jews and Christians, although the problem was not so much one of morality as of the possible apostasy from the Church. One of the reasons that badges had to be worn by Jews under Church ordinance was so that the Gentile prostitute could recognize her visitor as a Jew and thereby avoid him. If, however, intimacies did occur between a Jew and a Christian prostitute, the Jew could be burned alive. Jews generally accepted this prohibition, and in fact Rabbi Judah ha-Hasid advised the Jewish women in the presence of possibly "immoral" young Jewish men to conceal their Jewish identity and claim to be Christians, even displaying a crucifix on their chests, in order to intimidate the men against molesting them. In fact the Jewish writers as a whole were as hostile to intercourse between Christians and Jews as the Christians were. The Talmudic writer emphasized that the Jewish male who consorted with a

Gentile woman would not be released from Gehenna (Hell), and to emphasize the dangers, he prescribed flogging for those found involved. In fourteenth-century Spain, a Jewish widow charged with having sex relations with a Gentile was condemned to having her nose cut off by the Jewish court, and this apparently was not unusual.[64]

Avignon was just one of the many cities to establish more or less official brothels and to regulate the activities that took place there. Ordinances for brothels are extant from Nuremberg, Strasbourg, Munich, Constance, Nîmes, Ulm, as well as lesser-known places. Often the local executioner doubled as supervisor of whorehouses in order to supplement his income.[65] In the papal city of Rome the marshals of the pope were very careful to collect their fees from the brothel.[66] Occasionally some ecclesiastical officials were overzealous in dealing with the brothels under their control. For example, the Archbishop of Mainz in the twelfth century was said to have spent more time and money on prostitutes than in carrying out his official business. Usually, however, ecclesiastical officials tried to avoid direct connection with the operation of a brothel, although there were exceptions. An English cardinal in 1321 allegedly purchased a house with a brothel as an investment, and expressed no qualms about allowing it to continue operation.[67]

Bathhouses became a favorite center for prostitution in the medieval period. They were located in all the more important cities, often supported by the municipal authorities in order to allow the poor to bathe more frequently. It was because of the association of the public bathhouse with prostitution that ecclesiastics kept warning Christians in general and clerics in particular about the moral dangers of frequenting such places.[68] To cut down on illicit sexual activity taking place in the public baths, city authorities insisted on rigid seclusion of the sexes and periodic inspections. Despite these efforts prostitution continued to flourish, as indicated by the fact that the words *stew* and *bagnio*, originally English and Italian terms for bathhouse, have become euphemisms for brothels. As the popularity of the bath spread, kings and officials attempted to supplement city legislation. In England, Henry II issued regulations for those of London in the twelfth century. He stipulated that no bathhouse operator or his wife was to let any single woman come freely, that no woman was to live in the bathhouse, that no one engage in sexual relations in the bathhouse, and that the constable, bailiff, and other officials be allowed to search the stewhouse every week. Food and drink were also not to be served.[69]

Though prostitutes in areas under the jurisdiction of the French kings wore a special shoulder knot (usually red) that set them apart, there was no uniform agreement in medieval Europe as to the color or clothing assigned to prostitutes. In Toulouse, as indicated, they wore white. In Leipzig they wore yellow cloaks trimmed with blue, in Vienna a yellow handkerchief attached to their shoulder, in Bern and Zurich a red cap. In Parma prostitutes wore white cloaks, in Bergamo yellow, in Milan black wool. Any citizen meeting a prostitute improperly clad had the right to strip her of her clothes.[70] Once a street was designated as a center for prostitution it continued to keep that designation for centuries. In the nineteenth century Henry Mayhew found that Paris streets then designated as proper areas for houses of prostitution, such as the Rue Froidmantel, la Court Robert de Paris, Rue Charon, Rue Tyron, and Champ Fleury, had served the same purpose in the medieval period.[71] In Germany, where the locations of bordellos might have changed, the onetime association with prostitution was continued by such names as Frauengasse Strasse, Frauenpforte Strasse, or Frauenfleck Strasse. A standard name for streets on which brothels were located was Rose Street, since to "pluck a rose" was a euphemism for copulating with a prostitute in several European languages.

Wherever great numbers of people gathered, so did the prostitute. When the Council of Constance was held in the small city of Constance, Switzerland, between 1414 and 1418 in order to end the Great Schism and to deal with heresy and reform in the medieval Church, large numbers of prostitutes flocked to the town. Contemporary accounts claim the number of prostitutes was at least seven hundred.[72] Prostitutes also followed German, French, and other armies and in fact were regarded as essential for taking care of the wounded, and for doing the necessary chores for the fighting men, including the cooking, laundry, and keeping the camp in order.

The Medieval Prostitute and the Literature of Prostitution

Both the secular and religious ideal in the medieval period was to reclaim the prostitute if at all possible, and the medieval Christian was always conscious from the example of Mary Magdalene that a harlot could achieve salvation. Usually the machinery of the Church stood ready to assist women willing to leave the life of sin, although it was recognized that realistically chances for successful reform were slim. Still the hope of reform was there, and two major avenues were advanced. Favored by most reformers were attempts to induce the repentant prostitute to enter the religious life, to become a nun. From at least the twelfth century onward, if not earlier, religious houses were established with the particular purpose of serving as asylums for reformed prostitutes.[73] In 1198 Pope Innocent III urged that all good citizens attempt to reclaim prostitutes. In

1224 a concentrated effort began to create a special religious order of penitential nuns to harbor reformed prostitutes, and in 1227 Pope Gregory IX gave the highest ecclesiastical sanction to the Order of Saint Mary Magdalene, which subsequently established convents in numerous cities. The sisters wore a white habit; whence they were sometimes known as "the White Ladies."[74] Subsequent official patronage and encouragement was given to the Magdalenes by the fourteenth-century popes.[75] Convents for reformed prostitutes, not necessarily affiliated with the Magdalene order, received endowment and support from monarchs such as Louis IX of France.[76] One of the most famous of the Magdalene houses was established in Vienna at the beginning of the fourteenth century, although it was not chartered until 1384. Known as the Soul House, it was organized like a convent, although its inmates were not required to take a vow of either poverty or chastity, and many of the women left the house as brides of respectable citizens of the city. In 1480 Emperor Frederick III granted the inmates of the houses the right to sell the product of their vineyards, and in order to increase the sale, the women apparently began selling sex on the side. This led to the removal of the women from the house, which was turned over to Franciscan monks.[77]

A second method of dealing with the reformed prostitute was to encourage her to marry. Canon lawyers, however, were wary of this solution and usually proposed that a number of conditions be fulfilled before a prostitute be allowed to marry. In fact, the doctrine of the early Church had tended to discourage such marriage, and for a time a man who married a whore was regarded as idiotic and unreasonable. To be eligible for marriage the reformed prostitute had to do public penance for her sins and obtain a special dispensation.[78] If a man accidentally married a prostitute, believing her to be a chaste virgin, the marriage was legally valid, although if she continued to practice her trade it might not be. In 1109 Pope Innocent II lauded those who married harlots in order to reform them and described their actions as not "least among the works of charity." Those who rescued public prostitutes and took them to wife were performing acts that would count for the remission of their own sins.[79]

One of the most interesting ways to rescue prostitutes was that advocated by Fulk of Neuilly, one of the preachers associated with the Fourth Crusade. He secured an agreement with the Parisian authorities whereby they would give 1,000 livres (supplemented by an additional 250 livres agreed to by the students at the University of Paris) to each former prostitute who contracted an honorable marriage.[80] However, the Church was slow in allowing such marriages without strict guidelines because of potential abuses.

In effect, medieval authorities, both secular and ecclesiastic, regarded prostitution as a necessary evil, an evil that had to be tolerated in order to avert greater evils. Fearful of female sexuality, the ecclesiastical writers tended to demand a higher standard of sexual morality from women than from men, but aware of the double standard implied in this, did not overly punish the prostitute. Occasionally some official determined to eliminate prostitution, as Saint Louis did, but his failure added to the resignation. If prostitution was to be accepted, however, it had to be controlled, and in general the medieval efforts to confine it to certain quarters or to distinguish prostitutes from other women were successful. Much of the energy of the ecclesiastical authorities was spent in trying to deal with patrons of prostitutes, and they made a concerted effort to prevent clergy from having contact with prostitutes. Here they probably failed. For example, one of the papal legates sent to England to lead the efforts against clerical concubinage was found in bed with a harlot, though he had just finished celebrating mass.[81] By the end of the medieval period, prostitution was well established in most of the important towns of Europe, and regulated by well-defined customs and traditions. Some towns, however, refused to allow prostitutes in town after nightfall, and thereby confined their activities to just outside the city walls.[82] Other towns put prostitutes under the direction and control of the public executioner. This association, perhaps more than anything, emphasizes the ambiguous attitude of officials toward a "necessary" function that had connotations of evil and low status.

The ubiquity of prostitution is indicated in part through the vast number of terms associated with brothels. Translating these terms into English, we find women's houses, friendship house, daughter house, aunt's house, small house, rose garden, "Stockhaus" (jailhouse), temple house or temple, joy house, clap house, common house, abbey, lupanaria, great house, public house, bordello, and brothel, among others.[83] Bloch, in his study of prostitution, found some seventy-five towns and cities in medieval Germany with brothels;[84] other countries probably had as many if not more.

Prostitution in much of the medieval period lacked the romanticizing present in the Greek period, and though there were probably different levels of prostitution, the difference between the levels was not very great. But by the end of the medieval period the courtesan, the high-class prostitute, had again made her appearance. There are at least two explanations for this reappearance, one economic, the other cultural. Prostitution is a hard life, unless the prostitute is able to be selective in her choice of clientele. If she can become a romantic figure, if she can gain wealth and status by her accomplishments, then she becomes something more than an ordinary prostitute. Though early medieval kings had their mistresses, the market for high-class courtesans was limited. This changed with the growing prosperity in the later medieval period, with the growth of urbanization, and with a new mystique of romantic love. Scholars have spent a good deal of time and energy in trying to trace the sources of romantic love to Islamic lyric poetry, to Greek Platonism, to the Latin poet Ovid—all of which contributed—but welding these is an economic factor, the ability of women to act as patrons. Sidney Painter speculated that the whole thing started one day when a hungry minstrel wandering about the duchy of Aquitaine came to a castle where he hoped his tales of battles and his tumbling tricks would earn him a good dinner. The lord of the castle was absent, and the lady, who acted as his hostess, soon found the endless stories of battle rather tiring and his tumbling rather boring. It became evident to the minstrel that his stay would be very short unless he interested his hostess. Being somewhat inventive, he composed a song in praise of her beauty and virtue and described their effect on him in rather glowing terms. Not surprisingly, he found the lady was pleased. She rewarded him with a better bed and more ample food, and as word spread, other minstrels followed his example. It was not long before the baronial halls of southern France were ringing with songs in praise of ladies who were able to dispense lavish hospitality, and any lady who failed to have a minstrel singing her virtues felt out of fashion. Onto this scene came William IX, count of Poitou and duke of Aquitaine, who thought such songs might prove a pleasant accompaniment to his triumphs over feminine virtue, songs with which he could entertain his companions. The duke's accounts of his amourous adventures proved to be as interesting to his friends as his stories of battles, and with the example of a powerful prince who ruled a third of France to spur them, the fashion grew.[85]

Duke William's ideas were carried northward by his granddaughter, Eleanor of Aquitaine, wife first of King Louis VII of France (1137–1151), then after her marriage was annulled, to Henry II of England (1152–1204). Eleanor's place as patroness was passed on to her daughters, Marie, countess of Champagne, and Alix, countess of Blois. The minnesingers of Germany and the poets of Italy also adopted the idea of courtly love, and as it spread it was fortified with ideas from Ovid's *Ars Amoris,* newly reintroduced into Europe. These principles were embodied by Andreas Capellanus (Andrew the Chaplain), a member of Marie's household, in *The Art of Courtly Love.*

Love to Andrew was a passion that came from looking at and thinking too much about the body of a member of the opposite sex; it could be satisfied only by embracing and fulfilling love's commands, in other words, by sexual intercourse. Love was different from marriage;

marriage was a contractual obligation, and love was entirely voluntary. True love might become adulterous, but it need not end up that way. The fact that he might really be sanctioning adultery, or at the very least fornication, undoubtedly troubled Andrew. It was perhaps for this reason that in the latter part of his book he launched a bitter diatribe against women, as if to clear his hands, implying that it was all woman's fault that she was so sexual, and she, not he, should take the blame.[86]

Whether courtly love and the romantic ideal damaged the institution of marriage is debatable;[87] it did, however, along with the changing economic scene, help reestablish the courtesan as an important adjunct of society. This was also encouraged by the reinterpretation of Platonic philosophy. As indicated earlier, for Plato and the neo-Platonists, love began on the individual level as a desire for beauty, extended to a recognition that beauty was an intangible spiritual cognition. In Plato's dialogues, however, love was generally not the relationship that took place between a man and woman but between two men or between a man and a youth—homosexual love. When the study of Plato was intensified in the late Middle Ages, many writers were concerned with avoiding homosexuality. They could do this either by attributing only an intellectual and verbal fervor to those who loved members of the same sex, or by attributing not to men but to women the personal beauty that excited men to love and impelled the lover to seek the higher forms of beauty. Increasingly this latter course was pursued,[88] and the more materialistic concepts of courtly love were reinforced with the spiritual aspects of Platonic love.[89] It was through the love of ideal beauty and goodness that man realized his higher calling and divine purpose. This led to an idealization of beauty in women, well expressed by Guillaume Bouche, who stated that woman was "God's greatest gift to man," all the more so since by her strength and virtue the spirit was enabled to attain a contemplative state that led by degrees to a desire for things divine. It was due to woman that man was able to forget himself, since woman had been put on earth as an advance intimation of what the celestial habitation would be like.[90]

Such attitudes led to an enhanced ideal status for women. Some women were even given an education similar to that of men, although it was held to be more proper for women to work by influencing men rather than by engaging directly in political deeds. Grudgingly the misogynism of the medieval cleric gave way to a changing view of women. As part of this movement the courtesan received intellectual justification as the lady of charm and intelligence, education and manners, living in her own house holding court, the friend of men of influence both in politics and in art. In France under Francis I (1494-1547) the courtesan mistress reached her greatest heights in Europe since the time of the Greeks. Francis adored women; he enjoyed their company, admired their beauty, appreciated their wit, delighted in their perfume, and sought their favors. He is reported to have said that a court without women was like a year without a spring, or like a spring without roses. According to Abbé Brantôme, the sixteenth-century chronicler of the lives of fair and gallant ladies, Francis held that all noblemen of his court should be pursuing at least one courtesan; those who did not were simpletons without taste.[91] According to Brantôme, even the Cardinal of Lorraine took a special interest in any attractive young woman, married or single, who appeared at court for the first time, and usually offered to train her in the ways of the court.[92]

Being a mistress to a king was not without its problems. This is indicated by the case of Françoise de Chateaubriant, perhaps the most famous courtesan of the period, although she had a strong contender for the honor in the person of Anne, Duchess d'Etampes. Both were mistresses to Francis. Anne, however, had been chosen as the king's mistress by the queen, Eleanor of Spain, and was much younger. During a period of intense rivalry between Françoise and Anne, Anne attempted to demonstrate her hold on the king by requesting that he give her the jewels that he had earlier given to Françoise. Infatuated with Anne, the king attempted to grant her wish and sent a message to Madame de Chateaubriant asking the return of his gifts to her. Upset at such a request, she had them all melted down and gave the lumps to the king. This action, rather than angering the king, amused him and he forgave his ex-mistress for her "greatness and boldness of heart."[93]

Madame de Chateaubriant had first come to the attention of the king as the wife of Jean Laval, to whom she had been married as a young girl of eleven. Though she had given birth to her first child when she was twelve, she matured into an extraordinarily beautiful woman. Francis, always on the lookout for beautiful women, heard about her and requested that the Lavals visit him at his court, which was then traveling, in Blois. Jean Laval, suspicious of the king's motives, replied that his wife was much too shy to be presented to the king. Soon a second letter arrived requesting the appearance of the Lavals at court, and Jean, feeling that he could not ignore the summons, set out by himself. Disappointed when only the male Laval made an appearance, the king put pressure on him to have his wife join him. Under royal pressure, Jean wrote to his wife in the presence of the king, requesting her attendance. This invitation was turned down since Jean before leaving home had warned his wife to ignore any summons to the court unless the letter contained a ring identical to the one she wore on her finger. Unfortunately, Jean boasted of his successful scheme to his valet, and the valet, hoping for a reward, betrayed the secret to the king. On the king's orders the valet stole the ring, had it copied, and then restored to its hiding place. Again the king requested Jean to write his wife, promising that if he did, the king would send the letter by royal messenger. Jean did as requested, the king took the letter, inserted the duplicate ring, and in a short time Françoise arrived at the court in a state of great excitement, only to find her husband furious. As soon as the king saw her he took steps to have her as his mistress and spent three years of royal persuasion to gain his way. Jean went back to Brittany, where he brooded over his wife's infidelity. When the king died, Françoise returned to Brittany, but her husband apparently felt she was to blame, and shortly afterwards the ex-royal mistress was found murdered.

Not all courtesans met such calamitous ends. Agnes Sorel, the mistress of Charles VII (1403-1461) of France, dominated the king until her death in 1450. She is remembered today for introducing a new style of dress, bare to the waist, a style that spread throughout much of aristocratic France. Unfortunately, many of the ladies who adopted the style apparently lacked the well-rounded firmness of Agnes's breasts. Perhaps the most interesting example of the successful courtesan was Diane de Poitiers, mistress of Henry II, the son of Francis I. Unlike most courtesans Diane was much older than her royal paramour. In fact when Henry first met her she was thirty-one, and he was only eleven. Despite the difference in ages, the young man was smitten, and began to court her. Finally, when Diane had reached the respectable age of thirty-nine, she consented to become his mistress. Henry's much younger wife, Catherine de' Medici, put up with her aging rival until the death of her husband, whereupon she ordered Diane to return the crown jewels that Henry had given her. Catherine was fascinated by the tricks allegedly used by Diane to attract her husband, and in order to find out what these might be she had holes pierced in the ceiling of Diane's room. In this way Catherine could witness Diane and Henry in sexual intercourse, but she was unable to discover any special reason for the attraction the older woman had on the young king. Probably the real reason for Diane's success was that she was a mother figure as well as a mistress, rather than for any particular sexual ability that she possessed. Henry remained more or less true to Diane until his death, perhaps further proof that the tie was more than sexual.[94]

Stories similar to those of the Greeks were told about famous courtesans. One of the most famous courtesans of the city of Rome at this time was a woman known as "the Greek." Among her lovers was a certain French nobleman to whom she had taught all the arts of love. After serving her French lover, the woman sought to meet his wife, in part because she felt that the wife ought to make her a handsome present for educating her husband in the various ways of pleasing women.[95] Another famous courtesan at Rome, named Faustina, married a lawyer, but continued to welcome old clients and friends who could afford her services. Remaining true to the prostitute's creed, she refused to engage in sexual activity unless she was well paid.[96] The rationalization by men who went with courtesans in the Middle Ages (a rationalization the Greeks could not use) was that they might marry one, and thus they claimed, they could save a soul, and gain God's mercy.[97] Even popes turned to courtesans. The most notorious pope in this respect was Rodrigo Borgia, who became pope under the name of Alexander VI. A native of Spain, Rodrigo had been brought to Rome by his uncle, Pope Calextus III. Accompanying him was his mistress, Vanozza dei Cattanei, who gave birth to four of his children, including Cesare and Lucrezia Borgia. To camouflage their liaison, Alexander VI found her three different husbands. As she grew older, she was given a pension, and Alexander VI turned to Giulia Farnese, who at the time was only seventeen. Though Giulia was married, Alexander VI persuaded her to leave her husband and move into his apartment, where she allegedly participated in sexual orgies with him, including one in 1501 in which fifty nude prostitutes crawled among lighted candles, picking up chestnuts with their labia. She gave birth to three of Alexander's children and is commemorated in Pintoricchio's *Madonna* and Guglielmo della Porta's *Truth,* both of which she posed for. *Truth* is a marble nude that reclines atop the tomb of her brother, Pope Paul III.

The concept of courtesan, however, did not extend beyond the upper classes. The word itself originally meant one who was attached to the court, and is derived from the word *courtier*. It soon became synonymous with court mistress or high-class prostitute, and the courtesan restricted her attention to men of the upper classes. By so doing she also fitted into some of the stereotypes of the day. Andrew the Chaplain, the codifier of courtly love, taught that love was an emotion confined only to the nobility, and he apparently believed that it was unlikely that anyone in the lower classes would have the virtues necessary for love. If a nobleman desired a peasant woman so strongly that he could not resist the temptation, he was free to rape her on the spot since a courteous approach could only have been wasted on a woman who could not possibly feel love.[98] As for the ordinary prostitute, Andrew felt that she should be shunned. If occasionally a man had a need for her services, he did not have to waste his time courting her, nor did he have to instruct her.[99] These ideas were not confined to Andrew. Baldassare Castiglione in his *Book of the Courtier* held it was essential for the courtier to love apart from the common, ignorant sort of people.[100] Needless to say, the lower-class male who tried to have intercourse with an upper-class female found himself in deep trouble, much as black men in the South have.

Though upper-class writers tend to neglect the lower-status prostitute and to profane her character, she benefited from the rise of the courtesan. She also found her way into the literature of the fifteenth century through the writings of François Villon (1431-?), master of arts, thief, pimp, pickpocket, frequenter of brothels, recorder óf the lower levels of Parisian life. Villon, in his various poems and testaments, has given us some of the most moving portrayals of women of ill-repute in all literature. He had no developed philosophy of love, but was interested in the women who walked the streets or supplemented their income by prostitution. In the *Lament of Belle Heaulmière* Villon has an old prostitute giving advice to six would-be prostitutes. *Heaulmière* means the helmetmaker's girl; other prostitutes were often known by the names of the trades at which they worked or had worked. The backgrounds of Villon's six women are also worth mentioning. Belle Gantière sold gloves in her spare time; Blanchela Savetière was the wife of a cobbler; Gente Saulcissière worked in a sausage shop; Guillemette la Tapissière worked in tapestry; Jehanneton le Chaperonnière made hoods and horns, and Katherine l'Esponnière was married to a man who belonged to the spur-making guild. To all of them Belle had the same advice: Make your money while you can, spare no man, for an aged prostitute is of no more use than a worn-out coin. Villon also meditated on the nature of woman. He was convinced that love of women was the work of the devil, because for a moment of pleasure one has to suffer many moments of sadness. He concluded that for the woman it was still best to take while she could.[101]

Villon claimed that women loved only for money; his jaundiced view came from the fact that he himself had once loved a prostitute. In a poem about it, he reported that as soon as his pocketbook had been exhausted the prostitute cast him aside for a rich old man who was more "foul, ugly, and hideous" than one could imagine. Each part of his poem ends with the refrain that poverty counts you out, for the rich always have the advantage in love. In John Payne's translation of this poem, *Ballad of Ladies' Love*, the refrain "Riche amoureux a toujours l'advantage" is translated as "The wealthy gallant always gains the day." This is the second verse in the Payne translation:

> So chanced it that, whilst coin my purse did fill,
> The world went merry as a marriage bell
> And I was all in all with her, until,
> Without word said, my wanton's loose eyes fell
> Upon a graybeard, rich but foul as hell:
> A man more hideous never woman bore.
> But what of that? He had his will and more:
> And I, confounded, stricken with dismay,

Upon this text went glossing passing sore;
The wealthy gallant always gains the day.[102]

Despite his cynical attitude, Villon had a sympathetic feeling for many
of the women of the street, and in one of his poems he described both
his life as a pimp and that of his girlfriend, the prostitute Margo, who
after satisfying her customers,

claps me on the head,
says I'm cute and whacks my thigh.
Then, both drunk, we sleep like logs.
When we awake, her belly starts to quiver,
and she mounts me, to spare love's fruit;
I groan, squashed beneath her weight—
this lechery of hers will ruin me,
in this brothel where we ply our trade.[103]

The other verses in this poem also end with the refrain "in this brothel
where we ply our trade."

In the Paris where Villon wrote and lived, then a city of 100,000,
prostitution must have been rampant. One fifteenth-century observer
claimed that there were five or six thousand women engaged in prostitution,[104] and though this number is probably an exaggeration, the numbers
must have been vast. By the end of the Middle Ages prostitution was
not only accepted; the cult of the courtesan had romanticized it, at least
to some extent. The status of women was changing slightly, but women
still had a long way to go for any semblance of equality. They were
regarded as sex objects still, but to be a sex object was perhaps not
a bad thing; it was certainly better than to be "all crazy and full of fleas,"[105]
as Leone Battista Alberti, one of the learned men of the Renaissance,
expressed it. Prostitution was tolerated, even regulated in most of the
areas of Europe, and all attempts to eliminate it had been more or less
abandoned. Prostitution might be condemned but the prostitute herself
was not. There was always hope that she would abandon her ways, but
other than joining a convent or getting married, there was little a respectable
woman could do to support herself. Ordinary women worked in the shops
of their husbands or fathers, but even these opportunities were restricted.

8   THE POX AND REFORM

In traditional histories the sixteenth century in Europe is denoted as the Reformation, and the concentration is on changes yielded by alterations in religious attitudes. The religious reforms, particularly the rejection of clerical celibacy by the Protestants, affected sexual attitudes. But as we will demonstrate, especially significant as far as prostitution was concerned was the new fear of venereal disease.

Matrimonial and sexual questions in general did not play a dominant part in the religious controversies or literature of the sixteenth century, although almost to a man the reformers believed that the traditional demand for clerical celibacy was damaging the whole fabric of Christianity. Some went so far as to argue that celibacy was contrary to the laws of God. Even those Protestants who felt that there might be something worthwhile in adhering to the celibate life felt that irrevocable vows of celibacy were contrary to the nature of man. The Swiss reformer Ulrich Zwingli (1484-1531), for example, denounced compulsory vows of chastity, but at the same time held that continence was a gift from God. Those monks or clerics not granted this gift were committing a sin by not entering into matrimony. Martin Luther (1483-1546), the early leader of the Protestant movement, attacked clerical celibacy and monastic vows and advised those about to be ordained to avoid taking a vow of continence. He encouraged priests who had succumbed to the weakness of the flesh to cohabit with the woman if she was willing, since in the eyes of God they were already married.

Luther felt that the vows of chastity had originated in the belief that divine favor could be won by performing self-imposed disciplines; this in his opinion was a delusion. In a letter to a fellow reformer, Philip Melanchthon (1497-1560) he wrote that any prohibition of marriage originated with the devil.[1] According to Luther, continence was as little in our power as were God's other wonders and graces; some were gifted and others were not. The essential ingredient for salvation was faith, and not good works, even if perchance chastity could be regarded as a good work. John Calvin (1509-1564) argued in much the same way, though as usual he was somewhat more cautious than Luther. Calvin made it clear that he disapproved of celibacy vows only when such vows were regarded as acts of religious dedication or which were rashly taken by those who found they could not keep them.[2]

Both Luther and Calvin held marriage in much higher esteem than the early Church Fathers. To Luther, wedlock was God's gift to mankind, a state of life approved by him and possessing the authority of his sanction; marriage was implanted in our nature, instituted in Paradise, confirmed by the fifth commandment, and safeguarded by the seventh. It was a true, heavenly, spiritual, and divine estate. Nevertheless, Luther's attitude toward human sexual drives remained ambivalent. Marriage permitted the expression of carnal desires, but this did not mean that coitus was intrinsically good and pure. Sexual intercourse was still somehow unclean and could not be performed entirely in the knowledge and worship of God; it remained for most of mankind a regrettable necessity. Generalizing, perhaps from his own experience, he tended to regard marriage as a medicine, a hospital for the sick, the only effective antidote against, as well as cure for, the incontinence that troubled every man; for the human male to take a wife was as necessary as eating and drinking. Still, there had to be cautions, and the privilege of matrimony was to be used with moderation; otherwise marriage would become a pigsty in which the lecherous and sensual would wallow.[3]

Calvin, on the contrary, and perhaps surprisingly, was much more positive in his view of marriage. He repudiated Jerome's interpretation of Saint Paul's words that it was good for a man not to touch a woman (1 Cor. 7:1) and instead argued that coitus was undefiled, honorable, and holy, since it had been instituted by God. The reason sexual intercourse had been disparaged in previous ages as something unclean was, according to Calvin, that Satan had misled men to imagine that they would be polluted by intercourse with their wives. Despite such ameliorative views, Calvin remained uneasy about sexual intercourse, particularly the pleasure concomitant with coitus. This pleasure, he held, must inevitably be attended by a certain element of evil: the immoderate desire, the human corruption that produced the Fall from the state of grace in the Garden of Eden. On the other hand, God would not treat intercourse as sinful when it was sought or accepted as part of procreation. Calvin, therefore, covered carnal desires with the veil of matrimony, allowing the husband and wife to enjoy themselves, so long as they did so with modesty and propriety, but under no condition did this give them license to indulge intemperately. Marriage behavior should always be sober and appropriate to the dignity of the vows.[4]

Calvin and Luther also disagreed on women's position in society.[5] Though the propagation of the species was the special and characteristic end of matrimony, Calvin also taught that the primary function of marriage was social rather than generative. Women thus were not simply men's helpers in procreation, nor were they created as a "remedy" for male sexual impulses, but rather women were created as the inseparable associates of men for their whole lives. Luther, on the other hand, still saw women chiefly as the bearer of children and the divinely appointed means of sexual relief; he emphasized strongly the subordinate position of women in the marriage relationship.[6]

If the Protestants were less inclined to emphasize virginity and more inclined to praise marriage than the early fathers of the Christian Church, they were much more rigid, and far less tolerant, about sexual promiscuity. Luther and Calvin both emphasized the severity of punishment for those who strayed from the path of divine providence in the matter of carnal desire. Since prostitutes were women who encouraged men to stray, it was perhaps inevitable that some of the Reformers urged that prostitutes be punished by excommunication and perpetual exile.[7]

Luther had some definite views on prostitution. In a short tract titled "Thoughts Concerning Brothels," he attacked the whole practice of tolerating brothels as a means of curbing graver sins, a concept originally put forth by Saint Augustine. Luther said this might have been necessary when Saint Augustine wrote, since the people then lived under a pagan regime, but this was no longer the case.[8] In his "Address to the German Nobility" he stated that it was to be lamented that "Christians tolerate open and common brothels in our midst, when all of us are baptized into chastity."[9]

Luther was certain that God's commands did not allow men to compromise their marital vows by going to prostitutes just to make life pleasanter. Women to him should be wives and mothers, not prostitutes. His denunciations of prostitution were often put in strong terms. In 1543 he posted a notice warning students at Wittenberg about visiting prostitutes:

> Through special enemies of our faith the devil has sent some whores here to ruin our poor young men. As an old and faithful preacher I ask you in fatherly fashion, dear children, that you believe assuredly that the evil spirit sent these whores here and that they are dreadful, shabby, stinking, loathsome, and syphilitic, as daily experience unfortunately demonstrates.[10]

Luther added that if he were acting as a judge he would order severe punishments for the offenders, but since neither he nor other preachers were judges, he called on them to speak powerfully against such sins. Preachers were urged to apply public pressure, to appeal to the good consciences of public officials to enact and enforce laws against brothels.

> Let the government, if it wishes to be Christian, punish whoredom, rape, and adultery, at least when they occur openly; if they still occur in secret, the government is not to be blamed.[11]

Luther, however, was reluctant for clergy to become involved in state enforcement of morals, preferring to have the realm of the church somewhat separate from the realm of the state, one realm being for grace, the other for justice. Still Luther occasionally had to act more directly in sexual matters. When he did so, he came down on the side of tolerance. This is effectively demonstrated by the case of Philip of Hesse, his political ally, who entered into bigamy rather than commit adultery. Luther comforted him by emphasizing there were many examples of bigamy in the Scriptures. He advised Philip to keep calm and his marital crisis would blow over—perhaps one of his wives would die.[12] Elsewhere, however, Luther held that except in great emergencies, Christians should have only one wife, and that instead of marrying the second girl, Philip might have kept her as a concubine.[13] Luther at first was opposed to divorce, preferring bigamy or concubinage, but ultimately he came to allow divorce for adultery, desertion, interference with a spouse's religious life, and other reasons. Calvin also regarded adultery as a ground for divorce and eventually desertion as well, but was reluctant to go further. He was also more hostile to remarriage, even for the innocent partner, than Luther was.

Calvin was in a much more effective position to eliminate prostitution than Luther because of the power he had gained in Geneva. Under Calvin, Geneva became a theocracy, a city run by him and his supporters who hoped to create a society of saints. The Bible was adopted as the norm, and its provisions were enforced except for those Jewish ceremonies that Calvin considered abrogated by the New Testament. Elders of the church kept track of the activities of the citizens in their district, and those found to be failing in observance could be publicly censured, excommunicated, and forced to request forgiveness in a public meeting in church. When the activities were regarded as particularly dangerous, and if there was no indication of repentance, the consistory, a body of clergy and laymen, had the power to request the aid of the civil authorities to bring culprits to punishment. Adultery, blasphemy, witchcraft, and heresy were regarded as deserving of capital punishment. Attendance at plays was forbidden, as was dancing. The immoderate use of liquor was grounds for chastisement. Luxury in clothing was suppressed, and all matters of color and quality were regulated by law. Inns were put under the direct control of the government, and prostitutes driven out of the city. The result was a kind of dedication among the citizens that tremendously impressed visitors such as Bernardino Occhino and John Knox, although the standards were maintained only by continual surveillance. One skeptical historian, Preserved Smith, reported that the records of Geneva show more cases of vice after the Reformation than before,[14] probably because the officials were always on guard and punished people for activities that had usually been ignored in the past. Two of Calvin's own female relatives, for example, were convicted of adultery. Nevertheless, the effect of Calvin's vigilance was to drive out of the city those who could not or would not conform, and to attract new immigrants who wanted the austere way of life that Calvin imposed.

Few of the followers of Calvin were able to establish such standards among their followers elsewhere, although John Knox approached it for a time in Scotland and so did the American Pilgrims in New England. What Calvin demanded was the dedication of all believers to the same extent that the medieval Church had demanded only from monks and nuns. Although Calvin did not require celibacy, the personal code of morality was no less strict. The difficulty with Calvin's community of saints, however, was that each generation had children, and not all the children chose to follow the same rigid standards as their parents. Ultimately the society was put in the situation of abandoning those children who did not conform or abandoning the society that imposed standards that the children refused to follow. Inevitably the society itself crumbled, although there were small groups who continued voluntarily imposing such strictures on themselves. In England some of the adherents of Calvin's beliefs tried to reform English society to meet the moral level of Geneva, and when they failed, many emigrated to America rather than compromise their ideals. Some of these would-be reformers were extremely hostile to prostitution, and Philip Stubbes, the Puritan author of *The Anatomie of Abuses* (1582), urged that all whores be cauterized with a red-hot iron on their cheeks, forehead, and other visible parts of the body. Stubbes, like Calvin, wanted to establish a society of believers, and was intolerant of magistrates who winked at prostitution, who tolerated dancing and other "immoral activities" that he felt served as an "introduction to whoredom, a preparation to wantonness, a provocation to uncleanness and an introite to all kinds of lewdness."[15]

The new morality, however, was not just confined to Protestant countries; it also made its appearance in Catholic countries, where it ran into conflict with the relaxed standards associated with the late medieval Church and the "Renaissance" papacy. As indicated in the last chapter, many men of the fifteenth and sixteenth centuries had turned to courtesans for love and companionship. Some of the courtesans, like Veronica Franco, poetess by inclination, courtesan by profession, the friend of the painter Tintoretto, and others, became famous. Italy in the sixteenth century, however, remained a place of double standards. Benvenuto Italiano commented that though it seemed "repugnant to reason," Italian men kept their wives with care, circumspection, and jealousy, while they were free to roam where they would.[16] The poet Ariosto also protested against such practices and wondered why a woman should be "punished or blamed" more than a man when she has merely carried out what a man does with the same desires.[17] Still good women were forbidden from doing what only the bad women were allowed to do, and so prostitution seemingly increased in the fifteenth and early sixteenth centuries,[18] the courtesan reaching a new level of respect and consideration.[19] Many were admired for their education. Pietro Aretino in writing about the literary abilities of the prostitute Lucretia Madrenna compared her to Cicero and reported that she could recite by heart "all of Petrarch and Boccaccio and countless verses from Virgil, Horace, Ovid, and many other Latin poets."[20] So great was the popularity of the prostitute courtesans in general that for a time they took an active role in festivals,[21] and some courtesans were given choice seats or places in churches.[22]

Often prostitutes appeared together in groups, and when this happened traffic jams developed. A sixteenth-century Venetian wrote a poem about the carriages of the prostitutes:

> Majestically the carriages go through the narrow streets of Rome,
> The via Sacra is not free, nor is the via Lata.
> They go straight down each street, clothed in spendor,
> And are carried through the Ponte Sisto in insolent glory.[23]

Some prostitutes became so famous for their beauty and their wit that they went into business for themselves, establishing houses of their own where customers went to visit them, to stare and converse. Only rarely did the hostess, the sole occupant of the house, consent to have sexual relations with her visitors, who regarded it as a great honor. There were complaints that even common whores attempted to act as courtesans. A Venetian document of May 22, 1543, states that a prostitute, Lucieta Padovana, regarded herself as a courtesan and not as a whore. The essential difference was money. A Florentine list of 1569 separated the courtesan from the prostitute on the basis of income, dividing prostitutes into rich, moderately rich, and poor, and stating that the rich prostitutes regarded themselves as courtesans rather than whores.[24]

Pietro Aretino compared the prostitute to the soldier. She was paid for doing wrong, but was not condemned because that is what society needed from her. For Aretino, in this tongue-in-cheek dialogue, prostitution is pictured as the best life for women, preferred to the convent or marriage.[25] Moreover, if perchance a prostitute was troubled by her conscience, a few drops of holy water could always cleanse her soul. Aretino was not alone in praising prostitutes for the way in which they practiced their trade and for the services they performed for men. Antonio Panormita, usually called Beccadelli, celebrated the work of the devoted prostitute who, after having been seized coarsely and pierced by men, always gave them many kisses.[26] Brutality among customers was apparently not unusual, and Aretino warned would-be prostitutes that men did not always respect them or their bodies but rather invented brutal ways to abuse them. He also advised on methods for dealing with such customers.[27]

The life of a prostitute was not always pleasant. As Nanna, the old prostitute in Aretino's *Dialogues,* related to young Pippa, a prostitute

> never has an hour of rest, neither when she goes out nor stays in, neither at table nor in bed. For when she is sleepy, she cannot sleep; she must stay awake to caress some scruffy man, a huge, ugly buffalo, who has a mouth that smells like turds, and will bang away at all of her. And if she balks or refuses, then reproaches are the order of the day: "You don't deserve me, you're not worthy of me; if I were this rascal or that scoundrel, then you'd stay awake." If she is at table, every fly looks like a silkworm to him; and if she gives the tiniest morsel to someone else, he grumbles and fumes with rage, gnawing at his bread . . . We are prodded and pushed and manhandled by all avenues and in all ways, day and night, and any whore who does not consent to all the filth they can think of would die of hunger. One man wants boiled meat, the other wants roast; and they have discovered the "aperture behind," "the legs on the shoulders," the "Gianetta style," "the crane," "the tortoise," "the church on the belfry," "the stirrup," "the grazing sheep," and other postures more farfetched and extravagant than a play-actor's prancings, so finally I would cry: "O world, may God be with you!" though I am ashamed to say it. In short nowadays they make an anatomy of any lady whatsoever; so learn how to live, Pippa, and learn how to manage, or else I'll see you in hell.[28]

Inevitably with such an attitude toward life, Aretino's name is also associated with a sexual manual. He wrote the text for some sixteen drawings attributed to Guilio Romano, a painter in the school of Raphael, illustrating various sexual postures.

Also inevitably there was a reaction. Pope Paul III (1534-1549) although the father of bastards himself, attempted to deal with some of the more famous courtesans by forcing them to be classed as prostitutes.

Tullia d'Aragona, for example, the daughter of another courtesan, Giula Ferrarese, quickly fell from a position of influence when so classified. Aretino himself had to leave Rome for a time for safer pastures. Pope Paul IV (1555-1559) went to extremes in ordering the nude paintings by Michelangelo in the Sistene Chapel to be clothed with decent draperies, and for the next century several painters, collectively nicknamed breeches makers, spent their time painting clothes on unclothed old masterpieces or putting fig leaves on statues. There were limits, however, and prostitution was never abolished in the papal territories although under Popes Paul IV, Pius V, and Sixtus V, there were attempts to do so. The strongest effort was by Pope Pius V in 1566. He ordered everyone who engaged in prostitution to leave the city of Rome. But, allegedly, when such large numbers of people made preparations to leave, the city was thrown into panic and he was induced to rescind the ordinance.[29]

At the Council of Trent (1545-1563), which met to deal with the problems raised by the Protestant Reformers, prostitution was ignored but not sex in general. Celibacy was reinforced, the sanctity of marriage was stressed, and a series of edicts were issued to control loose living. The council edicts emphasized that it was a grave sin for single men to consort with prostitutes. Priests who continued to live with women after being warned by officials were to be removed from office.[30] Still prostitution continued to exist in Rome, and in spite of attempts of the popes to eliminate it, Roman officials still collected a tax on prostitutes.[31]

Prostitution was under attack not only by religious reformers but also by those growing fearful of syphilis. Venereal disease has a long history. The name *venereal* itself comes from *venery,* the pursuit of Venus, goddess of love, although what we now classify as venereal disease was not always recognized in the past to be spread through sexual intercourse. Gonorrhea is mentioned frequently in ancient medical records, and it probably caused most veteran prostitutes to become sterile eventually. In China there were attempts to counteract the dangers of venereal disease by discouraging the mistresses of rich patrons from having intercourse with lesser men.[32] The Greeks were conscious of some forms of venereal disease and Hippocrates, Galen, and other ancient authorities wrote at length about gonorrhea.[33] Often there was considerable confusion about how the disease was transmitted, and contagion was sometimes traced to air, to food, to breast feeding, to sleeping with another person, to wearing the same clothing, or eating from the same utensils as an infected person. But there was recognition that sexual intercourse helped contribute to the disease, and various methods including depilation, circumcision, special baths and salves were adopted or used in hopes of preventing infection.

Widespread mythology held that venereal disease in the male could be cured by sleeping with a virgin. In the late medieval period leprosy was also associated with excessive venery. A new type of venereal disease hit at the end of the fifteenth and the beginning of the sixteenth century, the disease we call syphilis, and it seemed more virulent and dangerous.

Syphilis is primarily a venereal disease spread from person to person by sexual intercourse although it technically (but rarely) can also be acquired by sharing a drinking vessel or by infection through a wound. The disease does not appear immediately upon infection but only after a ten- to ninety-day period of incubation. The first sign of the disease is a chancre usually on the genitals (hence its early association with intercourse), although chancres can also appear on other areas of the body where mucous tissue is found. As the disease exists today, the chancre is not particularly painful and will eventually disappear of its own accord within three to eight weeks, leaving only a slight scar to indicate where it had been. Soon after it disappears, usually from four to eight weeks later, the second stage of syphilis appears, and this is a more generalized reaction to the infection. Though the symptoms vary slightly from patient to patient there is likely to be a skin rash, sores in the mouth, a mild sporadic fever and headache, a sore throat, and ulcers or lesions that appear on the legs and other parts of the body. This second phase also eventually disappears, after which the disease enters a latent phase, although occasionally the symptoms of the second phase will reappear again. During the early latent phase the patient is highly infectious for about two years, after which the danger of infection declines. This late latent phase may last for several years, but if the patient does not die of other causes eventually the third stage of syphilis makes its appearance. This can take several forms. Often a lesion called a gumma appears, and it can be anywhere on the skin, in the bones, or in vital organs such as the heart. Blood vessels are weakened, allowing rupture of the supply to the heart or brain. The nervous system can be attacked, causing paralysis and insanity. Though there was no proof of the third stage of syphilis until the nineteenth century, people in the sixteenth century were concerned about the first and second stages of the disease because of its severity. Syphilis can also be transmitted from parent to child, and if the disease is in the active stage the mother will usually abort after the fourth month. If the disease is in a latent stage in the mother, the child will likely be born with a congenital case of syphilis, which could eventually result in deafness, blindness, insanity, or any of the other ills associated with the disease.

Because syphilis was in such a virulent form in the sixteenth century, it was a widespread topic of discussion, and both medical and nonmedical writers made copious references to it. The humanist Desiderius Erasmus looked on syphilis as a particularly horrible and terrible disease.[34] Since the disease seemed so horrible, and yet so new, many writers speculated about its origin, which the German humanist Ulrich von Hutten dated at 1493.[35] The Spanish writer Ruy Diaz de Isla agreed with the dating and claimed that it had been brought back to Europe from the New World by Columbus.[36] Whether syphilis is a "new disease" or whether it was an old one imported into Europe has long been the subject of debate. Barrels of ink and considerable emotion have been expended on the controversy, and only in recent years has the earlier emotionalism been replaced by hard evidence. There is still much speculation as to its origin.[37]

According to most accounts, the disease first broke out among the troops of the French King Charles VIII, who invaded Italy with a motley army of French, Italians, Swiss, and Germans, accompanied by camp followers. After capturing Naples, Charles was forced to withdraw because of illness among his troops. As he withdrew, his army spread the disease across Italy and France until it reached Lyons, where the army itself disbanded. Individual soldiers then carried the disease to their various residences in Europe. By the summer of 1495 the disease had made its appearance in Germany, and Emperor Maximilian condemned the "evil pocks" as caused by blasphemy. Both the French and the Swiss recorded its ravages in that same year. By 1496 it had reached Holland, England, and Greece, and in 1499 it was reported in Hungary and Russia. Some countries apparently escaped immediate infection. Though syphilis had reached Canton, China, in 1505, it was not reported in Japan until 1569. Iceland was free of the disease until 1753, and the Faeroe Islands until 1845.[38]

The physician Ruy Diaz de Isla was not the only one to attribute the origin of syphilis to the Americas; there were two other Spanish writers of the early sixteenth century, Bartolomé de Las Casas and Gonzalo Fernández de Oviedo y Valdés, who made that claim. Las Casas was in Seville in 1493, when Columbus came to that city; his father and uncle sailed with Columbus in 1493; and, superficially at least, his knowledge seems firsthand. Oviedo, who was fourteen when Columbus made his first voyage, but who nevertheless knew Columbus, was on hand to report events in Italy when the epidemic broke out in Naples. He later wrote:

> Many times in Italy I laughed, hearing the Italians speak of the French disease, and the French call it the disease of Naples; and in truth both would have had the name better, if they called it the disease of the Indies.[39]

Las Casas reported that he had asked the Indians with whom he came in contact in the Americas after 1502 if they knew the disease, and he

reported that they did, although he said the disease was much less dangerous to the Indian than to the Spaniards.[40] The difficulty with their testimony is of course that they were not physicians, and it is not always clear
how accurate their observations were. The physician Ruy Diaz de la Isla
did not write about the New World origins of the disease until 1539, at
which time he recalled that he had been witness to the arrival of the
disease in 1493,[41] and his recollections are suspect.

The French eventually became highly upset that the disease was called
the French sickness, and tried to call it the Neapolitan disease as Oviedo
reported. In spite of this the Italians and English persisted in calling it the
French disease or French pox, although other names such as the "great
pox" were also used. Compared to it, the other pox was a smallpox. Each
group tried to disassociate itself from the disease. The Turks called it the
Christian disease, the Chinese knew it as the Portuguese disease, and it
has also been called the German, American, Spanish, Syrian, Egyptian,
and English disease, as well as by hundreds of nonnational names.[42] The
name *syphilis* was first given to the pox by Giolamo Fracastoro (or
Fracastorius) of Verona (1484-1553), physician, poet, physicist, geologist,
and astrologist, who published a poem entitled *Syphilis sive Morbus
Gallicus* in 1530. The poem recounted how a dreadful drought afflicted
the island of Haiti, killing animals as well as their masters. A shepherd,
named Syphilis, who felt that the drought was a cruel punishment by the
sun god, Sirius, switched his allegiance to King Alcithous, an early mortal.
Alcithous, intoxicated by this sudden worship, decreed that the gods could
have the heavens, but that he was king of the earth. In retaliation for this
impiety, Sirius sent a new scourge to the earth, and Syphilis was its first
victim because he was the first to impugn the gods.[43] The term did not
come into popular use until the end of the eighteenth century.

Fracastoro also published a scholarly study of contagious diseases in
1546, *De Contagione et Contagiosis Morbus*. This included a discussion of
the "French disease," which was often transmitted by sexual intercourse.
Fracastoro, however, was not willing to attribute the origin of the disease
to America, and stated that it had existed in Europe before America was
known.[44] In fact, when the matter is examined in detail, the supporting
evidence for the New World origin of the disease can be challenged.
Probably the reason for the wide acceptance of the disease's origin in the
Americas was that guaiacum, a decoction of a West Indian wood, temporarily became widely popular as a cure for the disease. Since it was
assumed that God would not have allowed the cure for the disease to be
located in a place different from the one the disease itself was found, and
the cure came from the West Indies, by this kind of logic the disease itself
must have originated there.[45] Though there are accounts of syphilis being

present in America in the late fifteenth and early sixteenth centuries, all such accounts were written after the disease had made its appearance in Europe. The earliest dating of the disease is found in the biography of Columbus by his son, Ferdinand, the original of which is lost, and which has survived only in an Italian translation. This has caused some historians to doubt the reference. But even accepting it as accurate, all that Ferdinand states is that when his father arrived in Española on his 1498 voyage he found that some of the people he had left behind were dead, and the others were sick with the French sickness. This does not prove the disease came from the West Indies; the group may have brought it with them.[46]

Ferdinand also included an account of the cosmogony of the Arawak Indians based on the writings of a "Fray Ramon," which tells how their great folk hero had had great pleasure with a woman but then had to take to the bathhouse to wash himself because he was full of sores from the French sickness.[47] This, along with the writings of Las Casas, Oviedo y Valdés, and Diaz de Isla, is the chief source for the New World origins of the disease. For a time, discoveries of pre-Columbian skeletal remains showing syphilitic bone lesions reinforced that idea. This is no longer sufficient. Recent studies seem to indicate that the bone evidence is doubtful for at least two reasons: the confusion by early investigators of syphilis with leprosy, yaws, and bejel; and the difficulty of dating many clearly syphilitic bones to a pre-Columbian period.

The Columbian theory still has merit but there are strong alternatives. One theory holds that syphilis originated in Africa, and was introduced into Spain and Portugal by slaves brought from Black Africa, beginning in 1442 with the expeditions of Prince Henry of Portugal. Since the sale of these black captives served to finance other expeditions, syphilis and slaves spread throughout Spain and Portugal. The Spanish themselves shipped the disease to the New World either by carrying it themselves or, after 1502, by shipping black slaves. The assumption behind such an argument is the fact that yaws, an African disease, is bacteriologically indistinguishable from syphilis. It differs only in that it is chiefly transmitted by nonvenereal contact. Normally yaws is restricted to hot climates, and to accept this version of origin it is necessary to assume that the spirochete found refuge in the mucous membranes, where it became a venereal infection. If in fact yaws and syphilis are manifestations of the same disease, then the theory has some validity.[48]

A variant of the Africa theory of origin would put the introduction of syphilis much earlier; according to it, syphilis traveled from Africa through ancient Egypt, Arabia, Greece, and Rome, and in those times was confused with leprosy. One of the arguments for this is the fact that as leprosy disappeared from Europe or at least from European medical literature, syphilis took its place; both these diseases caused skin eruptions. The difficulty with this version of the disease is that syphilis also often affects the bones, and there is as yet no evidence of syphilitic disease in bones earlier than the fifteenth century. Moreover, the Europeans of the time felt they were observing a new disease.

Some recent investigators have adopted the view that syphilis is really the same as the nonvenereal illnesses called yaws in the tropics, bejel in the Middle East, pinta in Central America, irkinja in Australia, and so forth. The leading exponent of this view has been E. H. Hudson. His research has shown that all of these diseases are caused by a spirochete *Treponema,* all of which are identical under the electron microscope, are detectable by the Wasserman and other tests, and can be treated with antibiotics. The antibiotics created within the body of the host by one treponema serve to immobilize the others, and immunity to one seems to confer immunity to others. Though the symptoms of the disease are similar, neither yaws nor pinta involves the heart, brain, or other organs as does third-stage syphilis. The only way the treponemas can be distinguished from one another at present is by the symptoms they induce in laboratory animals. These are slightly different for each disease, but also vary from animal to animal.[49] Hudson would explain this by the fact that in the tropics it is a skin disease transmitted from child to child, whereas in northern climates it is a disease of adults transmitted by sexual contact or contact through mucous membranes, since the spirochete could not otherwise survive in the colder north. There is also nonvenereal syphilis that exists in certain areas.

Most experts are at present withholding judgment about the origins of syphilis. Obviously our current means of distinguishing among organisms is still not discriminating enough. For example, both cowpox and smallpox appear to be nearly identical under the microscope, and immunity to one is immunity to both (the whole basis of vaccination), but they are not the same disease. If the unitarian theory of Hudson and others does prove out, then it becomes necessary to explain the apparent sudden outbreak of syphilis. It could be argued, for example, that better sanitation and isolation (brought about by the fear of leprosy) would have eliminated the less adaptable treponemas, leaving only a venereal strain. This seems doubtful if only because sanitation was not that well developed. There is also the possibility that the treponemas living in the bodies of Europeans suddenly mutated, producing a new and deadly version of an old disease. It is also possible that the bringing together of strains of the African and Latin American treponemas gave birth to more deadly forms. In the latter case, we still end up with a New World connection.

Regardless of origins, syphilis hit Europe hard in the sixteenth century although its ferocity began to let up by the end of that same century. Jean Astruc in the eighteenth century, on the basis of sixteenth-century writings, broke down its appearance into several stages, stages that are important for any study of prostitution. The first stage he set from 1494 to 1516, when patients reported small genital ulcers followed by widespread rashes, and then gummy tumors and sores on the body, palate, uvula, jaw, and tonsils, agonizing pains in muscles and nerves, and often an early death. From 1516 to 1526 two new symptoms were added: bone inflammation and hard genital pustules resembling warts or corns. In the period between 1526 and 1540 there was a general abatement of the malignancy, the number of pustules tended to decrease and there was more recording of gummatous tumors. Inflamed swelling of the lymph gland in the groin became common as did loss of hair and teeth, although this might have been caused by mercury poisoning, since mercury replaced guaiacum as the most effective treatment for dealing with the skin sores. Mercury was rubbed on the body, applied through plasters, and swallowed in pills, in such quantities that the cure might have ended up worse than the disease. From 1540 to 1560 the more spectacular symptoms of the malady diminished to such an extent, in fact, that gonorrhea and syphilis were beginning to be regarded as the same disease. Although there was a continual decline in the deadliness of the disease between 1560 and 1610, reports of one new symptom appeared, namely noise in the ears. During the seventeenth century syphilis was regarded as a dangerous infection but not nearly so dangerous as it had been. By the time Astruc wrote, he was so encouraged by its declining virulence that he looked forward to its dissappearance.[50]

The recognition of the venereal nature of infection, and the fear of the disease, combined with the moral fervor of the various sixteenth-century Reformers, resulted in a reaction against prostitution. In 1536 the Imperial Diet of the Holy Roman Empire issued an edict that prohibited all concubines or other extramarital sex relations such as prostitution.[51] Following this, there was a whole series of imperial police ordinances providing for harsher and harsher punishments.[52] Cities also joined in the fight. An edict of 1530 in Frankfurt am Main provided for a fine of ten gulders for those caught with a prostitute.[53] In London the public houses of ill-fame were closed in 1546, and in Paris in 1560.[54] The Paris edict of 1560, which was not registered until September 1561, prohibited all citizens from lodging and receiving in their houses persons without employment for more than one night, and ordered all brothels closed.

One of the madams, "Mother Cardine" (*mother* being a common euphemism for brothelkeeper), opposed the closing law, and had sufficient money and backing to enter into litigation. The king, however, meant business, and despite the size of her establishment, which occupied a number of houses in the center of a quarter known as the Bourg-l'Abbé, it was closed down in February 1566.[55]

Punishments for prostitutes also became more severe in this period. Especially notorious was the *accabussade,* a type of punishment still practiced in Toulouse as late as the eighteenth century. According to descriptions of the punishment, a woman found guilty of prostitution was led to the town hall where her hands were bound behind her back by the public executioner, a sugarloaf bonnet adorned with feathers was pushed atop her head and a sign fastened on the back of her dress indicating that she was a prostitute. Bedecked in this way, she was marched through the town to the jeering accompaniment of her fellow citizens. When the procession reached the banks of the Garonne River, the executioner and his assistants transported the poor woman to a rock situated in the middle of the river, forced her to undress, then placed her in an iron cage especially made for the purpose. The cage and the prostitute were then dunked three times in the river, remaining under water each time until the woman was nearly but not quite drowned. After the third dunking, the cage was left on the rock where the sodden prostitute was viewed by the passing populace until she was dragged off to an almshouse to spend the rest of her sentence.[56] In Germany during the sixteenth century a prostitute named Helena Louboldin was flogged twice in 1581, had her finger cut off, and then was run out of town.[57] Not only was the prostitute punished, but so were her patrons. Twenty-four burghers who had committed "lewdness and adultery" with the wife of a tanner in one German town were confined to the tower for four weeks on a diet of bread and water. The woman in question, a professional prostitute, had to carry a stone around town as evidence of her adultery, and then was banished in perpetuity.[58] In both northern and southern Europe, brothels tended to disappear at the beginning of the sixteenth century,[59] but the disappearance was only temporary. Once the fear of venereal disease began to pass and the zeal of the Reformers to decline, prostitution went back to its old ways. In some places there never was any change.

This is indicated by the case of Seville, Spain, in the late sixteenth century. Here the brothel quarter, El Compás, was a collection of shacks owned by both the municipality of Seville and various ecclesiastical orders such as hospitals and religious houses. The owners, however, did not operate the brothels but leased their properties to others. The twenty houses owned by the city were rented to the public executioner, and he in turn collected a daily rent from each prostitute and selected the persons who were to act as brothelkeepers. Most of the brothelkeepers were men, but occasionally a woman is mentioned. Both men and women brothelkeepers had to take an oath before the town clerk to uphold the statutes of the brothel, and the position was one of some status and responsibility. All women who wanted to work as prostitutes had to be approved by the city. To do so, they had to prove that they were commoners of more than twelve years of age, had lost their virginity, were orphans of unknown parents or had been abandoned by their parents, and were in good health (this required a certificate from the brothel physician). Municipal officials were to try to dissuade candidates from becoming prostitutes, but failing this, they were empowered to issue documentation allowing entry to the brothel. Those women who attempted to practice independently on their own were expelled from the city. Many prostitutes were married, and their husbands were listed as living in the district. Some women are known to have served for twenty or more years. As prostitutes they were not permitted to wear hats, gloves, slippers or mantles, but only half-mantles (like modern-day mantillas), for which reason they were called the "ladies of the half-mantle." Throughout the sixteenth century municipal authorities stipulated that these mantles be yellow, as they had been in the Middle Ages, and it was not until the seventeenth century that they finally approved what had been the garb of prostitutes for many years—the short black mantle. This dress had to be worn by the public women at all times they were in public, except in church, when they were allowed to wear their "mantles long like respectable women." On Sundays and feast days the brothel was to be closed and the prostitutes were required to attend church, escorted there by the constable of the brothel. True to the medieval tradition there were periodic attempts to convert them, and occasionally a particular brothel was closed in order that the Jesuits might carry their message of redemption directly into the brothel. Those prostitutes who did repent of their life took refuge in the convent of Dulcísimo Nombre de Jesus, which had been founded for ex-prostitutes. Though figures on prostitution are notoriously unreliable, in 1601 it was estimated that there were some three thousand prostitutes in Seville, and undoubtedly many of them were out on the street and not in the brothels. In fact many of the streetwalkers were ex-brothel prostitutes who had been expelled from the brothel because of ill health. There were also other younger women who walked the street, working out of cheap rooming houses, although probably most operated in the section of the city just outside the walls designated for brothels.[60]

Though many other cities abolished the special statutes, clothing, streets, quarters, and even insignia of the prostitutes, others did not. Since the panicky fear of venereal disease had passed, many localities went back to regulated prostitution. In some areas, however, the illegal status of prostitution made it more difficult for the authorities to regulate; it also enabled people with the right connections to avenge themselves on unfaithful mistresses or tyrannize the lesser women of the streets by threatening to denounce them as prostitutes. When prostitutes were outlawed, personal mistresses became popular among the upper classes, and virgins were sought since they would be free of venereal disease. Once ensconced as a mistress, a woman found that her problems did not disappear. An amatory master could trade or sell her to others even though she was not technically classed a prostitute.

Though some of the reformers thought they saw a general improvement of morals during the sixteenth century, and there were undoubtedly real differences in the treatment of prostitutes from one area to another, prostitution continued to exist on a fairly large scale. But hard evidence for improvement of morals is difficult to come by. One investigator reported that the small German city of Dinkelsbühl was much improved in the period 1534-1545 when the reformers were in control, since only five illegitimate children were baptized during this period, a much lower rate than before.[61] Such statistics, however, are misleading since they do not indicate how many hasty marriages there were, how many pregnant women left town, or the incidence of similar factors. Probably organized prostitution declined in the sixteenth century in many parts of Europe, particularly in Protestant ones, but unorganized prostitution continued to function. Ultimately, however, organized prostitution was seen by many people concerned with venereal disease as a way of dealing more effectively with this problem.

A tolerant attitude toward prostitution is found in the writings of Michel de Montaigne (1533-1592), the French essayist, who was a skeptic in the midst of religious wars and who functioned as an intermediary between Protestant and Catholic factions. In his *Essay Upon Some Verses of Virgil*, Montaigne writes that as an old man he found himself inveighing against temperance just as once as a young man he was against sensuality. He believed one of the reasons women turned to prostitution was that women in general were treated so inconsiderately by men. Even though women were far more capable and ardent in the sexual act than men, male society censured them if they expressed such desires. The whole idea of exclusively female chastity was ridiculous, and even more ridiculous was the lack of contact most women had with men. He commiserated with Hiero's wife, who had failed to realize that her husband had a stinking breath because she believed that all men must have had such a breath. So under the control of men were women that some were deliberately prostituted by their husbands. Other women prostituted themselves for the love of a husband, to save his life, or to provide for him. Some women had to prostitute themselves to provide for their own necessities.

For these reasons, a woman categorized as being of loose behavior might be of "purer will and better reformed, than another who frameth herself to a precise appearance."[62] Women, in Montaigne's mind, were sexual creatures just as men were and should be accepted as such. He reserved his pity for those men who, by buying the body of a woman, were satisfied. For him a body without a soul, or without feeling, was a horrible idea, yet the will of a whore could never be for sale. Women were individuals, and as long as men regarded them as commodities, they were achieving only a fragment of the realm of love. Montaigne asserted that this was all that most men wanted, and that therefore prostitution would continue to exist regardless of the fears of disease or injunctions by moral reformers.

9 KINGS AND COMMONERS

Lord Acton, the distinguished English historian (1834-1902) claimed that "power tends to corrupt; absolute power corrupts absolutely."[1] That Acton had sexual examples in mind is doubtful, but the royal monarchs of the seventeenth and eighteenth centuries established sexual examples of that famous dictum. This was nowhere more true than in the France of Louis XV (1715-1774), although England under Charles II (1660-1685) was a strong second.

The new sexual mores of royalty were at least in part a reaction against the religious fervor of the sixteenth century. As arguments over doctrine sank into the background and fear of eternal damnation receded, people became more concerned with living in the here and now instead of worrying about the next world. Obviously sex was very much a part of this world. There were of course other influences on their behavior. In a period of royal absolutism fawning courtiers could gain, or believed they could gain, a near stranglehold on the person of their monarch if they catered to his every sexual whim. There was also an element of conspicuous consumption: what a king could do so could his courtiers, and it became almost pro forma for every striving noble to have a mistress in order to maintain his position in society. From the time of Louis XIV (1643-1715) what France and her king did was adopted throughout Europe, and the French kings' indulgence set the pace. If the French king had a mistress, then the king of Prussia must have one, and so must every other petty prince.

The French rise to dominance in this area started with the house of Bourbon, a line established on the French throne by Henry IV (1589-1610). Henry had succeeded to the throne after the War of the Three Henrys in which various factions, religious and otherwise, struggled for control. In order to secure his victory, Henry, a leader of the Protestant faction, converted to Catholicism because, as he allegedly said, "Paris vaut bien une Messe [is well worth a mass]." Henry's attitudes toward sex set the tone for his successors: During his lifetime he had some fifty-six mistresses, three of whom had been nuns. The most famous of his royal bedmates was Gabrielle d'Estrées, whom Henry had first met while staying at the castle of her parents in 1590. Gabrielle's father, anxious to save his daughter from a royal entanglement, married her off to Nicholas d'Amervals, but despite the marriage she soon became the king's mistress, living with him from December 1592, until her death in April 1599. For her services to the king she became the Marchioness of Monceaux, Duchess of Beaufort, and Duchess of Étampes, as well as the forerunner of a long line of more or less official mistresses.

Gabrielle's death was a blow to Henry, but he was assisted in his recovery by several other women. A month after the birth of the future Louis XIII in 1601, another of Henry's mistresses, the Marquise de Verneuil, also gave birth to a son. In the years that followed, the birth of the king's natural children either alternated or coincided with those of his legitimate offspring. When the young Louis was a boy of seven his father introduced his then-current mistress to him by saying that "this charming lady has just given me a son—he will be your brother."[2] This remark greatly upset the young prince, and perhaps helped turn him against women in his later adult life. Instead Louis XIII had a series of male companions but he also had a mistress, Madame d'Hautefort, for a time. Generally he ignored his wife, Anne of Austria, and he never had an "official" mistress.

Louis XIV, who succeeded to the throne as a four-year-old in 1643, had the longest reign in French history. Louis was dutifully married to his cousin, Marie Thérèse of Austria, the mother of his legitimate children, but the chief female influences at court were the mistresses who dominated the king—if that was possible. Louise de la Vallière was the official mistress from 1664 to 1670; she was then ousted from the royal bed by Madame Athénaïs de Montespan, the wife of a marquis, who nine years later was supplanted by Madame de Maintenon. Madame de Maintenon was the most successful of all the royal mistresses, since she became queen in 1684. It was perhaps because Louis was growing old that Madame de Maintenon was so successful, but whatever the cause, after her appearance on the scene, the king grew increasingly religious and moralistic, almost a model of moral rectitude, although there were brief interludes with such women as Marie Angélique d'Escoraille de Roussile, Duchesse de Fontanges, who became his mistress in 1679.[3]

Though Louis XIV settled into an increasing monogamous old age, his brother monarch across the channel, Charles II (1660-1685), king of England, seemed intent on wiping out the last vestiges of Puritan morality in England. Charles, whose father, Charles I, had lost his head during the

Puritan uprising, returned to England in 1660 following the death of Cromwell and soon became the master in a new age of English mistresses. Charles was well suited for his task and had started on his mistress hunting career long before he returned to England. The first of his many mistresses in England was Barbara Palmer, née Villiers, who for her services saw her husband, Roger Palmer, given the title of Earl of Castlemaine and Baron of Limerick, and then for her continued loyalty, she in her own right became the Baroness Nonsuch, Countess of Southampton, and the Duchess of Cleveland. It is as the Duchess of Cleveland that she is usually remembered.

Barbara had been Charles's mistress before he married Catherine of Braganza, and his proud new wife at first refused to recognize her extracurricular rival. Eventually, however, the queen became friendly with Barbara, so friendly that she was influential in the conversion of Barbara to Catholicism, a move that many Protestants thought threatened England's future. Barbara did not confine her attentions to the king and her husband; she had other lovers besides, and there is some doubt whether her first child, Anne, was fathered by her husband, by the king, or by Philip Stanhope. Among her other bedmates, both before and during her reign as royal mistress, were Henry Jermyn, a courtier, Charles Hart, an actor, Jacob Hall, a rope dancer, and John Churchill, afterwards Duke of Marlborough, and the sire of a distinguished line of Churchills. Despite her promiscuity, Barbara retained her hold on the king until 1674; she then moved to Paris and did not return to England until shortly before the king's death. She herself died in 1709 but not until she had seen all her sons created nobles and two of her daughters married into nobility. The third daughter, also named Barbara, entered a convent in France, although she was not the most chaste of nuns since she was the mother of at least one illegitimate child.

Another of Charles's mistresses, Louise de Kéroualle, had been presented to him by advisers of Louis XIV in an attempt to improve Anglo-French relations. The gift from the French court worked hard to carry out her tasks, first by coyly refusing the royal advances, thereby further inflaming the aging Charles II, and eventually by giving in at an opportune time. For her efforts on the royal behalf she was made Baroness Petersfield, Countess of Fareham, and Duchess of Portsmouth. She also encouraged the king's Catholicism, attempting to make certain that on his deathbed he did not die without confession and absolution. After Charles's death she retired to France where she lived out the rest of her life. When the English confiscated some of her estates, the French kings awarded her a pension for her patriotic services on behalf of France. Her son, born in 1672, was the first to bear the title of Duke of Richmond.

The most famous and most popular with the public of Charles's many mistresses was Nell Gwyn. Her story is the rise from bawdy house to royal bedchamber and indicates the rewards possible for a girl who could play her cards right. Nell Gwyn, born in February 1650, was the daughter of a Madam Gwyn, an enormously fat woman who smoked and drank to excess, and who was probably the operator of a brothel when Nell was born. Nell's father was a yeoman about whom we know very little, even his first name. Her elder sister, Rose Gwyn, was probably a professional prostitute, and it was through her effort that Nell was able to make some of the connections that launched her career. Nell, as a thirteen-year-old, began work as a servant girl in a sort of bawdy house, a cellar café furnished with a few plain tables, candles, some stools, and the necessary glasses and liquors. Close by were rooms where the waitresses could supplement their income. Customers ranged from nobility to tradesmen, from law students to king's companions. Her sister, who was then mistress to a shareholder in one of the Covent Garden theaters, utilized her influence to get Nell a job as an orange girl; that is, she was allowed to sell oranges, lemons, fruits, and sweets to theater audiences.

Once in the theater, Nell soon gravitated to the stage since it was at this period that actresses first began to appear. Previously female roles had been enacted by men, although all theater had been banned temporarily under the Puritans. By her ability as a comedienne, as well as by granting sexual favors to the right people, Nell managed to rise in the theater. In the process she acquired a valuable wardrobe, and learned how to wear fashionable clothes, both important in giving her social mobility. Equally important was her ability to attract the right man at the right time. She was mistress to a succession of important men; one of her actor-manager-bedmates traded her to Lord Brockhurst, and Nell, having reached the nobility, temporarily quit the stage. The affair proved of short duration, and Nell returned to the stage. She was then picked up by the Duke of Buckingham, not for his own purposes, but as an entry to Charles. Charles, like many other royal lovers of this period, rarely bothered to select his own bedmates. Instead he left the task to his court favorites, who used this method to ingratiate themselves. Along with Nell, Buckingham and his assistants selected another actress, Moll Davis, in an effort to interest the king, and in the first round of competition Nell lost out. Rumor has it that she was nosed out of the frontrunning position because she asked for cash on the line instead of waiting for royal favors to be bestowed on her. But though Nell did not get a full-time job as companion to the king, he was sufficiently impressed with her to invite her back for other visits. Once invited back, Nell made up for lost time, and shortly was set up in her own house by the king. From then on, Nell regarded herself as the king's whore, for as she often stated, even though she had been brought up in a bawdy house, she was only one man's whore at a time. It is this frankness coupled with her wit that has made Nell Gwyn one of the most-written-about women of the past.

Charles had a succession of mistresses, and he provided well for them and their offspring. Though lacking legitimate children of his own, he had numerous illegitimate ones. Not all the king's bedmates received the position that Louise de Keroualle or Barbara Palmer or Nell Gwyn did. Many served the king only for one night, and it was the duty of William Chiffinch, Keeper of the Privy Closet and Page of the Bedchamber, to supply the king when he needed a temporary diversion. Many of the temporary visitors came by boat from London and docked just below the king's bedchamber, which overlooked the river. For two years Nell herself had traveled down the river for an occasional visit, although more frequently than most of the other night visitors. Her determination to succeed was such that she came to be accepted by the inner throng of mistresses. She presented Charles with two sons, Charles, who was made Earl of Buford and later Duke of St. Albans, and James, who died before he reached maturity.

As Charles grew older, and still lacked a legitimate heir, it seemed increasingly likely that his brother, James, would succeed him. James, however, was an open and avowed Catholic, not just a secret one like Charles. Fearful that a strong Catholic king would restore his religion to England, the Protestants became worried; as the worry increased so did Nell's popularity among the London masses since she was one of the few Protestant mistresses at court. Many felt that if the king's growing Catholicism could be curtailed, Nell was the woman to do it. She came to be identified as a symbol of Protestant womanhood, courted, fawned on, and flattered in song, prose, and verse. Aphra Behn, dramatist, feminist, and devoted Protestant, dedicated her play, *The Feigned Courtesan,* to Nell in 1679, saying that when Nell speaks,

> Men crowd to listen with that awful reverence as to holy oracles or divine prophecies, and bear away the precious words to tell at home.[4]

In 1681 when Nell's carriage was mistaken by a London mob for that of one of the Catholic mistresses, the townspeople surrounded it and threatened to overturn it. With the mob all around, Nell stuck her head out the window and allegedly shouted, "Pray good people, be civil, I am the Protestant whore." Immediately the mobs cheered her, blessed her, and allowed her to pass. Nell, however, did not long survive after the death of her royal lover. She died in 1687, loved, if not respected, by a great portion of the English people.[5]

With the death of Charles II, the English court returned to a less flamboyant display of mistresses, although each succeeding English king continued to maintain at least one mistress until George III acceded to the throne in 1760. Under George I (1714-1727) the king's mistresses were extremely influential since the king, who prior to his accession to the throne had been elector of Hanover, hardly spoke any English and few of his English advisers spoke German. Communication was carried out through his mistresses, the most influential of whom was Ehrengarde Melusina, Duchess of Kendal. She had become his mistress about 1690 when he was elector of Hanover and managed, in spite of her lack of beauty, to hold his affection even when challenged by Charlotte Sophia, later Countess of Darlington; she also made a fortune by selling titles and public offices. Mistresses had to be careful, however, not to overplay their hands. Even queens had only limited power. George I, for example, had divorced his wife in 1694 for alleged infidelity and then had kept her prisoner for the remaining thirty-two years of her life. George II (1727-1760) was much more devoted to his wife than his father had been to his mother, but he usually also maintained a mistress as well. Few of his mistresses, however, received much financial reward from their service to the king. It was not until the reign of George IV in the nineteenth century that the mistress again reached a position of social respectability in England. But if the English kings became somewhat less ostentatious in their display of royal mistresses, the French monarch Louis XV set an impressive record.

Louis XV had succeeded to the throne of France in 1715 as a five-year-old on the death of his great-grandfather, Louis XIV. The young king never developed the strong personality characteristics of his forebear, and in fact showed little interest in state affairs. His chief occupation was hunting; next to hunting came his interest in beautiful women. His wife, the queen Maria Leczinka, daughter of the exiled king of Poland, after giving birth to several children, denied the king access to her bedchamber. When this first happened, the distraught king allegedly called in his valet and told him to go and find a woman—any woman—and bring her to his bedroom forthwith. Within a few minutes the dutiful valet had returned with a young woman who so satisfied the king that Louis forgot his wife's rebuff. For her temporary services, the young woman was given a favorable marriage settlement and soon disappeared from court. The king's advisers, however, certain that the king would require future feminine companions, attempted to find a mistress they could control, one who would confine her activities to the boudoir and leave matters of state to them. Their search eventually centered on Louise Julia de Mailly, née Nesle, a lady-in-waiting to the queen. The lady proved willing; the problem was to interest the king.

The Duc de Richelieu, Louis Armand du Plessis, one of the king's advisers, told the king that a man with his heavy responsibilities needed the constant solace of a loving woman. The young king quickly agreed that a devoted feminine companion might be helpful since the queen would have little to do with him, but indicated that he did not know where to find such a companion. The duke then proposed his preselected candidate, and a meeting was arranged. For some reason the affair did not come off, and Mme de Mailly lost her first opportunity to grace the royal bed. Anxious about their failure, the advisers caucused again only to find that though their choice had been the correct one their approach had been much too refined. For the second meeting, instead of presenting a demure young noblewoman making her curtsies before the king, their candidate was made to lie on a couch with her head resting on her arms, her dress arranged so that her leg was exposed to the thigh, and her bodice undone. Louis hesitated to enter the room when he first saw her, but his valet, who was involved in the scheme, pushed the young man into the open arms of the reclining lady. Nature took its course, and when the good lady appeared shortly afterwards with her dress in great disarray, she reportedly raised her skirts before the assembled conspirators, showed her legs, and said: "Just look what this rake has made of me."

The queen soon heard of this affair, and though she had regarded the appearance of a mistress as inevitable, she was upset that one of her own ladies-in-waiting had become the royal prostitute. The queen vented her anger on Mme de Mailly, making her life so unhappy that she attempted to resign her position. Louis, however, took the side of his mistress with the result that relations between the king and queen became extremely formal. The king found it best to absent himself from Versailles to carry out his assignations. He purchased the Château de Choisy for Mme Mailly and spent most of his time with her. His new mistress soon found that it was no easy matter to keep the king amused. Other than his hunting and his womanizing he seemed to be utterly bored with his life. She encouraged him to take up various hobbies, including the making of snuffboxes, but on the days when he could not hunt he was almost unbearable. Whether by accident or plan, she introduced the king to her younger sister, Mme de Vintimille. Also a married womn, de Vintimille's marital status did not prevent her from quickly supplanting her older sister in the king's affections. The Comtesse de Vintimille de Luc was a dominating woman, very different from her sister, and within a few weeks the king was clearly under her influence. The romance was tumultuous but short-lived since within a year the Comtesse died from the aftereffects of childbirth.

After grieving for a few short months, the king again turned to the

Nesle family; this time he chose Marie-Anne de Mailly de Nesle, Marquise de la Tournelle, a still younger sister of the Comtesse de Mailly. Madame de la Tournelle, a recent widow, tantalized the king by deliberately refusing his amorous requests. After withholding her services for a suitable period, she gave in on conditions that few mistresses before or since have achieved. She asked for full recognition of her position as chief mistress, the title of duchess, the legitimacy of her children, free access to the king's private purse, and the dismissal of her older sister, who was still a member of the court. The king complied and fell almost totally under her control. Her fall came not from any failure on her part but because the king became seriously ill and the Bishop of Soissons refused to administer the final sacraments until she was officially dismissed. Louis, fearful of dying without benefit of sacraments, dismissed her. But as soon as the king recovered he recalled the Duchess of Châteauroux, now her title, to active duty. Before she could return, however, she died, and the king was desolate.

The Nesle family had benefited greatly by the activity of its women. Three of the five daughters of Louis de Mailly, the Marquis of Nesle, had been regular mistresses of the king and a fourth, the Duchess of Lauragais, had been an occasional mistress. One sister never yielded, perhaps because her husband had publicly stated that any slur on his honor would be settled in "royal" blood. For serving the king so well, the Marquis de Nesle had all his debts paid and received a handsome sum from the king's privy purse as well. Having prostitute daughters had its advantages.

Louis's grief over the loss of his most recent mistress was eased by Jeanne-Antoinette d'Etoiles, née Poisson, a twenty-four-year-old beauty whom he met at a masked ball given in honor of his son's marriage. By the time she had attracted the king, Jeanne-Antoinette had already been married to Charles Guillaume la Normant d'Etoiles but conscious of the king's interest, and ambitious for advancement, she took advantage of the situation. She had her husband conveniently sent on business while she stayed with the king, demanding the position of chief mistress before she would consent to sleep with him. Even though she came from a bourgeois family, an unheard-of breach in royal etiquette, she won her case; when her husband returned, he was gently taken aside and told that he had to yield his wife to the sovereign. The new mistress was given the title of the Marquise de Pompadour, and it is as Madame de Pompadour that she is known in history.

Quite early in her career as royal mistress Madame de Pompadour realized that in order to maintain her position she had to keep the king continually distracted, not only by thinking of new ways to satisfy his physical desires but also by nourishing his mind as well. One of her lasting contributions to French culture was her patronage of the arts.

Pompadour also attempted to consolidate her position by easing the tensions between the king and queen, and eventually she was successful in bringing about a more cordial relationship between the two; she herself became a close friend of the queen. A fringe benefit to any royal mistress was her ability to help her family, and Madame Pompadour saw to it that her brother received a royal appointment and her father an estate. Her father, however, a rather blunt-spoken individual, spoke of himself as the "father of the king's whore."

Fully cognizant that her success lay in keeping the king happy, Madame de Pompadour soon found, as did her predecessors, that the king's attention was very short-lived. To revive his interest, she began to import other women to satisfy his needs. Acting as a sort of royal procuress she brought in Louise O'Murphy, the Marquise de Coislin, as well as others, still managing to remain the king's confidante and trusted adviser, and an extremely powerful figure. As the king became satiated, stronger measures were needed. To accommodate the king's growing taste for young girls, and to supply a constant variety, a house was purchased in the Deer Park (Parc aux Cerfs) district of Versailles. As royal houses went, it was a modest one, capable of housing only two or three girls at one time. The girls were procured by Lebel, the *valet de chambre,* under supervision of Madame Pompadour, and the house was run by Mme Bertrand, a reliable middle-aged woman, who was known as the "Mother Superior." Each girl, while resident in the house, had her own private room, a maidservant, and a footman, but she was never allowed to go out unchaperoned. The young women lived a rather secluded boring life, but to pass the time they were taught singing, dancing, and painting. When they attended the theater a special box was reserved for them. They were never officially told that their lover was the king, but rather were encouraged to believe that he was a Polish nobleman, a relative of the queen, who held a high position at court. To believe otherwise was dangerous. One of the girls who accidentally revealed the true identity of her lover was committed to a madhouse. Even though the inmates never officially knew the identity of their master, the rest of the court was familiar with what was taking place. As each girl ceased to attract the king, she was given jewels, a present of a few thousand louis, then married off to a willing man. Those who had given birth to royal bastards had their babies taken from them and had them sent to some accommodating foster mother. Those girls who interested the king beyond an occasional visit were taken from the Deer Park and given special houses by the king. One of the women in this second category overplayed her hand with the king, and her fate shows how tenuous the status of most of these women was. Mlle de Romans had given birth to a child whom the king accepted as his own, but once she antagonized him, he ordered her house searched and all documents relating to his paternity removed.

The extent of the king's activities are difficult to document, although it is known that at least six royal bastards were born in the early 1760s, all while Madame de Pompadour was officially unchallenged as the reigning mistress and Maria was still queen. When Madame de Pompadour died in 1764, there was a wide-scale hunt for a suitable successor, but it was not until 1768 that the new full-time mistress appeared. The position was filled by Jeanne, Comtesse du Barry, the daughter of a woman innkeeper and an unknown father. She had been brought to Paris as a child by her mother who had been engaged as a housekeeper by one of the leading prostitutes of Paris. Later her mother married a clerk who was wealthy enough to allow young Jeanne to be educated at a convent. After she left the convent, it is not clear as to how she lived. There are rumors that she went to work for the famous Mme de la Gourdan, one of the leading procuresses of Paris, although detailed evidence is lacking and contemporary memoirs are contradictory. It is clear, however, that she did have some contacts in the demi-monde, and in 1763, at the age of twenty, became the mistress of the Comte du Barry. M. du Barry was not a nobleman, but had adopted a title to further his own interests; he was accustomed to selecting young women who would benefit from his tutelage: teaching them the essentials of good grooming, and then selling them to the highest bidder. When he heard that the king's advisers were hunting for a royal mistress, he put forward Jeanne as a candidate, and carefully arranged the presentation to the king.

Jeanne was introduced to the king as the wife of M. du Barry's younger brother, and the well-tutored Jeanne so impressed the king that she was invited to stay on at Versailles. In fact the king was so much taken with her youth, her high spirits, and her charm, that by the time his advisers found out about her actual background, she had ingratiated herself in his favors enough to be accepted without question. Nevertheless to consolidate her position, and give her a more acceptable background, she was formally married to the younger brother of the Comte, a birth certificate was produced (thus removing any question about her legitimacy), and a fortune in diamonds bestowed upon her. After an official presentation at court on April 22, 1769, she became the king's official mistress. The Deer Park was abandoned as a diversion perhaps because Louis was growing older and Jeanne proved enough of a distraction for him. At any rate the king increasingly spent his time at the Petit Trianon, a small château where he could relax from the rigid court etiquette. To show his love for his new mistress the king lavished all sorts of presents on her, and she held her position until Louis died in 1774 after fifty-nine years of misrule. He said on his deathbed, "I have governed and administered badly, because I have little talent and I have been badly advised." His inheritance was autocracy, his reign a disgrace, his legacy a revolution.[6]

When Louis's grandson and successor, Louis XVI, attempted to continue to rule France in the old way, absolutism met its death. Within a few years the French Revolution swept Europe, toppling many of the old regimes. Before that happened most other kings had attempted to imitate the French example, but none achieved quite the level of Louis XV of France or Charles II of England. Augustus the Strong, king of Poland and elector of Saxony, who died in 1733, was a notorious womanizer. Though he left only one legitimate son, Frederick Augustus, he left more than a hundred illegitimate children, the most famous of whom was Maurice of Saxony, who became Marshal-General of France and is usually called Marshal Saxe. Philip III of Spain (1598-1621) was the father of 322 illegitimate children, and though his successor Philip IV (1621-1665) invoked a brief period of rigid moral restrictions on court life, this was soon abandoned and would-be mistresses flocked to the court. Even ecclesiastical dignitaries were caught up in the fever.

The French Cardinal Richelieu allegedly offered Anne de Ninon de Lenclos 150,000 livres to become his mistress. She declined on the grounds that such a sum was too much from a lover and too little from one she did not love. The list could go on to include most of the powerful and near-powerful figures of seventeenth- and eighteenth-century Europe. The woman who could attract a royal courtier or powerful man with her beauty or charm, acquiring polish and sophistication somehow, could go far in spite of her humble origins.

Prostitution at other levels of society, however, was not so luminous. In France, for example, though prostitution remained technically illegal, officials cognizant of the ineffectiveness of their ordinances and perhaps not unmindful of the royal model, modified the laws in 1684. The modification distinguished between the professional prostitute and the poor girls or minors who had no other way to earn a livelihood. Further modifications were made in the French law in 1713, by which promiscuous women were separated into two legal categories: professional prostitutes and those who led dissolute lives without being professional. The police remained free to move against any professional prostitute, but for the woman who was not so classified officials could only act against her when a formal complaint was made charging her with affronting public decency. Professional prostitutes could be condemned on the slightest evidence, sentenced to exile, imprisonment, whipping, or having their heads shaved. Those not so classified had all the privileges of other accused persons and their sentences were subject to appeal.[7] The distinction became a matter of police interpretation.

Only a few were classed as prostitutes even though the police themselves licensed brothels. Usually the police classed a woman as a prostitute only when some powerful and responsible person complained, and the penalties, after a lapse of a few years, became less and less severe. Still there was always the opportunity for blackmail. The most famous, most notorious and most publicized Parisian brothel of the period was the House of Madame Gourdan on the Rue des Deux Portes. The center of this brothel was the "seraglio," a great salon where the prostitutes were posed in the positions they would take to satisfy the visitors' whims. The brothel was not only an established house, but a recruiting and training center. Girls fresh from the country were sent to the "piscine," a bath-house of a sort, where they were bathed, powdered, and perfumed; they then entered the "Cabinet de Toilette," where they were taught the arts of their profession and then eventually elevated into official employees.

Madame Gourdan obviously ran a house catering to wealthy and powerful clients. She took care to see that they were well satisfied. A description of her recruiting methods comes from the pen of Pidansat de Mairobert, who wrote a rather scandalous book about Madame du Barry after the death of Louis XV in 1774. Though the book purports to quote Madame Gourdan herself, it is probably a complete invention. Nevertheless it portrays the way that a successful madam operated. According to Mairobert, Madame Gourdan after hearing of the arrival of a wonderfully beautiful shopgirl at the Maison Labille hurried to verify the report. When she saw the future Madame du Barry she could scarcely contain her excitement and quickly paid her a few louis d'or to undress.

I saw her naked as she was born! I drew closer. I saw a ravishing body, a throat . . . well, my hands have caressed a good many throats in their time, but never one of this elasticity, of this shape, of this irresistible softness. The plunge of her breasts threw me into an ecstasy; her dazzling white thighs, her delicious little buttocks—the Sculptors themselves have never produced anything more perfect. As for the rest, I was connoisseur enough to realize that the *pucelage* [maidenhead] was in a very equivocal condition to say the least of it, but with the application of certain astringents it might be sold a few more times![8]

To enable respectable clients (including women and clerics) to visit her house there was a secret passage that led to the brothel from a merchant's home on a different street. The brothel included devices designed to stimulate sexual appetites, including pornographic statues and pictures, amulets and salves, a peep room where voyeurs could watch couples engaged in intercourse, and even a chamber of horrors for those who liked to beat others or be beaten while engaging in intercourse.[9]

Madame Gourdan also maintained a private country house where she sent her sick and pregnant employees, but which also served as a secluded trysting place for her more favored customers. Ironically this country house was known as the "convent" by the peasants who lived in its vicinity. There were several other madams, then known as "bordel mothers," *matrone* or *mèreabbesse,* who achieved fame during the period. One was Anna Fillon, active in the first part of the eighteenth century, who became known as the *presidente* (lady president) because someone had once mistaken her for the real President Fillon of Alençon, who was in Paris on a short visit. Because of this accident, the term *presidente* became synonymous with Madame Anna, who in her later years married a count and closed her life as a respectable lady, although she did not acquire the fortune that Madame Gourdan did.

Another famous procuress was the woman known as Madame Paris, who was at the height of her fame in the 1740s and 1750s. Her establishment was at first located in the Rue de Bagneaux, which greatly upset the parish priest of the area. He complained to the police officers about the brothel, but they refused to intervene since the brothel operated under their protection. The priest then complained to his ecclesiastic superior, who passed the complaint on to higher government quarters, but nothing was done. Even the Bishop of Paris was powerless, and was told by the police that he had no reason to complain since the house was so well ordered that he could visit there himself.[10] Eventually, however, Madame Paris decided in July 1750 to move to the Faubourg Saint-Honoré, where she maintained the notorious Hôtel du Roule. Here the prostitutes sat around a central waiting room dressed in light provocative clothes, playing, singing, and chatting, waiting to receive their clients. The price for an overnight stay was twelve francs, twice what it was to have supper with a girl.[11] Eventually, however, Madame Paris ran afoul of the law. She was charged in 1752 with impairing the morals of a twelve-year-old girl who had been seduced for the purpose of prostitution.

Madame Paris's position was assumed by a new proprietress, a Mlle Dupuis, also known as Montigny. She had been seduced at an early age by an officer who had taken her to Paris only to desert her later. Before becoming a madam, she had in turn been the mistress of a physician, a banker, a musketeer, and an abbé. The center of the brothel was a large reception seraglio, where some fifty girls were separated into groups, each group wearing a different colored set of ribbons and accessories. The price of each girl was posted in order that the customers could avoid haggling over price. Mlle Dupuis also ended her career afoul of the law.

She expended much of her profits on a lover, who deserted her after the police had moved in, and she spent most of the remaining savings to avoid being charged as a common prostitute. She never recovered from the trauma, and shortly after gaining her freedom she was found dead in a gutter on a dark street.[12]

There were also special brothels. One brothel catered to clergymen, others had special rooms so that these gentlemen would run less risk of discovery of their extraclerical activities. Another brothel specialized in Black prostitutes. Still another specialized in virgins, although the virginity of most of the employees was probably fictitious. One brothel claimed that its women were recruited only from the upper classes.[13] In order to attract customers many of the less well-known brothels posted squads of men at busy intersections where, under the pretext of advertising washer-women, dressmakers, and other female services, they recruited for the various brothels and gave a concise summary of the specialties and inmates of the house.[14] Some brothels published directories, and one such directory gave names, addresses, and comments on 108 girls. Many of the individual descriptions went into great detail; others, such as the one on Rosine, were short and to the point: "She has 'crabs.'"[15] Individual prostitutes also passed out cards such as the one given by a certain Mlle Adelaide of Palais Royal, No. 88, which said:

> If for pleasure you're out,
> You'll find me always about.[16]

Our knowledge of the brothel of eighteenth-century Paris is based primarily on the weekly reports that the madams were required to submit to the police. Prostitution could not have existed without police sanction, and they kept very detailed accounts in order to maintain their share of income. One madam, Babet Desmaret, the proprietress of a house on the Rue du Faubourg-St. Honoré, carefully recorded the name of every client, the name of the girl he chose, and the length of time spent in the brothel. Other brothelkeepers were not quite so detailed, but the researcher who has the patience can find out how many customers visited each brothel every day.[17]

Not all the prostitutes were to be found in the brothels. Though the streetwalker was in somewhat more danger of arrest than the brothel inmates, there were still hundreds of women willing to sell their services. The most famous and most frequented center of assignation was the Palais Royal originally built for Cardinal Richelieu. It has been estimated that in the eighteenth century no less than fifteen hundred prostitutes gathered there each day. The many galleries, shops, restaurants, and theaters made it a natural haunt for men and women on the prowl. An eighteenth-century German visitor, Friedrich Schulz, made a distinction between five classes of prostitutes operating in the Palais Royal, two "respectable" and three "common." The better types described themselves as young widows and promenaded through the streets and galleries. Below them were the various workers in the stalls. In the more fashionable shops groups of young girls, scantily dressed, sat on great piles of fine silk and cloth, knitting, watching the passersby, waiting for customers of either goods or services.[18] Next to the Palais Royal were the great boulevards, the Tuileries, the promenades of Longchamp, and the theaters. Many of the nearby coffeehouses had part-time prostitutes who would take interested customers to nearby rooms reserved for such purposes. One well-known restaurant had some twenty small and tastefully decorated compartments reserved for private get-togethers of this sort. The lowest type of prostitute was found outside the limits of the city proper working at the roadside inns, waiting to serve any chance passerby.[19]

Casanova described the Palais Royal as a

> rather fine garden, walks lined with big trees, fountains, high houses all round the garden, a great many men and women walking about, benches here and there forming shops for the sale of newspapers, perfumes, tooth-picks, and other trifles. I see a quantity of chairs for hire at the rate of one sou, men reading the newspaper under the shade of the trees, girls and men breakfasting either alone or in company, waiters who were rapidly going up and down a narrow staircase hidden under the foliage.[20]

One of the needs of such large-scale prostitution was a steady supply of girls. Many were sold into prostitution by their parents. A Paris police investigator, François Guillotte, for example, obtained a contract with the parents of a seventeen-year-old girl that might be regarded as typical.

> We, the undersigned, François Ricard and his wife, Perrine Ricard, born Boette, faithfully assure M. François Jacques Gillotte, that we will make no trouble about any children that he may have by our seventeen-year-old daughter, Marie Ann Ricard, and agree that he may have intercourse with her as if she were his own wife, provided that he pay us the agreed sum of 300 livres in advance, and that he may acknowledge any children he may have by our daughter. Mutually agreed in Paris on May 13, 1729.

After encouraging the parents to sign such a contract, the policeman had them arrested but they were only in prison a short time before they were released.[21] Usually the police only intervened when it was to their advantage to do so or when under pressure. Abbé Prévost's famous novel,

Manon Lescaut (1731), tells the story of Manon, a girl who preferred luxury to faithful love, was arrested for prostitution at the behest of powerful enemies of her lover, the Chevalier des Grieux, and was deported to the French territory in America.[22]

Usually, however, the police were more interested in deriving revenue from prostitutes than punishing them. Some inspectors, a M. Berryer, for instance, in their attempts to keep a careful watch on the prostitutes, found it necessary to frequent the brothels as patrons, justifying their action on the grounds that it was only as customers that they could tell what was going on. Others, such as M. de Sartine, who became a police prefect in 1759, were said to have "Prohibited everything so hat everything would be permitted,"[23] but of course at a price. The police perhaps were only reflecting the ideals of Louis XV, who set an example difficult to ignore. Casanova, no moralist himself, expressed astonishment at the lax manners and morals of Parisians on his first visit there. As an illustration, Casanova reported that after being introduced to a Mlle Le Fel, a popular actress, he remarked that the three children around her certainly did not look like one another. The young woman replied that the reason for the difference was that the eldest boy was the son of a duke, the second the son of a count, and the third the son of still another man. Casanova apologized to the woman for mistaking her as their mother. Mlle Le Fel replied: "You were not mistaken, I am their mother." Casanova added:

> I was a novice in Paris, and I had not been accustomed to see women encroach upon the privilege which men generally enjoy. Yet Mademoiselle Le Fel was not a bold-faced woman; she was even rather lady-like, but she was what is called above prejudices. If I had known the manners of the time better, I should have been aware that such things were every-day occurrences, and that the noblemen who thus sprinkled their progeny everywhere were in the habit of leaving their children in the hands of their mothers, who were well paid. The more fruitful, therefore, these ladies were, the greater was their income.[24]

Whether more effectively to control prostitution or better to grease the hands of the police, French officials in 1778 passed still another law prohibiting public women from plying the street, squares, wharves, and boulevards of Paris, and which also prohibited any boardinghouse keeper from allowing men and women to sleep together unless they could show a marriage contract. That the law was designed more for harassment than control seems evident from the fact that the ordinance neglected to say anything about brothels per se, and in fact the police still continued to license brothels. About the only effect of the ordinance was to cut out the competition of the streetwalkers, although not for long.[25]

In England prostitution was almost as widespread as it was in France, and London could have given Paris a run for its money. Prostitutes plied their trade at public shows and feasts, churches, plays, parks, wherever there was likely to be a crowd. One English writer reported that during the May Day festivities only a third of the maidens who took part in them returned home virgins. One of the most famous houses in London in the seventeenth century was the one run by Mother Creswell, which was well described by Richard Head in *The English Rogue*. According to Head, Mother Creswell kept only the best of utensils to serve her guests, tried to maintain a certain modesty of manner in her harlots, and in general maintained an air of refinement. When customers entered her premises she served them special wines, meats, and other delicacies before attempting to find out what their needs might be. After they had imbibed, she chatted with her guests, selected one of her girls to visit and talk with each of them, but gave each of her customers the opportunity to accept or reject the girl. If the first girl was rejected, she retired gracefully and another girl was sent in. When the customer was satisfied, the two retired discreetly to a bedroom. As Head so quaintly put it:

> Withdrawing into another room, to heighten my thoughts, she declared to me her birth and education; that as the one was well extracted, the other had occasioned much cost and expense; that for her part, she associated with none but persons of quality, whose long patience and entreatments first procured a familiarity, and in fine, freedom in the exercise of love-affairs; and so would have (seemingly) put me off upon this score, that it was not usual for her to admit any to her embraces but such whose long aquaintance had gained her affection. I offered her a crown, which she refused with indignation; telling me, that she was not yet reduced to so low a condition as to become so poor a mercenary prostitute. At last, with much persuasion, I fastened on her a half piece; and so striving with her (she only seeming averse), I accomplished my ends.[26]

Descriptions of the more sordid conditions of brothels are not as common as their ubiquity might indicate. Robert Burton, in his *Anatomy of Melancholy* written in 1621, stated that bawds were everywhere and so common and so full of tricks and subtleties, and so many nurses, old women, panders, letter carriers, beggars, physicians, friars, and confessors were associated with them, that it was beyond his ability to describe.[27] Thomas Heywood, a contemporary of Burton, put the subject in a slightly different way by stating that he would not trouble his readers with accounts of prostitution for in these "corrupt days" almost every boy of fifteen or sixteen years knew more from his own experience about harlotry than he could illustrate in his writings.[28]

Though there was often a feeling that the prostitutes were more to be pitied than condemned, only occasionally do we get a condemnation of the role that the male played in prostitution—this in spite of the fact that lower-class women were considered fair game for young gentlemen, even though the women might not go willingly. Some attempt to deal with this involuntary prostitution was made during Queen Elizabeth's time by legislation that stipulated that no laundress or waitress could enter a gentleman's chamber in a public inn unless the woman was past forty years of age; that under no conditions could any other maidservant go into a gentleman's room; and that those gentlemen found in compromising positions were punished instead of the women they were found with.[29] Like most such legislation dealing with prostitution, however, it was only rarely enforced since males did the enforcing.

One of the new "professions" open to prostitutes in the seventeenth century was the stage, although the wandering entertainer had long been associated with prostitution. In fact, the very term *harlot* originally meant wandering person of either sex, although by the sixteenth century it was increasingly applied to a prostitute or strumpet. Because of the association of the stage and prostitution a special prologue had to be written for Desdemona in *Othello* when on December 8, 1660, the role was played for the first time by a woman on the English stage.

> 'Tis possible a virtuous woman may
> Abhor all sorts of looseness, and yet play:
> Play on the stage—where all eyes are upon her:
> Shall we count that a crime France counts as an honour?
> In other kingdoms husbands safely trust 'em'
> The difference lies only in the custom.[30]

Despite the proclamation of the possible virtue of the actresses, the quickest way to a royal bed, or to the title of duchess for a commoner, was the theater stage. Not all actresses acquired a title, but all had the opportunity to demonstrate their wares before the public. Though the common prostitute could be whipped and expelled from London, and even the brothel had to post sureties for good behavior,[31] the stage proved a new way of circumventing the law.

Though brothels were common in London, the prostitute might set up in her own house. In a Restoration play titled *The Whores Rhetorick* (published in 1683), Mother Creswell herself is made to advise a young would-be prostitute to get her own house in order best to avoid the rules imposed by the larger houses. To avoid being labeled a prostitute, however, she was to hire an old bawd to nose out customers, and then draw them to her mistress, for which service she was to be paid a proportion of the proceeds.[32] Such an operation, however, was costly and only the richest and most successful could operate thus.

Prostitution in general was a popular subject with writers, with many works bordering of pornography. *The London Bawd* carried such articles as "How a Citizen Went to a Bawdy-House for a Whore, and the Bawd Helpt Him to His Own Wife,"[33] and another surveyed *The Prostitutes of Quality or Adultery à la mode.*[34]

Some were written with tongue in cheek, and were a severe condemnation of the social conditions of the time. The Reverend Martin Madan, for example, wrote a short pamphlet titled "An Account of the Triumphant Death of F. S. A Converted Prostitute Who Died April 1763, aged 26." This told the story of a girl who was reduced to want in spite of her genteel education. To support herself she turned to the stage, then needlework, and finally prostitution at which she did very well. The woman then repented, became a farm worker, lost her job when the season was over, was reduced to beggary, became ill, and soon died.[35] By implication Madan seemed to be saying that prostitution was one of the few ways that a woman on her own could support herself, and that society rather than the prostitute was to blame.

To advertise the abilities of various prostitutes, directories were published, some of which are still extant. A *List of the Sporting Ladies,* dating from about 1770, is full of double entendres as are many other later lists.

> Miss Rattletrap, from Pall-Mall, London, is calculated for first rates; the rider must be very careful of her, as she starts at full speed. Price 15s. Bank notes taken, if good, but objects to paper currency in general. May be heard of at the Bagnio, Catch-all Lane.

or

> Miss D.G. . . .Y intends visiting the Races as usual; she is a strapping wench, and from her experience and high training, is possessed with every charm to render an Amour with her delightful. Her figure is handsome, has good eyes, and a melodious voice; is well legg'd and her dress decent. May be spoken with in the Fisher Row. She allows gin and peppermint in the room, and includes all charges at 10s 6d.

or

> Marston Nance of long standing in this town, has been some time in the country for her health, but is returned, for the races only, in prime order; she requires to be used gently, as she is very irritable; and having lately taken fresh instructions in the *pugilistic art,* from the celebrated B . . . k and B . . . r, at Friske, will be apt to treat her customers

roughly—Gets drunk and is quarrelsome in the evening. Price 2s 6d. May be met with after dark in St. Clement's.[36]

A more complete list of London prostitutes was known as *Harris' List of Covent-Garden Ladies,* which was more a book than a list and apparently was published almost yearly.

Miss B--rn, No. 18, Old Compton Street, Soho.

"Close in arms she languishingly lies,
With dying looks, short breath, and wishing eyes."

This accomplished nymph has just attained her eighteenth year, and fraught with every perfection, enters a volunteer in the field of Venus. She plays on the pianoforte, sings, dances, and is mistress of every Manoeuvre in the amorous contest that can enhance the coming pleasure; is of the middle stature, fine auburn hair, dark eyes, and very inviting countenance, which ever seems to beam delight and love. In bed she is all the heart can wish, or eye admire, every limb is symmetry, every action under cover truly amorous; her price is two pounds two.

A perusal of the list indicates some of the reasons for women becoming prostitutes. For example, a Miss H-rd-ye of No. 45, Newman Street, "borrows her names from her late keeper, who is now gone to the India's and left her to seek support on the wide common of independence." Some were quite young. Miss L-v-r, No. 17 Ogle Street, Queen Anne-street East is described as a young "nymph of fifteen." Many others were in their teens.[37]

Prostitutes were ubiquitous, and such writers as Samuel Pepys and William Hickey give accounts of their adventures. So did James Boswell, who reported in 1762 that he had vowed not to have anything to do with whores because he was concerned about his health, but unable to satisfy himself any other way he picked up a girl in the Strand. He went with her "with intention to enjoy her in armour," i.e., a linen prophylactic sheath, but since she had none with her he just "toyed with her."

She wondered at my size, and said if I ever took a girl's maidenhead, I would make her sqyaek. I gave her a shilling, and had command enough of myself to go without touching her. I afterwards trembled at the danger I had escaped. I resolved to wait cheerfully til I got some safe girl or was liked by some woman of fashion.[38]

Boswell, however, remained troubled and reported on December 14 that he had been in London for several weeks without ever enjoying the delightful sex, although he was surrounded by all kinds of good-hearted ladies "from the splendid Madam at fifty guineas a night, down to the civil nymph with white-thread stockings who tramps along the Strand and will resign her engaging person to your honour for a pint of wine and a shilling." Boswell, however, was unhappy that he lacked the money for the higher-class prostitute and was fearful of the diseases carried by the common prostitute.[39] Eventually Boswell found an actress by the name of Louisa to whom he was attracted. She, however, demanded 50 pounds and Boswell, unable to pay it, began courting her in an effort to get her to lower her price. Louisa, for her part, was accustomed to dealing with men like Boswell and managed to borrow two guineas (42 shillings) from him. She delayed going to bed with him for a month, when Boswell proudly reported that "five times was I fairly lost in supreme rapture. Louisa was madly fond of me; she declared I was a prodigy, and asked me if this was not extraordinary for human nature." Boswell reported that ten times might be extraordinary, but this was not, although in "my own mind I was somewhat proud of my performance."[40]

Boswell was even more proud that he had only paid eighteen shillings for his recreation. He had intercourse with her a couple of more times during the next week but began to lose interest, particularly on January 20 when he found that he had an infection in the "members" of his body "sacred" to Cupid.

> What! thought I, can this beautiful, this sensible, and this agreeable woman be so sadly defiled? Can corruption lodge beneath so fair a form? Can she who professed delicacy of sentiment and sincere regard for me, use me so very basely and so very cruelly . . . [41]

After being treated by a surgeon, he went to Louisa's to confront her with her infection. Louisa confessed that some three years earlier she had had a venereal infection but stated that she had not been bothered for fifteen months. She, moreover, said that she had not been with a man other than Boswell for some six months. Boswell, not certain that Louisa had given him the disease, left. But later, after he became convinced that she had, he asked her to return his loan of two guineas, since the surgeon had charged him five guineas for the cure. Louisa, after some delay, and after Boswell threatened to denounce her, did so.[42] Here again the laws were used to harass the prostitute.

More sympathetic pictures of the prostitute were given in some of the fictional accounts of the time. Daniel Defoe's *Moll Flanders,* published in 1722, for example, had a prostitute for a heroine. And though the story is fiction, Moll's life might be regarded as fairly typical of the many girls who turned to prostitution during the eighteenth century. Moll's mother was transported away to the New World as a felon when Moll was eighteen months old, leaving the infant girl without family or friends to care for her. Befriended by a band of gypsies who later deserted her, she became a ward of the local parish. At fourteen she was taken into the service of a kindly woman who treated her as one of her daughters; the eldest son, however, did not regard Moll as a sister; he became her lover and she his mistress. This type of encounter incidentally was apparently Boswell's initiation into sex as well, according to his journal entry of 25 November 1762. Moll, however, fared somewhat better than Boswell's servant, since she managed to marry a younger son of the family she served. After he died, Moll passed through a whole series of adventures indicated in the original caption of the work: *The Fortunes and Misfortunes of the Famous Moll Flanders, Who was Born in Newgate, and during a Life of Threescore Years, besides her Childhood, was Twelve Years a Whore, five Times a Wife (whereof once to her own Brother), Twelve Years a Thief, Eight Years a Transported Felon in Virginia, at last grew Rich, liv'd Honest, and dy'd a Penitent. Written from her own Memorandums.*[43]

Moll was a whore, even though she found the word *whore* "harsh" and "unmusical." Another of Defoe's heroines, Roxana of *Roxana, or the Fortunate Mistress,* could be classified as a courtesan, that is, she moved at higher levels of society, had good manners, was well dressed, and was both more seductive and more insincere than the forthright Moll. Roxana, like Moll, lost her virtue at an early age, but she was more successful in selling herself to the rich and renowned. She reasoned that since nature had given her a beautiful body as well as agreeable features, both of which aroused the male, there was no reason why she shouldn't make use of them to her own best advantage once she found it necessary to prostitute herself.[44]

A far more detailed description of the life of a prostitute than either *Moll Flanders* or *Roxana* can be found in the novel *Fanny Hill* by John Cleland, first published in 1748. Though widely circulated at the time, *Fanny Hill,* unlike the novels of Defoe, was regarded as pornographic in the nineteenth and twentieth centuries and until recently circulated only underground. Fanny's tale of woe is realistic enough. She was the daughter of very poor parents, in a small village near Liverpool, who died of smallpox when she was only fifteen. She was induced to move to London by a scheming friend who deserted her when they reached the city. Left on her own, Fanny applied for employment at the home of a Mrs. Brown who, unknown to her, was the operator of a bordello. Her first initiation into the trade was a lesbian experience. She was then sold to a lecherous merchant, but he failed to seduce her. She soon lost her maidenhead to someone else, entered another brothel, this time willingly, managed to inherit a large fortune by giving assistance to an old man, married a handsome young man, and became a great lady. The story differs from *Moll Flanders* or similar novels in its rather explicit but also chaste descriptions of the sexual act. Fanny is a whore, but she enjoys her work and eventually achieves a station worthy of her talents. Cleland hints at the ugliness and squalor of prostitution, but never really delved into it.[45]

Still another view of prostitution is given by Samuel Richardson, best known for his novel *Pamela; or Virtue Rewarded,* published in 1740. Both Pamela and Clarissa, the heroine of his novel *Clarissa* (published in 1748), are the opposite of Fanny in that they are virtuous girls who attempt to delay their submission until marriage. In *Clarissa* Richardson has a passage about prostitutes gathered around the bed of a dying sister. He describes them as having just risen from their nocturnal work beds, their faces streaked with paint, their skins wrinkled, their hair streaked; they were slipshod, stockingless, from a "blooming nineteen or twenty" to haggard well-worn strumpets of thirty-eight or forty.[46] Some women might find prostitution attractive after reading Cleland but not after reading Richardson. The virginal Clarissa, raped by her lover in a brothel, wastes away and dies. If the choice is between the virtuous but ravished Clarissa and the fun-loving Fanny Hill, it is obvious which is the more attractive life.

Prostitution in the eighteenth century was simply a fact of life, accepted as a necessity. Jean Jacques Rousseau, on his stay in Venice in 1741, for example, wrote that he had always disliked common prostitutes but in Venice there "was nothing else within my reach."[47] In the course of a dinner-table conversation with some of his male friends, Rousseau's period of enforced abstinence was noted, which the group set out to remedy immediately by going to the home of one of the distinguished courtesans of the city.

> The *padrona,* to whose house we went, was good-looking, even handsome, but her beauty was not of the kind that pleases me. Domenico left me with her. I sent for *sorbetti,* asked her to sing to me, and, at the end of half an hour, I put a ducat on the table, and prepared to go. But she was so singularly scrupulous, that she refused to take it without having earned it, and, with equally singular foolishness, I satisfied her scuples. I returned to the palace, feeling so convinced that I had caught some complaint, the first thing I did was to send for the physician and asked him to give me some medicine.[48]

Rousseau, however, was not infected, and there were two other sexual adventures in Venice. Dining on a boat in the harbor he was entertained by a prostitute who was "flattered by the price men put upon her favours." Attracted to her, Rousseau made an appointment.

> I entered the room of a courtesan as if it had been the sanctuary of love and beauty; in her person I thought I beheld its divinity. I should never have believed that, without respect and esteem, I could have experienced the emotions with which she inspired me. No sooner had I recognized, in the preliminary familiarities, the value of her charms and caresses than, for fear of losing the fruit of them in advance, I was anxious to make haste to pluck it.[49]

Before he could reach a climax, however, Rousseau noticed that the woman had only one nipple, and he became so obsessed with this physical defect that he left the bed. She advised him to "Give up the ladies, and study mathematics [Lascia le donne, et studia la matematica]." Still he yearned for her, but she refused to meet with him again. Finally in order to satisfy his needs, he and his friend, Carrio, purchased a little girl of between eleven and twelve years from her mother. Rousseau reported that he was content to simply chat and innocently play with the child and that he engaged a singing master for her in order to give her a means of livelihood when he left. Rousseau also reported that he was convinced that if he had remained in Venice he would have been a preserver of her virtue rather than a corrupter of her innocence since he felt to have had intercourse with her would have been like incest.[50] We have to accept Rousseau's word for it, but when it is possible for a man, any man, to purchase a young girl to do with as he will at very "modest" cost, then it becomes obvious why prostitution was so widespread. Women had little control over their own affairs, and in a man's world the only thing women had to advance themselves was their sex. The problem of the eighteenth century becomes a question, not of why some women became prostitutes, but rather of how some managed to avoid it.

Widespread prostitution in the eighteenth century coexisted with a rise in illegitimacy, and the two are undoubtedly interrelated. Demographic research of the past few decades has tended to show, as much as it can be shown, that the rate began to increase most notably in 1750 and continued its upward ascent until 1850, when it began to decline.[51] Though the increase might in part be due to more effective record keeping, most demographers would argue that there was an actual increase. Several explanations have been advanced to account for this, and these explanations also help account for the increase in prostitution. One explanation quite obviously is a change in sexual mores.[52] The kings and their mistresses are merely one example.

For illegitimacy to increase, the change need not be that radical. It might well be that instead of marrying, a couple would enter into an informal style of marriage, cohabitation if you will, but the children of such relationships would be regarded as illegitimate, even though the parents regarded themselves as married and might eventually become formally married. There is some evidence for this style of relationship in the eighteenth century, and it should be noted that the increase in the illegitimacy rate seems to be concentrated in women under thirty years of age. Any such change in marriage relationships, however, would imply that the religious impetus for marriage was no longer so strong, and there is other evidence that this was the case.

The increasing social disorganization obviously had an effect on morals, prostitution, and illegitimacy.[53] It was, after all, in the eighteenth century that industrial capitalism made its appearance, and the initial result was great economic deprivation and exploitation. Friedrich Engels (1820–1895) summed up the influence of these factors on sexual mores at the end of the nineteenth century,[54] but many non-Marxists as well as anti-Marxists have also looked to social disorganization as a cause of prostitution, illegitimacy, and family disintegration.[55]

Demographers have also advanced other factors. Edward Shorter, for example, has argued that the European population during the eighteenth and early nineteenth centuries was growing not only larger but younger. This, he postulated, tended to lessen the influence of the elders, and encourage the development of a kind of youthful counterculture. Encouraging this counterculture were rapid changes in the class structure due to the increase in landless laborers, proletariat if you will, in both urban and rural areas, although the change was most noticeable in the urban areas. The increasing urbanization of Europe also weakened traditional family ties and authority figures, and provided increased possibility of sexual experimentation. Also challenging traditional leadership was the growth of centralized government, which spread its tentacles—the bureaucrats, the emissaries of central rule—ever further, and in the process undermined traditional local elites. These structural changes furthered the alienation of the lower classes, which joined the challenge to traditional patterns. The new counterculture, most noticeable in urban areas, exalted the individual over the family, emphasized romantic love, and deemphasized traditional obedience to the communal authorities.[56]

The nexus of illegitimacy and prostitution was perhaps inevitable, although not every mother of an illegitimate child became a prostitute. Any increase in premarital sexual activity will lead to an increase in illegitimacy in an almost predetermined pattern. Estimates indicated that a woman engaging in sexual intercourse on a fairly regular basis is likely to find herself pregnant once in every thirty acts or so of intercourse or three times in every hundred. Since the rate of intercourse declines for males as they grow older, the appearance of greater numbers of promiscuous young men would in itself increase illegitimacy. It would also increase prostitution since in the eighteenth century there was often a male-heavy sex ratio in the rapidly increasing urban areas where prostitution was generally the accepted sexual outlet. Moreover, the fear of venereal disease, which earlier had reinforced traditional moral prohibitions against promiscuity and prostitution, was not the inhibiting factor it had been as the horrors of the disease seemed to diminish.

Reformers and moralists, intuitively aware of the increase in promiscuity, illegitimacy, and prostitution, wrestled with solutions. Usually they thought in traditional terms of preserving the family, and this to many implied "protecting good women" from the promiscuous male. Prostitution seemed acceptable as the traditional way of avoiding greater evils. One of the more elaborate schemes was put forth in a 1724 pamphlet attributed to Bernard Mandeville, titled *A Modest Defence of Public Stews.* Mandeville, a physician, is best known for "The Fable of the Bees," and the rather biting wit evident in that work is evident in this account as well. Mandeville felt that the greatest evil attached to prostitution was the spread of diseases to innocent spouses and children. The solution to this, and the other evils of promiscuity, was the establishment of public brothels since public whoring was "neither so criminal in itself, nor so detrimental to Society, as private Whoring." Unregulated prostitution, he claimed, had led to an increase in illegitimate births, alienated affections of wives and husbands, tempted people to live beyond their income, debauched married women, warped virtue, and ruined young virgins. These evils, however, were not intrinsic to prostitution, only to the "abuse and ill management" of prostitution. All could be eliminated by legalizing prostitution:

> The mischief a Man does in this Case is entirely to himself; for with respect to the Woman, he does a laudable Action, in furnishing her with means of subsistence, in the only, or at least most innocent way that she is capable of procuring of it.[57]

Mandeville had worked out his plan in great detail. He proposed that a hundred or more houses of prostitutes be set up in London, housing two thousand women, and a proportionate number be established in every city and market town. Each house, holding twenty women, was to have a matron, and was to be associated with an infirmary with at least two physicians and four surgeons in attendance for regular inspections.

Supervising orgnized prostitution would be a body of three commissioners who were to redress the complaints of the women and of their clients. Each house was to have four classes of prostitutes, selected according to beauty or other qualifications, and the price for each group would vary. The first, or lower, class of prostitutes would total eight women and their fee would be half a crown (two and a half shillings); the second class would consist of six women who would charge a crown; the third class of four women were to be paid half a guinea, and the fourth class of two women would be reserved for "persons of dignity" who could offer to pay a guinea. Medical inspection of women would be paid for by a tax on the public brothels. To protect the morals of minors, no children would be admitted into the house. Any prostitute who became pregnant was to be removed in order that her delivery take place in a better environment. If after the delivery the mother elected to return to the brothel, the child was to be sent elsewhere.

Mandeville argued that the adoption of his plan would prevent boys from masturbating, cut down "too frequent" or immoderate enjoyment of intercourse, protect against venereal disease, halt debauching of modest women, and eliminate a host of other evils that he enumerated in great detail.[58] Women for the houses would come from those who were already practicing prostitutes; if the supply became insufficient there would be an increase in private prostitution, and the houses would soon be adequately stocked. He believed also that it would be good to import foreign women into England, which would help keep the English girls more moral, and at the same time satisfy people's curiosity about foreign girls without having to go abroad. He concluded that the public brothels would not "encourage Men to be lewd," but on the contrary encourage them to "exercise their Lewdness in a proper place."[59]

A French work, attributed to Nicolas Edmé Restif de la Bretonne, urged a plan similar to Mandeville's. One of the variations he advocated was that the state prostitutes be examined every day by experienced former prostitutes, and weekly by physicians.[60] Other writers were more original. Martin Madan, mentioned elsewhere in this chapter, urged the adoption of polygamy as an antidote to prostitution. As Madan saw it, polygamy was a big improvement over adultery. Adultery, in fact, he felt to be deserving of capital punishment, whereas polygamy was an expedient in some cases, and in some individuals an absolute necessity to prevent greater sins. Besides, polygamy was only in line with the Biblical injunction that required a man to keep, maintain, and provide for "the women he seduces,"[61] Madan's proposals did not go unanswered,[62] and from the nature of the responding pamphlet literature it appeared that the average English writer much preferred prostitution to polygamy. Some of

Madan's critics argued that polygamy would not solve the problem since a man might well continue to lust after women even though he had several wives. Some questioned how a polygamist was to support his wives. It was felt such a man might encourage them to sally forth in the streets to sell themselves, so that the Madan proposals would add to the problem rather than cure it.[63]

Part of the difficulty with any serious discussion of the problem of prostitution is that those most articulate about the "immorality" of the "lower-class" women belonged to the upper classes. They adhered to a double standard, not only between the sexes but between the classes. Lower-class women were often considered fair game for young gentlemen, even though many of them protested the unwanted attentions thrust upon them. The rich man often kept a mistress for his own pleasure, as well as for the pleasure of his friends, but this was separate and distinct in his mind from the prostitute. Several upper-class London prostitutes such as Fanny Murray, Kitty Fisher, Nancy Parsons, Kitty Kenedy, Grace Dalrymple Eliot, and Gertrude Mahon became more or less famous,[64] patronized by the great and the near great. In the minds of their patrons they did not pose any problem to public morals. A tract by a Father Poussin, said to have been written originally in French and translated into English under the title of *Pretty Doings in a Protestant Nation,* included a sample letter of the kind that various nobles allegedly sent to their mistresses after a drinking bout or when a friend was in need of consolation:

August 23, 1734

Dear Molly

On sight hereof permit the Bearer, to immediately enter a Pair of Holland Sheets with you; let him have Ingress, Egress, Regress to your Person, in such manner as to him shall seem meet, for the space of twenty-four Hours, and no longer, and place it to the Account of

Your Kind and Constant Keeper
Edmund Easy

King's Arms Tavern
Four in the Afternoon

P.S. Child, go through all your Exercises and Evolutions as well for your own as my Credit.[65]

Another of the difficulties reformers had was in finding alternatives to prostitution for the women they wanted to reform. Many showed considerable sympathy with the plight of the prostitute and argued that she was not to be blamed for her condition since she had often become a prostitute after being deceived by a hypocritical man. In the minds of many reformers, once such a woman was able to gain employment or find a husband she would leave prostitution.[66] John Campbell, who wrote under the pseudonym of M. Ludovicus, thought that a Foundling Hospital should be established for young girls and other females.[67] Others advocated the establishment of Magdalen Houses. There, women leaving the field could be afforded means of employment, learning "habit and industry" so that they could make their way in the world without resorting to prostitution.[68]

John Fielding, brother of the novelist Henry Fielding, and with him co-founder of the first police system in London, went into great detail about a plan to rescue prostitutes. John Fielding believed that the basic reason for the high crime rate in England was the existence of large numbers of foundling children. Inevitably boys became thieves from necessity and their sisters "Whores from the Same Cause."[69] In his investigation of London prostitutes, Fielding found that large numbers of them were girls under eighteen, many of them twelve or thirteen. To give the female children without parents some alternative to prostitution, Fielding proposed a "Public Laundry," which would help

> preserve the deserted Girls of the Poor of this Metropolis; and also to reform those Prostitutes whom Necessity has drove into the Streets, and who are willing to return to virtue and obtain an honest livelihood by severe industry.[70]

The laundry, to be established by public subscription, was to be inspected periodically by a board of lady visitors. Fielding wanted his girls to learn as well as work, and part of his plan called for teaching girls under twelve to read, those between twelve and sixteen the housewifely tasks of knitting, cooking, and so forth, and only those over sixteen were to work in the laundry, helping to support themselves until they were married.[71]

Fielding's proposals did not go unchallenged, in part because some were upset by his "charity" toward the prostitute, and in part because he provided for the education of the lower classes. Many social critics of the time were convinced that prostitution stemmed from girls being spoiled by "the false good nature of their superiors." Too many society women gave their servant girls castoff clothing, and this soon led these girls to putting on airs, and it was such pretense that led to prostitution. Even some of the severest critics, however, felt that repentant prostitutes ought to be given asylum, although any prostitute who refused to work was to be beaten or transported to the penal colonies. It was only by a "due mixture of mildness and severity" that England could eliminate the great "enormity" of prostitution that had so long infested the streets.[72]

Saunders Welch also criticized the Fielding plan for ignoring bawdy houses. Moreover the laundry in itself could not attract sufficient backers to be practical. Instead Welch urged the erection of a hospital by public subscription to hold prostitutes until they repented. To encourage donations he provided that every person who subscribed 50 pounds be given the title of governor for life.[73] Jonas Hanway, another critic, felt that Fielding's idea of a laundry was not adequate and instead proposed a factory for manufacturing carpets. He reported that the Turks had already found that carpet weaving was a way to keep the harem women busy, and would work equally well in England. Such a factory would enable the prostitutes to work for

> their benefit, that they may be the farther removed from temptation; and next for our own sake that by their labor they may repay the husbandmen and manufacturer for their food and raiment, and ease the community by supporting themselves by their industry.[74]

Hanway believed that one of the causes of prostitution was the obligation of girls to furnish a dowry when they were married, and since many girls in the lower classes could not afford dowries their only alternative was prostitution. He urged that the English royal family give a number of poor girls dowries whenever an heir to the crown was born.[75] Hanway was especially concerned with those citizens who felt that any steps to alleviate the conditions of the prostitute was against the will of God, since many people believed that vice carried "its own affliction along with it" and that the "order of Providence" should not be counteracted. His clinching argument was that Protestant countries could not lag behind the Catholic countries in Europe, where there were several convents established to reclaim the transgressors.[76]

The difficulty with all these schemes is that they looked on prostitution as a woman's problem, and such a point of view simply made the problem insoluble. Women were human, but they were also property and were clearly subordinate to men. Few women effectively challenged this subordination before the twentieth century. To look on prostitution as a class problem, which it also was, required a radical reorganization of society, which the middle and upper classes refused to contemplate. The truth was that sex was commonly merely a commodity for the male, to be purchased if necessary, to be taken freely if permitted. It was a buyer's market. Casanova, for example, cast aside the expensive Madame Prote in Saint Petersburg, Russia, for Zaire, whom he bought from her father for 100 rubles to do with as he wished.[77]

Women who played their cards right, such as Madame de Pompadour, could acquire fame and fortune, and undoubtedly many young girls adopted these glamorous women as models. In prostitution, however, almost none of the successful courtesans started at the bottom and worked their way up; most of those who started at the bottom remained there. It is not clear, however, that the lower-class prostitute was necessarily worse off than the lower-class wife, nor that the upper-class prostitute was any worse off than the upper-class wife. Prostitution was one of the few ways a woman could make it on her own, and if she had intelligence, sophistication, talent, and the right contacts, she could go far. Most failed because they lacked the contacts. Often the woman's family pulled strings for her to become a mistress to a powerful man, since in such a position she could do much in return. A rough survey of the English nobility reveals that a significant proportion of the nineteenth-century nobility either possessed an ancestor (usually female but sometimes male) who had moved the family up the aristocratic ladder by performing sexual services for royalty, or else the family itself descended illegitimately from royalty.

Probably the principal deterrent to male promiscuity was fear of venereal disease, but this fear was not as powerful in the eighteenth century as it had been earlier or as it was to become later. Since prostitution thus seemed inevitable to most authorities, they turned to regulation and control, thereby curtailing the "dangers" of venereal disease and the "abuses" of prostitution. This "solution" as we will show was highly selective.

10 REGULATION AND THE STATUS QUO

Napoleon Bonaparte once stated that "prostitutes are a necessity. Without them, men would attack respectable women in the streets."[1] In spite of the revolutionary fervor of the last part of the eighteenth century, traditional attitudes toward women and sex remained. Unlike the kings who preceded him, Napoleon did not keep a large number of mistresses but rather preferred brief affairs, and was particularly partial to actresses. Though the Revolution failed to change basic attitudes, it did sweep away many of the laws of the *ancien régime*.

As indicated elsewhere in this study, prostitution in France, though technically illegal, had not been prosecuted with any great fervor by the police, who in fact supervised the brothels of Paris. In 1778 under the pretext of reinforcing ancient laws against prostitution, Lieutenant Lenoir of the Paris police, with the approval of the king, issued a series of regulations that extended this regulated system.[2] Technically the new regulations, among other things, prohibited the renting of rooms to prostitutes. The whole system disappeared, however, in 1791 when all the ancient regulations dealing with prostitution were abolished. In 1795 the Director requested the legislative body to define prostitution and "give judicial proceedings a special form," but nothing came of the request. Failing legislation, Parisian officials began a new Register of Prostitutes in 1796 and employed agents to find and register women. In 1798 two private physicians were given the task of examining the Parisian prostitutes and were to report any cases of infection. In 1802 a dispensary was established. All public prostitutes were required to submit to semiweekly examinations at the facility, but since the operational expenses for the dispensary were left to the physicians themselves to collect, the method did not work out very well. Napoleon included the prostitutes in his Workmen's Guilds, where under the control of the police they were kept as a distinct caste in a prescribed quarter of the city. Under this system the prostitutes themselves had to pay a fee to the police, who then turned it over to the physicians.

All this, however, was a matter of regulation rather than law—*Réglementation* is the technical term. The Napoleonic Code of 1810, for example, did not mention prostitution, and neither for that matter did efforts made in 1811, 1816, 1822, 1848, 1877, and 1895 result in any change. Inevitably the police returned to their old methods of dealing with prostitution, and with only slight modifications continued the system that had been in existence prior to the Revolution. Essentially the system attempted to confine prostitution to licensed houses, although the police ultimately had the power to make exceptions. Control of prostitution in Paris was in the hands of Le Bureau des Moeurs (Morals Bureau), although outside Paris each local administration had its own system. The justification for attempting to confine prostitution to brothels was the assumption that the brothelkeepers, by reason of their investment, would have a property stake in keeping prostitution under control. At first prostitutes who had lived in isolated quarters were ordered to take themselves to brothels, and solicitation on the streets was forbidden. Such a prohibition proved almost impossible to police. There were other difficulties. In 1828, for example, the tax levied on prostitutes for meeting the expenses of the sanitary control was abolished, because so much of the time of the special agents of the Morals Bureau was spent in hunting down prostitutes who were delinquent in their payments. The police felt, too, that requiring registered prostitutes to pay the tax served as a deterrent to voluntary registration and medical inspection.[3]

Even with the abolition of fees, there were problems. Police at first registered any woman as a licensed prostitute who requested such a designation as well as any female they arrested for promiscuity. No inquiries were made as to age, civil status, or antecedents. This approach proved impracticable when it was found that girls of ten who had been arrested for lewdness were classed as prostitutes, and as public pressure mounted the policy was changed. As the nineteenth century progressed the trend was to refuse to register girls under sixteen or to allow boys under eighteen admission to licensed houses. In the long run, however, attempts to confine prostitution to brothels failed, and police were forced to relax their restrictions on non-brothel prostitution. They tried to bring the freelance prostitute in line with the system by requiring each woman to own the furniture of her own apartment and to use designated licensed houses for her assignation, again on the assumption that a property investment would make it more difficult for the prostitute to escape the attention of the police.[4] They were not particularly successful here either.

The most important part of the plan was compulsory medical inspection. A sanitary department associated with the morals bureau was reorganized in 1828. Prostitutes found diseased were sent at first to Saint Lazare Hospital for treatment (later there were others), and when cured, were allowed to resume their occupation. By the middle of the century, inspection took place once a week for prostitutes in licensed brothels and every other week for prostitutes who practiced independently. Though the number of physicians associated with the dispensary varied, the administration was rather elaborate. The Paris dispensary had a chief, an assistant chief, as many as fourteen regular physicians (or surgeons) and ten assistants. Each independent prostitute carried a card with her signed by the medical inspector and stamped with the date, a sort of guarantee of the clean bill of health. Prostitutes had to show these cards to anyone requesting it.[5]

One of the reasons for the growing concern over disease was a realization of the complexities of venereal disease. After the large-scale epidemic of syphilis in the sixteenth century, fears about the disease had begun to decline, only to reappear at the end of the eighteenth century. One reason for this was renewed attention given to the debilitating aspects of venereal disease by military authorities. Gonorrhea, in particular, temporarily incapacitates when the urethra is inflamed, causing extreme pain on urination. The mass mobilization of men in the Napoleonic Wars at the end of the eighteenth and early in the nineteenth centuries spread the contagion throughout Europe and venereal disease again reached epidemic proportions. There was also increased knowledge of venereal disease. Benjamin Bell at the end of the eighteenth century had differentiated between syphilis and gonorrhea. It was not, however, until 1837 that Philippe Ricorde effectively proved that syphilis and gonorrhea were separate diseases, thus ending the confusion perpetuated by the famous John Hunter, who in 1767 had innoculated himself with gonorrhea pus and found himself infected with syphilis as well. Though this was due to the fact that the patient he had taken the gonorrhea pus from was someone who undoubtedly had an unsuspected case of syphilis, Hunter's evidence that both were the same disease was widely accepted. Not all physicians adopted Hunter's ideas, but his influence was such that few dared openly to challenge his conclusions, until Ricord showed otherwise. Ricord also described the characteristic three stages of syphilis, emphasizing the dangers of the third stage.[6] Not all third-stage variations, however, were described by Ricord. Syphilitic aortitis (inflamation and possible rupture of the large artery leading from the heart) was not described until the end of the nineteenth century. Though some forms of mental illness for a long time had been associated with sexual activity, the definite association of tabes dorsalis (degeneration of nerve fibers affecting motion) and paresis (paralysis) with syphilis, were not demonstrated until the end of the nineteenth century by Jean Alfred Fournier, a pupil of Ricord and director of the venereal clinic in the Hospital Saint Louis. Fournier also emphasized the dangers of congenital syphilis.

As the horrors of syphilis began to be emphasized, there was more and more a demand for medical inspection of prostitutes, and medical inspection implied some form of regulation. Often the medical community took the lead in demands for inspection, although there were other factors involved as well. Berlin is a case in point. Berlin had established a system of regulation similar to that of Paris in 1792, although the Prussian king had insisted such regulations not be written into the law. In agreeing to regulation, the king claimed to do so only because prostitution could not

> without impropriety and consequences injurious to morality, be established by the public laws, which must not contain any sanction whatever for prostitution.[7]

The Berlin regulations of 1792 stipulated that no one could open a brothel without first receiving permission from the police, nor could any landlord rent a room to a prostitute without police permission. Prostitutes at large were compelled to live in certain streets and the person who lent them lodgings, by custom elderly women, whether single, widowed, or divorced, had to undertake responsibilities similar to those of the tenants of a licensed house, including responsibility for any crime committed on the premises.

To enforce medical inspection, prostitutes were not only threatened with three months in jail for transmitting venereal disease to a client but had to pay the cost of the client's medical treatment as well. As compensation, the Berlin law also provided penalties for the man who infected a prostitute with venereal disease, and there were also fines to the brothelkeeper involved. Obviously the Prussian authorities were determined to cut down the incidence of venereal disease, but unfortunately the medical science of the day was not up to such rigid standards. It would be difficult if not impossible to tell which client infected a prostitute, and for a client with an active sex life the source of contagion would be equally difficult to trace. Only the most obvious cases could be detected and for this purpose every prostitute was required to be examined weekly by an official surgeon whose salary was paid by taxes imposed on the licensed houses. Since the surgeons of the time as yet knew nothing about aseptic techniques, the inspection probably resulted in greater infection rather than less, with the surgeon spreading the infection. Nonetheless the system became widely imitated.

In some respects the Berlin regulations were much stricter than the Parisian ones since a woman under twenty-four years of age could only be registered as a prostitute if she was a case of "utter depravity." The police alone, however, were the judges of whether a woman qualified for this designation. Clandestine prostitution was punished by three month's imprisonment, followed by confinement in the workhouse until the woman demonstrated a desire or found an opportunity for other employment. Sale of intoxicating liquors, dancing, and games were prohibited in the brothels, in order to prevent them from becoming places of entertainment.

At first houses of prostitution had been deliberately scattered through-out the city although prohibited in the vicinity of churches and schools and on crowded thoroughfares. A considerable number of them had located on a small street known as the Königsmauer, and in 1839 the police decided to concentrate all the city's thirty-three brothels on this street in order to cut down law-enforcement problems. The concentration of the houses soon resulted in the area becoming the center for much of the illegal activity in the city, something that the police had anticipated, but the police had not realized that the high crime rate in the district discouraged many would-be customers. The result was an increase in clandestine prostitution, i.e., prostitution outside the district. Convinced that police regulation of brothels was a failure, the Minister of the Interior ordered all licensed brothels in Berlin to close as of January 1, 1846. This order was not intended to outlaw prostitution but rather to remove the police license; prostitution was still tolerated and a register was maintained of the current state of health of all prostitutes.[8]

Pressure to reopen the brothels then took place, led in part by military authorities who believed brothels a much more satisfactory way of controlling venereal disease than through the freelance practitioner. It was also believed by many that brothel prostitution cut down on illegitimacy, although the figures did not support this. For example, in the two-year period ending in 1841 there were 5,652 illegitimate births in Berlin compared to 34,450 legitimate ones, a ratio of one to seven; in a three-year period when prostitution was confined to Königsmauer, there were 10,175 illegitimate births and 54,696 legitimate ones, a ratio of one to five; in the years 1847–49 when official brothels were closed there were 5,053 illegitimate births and 26,782 legitimate births, or a ratio of one to five. Though different time periods were compared, and all other factors ignored, such as the Revolution of 1848, the period of nonregulation did not basically result in any radical change in illegitimacy despite claims to the contrary.[9]

Nevertheless, in 1851, under pressure from military and other authorities, the licensed houses were opened again, only to be closed once more in

1856. Registration, however, continued to be under police control. To enforce registration, the police established a specialized police division known as the Sittenpolizei, or morals police, similar to the modern American vice squads. These police were charged not only with watching the registered women but in dealing with all unregistered women whose actions aroused suspicions, i.e., who were soliciting on their own. Unregistered women suspected of engaging in prostitution were arrested and questioned, and if they were over 18 years of age steps were taken to inscribe them, although, if they were under 21, the police had to communicate with the parents or guardians of such girls. Until a woman was inscribed a prostitute she was acting illegally if she solicited. If picked up for a second offense she could be punished with imprisonment and hard labor. The inscribed prostitute was not to loiter in streets or public places, was forbidden to appear in certain areas or to linger near schools, churches, or royal buildings, and was prohibited from attending the theater, circus, and so forth. An inscribed prostitute had to admit police officers into her dwelling at any time and give police information about persons discovered with her. She had to keep police informed of her address, was to refuse to have intercourse with a minor, and avoid being seen publicly with other prostitutes or pimps. Though inscription was nominally voluntary, a police official could also enter a woman on the list over her protests if he regarded her as a practicing prostitute. Prostitutes were required to have periodical medical examinations, and if they missed one, the morals police sought them out.[10]

Most of the continental European cities adopted similar systems although there were wide variations in particular details. A married woman, for example, could be forcibly enrolled in Paris and Berlin, while in Budapest she could be enrolled only with her husband's consent. On the other hand, married women, even if they requested inscription, could not be enrolled in Munich or Vienna. Women who were only part-time prostitutes, that is, who had other means of employment, were enrolled in some cities and not in others. Authorities in Bremen, Stuttgart, Munich, and Budapest, for example, took barmaids and other employed women off their rolls on the assumption that such employment was a sign that the woman intended to leave prostitution. A prostitute could be removed from the police lists in many cities at her request, while in other cities she could not do so until the police were satisfied that she had left the life. In Stockholm, police removed a woman from the list "until further notice" and for three months she was under police surveillance.[11] In some of the smaller cities prostitutes were confined to a single street, and other cities confined them to special quarters, but this kind of control proved difficult in the larger cities.

Similar differences existed in medical examinations. Bordeaux, Cologne, Danzig, Dresden, Brest, Toulouse, Marseilles, Leipzig, and Amiens required medical examinations once a week; Frankfurt on the Main distinguished two classes of prostitutes and required those in the first class to be examined twice a month, while those in the second class underwent weekly inspections. Geneva required an examination every five days, whereas Hamburg stipulated two a week as did Madrid, Milan, Rome, Prague, and Vienna; Nantes required two a month.[12] Though medical control was one of the justifications for inscription, the medical examination probably did very little to guarantee the security of the client— partly because of the nature of venereal disease and partly because of the inadequacies of the medical examination. Though the prostitute might contract syphilis only once, she could act as carrier even when she herself was not in an infectious stage by passing it from a diseased customer to one who was not. Moreover, even when syphilis was apparently latent, it was often actually florid, since the methods for determining this were so inaccurate at the time. Gonorrhea, though not as dangerous as syphilis, was also difficult to contain since reinfection was so easy. Though there were fewer noticeable cases of gonorrhea, among hardened prostitutes as they grew older (the disease was more difficult to diagnose because of low-grade infection), few were ever really cured. Moreover, as indicated, the medical examination itself was often a way of spreading the disease. Rubber gloves and aseptic techniques appeared only at the end of the century and physicians sometimes spread the disease from one prostitute to another by their very inspection. The examination was also slipshod in other ways. Abraham Flexner, who made a study of prostitution in Europe just prior to World War I, found, for example, that the city physician of Geneva managed to examine some 86 inscribed women in less than an hour. He concluded that most examinations would have disclosed primary syphilis or virulent gonorrhea but little else.[13]

Among the strongest advocates of some form of medical inspection were the military authorities, who increasingly expressed concern about venereal disease among the troops. The assumptions behind much of the regulation were that men needed and wanted sex, that good women would not give it to them except in the confines of marriage, and that therefore prostitution was necessary. For example, it was more or less standard custom in the British navy in the nineteenth century to invite prostitutes on board ship as soon as one reached port. In fact, in some of the English port towns, the launch captains carried out boatloads of women to meet the incoming ships, and were paid for their efforts by the sailors who took the prostitutes off their hands.[14] As military authorities became more and more concerned with venereal disease, British authorities turned to medical inspection as an answer. Rather than leaving the problem to local officials, however, the British Parliament itself entered into the arena with a series of Contagious Diseases Prevention Acts passed in 1864, 1866, and 1869. The first Act of 1864 gave control of prostitutes in some eleven designated port cities to the Admiralty and War Offices in order to prevent "contagious disease" at military and naval stations. In the designated cities any woman believed to be a common prostitute by the police or by any informer could be ordered by a magistrate to undergo a physical examination at one of the certified hospitals. If any woman so designated refused to go voluntarily she could be forcibly detained, and any person harboring a prostitute known to have a venereal disease could be fined or sent to prison.

The original law had been enacted on a three-year basis, and to supplement and extend it another bill was passed in 1866, covering another district, making a total of twelve areas. The 1866 Act required regular medical inspections and established a register of prostitutes. Women who passed inspection were given a certificate indicating their freedom from contagious disease, and this resulted in some of them regarding this as a license to operate as "Queen's women." Infected women could be detained for some six months without benefit of a magistrate's hearing. In 1869 the legislation was extended to cover six more areas and the period of detention was increased to nine months. To enforce the law, the Act created a special body of police who circulated in plainclothes among the people, especially the poorer classes, to make certain that every prostitute was examined. Once they classed a woman as a prostitute, her name could not be removed from the roster without going through a rigidly formal procedure. Any woman, regardless of whether she was a prostitute or not, could be ordered to submit to an examination or suffer imprisonment.[14] Inevitably the police classed almost any poor woman as a prostitute.

Since the impetus for the act came from the military, the regulations originally were limited to military and naval towns. London, the largest city in Europe, was not included nor were most of the other larger cities although momentum built up to extend the law to include non-military areas. The first step in this direction was the organization in 1868 of the Association for Promoting the Extension of Contagious Diseases Act, 1866, to the Civil Population of the United Kingdom. The group, under the leadership of its secretary, Berkeley Hill, had the support of many medical and ecclesiastical figures. By the end of 1868 the organization had some 43 local branches, and Hill was campaigning everywhere, arguing that control would not only bring down the incidence of venereal disease but benefit the prostitutes themselves.[15] Reaction soon set in, however, and in 1869 two groups formed to contest the principle of regulation, the National Association for Repeal of the Contagious Diseases Acts and the Ladies National Association for the Repeal of the Contagious Diseases Acts. During the next decade the campaign to repeal the acts was waged. Finally in 1883 a resolution of Parliament condemned compulsory medical examination, although the Act itself was not formally repealed until 1886.

Though many individuals attacked the law from the beginning because, as one writer said, England had "solemnly recorded in the Statute-book of a Christian nation" that prostitution was legal, there were other factors more responsible for its defeat. Among these was an increasingly vigorous movement demanding the emancipation of women, working-class resentment of the class character of the legislation, and ultimately also a series of medical and legal arguments challenged the whole basis of the law. As far as the venereal disease rate itself was concerned, the justification for the Act, official statistics show an initial decline followed by a slow but steady increase at the end of the period. In short, the results were ambiguous. Even the defenders of the act found it difficult to defend the way the law was being enforced. It required women labeled as prostitutes to undergo periodic inspections, but as in other countries the examinations themselves left a lot to be desired. Investigators found that the average physician spent only from three to five minutes in his examination of the prostitute, and that the thoroughness of the examination was not consistent.

Originally the Admiralty had issued instructions to examining surgeons to use the speculum, a device for looking inside the vagina, but these instructions were later withdrawn when it was found that a great number of women were injured during the examinations from the carelessness of the surgeons. It was also found that many of the attending medical personnel were so slipshod in their investigation that women were being infected with venereal disease at the dispensary. To make matters worse, police officers enforcing the Act were found to be blackmailing and intimidating innocent women as well as prostitutes. Many women who could not read were talked into signing a statement that they were prostitutes. Once signed, even if under a misunderstanding, there was little possibility of rectification. Moreover, even if a prostitute attempted to give up her way of life for more respectable employment or for marriage, the only way she could remove her name was by getting a magistrate's order, the securing of which was extremely difficult. Many minors signed papers stating they were prostitutes, often not knowing exactly what a prostitute was.[16]

Though the experiences of the English attempts at regulation were similar to those found in many parts of Europe, none of the European states (except for Norway in 1890) followed the English practice in repealing their ordinances regulating prostitution. Critics continually pointed out that regulation never accomplished what its advocates held it would do. It never dealt effectively with venereal disease if only because nineteenth-century medical knowledge gave only an inadequate understanding of how to deal with it. It failed to curtail illegitimacy or to contain prostitution or to eliminate the abuses associated with it. Worse yet, it was also not a particularly economical way of dealing with prostitution. In spite of large-scale police efforts spent in getting prostitutes to register, to be inspected, or confining them to certain areas, it seems clear that the majority of prostitutes were never inscribed even in regulated countries. Why then did registration have so much support behind it?[17]

The answer to this question probably lies in the whole nature of the social transformation taking place in the nineteenth century, a change already well in advance in certain areas in the eighteenth century. The massive urban growth of the time and the subsequent dislocation of society challenged traditional attitudes. Looked at dispassionately from the point of view of today, nineteenth-century prostitution does not seem to have threatened any fundamental principle of the state; it did not impair economic or industrial activity; nor was it a greater threat to public health than bad sewage, cholera, tuberculosis, or any other illness of the time. Still prostitution was certainly visible and became a symbol of urban illness. It was the "Great Sin of Great Cities."[18] which seemed to be "alive with lust."[19] Rather than dealing with the basic sources of the malaise that afflicted society, although many of them were unknown at the time, it was much easier to deal with such a visible symptom as prostitution. Yet at the very time prostitution was under attack, it was considered a necessary evil. William E. H. Lecky, in his *History of European Morals,* originally published in 1869, summed it up when he called the prostitute, the symbol of degradation and sinfulness, "ultimately the most efficient guardian of virtue."[20]

Prostitution was not the only urban evil attacked by reformers. Alcoholism was another crusade, pornography another, exploitation of children still another. Perhaps would-be reformers in most periods can really only deal with symptoms rather than root causes. In the process of dealing with symptoms, of course, some of the causes of the illness are also removed. The nineteenth century was the great age of reform, and though we can be critical, the accomplishments were significant: the abolition of the slave trade and much of slavery, and the laying of the foundation for modern social legislation.

To bring about reform, it was necessary to publicize the ills of society, and inevitably many of the would-be reformers were prone to exaggeration. Michael Ryan, who wrote about prostitution in London in 1839, for example, estimated that there were some 80,000 prostitutes working in the city.[21] A skeptical contemporary, however, estimated that, since the total female population of London at that time was 769,628, of which 394,814 were women between the ages of fifteen and fifty, Ryan's estimate would have made one of every five adult women a prostitute. Ryan, however, went further in his claims and estimated that fully two-thirds of the women on the streets were under twenty years of age. Since there were an estimated 78,962 females between fifteen and twenty in London, Ryan would have had almost every one a prostitute.[22]

Often, too, the causes of prostitution were simplified. Ryan, for example, said that prostitution was caused by seduction, neglect of parents, idleness, the low price of needle and other female work, the employment of young men milliners and drapers in shops in place of women, the facilities of prostitution, the prevalence of intemperance, music, and dancing in public houses, saloons, and theaters, the impression that males are not equally culpable as females, female love of dress and of superior society, the seductive promises of men, the idea that prostitution is indispensable, poverty, want of education, ignorance, misery, innate licentiousness, improper prints, books, obscene weekly publications and the profligacy of modern civilization.[23] Mixed with the superficial causes were basic ones, but many root causes were ignored entirely.

Other investigators, more sophisticated than Ryan, did not overlook them. William Watts testified in 1834:

> It is impossible for young women to produce the necessaries of life, exclusive of dress, by the present wages they can earn as lace-runners. The consequence is that almost all become prostitutes, though not common streetwalkers. This is an usual and, witness believes, a true cause assigned by young women for losing their virtue.[24]

William Osburn added:

> Vast numbers of girls who have wrought in factories are driven to prostitution when they are deprived of employment; girls not belonging to the parish of Leeds, probably to distant parishes, in some cases to no parish at all, have absolutely no other alternative but that of prostitution when trade is low and times are bad, so that they have no employ in the mills.[25]

Besides economic factors and the consequences of social disorganization, the marriage patterns of the period contributed to prostitution. An

Austrian law of 1821, for example, stipulated that no male could be married who was unable to read, write, and understand arithmetic.[26] Legislatures set out to improve literacy, a laudable enough aim, but in the process they also encouraged prostitution, or at least illicit sexual relations (thought of as one and the same in the nineteenth century). Bracebridge Hemyng in his study of London prostitution designated a class of prostitutes as "Cohabitant Prostitutes," which included those who could not afford marriage fees, those who married a relative forbidden by law, those whose paramours objected to marriage, and those who did not believe in the sanctity of marriage for some reason or other.[27] Some of the authorities of the time included all mothers of illegitimate children as prostitutes.

An error made by most investigators of the nineteenth century was to regard prostitution as just a lower-class phenomenon. In a sense it was, since most of the women who were prostitutes came from the lower ranks of society. But prostitution could not function without customers, and most of these came from the middle and upper classes. In fact, men from the lower classes could not afford to visit a brothel frequently, and what many in this class did was to live with a woman or a series of women in informal marriage arrangements. Though this was looked on as prostitution by the authorities of the day, and it certainly increased the illegitimacy rates, those involved did not necessarily consider it as such. Still the assumption that once a woman was promiscuous she would become a prostitute and fall on evil days was widely believed. Indeed, one of the purposes for which William Acton wrote on prostitution was to challenge just this belief.[28] On the contrary, most women who were promiscuous did finally marry.

The fact that so many customers of prostitutes came from the middle and upper classes or from the skilled trades was probably a significant reason for official concern with regulation and inspection; regulation represented a way of dealing with the upper-class fear of the lower classes. Contemporaries were aware of this. Patrick Colquhoun estimated in 1800 that some 40,000 young men of the middle and upper class arrived yearly at puberty and either lived in or moved to London, where few of them married immediately.[29] In fact, marriage for the young man on the make was delayed more and more in the nineteenth century as higher and higher economic standards were imposed on him by the parents of prospective brides. Not infrequently, marriage for the man was delayed until he was in his thirties, and then he married a much younger woman. Usually men who married at such ages attempted to limit the size of their families, some by continuing to resort to prostitutes, others by utilizing contraceptives, a practice regarded as worse than prostitution by many

authorities of the day. Benjamin Bradshaw, for example, testified to a
Parliamentary Commission that the reason certain factory women had
fewer children than others was that "there are certain books which have
gone forth to inform depraved persons of a way by which they may
indulge their corrupt passions, and still avoid having illegitimate children."[30] One of the culprits, regarded as a promulgator of promiscuity, was
Richard Carlile, who encouraged women to use contraceptive to cut down
on family size. His methods were fairly effective. He advocated the insertion into the vagina of a piece of soft sponge attached to a ribbon. If the
sponge, inserted just before sexual intercourse, was

> large enough, that is, as large as a green walnut, or a small apple, it will
> prevent conception, and thus, without diminishing the pleasures of mar-
> ried life, or doing the least injury to the health of the most delicate
> woman, both the woman and her husband will be saved from all the
> miseries which having too many children produces.[31]

It was not economics alone that encouraged lower-class women to
view prostitution as a possible livelihood. Upper-class men considered the
poorer classes fair game. Women of these groups were subject to all kinds
of propositions and overtures, many of them quite vulgar and overt.
When respectability was measured by wealth and status, by definition, no
woman of the lower classes could be respectable. Police, even though they
often came from the lower classes, usually had the same attitudes; women
who lived in poverty or near poverty were harassed for activities that
would be glossed over in upper-income groups. On the other hand, those
women who became glamorous and successful as prostitutes, who restricted their services to the upper ranks of society, rarely if ever had to
concern themselves with the police. And there were a great many successful courtesans in the nineteenth century, more than in the eighteenth,
because there was greater wealth and a larger number of well-to-do
patrons. We also know more about the courtesans of the nineteenth
century than those of an earlier period, in part because literacy was more
widespread and because of the great increase in the publication of literary
materials. Many courtesans wrote accounts of themselves, and others
became the focus of gossip recorded in memoirs, letters, diaries, and even
newspapers of the period.

At the top of the prostitute ladder were the royal mistresses, and
these remained as plentiful as in the past. The pacesetter in England was
George IV, who had served as regent for his insane father (George III)
before succeeding to the throne. As a young man, George had fallen
in love with a widow, Mrs. Maria Anne Fitzherbert, who was also a
devoted Catholic. Unable to marry her officially, he married her in a

secret ceremony of doubtful legality in order to go to bed with her. Later
he denied the marriage, and formally married Caroline of Brunswick,
whom he eventually accused of adultery, and then Charlotte Augusta. He
continued to have a succession of mistresses including Lady Jersey, then
the Marchioness of Hertford, the Marchioness of Conyngham, and numerous
others.[32] George was a leader of a group of men known as the Bucks, or
Corinthians, who imitated his sexual exploits. Though most of his friends
were married, they, like the king, regarded their wives as the begetters of
their heirs, and though they occasionally escorted their wives to a Court
Ball or other formal affair, they spent much of their time with what were
known as the "Fashionable Impures," or Cyprians, the high-class courtesans. Queen of the "Fashionable Impures" was Harriette Wilson, née Dubochet, the companion of kings, dukes, barons, and even lesser citizens
whom she liked or who could meet her price. At the height of her glory
she was a merry, radiant, healthy woman who apparently enjoyed her
calling and enthralled a string of lovers. In her middle age, however, she
began to lose some of her glamour, and hard-pressed for money, she
decided to sell her memoirs. Rather than expose her former lovers to
unwanted notoriety she advised each of them that for 200 English pounds
she would edit them out of her book. Some of them paid, relieved to be
let off so lightly, but others did not. The Duke of Wellington, the hero of
Waterloo, was one of those who refused to pay. When Harriette sent him
a letter requesting payment he scrawled across it in red ink, "Publish and
be damned." Harriette, however, had her revenge. In her *Memoirs* the
Duke is portrayed as a rather poor egotistical type of creature.

> Wellington was now my constant visitor:—a most entertaining one,
> Heaven knows! and, in the evenings, when he wore his broad red ribbon,
> he looked very like a rat catcher.[33]

She also told how she and one of her lovers kept the Duke of Wellington
outside in the rain, pretending they did not recognize him, and ultimately
forced him to leave, trembling with rage and impatience.[34]

Even though her *Memoirs* were written with an eye to possible blackmail, they are invaluable as a social picture of the time. While Harriette
undoubtedly exaggerated, as in the case of Wellington, her caricatures
have the ring of authenticity and usually manage to impart an idea of the
character of the men she was dealing with. Harriette reached her height
during the age of the "Dandy," in which male fashions and manners
dominated, so that most women seemed pale in comparison, particularly
the legitimate wives. The leader of this new style of masculine sartorial
excellence was Beau Brummell. Brummell's dress and manner were copied

by the Regent, the eventual George IV, and with royal patronage they were widely adopted, imitated and exaggerated by the male English upper classes.[35]

In such company, it was hard for an ambitious woman to get ahead, but Harriette and other Fashionable Impures managed it. The height of the social season in London was an annual Cyprians Ball, where the prominent courtesans played hostess en masse to their admirers and protectors. George Cruikshank illustrated just such a ball, emphasizing the bosoms, shoulders, and bodies for sale. The star in this firmament for a time was Harriette, born one of fifteen children in 1786, only nine of whom survived into adulthood. Three of Harriette's six sisters followed her into prostitution and all of them managed to achieve a much higher social standing than they had been born into. One of the sisters, Sophia, married Lord Deerhurst, and in her later years attempted to cut herself off from her sisters, none of whom managed to reach quite such a height of legitimacy.

Harriette's mother had operated a shop that repaired gentlemen's stockings, and it was a fairly good business until knee breeches went out of fashion in 1820, partly the influence of Brummell. Her father was a Swiss watchmaker, who worked only occasionally, preferring to live off his wife's earnings. Her elder sister Amy started the family interest in prostitution, beginning as a London streetwalker, but quickly rising to serve a more select clientele. Fanny, another sister, became the mistress of the Marquis of Hertford at an early age. Harriette, at least according to a story she supposedly told Julia Johnstone, her rival and friend, first fell in love with a washerwoman's son who kept a boat on the Thames. From him Harriette drifted to a recruiting sergeant with whom she eloped, but after he made off with her best clothes and watch, she determined that as long as she had lost her virtue, she ought to "look higher." She did. Harriette, Fanny, and Julia Johnstone were popularly known as the Three Graces, while Amy was rather unkindly known as one of the Furies. They all took a kindly interest in introducing Sophia, the younger Dubochet sister, into the profession.[36]

After reaching the height of her "profession," Harriette acted accordingly. Prospective clients who called without being correctly introduced were given the short shrift. Occasionally she unbent sufficiently to say that a fifty-pound note would do as well as a regular introduction, but this was only when the caller was presented in such a way as to fascinate her. Once a peer of the realm sent his footman with a note to Harriette's house requesting the honor of her company for the night. Harriette read the letter and then ordered the servant out saying:

This letter could not be meant for me, to whom his Lordship was only presented yesterday. Take it back, young man, and say from me that I request he will be careful how he misdirects them in future—an accident which was no doubt caused by his writing them after dinner.[37]

If a man caught Harriette's favor, however, she made her own approaches, and only rarely suffered rebuffs.

She had entered London high society as the fifteen-year-old mistress of Lord Craven, passing from him to a succession of other titled or rich Englishmen. She later fell in love with, and apparently married, William Henry Rochfort, a bogus colonel and bastard nobleman. The two went to Paris to start life anew, but he wasted what money Harriette had accumulated on liquor and gambling, and to add insult to injury, on other women. It was in these circumstances that Harriette, encouraged by her husband, agreed to write her memoirs. With their publication in 1825, her financial worries were over, since she received an estimated 10,000 pounds for them.[38] The *Memoirs* appeared in installments, and before each section was published, there were advertisements about the people who would appear in them starting with dukes and going down the line to marquises, barons, honorables, colonels, captains, and ultimately esquires.[39] This prepublication technique gave some of those she threatened to expose a chance to make last-minute decisions to buy themselves out.

Though her publisher was sued for libel and other damages, Harriette was not bothered by such suits; perhaps her past patrons felt lucky to get off as lightly as they did. Thirty-one editions were sold in the first year and pirated editions appeared all over Europe. Encouraged by her maiden efforts in writing, Harriette tried her hand at a couple of novels, but none of them were very successful. Her *Memoirs* had outraged a great many Englishwomen, and when she returned to England from France, one such female knocked her down and pulled out her hair in fistfuls. Since Harriette had succeeded in destroying the peace of mind of many married women, who were not supposed to read her *Memoirs* but probably did anyway, it is little wonder that she again returned to Paris to sink into gradual obscurity. She appeared in a Paris court in 1829 after accusing her brother of having improper relations with her maid. After 1832 she more or less vanished from sight, though it is believed that she returned to England about this time and died sometime in the 1840s; undoubtedly many of her former lovers knew of her wherabouts, but they were only too happy to let her live quietly.[40]

Julia Johnstone, a friend and rival of Harriette, also published an account of her life. Her *True Confessions*, which differs from Harriette's account in many significant aspects, is neither as accurate nor as witty as that of her rival. During her career she gave birth to some twelve children. Her background was only slightly different from Harriette's. Brought up in genteel poverty as the daughter of a maid to Queen Charlotte, she was in a position to meet the "right men." When she was fourteen she became the mistress to a Colonel Cotton, who had seduced her on the staircase. For a time she was governess companion to Cotton's wife and children, but when she became pregnant he set her up in a separate cottage and she passed as Mrs. Johnstone. Since her cottage was close to one occupied by Harriette, then the mistress of the Honorable Fred Lamb, the two women became friends. As they moved up in the world of the demi-monde they remained friends, sharing boxes at the opera, clothes, and confidences.[41]

Though Harriette was the most famous courtesan of her day, the woman who today is known even to schoolchildren, although not for her sexual activities, is Emma Hart, better known as Lady Hamilton, mistress of the national hero Admiral Horatio Nelson. Emma's father and mother are known, as is the date of her birth, May 13, 1765, but there is little knowledge of her early life. It is believed that she served first as the mistress of a Captain Willet Payne, after which she passed through the hands of a succession of men, until she met Charles Greville. Greville saw her potential, encouraged her to become educated, taught her to sing, dance, and act, and in 1782 introduced her to his friend George Romney, the portrait painter. Romney made numerous portraits of her and was enchanted. Two years later Greville took her to his uncle, who was then British minister in Naples, as part of an understanding between the two: Lord Hamilton agreed to pay off his nephew's gambling debts in return for his nephew's ceding him his mistress.

Since Emma had not been consulted in the transaction, she at first was resentful, but seeing there was little point in objecting, finally acceded to the arrangement. Her beauty and spirit soon made her a great favorite in Neapolitan society and Queen Maria Carolina became closely attached to her, although Emma could not at first be presented at court since she was Hamilton's mistress and not his wife. In order to strengthen her (and his) influence with the queen, Hamilton married her in 1791, and Emma became Lady Hamilton. The marriage proved helpful to England since Naples was a significant port during the French Revolutionary and Napoleonic Wars, and Lady Hamilton helped encourage a strong pro-British policy. The queen often communicated to Lady Hamilton information about her husband's policies and plans, sometimes in opposition to his wishes. It was probably because of Emma's influence that the British fleet in 1798 was able to obtain supplies and water in Sicily, which enabled it to win the Nile campaign.

When Nelson, the hero of the Nile campaign, visited Naples in 1798, he and Lady Hamilton resumed a love affair which had begun in 1793 but which had been carried on mainly by correspondence. She had a child by him, Horatia Nelson, in 1801, even though she was still married to Hamilton. Despite this, Hamilton, on his death in 1803, left her a good-sized bequest as well as the furniture of his house. Lady Hamilton then lived openly with Nelson (who was married) until his death, when he too left her a sizable endowment and control of the 4,000-pound legacy he willed to their daughter. She was, however, almost continually in debt, and in 1813 was put into debtors' prison; shortly after her release she died in distress if not in want.[42]

Another famous courtesan, one of the few besides Harriette Wilson to make the *Dictionary of National Biography,* was Cora Pearl, England's gift to France. She was born Eliza Elizabeth Crouch in 1836, near Plymouth, the daughter of a musician father and songstress mother. Cora was put into a French convent after her father had run off to America with his mistress. Later she went to live with her grandmother in England. Like Harriette Wilson, Cora Pearl also wrote her memoirs late in life, but she lacked Harriette's aptitude for either blackmail or literature. According to her own story, she lost her virginity at fourteen while returning from church one Sunday. A gentleman inquired of her if she liked cakes, and when she replied in the affirmative, he took her to a room and gave her not cakes but gin and water that she said was drugged. When she awoke the next morning, somewhat the worse for wear, the kindly gentleman asked her if she would like to stay with him; when she replied negatively, he laughed, gave her five pounds, and left, saying: "Just as you like, my dear . . . I never forced anyone."[43]

Although she refused to stay with her first customer, she did not return to her grandmother. Instead she moved into a room of her own and within a year became the mistress of William Buckle. She lived with Buckle for two years, and he took her to Paris for a holiday where she decided to remain. She began her stay in Paris with several disadvantages: she was not particularly beautiful, her French was poor and she spoke it with a Cockney accent, and her name, Crouch, had many unpleasant ambiguities in its French pronunciation. She changed her name to Pearl, and used her assets: her figure was beautiful, her red hair attractive, and her skin and teeth excellent. Cora decided not to compete with the "gentle beauties" of Paris,[44] but to create a following of her own, devoted to a spirited, gay, young girl who would do anything. She quickly climbed to the top of her profession, moving from bed to bed until she reached that of Prince Jerome Bonaparte, cousin of Napoleon III.

One of her favorite recreations was to invite some of her most respected patrons to dinner, and then offer herself for dessert. One of her admirers recorded such a dinner where the meal progressed in fine spirit until

> the door flew open and our footman in her livery brought in a life-size dish with a cover. They placed this in the middle of the long table and on taking off the cover there lay Cora Pearl nude . . . She had such a wonderful figure . . . that all the guests gasped with admiration.[45]

Cora reached the height of her career about the year 1867 when Prince Jerome Bonaparte installed her in a mansion in the Rue de Chaillot, known as Les Petites Tuileries, which Cora boasted had cost her lover 80,000 pounds.

Her downfall coincided with the defeat of the Second Empire during the Franco-Prussian War. Cora's royal patron had to flee Paris for London, but when Cora tried to visit him she was refused admittance. She returned to Paris, where she raised the British Union Jack over her house and turned it into a hospital for wounded officers. Her neighbors, who previously had paid little attention to her activities, were scandalized at such conduct, and there was an attempt to deport her as an undesirable alien. Though the prince was still nominally her patron, he was in England, and Cora, in need of friendship and support, had an affair with Alexander Duval, a young Frenchman who had just inherited a fortune of several million dollars. He spent the money on Cora, and when it was gone, she instructed her servants not to allow him entrance to her house. When the young man attempted to commit suicide, the family used its influence to have Cora ordered to leave Paris. Prince Jerome reluctantly told her he could no longer support her, and she passed from London to Monte Carlo, Milan, Rome, Nice, and Baden-Baden, attempting to relive the glories of her youth. She eventually returned to Paris, where she died of cancer in 1886.[46]

Even more successful than Cora Pearl was Elizabeth Howard, another English prostitute who made good in France. Elizabeth's origins are obscure, but she had the ability to attract men, and was left a fortune by one of her admirers whose son she bore. She later met Louis Napoleon, then in exile in England and when the Revolution of 1848 drove King Louis-Philippe from the French throne, Miss Howard financed the return of Louis Napoleon to France. He was elected president and soon proclaimed himself the Emperor Napoleon III. His new position, however, made his old alliance with Elizabeth Howard unacceptable, but his affection remained. To console Elizabeth for their separation, he created her Countess of Beauregard, gave her a château, and about a million dollars as a farewell present. She temporarily deserted her former life, married, but did not settle down since the marriage ended in divorce. She died in 1865 at the age of forty-three and was buried in England under the name of Elizabeth Ann Haryett.[47]

Another famous French courtesan was the Italian Virginia Oldoini, better known as the Countess of Castiglione. She was born in Florence sometime between 1835 and 1840. In 1854 she was married to Francesca Verasis, Count of Castiglione. The count had been directed to her by the French ambassador to London, who reported that she was the most beautiful woman in Europe. After catching a brief sight of her the impatient count quickly arranged with her parents to marry her; they acceded to his hasty demands for marriage because the count was an aide-de-camp to King Victor Emmanuel II, and Virginia's father was ambitious for a diplomatic appointment. The marriage was a fiasco, and the couple soon separated; the count's social contacts, however, had brought Virginia to the attention of the king. She became good friends with Victor Emmanuel II, who, like Charles II of England in an earlier period, could with justification be called the physical "father" of his people. Though there is no evidence of a liaison between the countess and the king, there is also no evidence against it, and knowing the king and the countess, the gossips had a field day.

The countess was sent to Paris by the king and his minister, Camillo Benso, Conte di Cavour (who was also her cousin) to secure French aid for Italian unification. She arrived in 1855, and after her first official reception she became the sensation of Paris. The emperor, Napoleon III, invited her for the first waltz, and then neglected to meet his other dance partners. Soon Napoleon began visiting her, and not so coincidentally France began backing Cavour's diplomacy. Though Napoleon III had his own political motivations for his actions, popular opinion attributed some of the change to the countess. Later her pro-Italian sentiments made difficulties for her, and in 1860 she temporarily left France to retire to her villa near Turin.

Her retirement from imperial favor did not halt her activities. Rather it opened new markets for her company since her prospective customers no longer had to compete with the emperor. Lord Hertford is said to have offered her 40,000 pounds for one night in her apartment, a price to which she agreed, but he demanded so much in return that the countess had to spend three additional days in bed recovering. She soon returned to Paris, where her list of patrons grew. One of them, the banker Charles Lafitte, loaned her 450,000 francs, and was somewhat shocked and surprised when she did not repay him. With the overthrow of Napoleon III, she lost much of her influence, and she retired from public life into virtual seclusion. Her last years were spent in a mirrorless apartment that she kept shuttered, acting as if she was a pauper (she was in fact very rich) and very ill (she was a hypochondriac). She died in 1899, leaving her documents to the Italian embassy in Paris. The embassy officials speedily destroyed many of her papers, an action that has since convinced many writers that she had not been without the political influence popular gossip attributed to her.[48]

The longest lived, and perhaps the most loved of the famous prostitutes of the nineteenth century was Catherine Walters, known to her public as "Skittles." She was born in 1839, and supposedly received her nickname by working in the Black Jack Tavern, where the patrons played skittles, a form of ninepins. Little is known about her background until she achieved fame in the 1860s. She too went to Paris, but her greatest triumphs were in London, where the Prince of Wales, the son of Queen Victoria, and other dignitaries became her patrons. When she was forty, she met and fell in love with Gerald Saumerez, who was half her age; they remained lovers to the end of her life. She, nonetheless, remained on good terms with most of the men with whom she had professional relations; many of them liked her as well out of bed as in it and regarded it as an honor to be in her company. She had eccentric tastes, and among other things, padded her toilet seat with swansdown so it would be softer to touch.[49]

One courtesan probably cost her lover his throne, namely, Marie Dolores Eliza Rosanna Gilbert, better known as Lola Montez. The daughter of a British army officer and a mother who probably had some Spanish blood, Lola was born in Limerick, Ireland, in 1818. As a child she accompanied her parents to India. Her father died when she was seven, and when her mother remarried she was sent back to Europe to be educated. In 1837 she eloped with a Captain James of the Indian Army and returned with him to India. The marriage soon broke up, and Lola came back to England without her husband. She became an actress, billing herself as "Lola Montez, Spanish dancer." Unsuccessful in London, she toured the continent with more success, both with her audience—and with men.

In 1846 she appeared in Munich, where Ludwig I of Bavaria, tired of some of his other mistresses, became thoroughly captivated by her. She soon became his mistress. In the course of events Lola became involved in the local power struggle that led to the dismissal of the king's Jesuit-oriented advisers. Lola for a time seemed to be on the winning side. She was made a naturalized citizen of Bavaria, created the Countess Landsfeld and given an income of $10,000 a year. Either as a testimonial to her influence, or the officials' lack of status with the people, the cabinet was dubbed the "Lolaministerium." In 1848, stimulated by the news of the Paris revolution, riots broke out in Munich, Ludwig I was forced to abdicate, and Lola was banished from Bavaria.

She returned to England and married George Heald, a young officer of the Guards, but his family guardian instituted a prosecution for bigamy against her on the grounds that Lola had never been legally divorced from her first husband, James. Lola and Heald fled first to Spain; then Lola, unaccompanied by her husband, went to the United States, where she appeared on the stage in a play entitled *Lola Montez in Bavaria*. She was especially popular in the California gold fields. When Heald drowned in 1853 in London, Lola married a San Francisco newspaper proprietor, but she did not live long with him either. She went to Australia for a time, only to return to the United States in 1857. By this time her health was none too good, and she devoted the remainder of her life (she died in 1861) to rescue work among the prostitutes in New York City.[50]

Prostitutes also served as the model for fictional heroines. Such was the case of Delphine Couturier, the daughter of a French farmer, who became the second wife of a well-to-do French physician, Eugene Delamare. Bored by her marriage, Delphine committed adultery with a neighbor, a farmhand, a clerk, and then with anyone who would pay. She neglected her husband, her little daughter, her friends and neighbors, and spent far beyond her husband's income. After some nine years of marriage, with her husband's finances in ruin, and unable to attract many admirers, she took a fatal dose of arsenic. When later her husband found the extent of her extravagances and her infidelities, he killed himself. Gustave Flaubert used her story as a basis for his novel *Madame Bovary*, first published in 1857.[51]

Similarly a Paris courtesan, Marie Duplessis, served as the model for Alexandre Dumas fils's heroine, Marguerite Gautier in *La Dame aux camélias*. She was born Rose Alphonsine Plessis in the Normandy village of Saint Germain-de-Clair, the daughter of a drunken draper, who exploited her after her mother died. When Marie was thirteen, her father sold her to a wealthy, lecherous bachelor friend, who kept her for a year before sending her back. She had supposedly lost her virginity before this to a young farmhand, and her treatment by her father's friend had further initiated her into the life of prostitution. When she was sent back to her father, he sent her on to Paris to live with relatives. She soon went out on her own, supplementing her income as a clerk and messenger by prostitution. Her first step toward success came when she moved in as mistress to a restaurant proprietor. She then moved on to become the mistress of Count Ferdinand de Monguyon, who had seen her at the theater. She left the Count for Agenor de Guiche, later to be the Duc de Guiche-Gramont. When she parted with Guiche-Garmont, she was supported by a syndicate of seven ardent lovers, who established her in a lavish suite of rooms at 11

Boulevard de la Madeleine. Other lovers soon appeared. Her trademark was the white camellia, and she had a fresh vase of camellias placed in her apartment daily. Alexandre Dumas fils saw her first in 1842 when he was eighteen and she was the same age. Within two years she had become his mistress and their turbulent affair lasted for a year. By the time he left her she was ill with tuberculosis, of which she died in 1847 at twenty-three years of age.[52] Giuseppe Verdi further immortalized Mlle Duplessis in his opera *La Traviata.*

During the period of the Second Empire in Paris the courtesan reached a new height. Collectively, these high-status prostitutes were known as *la garde.* Queens of their profession, they were among the most influential women of their time. In addition to furnishing heroines for Flaubert and Dumas, several also served as models for other fictional creations. Blanche d'Antigny (1840-74) served as the model for Émile Zola's *Nana,* and Aglaé-Joséphine Savatier/Apollonie Sabatier (La Présidente) was the inspiration for many of the poems of Charles Baudelaire.[53] The list could be extended. None of the more famous prostitutes was inscribed on the common police lists of the day. These were restricted to a different class of women who had not reached their heights.

As the nineteenth century progressed, however, there was a tendency to be less flamboyant in the display of sexuality. In England we associate this with the word *Victorianism.* At least as far as prostitution is concerned, the association is justified. The mere fact that Queen Victoria was a woman cut down on some of the more flamboyant aspects of prostitution in court circles. The elderly gallants of an earlier day were old and dying, and the Queen (along with her consort, Prince Albert) frowned on the kinds of diversions that had gone on before. It was not until the young Prince of Wales reached manhood (he was born in 1841) that the amorous tendencies of an earlier period were again noted in court, but these were still restricted by the hostility of the Queen. Many, in fact, began to question the need for prostitution altogether.

11 THE AMERICAN SCENE

Sex attitudes in colonial America in general were similar to those of Europe. This was to be expected since Americans were only Europeans who had left Europe. Though some of the early European settlers in America, such as the Puritans and Pilgrims, were in rebellion against certain European trends, even their rebellion had been shaped by the old country. The Puritans, like their counterparts in Geneva and in Scotland, were interested not only in saving their souls but in establishing a "visible" kingdom of God, a society where outward conduct would be according to God's laws. Nevertheless most of their normal legislation had direct English antecedents.

The American setting, however, forced some modifications in the European patterns. The United States before 1800 was primarily a rural country, and though prostitution is not unknown in rural areas, commercialized prostitution is more widespread in urban than rural areas. On the other hand, most of the early American colonies had a disproportionate sex ratio with far more men than women, and this distorted ratio lasted in many areas of the country until the twentieth century. Not all eligible women were married, however, and there were always unattached females willing to look with favor on the sexual approaches of unattached males. What was true of women of European descent was also true of Indian and Black women.

Many in fact were in no position to protest until conditions got out of hand. Sarah Lepinwell, a servant, complained that Thomas Hawes, her master's brother, had violated her, and that she had hesitated to call for help because she "was posesed [sic] with fear of my master least my master shold think I did it only to bring a scandall on his brother and thinking they wold all beare witness agaynst me." Ultimately, however, she brought a complaint, and in spite of the opposition of the Hawes family, Thomas Hawes was found guilty.[1] Contributing to sexual promiscuity in the colonies was the fact that servants, whether hired, indentured, or working off a criminal sentence, were not allowed to marry. Neither were apprentices. Even when a person finished his or her indenture or apprenticeship, marriage was unlikely since money was needed to start a family. Most slaves were also unmarried, although an owner of slaves was more likely to permit them to marry than his servants. Only "through marriage" could slaves contain their lust. As the price of slaves rose there was also an economic reason to encourage breeding.

Servants found other ways to satisfy their sexual drives. Many took time off when their masters were away, but even when a master of the house was at home, servants might slip out at night to a nearby tavern or elsewhere to find congenial company. Here they spent the tips they received from visiting guests or money that otherwise had come into their hands, since servants, except for hired ones, had no salary. In the larger households where there were many servants, sexual promiscuity was more difficult to control. Often both men and women servants slept in the same room, and since it was the custom to sleep without nightclothes, many found it difficult to overcome temptation. Undoubtedly many of the servants had what amounted to marital attachments, but regardless of the state of their entanglements many consummated their affairs in a crowded bedroom, often even on a bed on which other people were sleeping. If they were caught they were punished, although actual punishment was usually left to the discretion of the court. Judges could require a couple to marry, pay a fine, or give them corporal punishment. In practice, a fine or a whipping was the normal sentence, but if a pregnancy resulted, the law also required the father of the child to pay for its support and education. According to statute, the father was the person whom the mother accused when questioned during her labor. If a servant had to pay a fine or pay for the support of the child, the payment fell on his master, and the servant had to contract to work for an even longer term before gaining his freedom. To cut down on expense, the child itself might be turned over to a master as an indentured servant or put out to indenture elsewhere.[2]

Inevitably, however, there were individuals willing to profit from the sexual desires of the great number of unmarried, as well as perhaps from some of the married. The problem of prostitution, for example, was a matter of concern to the authorities almost from the beginning of the settlement. Several people in seventeenth-century New England were charged with keeping a "disorderly" house or for being prostitutes. Prostitutes were at times stripped to the waist, tied to the tail end of a cart, and whipped as the cart moved through town. In Plymouth,

Sarah Ensigne, for combining a whordome agrevated with divers cercumstances, was centanced by the Court to bee whipt att the cartstaile:

and that it be left to the discretion of such of the majestrates as shall see the said punishment inflicted for the number of stripes, but not to exceed twenty, which accordingly was afflicted by this Court.[3]

One of the most notorious of the Boston brothelkeepers was Alice Thomas. In 1672 she was found guilty of being an accessory to burglary, selling liquor without a license, profaning the Lord's Day, entertaining idle persons, and most notoriously of

giving frequent secret and unseasonable Entertainment in her house to Lewd Lascivious and notorious persons of both Sexes, giving them opportunity to commit carnall wickedness, & that by common fame she is a common Baud.[4]

She was whipped through the streets of Boston, and sent to prison to serve as long as the court deemed necessary.

Jolted by the case of Alice Thomas, the General Court, meeting in Boston, October 8, 1672, declared:

Whereas by sad experience, it is too obvious to all our people and others, that the sin of Whoredome and Uncleanness grows amongst us, notwithstanding all the Wolsome Laws made for punishing and suppressing such land Defiling Evils; And whereas there is of late, too just ground to suspect a greater Evil growing upon us, by the bold and audacious Presumption of some, to erect a Stews, Whore-House, or Brothel-House; for the nourishing such wickedness, the encrease of which Evil, if not timely prevented, may tend to the debauching of multitudes of persons, and tend to the utter ruine of their Estates, Soul and Body. It is therefore Ordered by this Court, and the Authority thereof: That if any Person, Male, or Female, shall presume to set up or keep any such House, wherein such wicked lusts may be nourished, and Whoredome committed, every such Baud, Whore, or vile Person . . . shall be severely whipt at the Carts-tayle, through the Streets, where such Offence, or Offences hath been committed, with Thirty Stripes, and thence to be committed to the House of Correction, and by the Master of the said House to be kept with hard fare, and hard labour, by dayly Task, and defect of their duty to be severely whipt every night with Ten Stripes; and once at least in every week, the said Baud and his Complices in such vile and sinful Courses, the Baud to be their leader, and the other two and two in hair Frocks and blew caps by the Executioner to be fastned to a hand Cart, and forced along to draw all the filth laid up in the Cart, through the Streets, to the Sea side going to the Gallows in Suffolk, and in all other Counties where the Court of each Shire shall appoint, and so returned to the House of correction, to be alike kept with hard Faire and Labour, according to the Custome of the House during the Courts pleasure, there to remaine.[5]

In spite of such laws prostitution continued to exist since the authorities only occasionally enforced the laws. Cotton Mather became so concerned about this lack of enforcement that in 1702 he organized a Society for the Suppression of Disorders in Boston. To help point out the areas of possible disorder for society members, he then proposed a short pamphlet *Methods and Motives for Societies to Suppress Disorders,* which he sent to interested individuals throughout the country. The society did not seem to have been particularly effective although in 1706 Boston had some three branches of the society with some forty members all told. By 1714 none of these was still functioning but Mather, undaunted, was still making plans for the society to check on houses of prostitution and to admonish the patrons who went there.[6]

The situation in the southern colonies was not much different. The first voyagers to Virginia had come without women; in order to make the colony more stable, the proprietors began to send out young women to serve as wives or companions of the Virginia adventurers. Some ninety women came in the first shipment, carefully selected as to character, although not all had come willingly. Even though the shortage of women made it comparatively easy for any woman to find a husband, the governors still found it necessary to deport two of the first boatload because of sexual transgressions. This punishment apparently was not sufficient since future colonists of Virginia were warned that there "were severe and wholesome laws against whoredom."[7]

Periodically the records of seventeenth- and-eighteenth-century America make reference to prostitution. In New York by 1680 a small path beyond Wall Street had acquired the name Maiden Lane because so many maidens went there during their courting activities, and not all of them married the men they courted. A New York visitor in 1695 spoke of the "wandering liberties" taken there.[8] In 1744 Alexander Hamilton reported that the New York Battery was a rendezvous point for the city's prostitutes, and that patrons had a "good choice of pritty lasses among them, both Dutch and English." Newport, R.I., had streetwalkers in 1744, and one observer described one "in a flaunting dress" who raised such blushes on his companion that it was determined he was one of her patrons.[9] In Boston a certain Hannah Dilley, the wife of a feltmaker, was accused of permitting "men and other suspected persons" to come to her husband's house where they "Carnally layd with whores, which the said Hannah then and there procured for them."[10]

As the eighteenth century progressed Americans became less concerned with punishing prostitutes. It was not uncommon for men who could afford to have mistresses to have them, and, inevitably, those who could not turned to prostitutes or perhaps to slave women. Benjamin

Franklin in his *Autobiography* explained that the "hard-to-be governed passions of youth" hurried him frequently into "intrigues with low women that fell in my way" and these caused him "some expense and great inconvenience, besides a continual risque" to his health. He also fathered at least one illegitimate son. His solution to his problem was to get married, a remedy he later offered to others in his pamphlet *Advice to a Young Man on the Choice of a Mistress*. After first advising his fictional young friend to seek out marriage as the proper remedy for "violent natural inclinations," Franklin said that if the young man could not take such advice but persisted in "thinking a commerce with sex inevitable," he should choose a mistress, preferably an older woman. This was because an older woman would likely be more prudent, far more knowledgeable, and less likely to have children. He added that the young man could also make an old woman more happy than a young one, and besides all mares looked the same in the dark.[11] Though America in the eighteenth century lacked the great wealth that supported some of the more lavish houses of prostitution in Europe, the emerging metropolises did not lack for them. The French traveler Moreau de St. Mery in 1795 noted that Philadelphia had several houses of pleasure as well as numerous freelancing procuresses who arranged assignations, often with prominent young women who otherwise were known as models of propriety.[12]

Prostitutes were sent to America as part of their punishment in Europe. The fictional Moll Flanders mentioned earlier serves as a case in point. In 1721, twenty-five prostitutes were sent from Salpêtrière, a house of correction in Paris, to become wives of the French residents in the Louisiana territory. It was assumed that the women would undergo a metamorphosis when they arrived in America—those who failed to do so were whipped or otherwise punished.[13] Where there were not enough European women, Indians and Blacks served as prostitutes, often unwillingly. Slaves had little choice in the matter, and neither did many Indians. Richard Henry Dana in his *Two Years Before the Mast* reported that when the ships put in at California ports, Indian women often met them.

> I have frequently known an Indian to bring his wife, to whom he was lawfully married in the church, down to the beach, and carry her back again, dividing with her the money which she had got from the sailors. If any of the girls were discovered by the alcalde to be open evil-livers, they were whipped, and kept at work sweeping the square of the presidio, and carrying mud and bricks for the buildings; yet a few *reals* would generally buy them off.[14]

Until the end of the eighteenth century, however, it seems clear that most of the prostitution existing in America was unorganized and more or less haphazard. This began to change for many of the same reasons that had brought about change in Europe. Industrialization and urbanization and dislocation became a prominent part of the American scene, although since America had been settled by immigrants from Europe, some dislocation had always been present. The nineteenth-century dislocation, however, was of a different kind. The American phase of the industrial revolution started in New England and the Middle Atlantic states, and many, perhaps the majority, of early factory workers in some of the textile areas were women, most of them young and unmarried. Early factory labor was not only extremely difficult but low-paying. After working a twelve-to-fifteen-hour day, many of the women found their wages were lower than what were considered starvation wages for men. In spite of this, most of the women preferred work in the factory to the other alternative, domestic service, if only because they had more freedom. Moreover most of them looked on it only as a temporary stage until they could marry and settle down. Conditions, however, left much to be desired. When the women left the factory in the evening, they were free to do as they wanted, but there was little for most of them to do. Many of them lived in boardinghouses with six to eight persons in a room, often three sleeping in the same bed. To make matters worse, in many of the smaller New England towns, including some of the textile towns, there was a sexual imbalance, more women than men, as the men moved to the frontiers or to the cities to make their way. Some women turned to prostitution either for affection or to escape, but the outraged citizenry ignored the causal conditions, and instead rioted and tore down houses of ill-fame, as they did in Portland, Maine, and Boston, Massachusetts.[15]

In the growing cities where the sex ratios showed a predominance of males, many of the males were not regarded as husband material by the country girls because of the language difficulties or differences in social status. Inevitably, a significant number of women never married, and the spinster aunt became an important institution in nineteenth-century American life. Other women, however, turned to prostitution as a temporary occupation, hoping to get a husband in that way, and migrated to the cities or to the frontier. In the rapidly expanding cities the prostitute found a large class of customers in the newly arrived immigrants who had left their womenfolk behind in Europe or elsewhere. The first big immigrant wave was the Irish, most of whom had left their homeland in dire economic straits. Once they had a job, they saved a percentage of their wages to send back to Ireland in order to bring the rest of the family over including girlfriends or wives. Not all their money was sent overseas, however; a percentage was used to escape their sorrows and their loneliness. Drink seems to have been a univeral remedy for the ills of many an immigrant. Payday was Saturday night, which by Puritan custom had been considered part of the Sabbath, and on that evening large segments of the immigrant community repaired to bars and taverns, much to the disgust of the older American residents who sat secure in the bosoms of their families. As the older generation of immigrants married and settled down, they were succeeded by new waves of immigrants, who again were mostly male, and the process was repeated. Often the first women to arrive from the old country were prostitutes, or perhaps prostitution was the only way that an immigrant woman without a man to support her could earn a living.

At any rate, for many of the newly arrived immigrants the only feminine companionship readily available was that of prostitutes, either full or part time, although few women either planned to or did make a career out of it. On the moving western frontier there were also vast numbers of men without women who worked hard and were anxious to forget their ordeals on paydays. The prostitute moved here also. Almost every immigrant community, whether on the East Coast or on the frontier, passed through a period of drunkenness and revelry,[16] possessing large surpluses of males over eligible females. Prostitution was regarded by most members of the establishment as essential to preserve the integrity of the "proper" woman.

Inevitably the attitudes of Americans toward prostitution became as contradictory as their European counterparts. Many accepted it as inevitable, but at the same time advocated celibacy as the ideal and publicly opposed prostitution. Still, evidence of prostitution appeared everywhere, and the American newspapers of the period are literally peppered with "items on prostitution, on sexual abnormalities, on cures for venereal disease, on refuges for expectant but unmarried mothers, on suits for seduction or for the support of illegitimate children, on prosecution of abortionists, and on cases of deserted children."[17] Brothels also served as a magnet for other crimes, and it was not unusual for patrons of brothels to be robbed or beaten. Many houses had sliding panels, which gave access to the man's wallet, and not infrequently a partly unclothed couple were confronted by a fake brother or husband. Blackmail was always a possibility, particularly if the customer was well-to-do. Often violent crimes took place. One of the most notorious crimes was the ax killing of the prostitute Helen Jewett, allegedly by the socialite R. L. Robinson, in New York in 1836. Though the circumstantial evidence was strong, most of the testimony depended on the words of prostitutes; this was in contrast to the appearance of the defendant, the handsome, nineteen-year-old socialite who did not testify himself, and it decided the outcome. When the jury brought in its verdict of "Not guilty," the crowded courtroom cheered.[18] Prostitutes could not be trusted, and it was more or less permissible for a young man to be sexually promiscuous.

However there was compassion for prostitutes on occasion; and some of it was found in such poetic expression, as "a ruined female is like a beautiful star, turned aside from the glorious path in which she rolled in music around the sun."[19] There were even elegies:

The Dying Prostitute—An Elegy

Weep o'er the mis'ries of a wretched maid,
Who sacrific'd to man her health and fame:
Whose love and truth, and trust were all repaid
By want and woe, disease and shame.[20]

Both Protestant and Catholic groups established institutional homes for girls who might otherwise end up in prostitution. Best known of the institutions designed to protect young girls was the American Female Guardian Society.[21] Prostitutes themselves were a matter of concern. Special missions were established, such as the Five Points Mission in New York, to deal with them and other members of the social underground. Even smaller cities got into the act. A Galesburg, Illinois, society reported in 1845:

Although we have not been called upon to mourn the fall of any members of our society, yet some circumstances lead us to apprehend that there have been recent outrages upon the cause of moral purity within the bounds of our congregation.[22]

Many of the societies, often called Magdalen Societies or Female Reform Societies, established homes for prostitutes where women were given training, usually in housework, and then placed in jobs, preferably at some distance away from their past haunts.[23] A Minnesota State Magdalen Society was established in Saint Paul in October 1873, and by May, 1874, eleven Minnesota communities had sent women there for rehabilitation.[24]

What made the American situation somewhat different from the European was the existence of brand-new settlements in previously unsettled areas and the mass immigration from other countries; many of the immigrants were single men working so they could bring their wives or families over or to support a wife of their own here. San Francisco, at the time of the rapid growth of the city caused by the gold rush, is a case in point. Gold was reported in January 1848, on the south fork of the American River, and as word spread there was a mass movement of men into northern California. Most of the early female arrivals were prostitutes of Mexican, Spanish, or French descent, who came from Mexico, Central and South America, particularly Peru and Chile, where there were also large French colonies. In 1849 Patrick Dillon, later to be French consul in San Francisco, observed that "weeks never pass that some Chilean or American brig loaded by speculators does not discharge here a cargo of women. This sort of traffic is, they assure me, that which produces at the time the most prompt profits." By 1852 these arrivals were commonplace, and one "respectable" woman of San Francisco noted matter-of-factly in a letter to a daughter back East: "May 30th Capt. Mann arrived today with a cargo of Chile women."[25] In California men at first outnumbered women fifty or one hundred to one and though the ratio between the sexes began to close somewhat, for decades there was a three-to-one ratio of males to females in the state, and not until the twentieth century did the radio begin to approach equality.

Under such circumstances, it was difficult for a woman to turn down the many suitors who besieged her. Sarah Royce, a leader of San Francisco society, accepted the necessity of prostitution, but still worried about the dangers that respectable married women had to face, since every woman was offered presents and given attention by all kinds of men. A Sacramento woman about the same time wrote that

> Every man thought that every woman in that day a beauty. Even I have had men come forty miles over the mountains, just to look at me, and I was never called a handsome woman, in my best days, even by my most ardent admirers.[26]

In the mining camps the women were even more scarce. Bret Harte's stories give vivid pictures of life in the mining settlements, and the prostitute appears in several of them. Perhaps the most famous of his stories, "The Luck of Roaring Camp," recounts the effect of the birth of a son to the camp prostitute, Cherokee Sal, who died after giving birth to the baby. Harte, following the more respectable conventions of his time, never quite calls Cherokee Sal a prostitute, but he made his meaning clear by referring to her as "a coarse" and "very sinful woman," one of the two females in the area, the other being a donkey. The infant died within a year, but not before he had changed the miners' attitudes, and brought tremendous luck to the camp. Almost all Harte's stories about prostitutes are tragedies, but he is sympathetic to their plight. In "The Outcasts of Poker Flat," two prostitutes, Mother Shipton and the Duchess, are isolated during a snowstorm with an innocent young bride-to-be. The failing effort of the two to survive and protect the girl led the narrator to conclude that the rescuers, who arrived a little too late, would have been unable to tell by their devoted faces which of the women had "sinned." In "Miggles," the prostitute left her former life to care for her onetime devoted customer, Jim, who had been struck with a paralytic stroke. Miggles delighted in caring for the helpless Jim since it finally gave her a chance to be a mother.[27] Later mining camps throughout the American West, up into Canada and Alaska, went through much the same pattern of life as did the cow towns on the western trails, although few of them had a Harte around to record their doings.[28]

Most of the women on the frontier who served as prostitutes were young, most were white, and most were unmarried, although there was a sprinkling of Blacks, Indians, Chinese, and others. The only real criterion was being female; everything else was incidental.

Some girls became prostitutes at fourteen, others were still prostitutes at the age of forty, but in the western cow and mining towns, the average age was somewhat below twenty, and after that they married, became ill and died, or committed suicide. Most probably married. In the post-Civil War period, a surprising number of western prostitutes had the last name of Lee, probably as an advertising gimmick since many of the customers were former Confederates. Many went by first names only, and such names as Minnie, Katie, Hattie, Mattie, Annie, Fannie, and Jennie were common, although some used euphemisms such as Tit Bit (a prostitute in Wichita), Dutch Jake, Black Pearl, Wicked Alice, and Little Gold Dollar. A Dodge City prostitute went by the name of Squirrel Tooth Alice. Newspapers of the day referred to their town prostitutes by various euphemisms: nymph du prairie, woman of the town, Mary Magdalen, our girl, soiled dove, frail sister, nymph du pave, scarlet lady, fair dolcina, Calico Queen, and girl of the night. In the census records they are usually listed as housekeepers or laundresses.[29] An exception to this was the case of Ellsworth, Kansas, in its census of 1870. The census taker using red ink listed, among others, Libby Thompson who "diddles," Harriet Parmenter who does "horizontal work," Ettie Baldwin who "squirms in the dark," and Lizzie Harris who "ogles fools." All lived in what the census taker called a "house of ill fame."[30]

Most of western prostitution was centered in the brothels, which were usually run by a madam who often ran a dance hall on the side and made money serving liquor as well. A large number of western saloons included side rooms for prostitutes. Many houses carefully controlled financial dealings, and to prevent any infringement on the house take, brass checks were issued, some of which still survive. In the morning the madam counted up the prostitute's brass checks and then reimbursed her at a percentage rate.[31]

Urban prostitution differed from that of the frontier only in its extent, and since there was a larger population of potential customers to draw from there was also greater variety. Urban prostitution was the subject of many scholarly studies in the nineteenth century. One of the most important of these was made by W. W. Sanger in 1855. With the assistance of New York City police, he had some 2,000 prostitutes in that city fill out questionnaires, giving such information as nativity, age, economic conditions, and the reasons for "entering the life." He found that immigrant women furnished a significant proportion of the prostitute population, indicating that the female newcomer as much as her male counterpart had to deal with problems of dislocation and change. In his sample, some 1,238 women, or 61 percent, had been born in foreign countries. By far the largest number, some 706, were from Ireland; it was the Irish who at this time were arriving on American shores in the greatest numbers. Germany furnished the next largest number of prostitutes, 257. Only one claimed Italy as home, three said they came from Poland, and one from Austria. None listed Russia or southeastern Europe as their birthplace, although a significant number were American born, primarily from New England, probably from those same towns in which there was a surplus of females.[32] In 1912 George Kneeland made a similar study of New York City prostitutes. Of his sample of 2,363, the majority were native Americans and only 664 (28 percent) were foreign born. Russia led all countries with 197, Germany with 122, then Austria-Hungary with 110, followed by Ireland with 58. Again the prostitutes, except in the case of Italy, probably reflected the change in the immigration picture.[33] It was not until later that Italian prostitutes began to appear in greater numbers. Included in the native Americans were 113 Blacks, a group that had not appeared in Sanger's list, which serves as an indication of the increased northward movement of American Blacks.

Another indication of the effects of immigration on prostitution is the appearance of Chinese prostitutes in San Francisco. The largest Chinese settlement in the United States was in San Francisco, and there were regular boatloads of women from China imported by merchants and tradesmen to serve as wives and as prostitutes. Women were sold for prices ranging from $200 to $500, and it was not always clear to the woman whether she would end up as a wife or as a prostitute.[34] Some prostitutes later were purchased as wives but many remained prostitutes and their fate was not particularly pleasant, for when they outlived their usefulness or had contracted diseases or otherwise became ill, they were sent to Cooper Alley, a back alley in Chinatown, where they awaited death. A reporter for the *San Francisco Chronicle* described the place in 1869:

The place is loathsome in the extreme. On one side is a shelf four feet wide and about a yard above the dirty floor, upon which there are two old rice mats. There is not the first suggestion of furniture in the room, no table, no chairs or stools, nor any windows. When any of the unfortunate harlots is no longer useful and a Chinese physician passes his opinion that her disease is incurable, she is notified that she must die. Led by night to this hole of a "hospital," she is forced within the door and made to lie down upon the shelf. A cup of water, another of boiled rice, and a little metal oil lamp are placed by her side. Those who have immediate charge of the establishment know how long the oil should last, and when the limit is reached they return to the hospital, unbar the door and enter. Generally the woman is dead, either by starvation or from her own hand; but sometimes life is not extinct; the spark yet remains when the "doctors" enter; yet this makes little difference to them. They come for a corpse and never go away without it.[35]

Following the example of Europe, Americans after the Civil War attempted to confine prostitutes to certain segregated areas of the city, to register them, and to provide for compulsory physical examinations. One of the leaders in this was a New York physician, W. W. Sanger, who even before the Civil War had become a firm advocate of regulation as essential for the prevention of venereal disease. He wrote that though

history proves that prostitution cannot be suppressed, it also demonstrates that it can be regulated and directed into channels where its most injurious results can be encountered, and its dangerous tendencies either arrested or materially weakened.[36]

Sanger made his study of prostitution just to bring about such regulation, but his report to the Board of Governors of the Alms House of New York City was ignored by all but the army until after the Civil War. The Union Army leaders, like their counterparts in Europe, were in favor of regulation, and when the army occupied Nashville and other cities they instituted regulation of prostitution. Once the army left, however, regulation was abandoned. After the war others, including such publications as the *Nation,* spoke favorably of regulation.[37] In New York, the scene of much of the agitation, a bill providing for reglementation was passed by the New York legislature, but it received a pocket veto from the governor. In 1875, after a Legislative Committee on Crime had reported in favor of reglementation, another bill was introduced, but this measure failed to pass in part because of the concerted opposition of women's groups, an indication of the budding political clout of the women's movement. The women argued that the licensing system was a failure as a sanitary measure since at best only a small percentage of prostitutes were licensed and dissolute men were neither inspected nor restrained. In 1876, an all-male New York City grand jury again urged the legislature to permit the reglementation system, but delegates from the British, Continental, and General Federation for the Abolition of Government Regulation of Prostitution were in New York City at the time and their influence in pointing out the deficiencies of the European system helped to bar any legislative act.[38]

The only city in the United States officially to adopt the European regulation system was Saint Louis, which enacted it in 1870. Taking advantage of a specially enacted provision in the City Charter that allowed the city "to regulate or suppress" prostitution, the City Council on July 5, 1870, passed the so-called Social Evil Ordinance. The provisions were similar to those of Berlin. Six physicians were appointed to the Board of Health to inspect the registered public women in each of six districts in the city. Those women found afflicted with venereal disease were committed to a special Social Evil Hospital until certified cured. The ordinance, with some amendments, remained in effect until 1874 when it was nullified by the Missouri state legislature. Then for several years after the nullification of the law, some medical inspection continued and the Social Evil Hospital operated on a voluntary basis. Under the ordinance, prostitutes were divided into three classes: the inmates of brothels, the occupants of rooms outside such houses, and the "kept women," or mistresses. No registered woman was permitted to change her residence without first giving notice to the authorities. Repeal came primarily because some 100,000 people signed a petition, and those who wheeled the petition into the state legislature were accompanied by young girls attired in spotless white gowns. Against such tactics the legislators proved helpless.[39]

For a time, however, regulation seemed to be the wave of the future as cities across the country contemplated such programs. Not only New York City, but Chicago, Cincinnati, San Francisco, and Philadelphia all witnessed strong efforts toward regulation. In the mid-1870s, for example, a renowned Philadelphia surgeon, Samuel D. Gross, addressed the American Medical Association in favor of some legal regulation:

> We send missionaries among the heathen in foreign lands, but neglect this fearful plague-spot at our own doors and at our own fireside . . . we permit our own brother to contract a loathsome disease . . . taint and infect his offspring unto the third or even unto the fourth generation. The only remedy for this evil is the licensing of prostitution.[40]

Two years later J. Marion Sims, in his presidential address to the AMA, added his voice to those urging regulation. He felt that with the new knowledge of syphilis, it became essential that the physician become involved in politics to bring about better public health measures.

Shall it be said that we, the representatives of the medical profession of a great nation, the custodians of the health of forty million of people, cognizant of all these facts, will longer let the people remain in ignorance of the dangers that surround them? . . . We must sound the alarm.[41]

In spite of such support, however, regulation failed, primarily because of opposition by newly organized women's groups. In 1874 a bill giving Pennsylvania cities power to segregate prostitution was introduced into the legislature but failed to pass; in Cincinnati an ordinance to regulate prostitution was defeated in 1874 after considerable publicity and public protest; similar efforts in Chicago failed in 1871. Unsuccessful attempts were also made in several other cities including Baltimore and Washington, D.C.[42] The repeal of the English regulatory acts in 1885 more or less ended effective American attempts to officially regulate prostitution.

With the failure of reglementation, most of the urban centers in the United States turned to segregation, the confinement of prostitutes to certain quarters, often known as red-light districts, a term allegedly derived from the practice of trainmen leaving their signal lanterns in front of a house or shack while making a visit there. The difficulty with the segregated district is that in most states (except for Louisiana, Arkansas, and New Mexico) such districts were against the law. Still law-enforcement officials favored such districts since they believed that confinement would not only protect the community against immoral influence but it would also allow them to keep track of dissolute persons and control organized vice. The "tolerated" districts, since they were against the law, could be raided at any time, theoretically always keeping things on the up and up. Inevitably, of course, police corruption was a sideline. Most of the cities that established such tolerated disticts underwent periodic crusades, usually touched off by local clergymen or by women's groups, which caused the police to raid the brothels or to arrest a specified number of prostitutes. Reform groups came in and closed houses officially only to have them open within a few weeks or months since the whole system was encouraged by the police and other officials.[43]

In spite of these difficulties, at least seventy-seven cities and towns had such districts, the overwhelming majority of them the larger American metropolitan areas. Some of the tolerated districts, such as the Barbary Coast in San Francisco, Bourbon Street and the French Quarter in New Orleans, became famous and still retain their fame. Others, like the Levee in Chicago, have disappeared. By the turn of the century, however, segregation began to lose out and according to a May 1916 survey of the American Social Hygiene Association, some forty-seven areas that once had regulated districts had dropped them.[44]

In a 1917 survey of prostitution in some forty cities, Howard Woolston found that only ten of them still had such districts: twenty-six of his sample cities once had had districts but closed them; only four had never established segregated areas. Included in his survey were all the chief metropolitan centers, but he also included Bisbee, Arizona; Butte, Montana; Savannah, Georgia; and Salt Lake City, Utah. Several of the cities, primarily in the South, had two or more designated districts, one reserved for whites, the other for blacks.[45] Some of the designated areas consisted of a single block; others encompassed a number of streets. There were also area variations. Most of the districts in the West and Northwest featured cribs, i.e., single rooms, where the prostitute worked but did not live. Often the cribs were located in large multistoried buildings, sometimes housing three to four hundred prostitutes, in which the bedrooms opened off a court or corridor. In the South and Southwest the prostitutes also worked out of cribs, but here they were a row or rows of one-story, one-room frame buildings or shacks, opening directly on the street. Regardless of the exterior, the crib contained little furniture except beds, since the women only remained in them during working hours. In a few cities the red-light districts were limited to two prostitutes and their attendants, but in most cases there were also saloons, dance halls, shops, and even other residents who were too poor to escape the district. In some cities the prostitutes lived outside the section and rented the cribs by night or during business hours; in other cities the women were compelled to live within the segregated section.

To maintain these districts the police usually employed some system of registration; at the very minimum they kept track of the names and addresses of the recognized madams and their houses. Landladies, or madams, were usually required to furnish the names of all their inmates and to notify the police of any departures or arrivals. Several cities required prostitutes to appear at police headquarters when they began operating in the city. The prostitute had to give her real name plus alias or aliases, age, birthplace, birthdate, place of last residence, the number of years she had been in the "sporting life," the name of the house to which she was going, and other physical data for personal identification. In one city the prostitute had to pay a monthly fee for a license certificate.[46]

Within a district there were distinctions among the houses and among the prostitutes. Some prostitutes worked under better conditions and were paid more for their services than others. Sanger in his study of New York prostitutes has an elaborate classification scheme, which indicates his own prejudices as much as it does reality. He had two main classifications, parlor houses and places of assignation, and each of these was divided into four groups. The first-class parlor houses were furnished lavishly, although he felt such luxury was not always in good taste. The women in these houses were invariably young and beautiful, were always well dressed, and could pass through the streets without anyone suspecting their occupation. Next were the second-class houses of prostitution, many of whose inhabitants had started in first-class houses but left them as "their charms began to fade." Women in these houses, he reported, had coarser manners because of their long association with prostitution, and the houses themselves were more tawdry. The third-class houses—and this is where his prejudices become most evident—were equal to or better than second-class houses but were staffed by immigrant women. The clients were also largely immigrants or transients, since many third-class houses were located in the harbor area and catered to sailors. Sanger called these third-class "public" houses because "neither women or keepers" sought to disguise their purpose. The fourth-class houses were where prostitution in its most "repulsive form" was found. Usually such a house was run by an old prostitute who gathered around her others of her "debased class and rented an old cheap basement, erected a small bar, and partitioned off one or two small cribs." These basement brothels, Sanger felt, were dangerous for a stranger because all kinds of petty criminals were associated with them.

He had a similar ranking of houses of assignation. In the first-class houses prostitution was carried on by appointment and in secrecy. The women involved could "scarcely be called prostitutes," but he nonetheless did so. Second-class houses of assignation were more likely to be hotels and boarding houses, but again these involved "respectable" women. Third-class houses were where shopgirls supplemented their income, and the fourth class, the lowest of assignation houses, were those used by streetwalkers who were also in league with petty criminals.[47]

Though few cities had the variety of New York, almost every city of any size had at least one exclusive house such as the one the Everleigh sisters ran in Chicago.[48] In many cities there were guidebooks issued to orient prospective customers. The earliest-known American guides were put out by restaurants, taverns, and other such places, but in some cities these came to be almost official guides. One of the most famous was the *Blue Book* (which had a green cover), which was first issued in New Orleans in 1895 and which continued to be published until 1915. The first issue of the New Orleans guide had forty unnumbered pages and was subtitled the "Tenderloin 400, or a gentleman's guide to New Orleans." The last issue had some 96 unnumbered pages. The 1903 edition included a couplet at the bottom of the title page:

> Give them a call, boys,
> You'll get treated right.

In the various books the houses and inmates were listed, some simply by name and address, others with more elaborate descriptions. Perhaps typical is the description of May Evans, who kept a house at 1306 Conti Street:

> Miss Evans is one woman among the fair sex who is regarded as a jolly good fellow, and who is always laughing and making all those around her likewise. While nothing is too good for May, she is clever to all who come in contact with her. Miss Evans also has the honor of keeping one of the quietest establishments in the city, where beautiful women, good wine and sweet music reign supreme. What more can a person expect? Just think of it! Pretty women, wine, and song . . . The signal of May's mansion is "All the Way." Phone 1190 Main.[49]

A guide called the *Souvenir Sporting Guide,* issued for Los Angeles in 1897, was much smaller but descriptions were similar. A Miss Ella Rorich was described as a

> popular young lady . . . occupying the mansion at 419 Commercial Street where you will be entertained in a royal manner. She also has four beautiful young ladies who assist in making it pleasant to gentleman callers. Miss Ella is very popular among the sporting fraternity and that alone is recommendation enough.[50]

Some prostitutes as well as brothels issued calling cards, or otherwise advertised. Nell Kimball, a San Francisco madam, advertised her girls as "Two bits for Mexican, Nigrah, Chinese or Japanese asked 50¢. French asked 75¢, and the American Yankee was $1.00."[51] In Goldfield, Nevada, "Big Matilda" issued a card advertising herself as "300 lbs of Black Passion," available at all hours, at 50¢ or three for $1.00. The Everleigh sisters in Chicago issued what has been called the most artistic, comprehensive, potent brochure of all, one that so irritated the mayor of the city that he finally ordered the house closed,[52] an indication of the tenuous ground on which the tolerated houses operated.

Zoned prostitution gradually disappeared from most of the towns and cities as presssure came to be put on the political authorities. Aiding and abetting the closings were the various vice commissions formed in many of the larger cities. In 1911 the Chicago Vice Commission aroused that city to the "evil conditions" that existed and vigorously urged a policy of repression.[53] The Chicago action was similar to actions in New York City and elsewhere. By 1920 some forty cities and/or states had conducted investigations and their reports were practically unanimous in denouncing zoning, and all but one city had closed its red-light district.[54]

The closing of segregated districts decreased, but did not eliminate, parlor houses, dwellings used exclusively for prostitution. Woolston found 168 brothels in the forty areas he visited in 1917, a large number but a considerable decline from an earlier period. New York City alone in 1912 had 142 such houses, only three of which reportedly remained in 1917.[55]

As in Europe there were a number of American women who became famous or notorious as prostitutes. Almost every community of any size had at least one prostitute whose beauty or notoriety is still remembered. Perhaps the most successful pre-World War I women engaged in prostitution, however, were not prostitutes but madams: the Everleigh sisters of Chicago. The two sisters were natives of Kentucky who had married unsuccessfully, turned to the stage, and ended in Omaha in 1898 at the time of the Trans-Mississippi Exposition. Taking advantage of the influx of visitors, and using money that they had inherited as well as earned, they opened a successful bordello. When the exposition closed, the sisters decided to move on to Chicago where they opened the Everleigh Club on February 1, 1900. At that time Ada, the elder sister, was 24; Minna, the younger, was 21. Everleigh was their adopted business name, not their real one. Even before the club opened, it had cost some $55,000 to equip, and the opening changed the nature of prostitution in Chicago. The sisters charged a scale of fees from $10 minimum to the more normal $50. Champagne and other drinks were also sold at steep prices. The first evening played to a gross business of $1,000, of which the Everleigh sisters kept only $500 since they refused to take a percentage of the fees that their prostitutes had earned on opening night. Later, however, they were not so reticent and profits mounted.

The Everleigh Club was a three-story house with quarters for some of the servants in the basement. There were numerous parlors with colors and styles to match their names: Moorish, Gold, Silver, Copper, Red, Rose, Green, Blue, Oriental, Japanese, Egyptian, Chinese, and Music Rooms and Ballrooms. The Gold Room, for example, had a miniature gold piano and gold furnishings everywhere. All rooms were stocked with expensive art and books. Upstairs were the bedrooms in each of which was found lavishly decorated marble-inlaid brass beds. Some of the rooms had mirrors on the ceiling to enable the customers to observe what was taking place. There was a host of employees, from barbers to masseurs, to aid the customers to relax.

Admittance required a letter of recommendation, an engraved business card (carried by only the "best people"), or a formal introduction. The house remained open until October 24, 1911, and during the eleven years of its existence, the sisters are estimated to have accumulated a profit of $1 million. When ordered to close, the sisters did so gracefully, and after first trying to retire to anonymity in Chicago, moved to New York City, where they lived quietly and respectably until they died.[56] Few of the prostitutes or madams could keep the assumed gentility of the Everleigh sisters or live quite so respectably afterwards; however, many "ladies" who practiced the trade retired in wealth and lived comfortably if not happily to the end of their lives. Many others, however, died young, many by suicide, others by disease. Still others married and settled down.

Equally famous, but more mysterious, was Mary Ellen Smith, a light-skinned Black who as "Mammy Pleasant" owned much of the Barbary Coast property in San Francisco. She built an ornate thirty-room, three-storied mansion in Octavia Street, which was known as the House of Mystery until it was destroyed by the great fire of 1906. Like the Everleigh sisters, she seemed to have made her money through control of prostitution rather than through prostitution itself.[57] Another famous San Francisco madam, Nell Kimball, ran a high-class house between 1898 and 1901. At one time in her career Nell had been engaged to Paul Dreiser, the brother of Theodore Dreiser, who wrote *Sister Carrie*.[58] Just how much Dreiser was inspired by her is not clear since there are many differences between the real Nell and Dreiser's heroine, Carrie Meeber, who technically, was not a prostitute but a kept woman. Dreiser, however, ran into censorship trouble with his novel because Carrie, though unhappy and discontented with life, ended as a successful actress with money, friends, and admirers,[59] much as was the case of Nell Kimball.

Many prostitutes, particularly the more famous ones, have been the subject of popular biographies that are often based as much on legend as truth. Apparently Americans, like the ancient Greeks, enjoy glamorizing famous courtesans, giving a misleading picture of prostitutes. Sometimes the role of prostitution is laundered away altogether. A case in point is that of Martha Jane Cannary, who has entered popular mythology as Calamity Jane, and it is difficult to differentiate fact from fiction. A confirmed alcoholic by the time she was twenty-four, she had served as a prostitute and dancer in various western towns such as Virginia City, Nevada; Cheyenne, Wyoming; Ogallala, Nebraska; Hays City, Kansas; and elsewhere. Her fame comes from her later association with James Butler (Wild Bill) Hickok. Their relationship remains ambiguous, but it is mainly her story of events that has survived rather than his. Part of the difficulty is that Jane was a character. A crack shot, she took to wearing men's clothes, and refused to conform to the traditional female role either as a good woman or a bad one. As an eccentric and notorious character, friendly with other characters of the time, she was much interviewed by newspapermen, who sent back to their editors her increasingly fictionalized versions of what happened in the Deadwood Saloon. In the process of her embellishment, her own past was glossed over.[60]

We know that in her alcoholism, Jane was typical of many another prostitute. Suicide was not infrequent, alcoholism and even drug addiction were common, and serving time in jail a fairly regular occurrence. Fortunately, for many, prostitution served as only a temporary steppingstone to a husband, but those who stayed in it found their careers shortlived since disease was rampant. Their problems were compounded by ostracism from most of society, particularly as sex ratios equalized. This ostracism appears even in the popular fiction of the time. A good example of this is Edward Z. C. Judson, who wrote under the pseudonym of Ned Buntline. He tantalized and titillated his readers by offering glimpses of the prostitutes who peopled New York's "garden of corruption." After giving rather sensational details he always injected a strong moral note of condemnation against the prostitute.[61] Nevertheless Buntline and his competitors gave some insight into prostitution. Most of the prostitutes they wrote about were poor country girls, or poor underprivileged slum dwellers in the wilderness of the city. In the stories they are always seduced; where upon they either voluntarily or by coercion enter into the life of prostitution.

There were also more realistic works that attempted to educate the public. Rebecca Harding Davis, the mother of the well-known Richard Harding Davis, was a novelist in her own right. In her novels she tried to portray the problems of industrial workers, the Black, and women caught up in the growing industrial cities. In her novel *Margaret Howth* (1862) she gave a sympathetic glimpse of the women inhabiting a brothel.[62] Other novelists followed her example, providing more or less realistic backgrounds for their heroines but usually sticking to the conventions of the day by having them either undergo redemption and rehabilitation, or suffer degradation and death. This was the formula of the best of the sociological novels of the period, namely, Edgar Fawcett's *The Evil That Men Do* (1889). Fawcett wrote about poor housing—the tenement buildings, the rent gouging—and other social and economic factors that led to girls becoming prostitutes. Inevitably the wages of such sinning were disfigurement, dissipation, and death.[63]

Best known today is the work of Stephen Crane, whose *Maggie: A Girl of the Streets* was privately published in 1893 under the pseudonym of Johnston Smith. Maggie Johnston, the chief character in the novel, found herself caught in a web of forces over which she had no control. The daughter of a brutal father and drunken mother, she fell in love with Pete, a friend of her brother, who seduced her. She was then disowned by her family, turned to prostitution, became increasingly depressed, finally killing herself.[64] Though melodramatic, the novel represented reality as did Dreiser's *Sister Carrie*.

In sum, though the American scene created some unique experiences, primarily because of the influence of immigration and the expanding frontier, the problems of prostitution were not much different from those of Europe. Americans held essentially the same attitudes, had adopted the same institutions, and looked to the same kinds of solutions.

12 MEDICINE, SEX, AND WOMEN

In the nineteenth century several factors came together to help bring about a change in attitudes not only toward prostitution but toward sex in general. One such factor was the beginning of scientific investigation of prostitution, primarily by physicians; another factor was a new medical view of human sexuality; ultimately the most important was a changing role for women and the assertion of equal rights for women. Both of the first two factors are interrelated and might be discussed together; the new role of women will be discussed in the last section of this chapter.

Perhaps the main reason for the new attention given to prostitution by the scientific community was the awareness that many of the ills of society were not necessarily inherent but were curable. Edward Jenner (1749-1823), for example, had demonstrated that vaccination could prevent smallpox. Ignaz Philipp Semmelweis (1818-1865) showed how using certain simple aseptic techniques such as a physician washing his hands with chlorine water could cut down on maternal mortality. The explanation for many of these breakthroughs came when Louis Pasteur (1822-1895) found that the air we breathed, the food we ate, the water we drank, and the earth we lived on contained masses of microorganisms, some of which were harmful, others harmless, and some helpful. He also found that these microorganisms could be killed by heat, and he developed a heat treatment, called pasteurization, which he applied first to wine, then to milk.

Pasteur's practical achievement soon produced results in other fields, in part through his own work, and in part through the efforts of Robert Koch (1843-1910), who described the life cycle of a contagious organism. Koch then postulated that a particular bacillus always caused a particular disease; by implication infectious disorders were caused by a specific organism. Koch himself isolated the tuberculosis bacillus, proving that tuberculosis was not a nutritional deficiency, as was often believed, but an infectious disease. Causative agents of other diseases began to be discovered in rapid succession. By implication prostitution itself might be a disease, and if it could be looked on as a disease, it too could be cured. Increasingly a medical model of sexuality began to replace the religious model, which had emphasized sin and salvation.

Encouraging further medical intervention into prostitution was the long association of prostitution with venereal disease. Most reglementation schemes had included medical inspection as their main justification. Physicians had been among the strongest advocates of such schemes, and their advocacy had increased with the realization of the dangers of third-stage syphilis. Moreover, the medical community could argue that there was a possibility that venereal disease could be cured. Albert Neisser, for example, had observed the gonococcus that caused gonorrhea in 1879. This was followed by the discovery of August Ducrey in 1889 of the bacillus causing soft chancre, and by Fritz Schaudinn and Erich Hoffman in 1905 of the spirochaeta pallida, the source of syphilis. Diagnosis of syphilis was materially assisted in 1906 by the invention of the complement fixation test for syphilis by August von Wasserman.

Since syphilis was the most serious of the venereal diseases, the search for cures concentrated on it. The key investigator was Paul Ehrlich, who with the help of his Japanese assistant Sahachiro Hata, experimented with a number of compounds that would kill the spirochete yet keep the patient alive. In 1910, the 606th experimental compound, an arsenic derivative that Ehrlich named Salvarsan, proved successful in both respects although it was a close race as to whether the patient or spirochete would expire first. Ehrlich continued to experiment until, with the 914th compound, a substance was found that was less dangerous to man but equally dangerous to the spirochete. He named it Neosalvarsan. Ultimately, however, penicillin and various sulfanilamides were found to be almost totally effective in bringing about cures of both syphilis and gonorrhea, but this did not take place until the end of World War II in 1945. Some of the incidental effects of venereal disease were also cured, such as the infant blindness associated with newborns whose mothers had gonorrhea. Karl Siegmund Crede found that by using a silver nitrate solution in the eyes of the newborn the gonococcus was destroyed.

Further encouraging medical interest in prostitution was the growing public health movement of the nineteenth century. Though public health is usually associated with the efforts to isolate contagious diseases or to gain better sanitation, it was also concerned with many social issues: alcoholism, the welfare of infants and children, incarceration of prisoners, improvement of mental hospitals, and prostitution. Probably the original public health concern came from the association of prostitution with venereal disease, but it was also strengthened by growing fears of the dangers of "excessive" sexuality. With the hindsight of history we can see that much of what the ninteenth-century physician diagnosed as caused by excessive sexuality was in reality often the symptoms of what we now know to be third-stage syphilis, such as tabes dorsalis (a failure of the locomotor muscles), but "lewd" and "dissolute" conduct itself was regarded as a causal factor at that time, and prostitution was part and parcel of what was regarded as dangerous to health and well-being. If science could cure venereal disease, it might also cure prostitution, and alert people to the dangers of excessive sexuality.

The reasons for the fear of excessive sexuality are not too difficult to understand, and have their origins in the eighteenth century. Since a real understanding of the nature of disease was impossible until the last part of the nineteenth century, physicians in the past often looked to philosophical systems to find cures. Physicians were taught that like heals like (heat heals heat-associated problems), or opposites heal (dry heals wet), or similar philosophies. As medicine grew more sophisticated, explanations became more complex, and the eighteenth century in particular saw the origin of many new philosophical schools.[1] According to some, beliefs about sexual activity played an important part.

The founder of modern studies of the reproductive system was William Harvey (1578-1657), whose *Anatomical Exercitations Concerning the Generation of Living Creatures* was published in Latin in 1651 and translated into English under the above title in 1653. Harvey had observed the hatching of hens' eggs, and also done considerable anatomical work on the deer in the royal deer park. From his studies he concluded that the one reproductive principle common to all living creatures was the ovum, and that in many animals the semen was irrelevant. This view was summarized somewhat later by the Swedish biologist Carolus Linnaeus as *Vivum omne ex ovo*—all life from the egg. Others came forth with supporting conclusions, particularly Marcello Malpighi, whose study of the embryo in hens' eggs was published in 1675, about the same time that Reynier de Graaf observed the changes taking place in rabbits' ovaries in the first days after fertilization and concluded that similar changes probably took place in the human female.

The growing tide of the "ovists" ran into a roadblock in the studies of Antony van Leeuwenhoek (1632-1723), whose life coincided with the invention of the microscope and whose microscopic observations were not equaled until the nineteenth century. Johan Ham, a medical student, brought Leeuwenhoek a glass bottle containing the semen of a man who had suffered from nocturnal emissions, in order to confirm the existence of little animalcula that Ham had observed in it. Leeuwenhoek not only confirmed the existence of such creatures, but noted that they were different from the animalcula he had observed in other solutions. He accurately described them as having round bodies with tails five or six times as long as their bodies and stated that they made swimming movements like an eel. To make certain that these animalcula were not the result of any sickness, Leeuwenhoek proceeded to examine the semen of healthy males. Here he observed the same kind of creatures, so many that he estimated there were a thousand or more in the space of a grain of sand. Through a series of other observations, he found that the animalcula died within 24 hours if kept in cold temperature but if they were kept in warmed conditions they survived several days. Leeuwenhoek gave the name spermatozoa to these animalcula, and the results of his discoveries were published in the proceedings of the Royal Society in 1678. Almost immediately other individuals turned to examining semen. One observer reported that he had seen a miniature horse in the semen of a horse, another reported seeing a minature donkey in the semen of a donkey. Still others distinguished male and female sperm, and some even believed they saw male and female sperm copulating, giving birth to little sperm. A decrease in the number was noted when ejaculation was frequent, and it was seen that age, health, and other factors also tended to affect the number and activity. The effects of the discovery was to emphasize the importance of the male in the procreative process, and to give a renewed emphasis to semen in some of the medical systems.[2]

One of the earliest writers to express concern with the dangers of sexuality was the great Hermann Boerhaave (1688-1738), who was a dominant figure in eighteenth-century medicine. Boerhaave was not a system builder but emphasized that the principal aim of medicine was to cure the patient. Nevertheless some of his ideas were seized on by the late-eighteenth- and early-nineteenth-century system builders. In his *Institutiones Medicae* (1708) Boerhaave had written that the "rash expenditure of semen brings on a lassitude, a feebleness, a weakening of motion, fits, wasting, dryness, fevers, aching of the cerebral membranes, fatuity, and other like evils."[3] The basis for the statement undoubtedly was the observation that the male after orgasm has a period of lassitude, but most of the claims seem to have no real basis in fact. Still, since Boerhaave had expressed such thoughts, others felt free to do so.

Building upon Boerhaave, several of the system builders of the eighteenth century, such as Georg Ernest Stahl (1660-1734), Frederick Hoffman (1660-1742), and John Brown (1735-1788), all managed to equate some aspects of sexuality with illness. Brown, whose system of Brunonism was influential, might be taken as an example. Basic to Brown's system was the notion of excitability, the seat of which lay in the nervous system. He explained all bodily states in terms of the relationship between excitability and lack of excitability. Too little stimulation was bad, but excessive stimulation could be worse because it might lead to debility by exhausting the excitability. A favorite example of the Brunonists was fire. Insufficient excitement was compared to a lack of air that would cause the fire to smolder and go out whereas too much excitement was like a forced draft that would cause the fire to burn excessively, become exhausted, and go out. Thus there were two kinds of diseases, those arising from excessive excitement and those from deficient excitement. Mutual contact of the sexes as occurred in kissing or close intimate contact gave an impetuosity to the nerves, while intercourse could give temporary relief, provided it was not engaged in excessively. Too frequent orgasm would release too much energy and excessive loss of semen was to be avoided.[4]

Though novelists, poets, and religious writers have often claimed that the company of wanton women weakened the sight, exhausted the marrow, and weakened the wit, such statements could be ignored as poetic license until the scientific community gave them credibility. The physician who more than anyone else furnished an intellectual basis for such beliefs was S. A. D. Tissot (1728-1787). Seizing on the ideas of Boerhaave, Tissot systematized them. He taught that man's physical body suffered a continual waste, and unless the losses suffered in such wastage were replaced, death would inevitably result. Normally much of the wastage was restored through nutrition, but even with an adequate diet the body could waste away through diarrhea, loss of blood, and seminal emission. Semen was a precious substance, and the loss of it under any condition imposed dangers, but unlike bleeding and diarrhea, it could be voluntarily controlled. Some loss of semen was necessary to propagate the human race, but other than this necessity the male was advised to carefully husband his semen, making absolutely certain that any loss went toward the constructive purpose of procreation. In fact, one of the most dangerous activities that men could engage in was the loss of semen from practices not aimed at procreation. Though Tissot used the term *masturbation* to describe such activity and his English translators used the term *onanism,* both terms were defined to include all types of nonprocreative sex. Tissot wrote that the semen lost through nonprocreative sex resulted in or would lead to (1) cloudiness of ideas even to the point of madness, (2) decay of bodily powers eventually resulting in coughs, fevers, and consumption (i.e. tuberculosis), (3) acute pains in the head, rheumatic pains, and an aching numbness, (4) pimples on the face, suppurating blisters on the nose, breast, and thighs as well as painful itching, (5) eventual weakness of the power of generation as indicated by impotence, premature ejaculation, gonorrhea, priapism, tumors in the bladders, and (6) disorders of the intestines, constipation, hemorrhoids, and so forth.

Though he was less concerned about female sexuality, Tissot was convinced that females who engaged in nonprocreative sex were affected in much the same way as males; they also suffered from hysterical fits, incurable jaundice, violent cramps in the stomach, pain in the nose, ulceration of the cervix, and uterine tremors that deprived them of decency and reason, lowered them to the level of the most lascivious brutes, and caused them to love women more than men.[5] With Tissot's "evidence" before them, a significant section of the medical community rushed to amplify his ideas, particularly in the following century, and the result was an ever-growing concern with the dangers of human sexuality and by implication of prostitution.

One of the investigators who exemplifies this is Michael Ryan, who wrote a study of *Prostitution in London* in 1839. This work, in spite of its title, is mainly devoted to the dangers of "excess venery," and along with some discussion of prostitution repeats most of the data gathered by Tissot and his successors. The implication is clear; those who engage in sexual intercourse with prostitutes are not only in danger of contracting venereal infection but of becoming debilitated by their excessive venery, some to the point of insanity.[6] Other medical writers tried to make their point by referring to prostitution only indirectly. This was the case of S. A. Graham, who is best remembered today through Graham crackers, originally based on his advocacy of unbolted (i.e. unsifted) flour. In a series of works Graham voiced his belief that many of his contemporaries were suffering from an increasing incidence of debility, including skin and lung diseases, headaches, nervousness, and weakness of the brain, all in large part due to sexual excess. He taught that sexual intercourse drew resources from both the animal parts of man (which he equated with the powers of sensation, motion, and volition) and the organic parts (those concerned with respiration, digestion, circulation, secretion, absorption, and excretion). Both the animal and organic aspects of the body were controlled by networks of nerves. Those pertaining to animal life were connected with the brain and spinal marrow, and from here were distributed to the muscles of voluntary motion and to the "sensitive surface of the body, or external skin." Organic life was controlled within the organs themselves by a kind of rudimentary brain or bulbous enlargement of the nervous system, which he called a ganglion or knob, of which there were a "large number in different parts of the body."

Since the production of semen and ejaculation in the male were the products of organic life, and the actual exercise of the organs in the "sexual performance" was a function of animal life, reproduction, almost alone of the bodily functions, was related to both functions of the body.

Though he realized that there was a need for intercourse for procreation, Graham told his readers that intercourse once a month was adequate and in no case should it exceed once a week. This advice was restricted to married couples; nonmarried individuals should abstain altogether because any sexual activity would prove dangerous to them. This was because it was not only the loss of semen that was dangerous "but the peculiar excitement and violence of the convulsive paroxysms, which produce the mischief."

> Young men, in the pursuit of illicit commerce with the other sex, generally contemplate the act, for a considerable time before its performance— their imagination is wrought up, and present lewd and exciting images— the genital organs become stimulated, and through their peculiar influence over the whole system, and this, to the full extent of its power, acts on mental and moral faculties, and is thence again reflected with redoubled energy upon the genital and other organs. . . . But, between the husband and wife, where there is a proper degree of chastity, all these causes either entirely lose, or are exceedingly diminished in their effect. They become accustomed to each other's body, and their parts no longer excite an impure imagination, and their sexual intercourse is the result of the more natural and instinctive excitements of the organs themselves.[7]

Even married couples had to be ever watchful, however, and if a man exceeded the bonds of that "connubial chastity which is founded on the real wants of the system," danger would result.

> Languor, lassitude, muscular relaxation, general debility and heaviness, depression of spirits, loss of appetite, indigestion, faintness and sinking at the pit of the stomach, increased susceptibilities of the skin and lungs to all the atmospheric changes, feebleness of circulation, chilliness, headache, melancholy, hypochondria, hysterics, feebleness of all the senses, impaired vision, loss of sight, weakness of the lungs, nervous cough, pulmonary consumption, disorders of the genital organs, weakness of the brain, loss of memory, epilepsy, insanity, apoplexy—and extreme feebleness and early death of offspring—are among the too common evils which are caused by sexual excesses between husband and wife.[8]

Graham believed, as did many others, that the loss of an ounce of semen was equivalent to the loss of several ounces of blood. Every time a man ejaculated he lowered his life force, thereby exposing his system to disease and premature death.

Reinforcing Graham's were the theories of Claude-François Lallemand. Lallemand was concerned with involuntary loss of male semen, a phenomenon he called spermatorrhea, and which ultimately, he said, resulted in insanity. Since nocturnal emissions, or wet dreams, were a natural consequence of youthful excesses, parents had to be ever vigilant, and prevent youthful minds from reading lascivious books, daydreaming erotic thoughts, or masturbating.[9] Lallemand's theories apparently led some physicians to advise young men troubled by spermatorrhea to visit prostitutes, a practice reported and condemned by J. H. Kellogg, whose Battle Creek Sanitarium perfected the breakfast foods sold by his brother. He said:

> There are hundreds of young men whose morals have been ruined by such advice. Having been educated to virtuous habits, at least so far as illicit intercourse is concerned, they resist all temptations in this direction, even though their inclinations are very strong; but when advised by a physician to commit fornication as a remedial measure, they yield their virtue . . . and begin a life of sin . . . In pursuing this course, one form of emission is only substituted for another, at the best; but more than this, an involuntary result of disease is converted into a voluntary sin of the blackest character . . . and which is not only an outrage upon nature, but against morality as well.[10]

Though it was accepted by most medical writers that sexual intercourse with a female prostitute was less dangerous than masturbation or homosexuality, still it was believed that intercourse with a prostitute also led to physical diseases, mental depravity, and moral corruption that would crush the human race.[11] So dangerous was sexual intercourse, in fact, that the only way a male could avoid damage was to engage in sex infrequently and then without prolonging the sexual act. William Acton, the nineteenth-century authority on prostitution, held that the dangers of sexual activity had been lessened for males because females as a group were indifferent to sex, and in fact had been created with this indifference in order to prevent the male's vital sexual energy from being overly expended. Only out of fear that their husbands would desert them for courtesans or prostitutes did most women waive their own inclinations and submit to their husband's ardent embraces. Women's reluctance forced their husbands to perform the necessary biological duty of reproduction in as expeditious a way as possible, thus avoiding severe damage to the nervous system. Still, there were dangers if the act was repeated too frequently, and any kind of seminal emission, even that aimed at procreation, posed dangers. The worst kind of emission, however, was masturbation, and the only way to keep biological man and woman under control was to insist that their sexual energy be used almost totally for the purpose of procreation.[12] Still, for those unable to have wives, Acton accepted prostitution as an inevitable factor in densely populated urban areas.[13] He hoped, however, that schools, churches, and other institutions would instill in young men the dangers of sexuality. He felt that prostitution resulted from unnatural marriage customs, which required young men to earn enough to support a wife, thus often delaying marriage until the age of thirty-five. The consequent celibacy imposed on them was almost impossible to achieve and prostitution thereby became more widespread than it otherwise would have been. Though he believed that women were less sexual than men, they had a "weak generosity" that they could not deny to men,[14] and to put the burden of preserving their own innocence on them was to invert the order of nature since woman was the weaker sex, designed by God to please the male. He felt it was intolerable that society tolerated the seducer and labeled the seduced a whore. Nevertheless, because this was a fact of life, and in spite of the dangers of sexuality, he felt that prostitution had to be tolerated because the alternatives were so unattractive.[15] Much to his own surprise also he found that most prostitutes did not enjoy sex.

Acton, however, believed that prostitution was only a temporary transition phase for most women, and ultimately most of them would marry. Women became prostitutes not through any deficiency in their character but because of the innate desire of women to please men, and men often led them astray. Though few investigators of prostitution would go quite as far as Acton in this respect, many agreed with him that the prostitute, except for her occupation, was more or less like other women. Others, however, viewed the prostitute as a pathological case. Cesare Lombroso maintained that the criminal and the prostitute were identical from the physiological and psychological point of view. Prostitution for him was merely the female form of crime.[16]

A somewhat less extreme position was taken by Charles Féré, who agreed that though some "prostitutes are more abnormal than the criminals," prostitution was different from other criminal activities because it was the clients of the prostitutes who were the aggressors, not the prostitutes themselves.[17] Since similar views were expressed by other writers, most nineteenth-century authorities did not consider the prostitute herself as an ill person.[18] Still there was something wrong with her in the mind of many investigators. The German neurologist and authority on psychopathology, Richard von Krafft-Ebing (who formalized the medical model of deviance), did not discuss prostitution as an example of "contrary sexual instinct," but he did imply that somehow the prostitute was abnormal. He wrote, for example, that sexual desire in woman was small.

> If this were not so the whole world would become a brothel and marriage and a family impossible. It is certain that the man that avoids women and the woman that seeks men are abnormal . . . The need of love in her is greater than in man, and is continual, not intermittent; but his love is rather more spiritual than sensual . . . Sensuality disappears in the mother's love.[19]

By implication then, Krafft-Ebing implied that prostitutes had a distorted sexual drive, a supposition that Havelock Ellis disagreed with. Havelock Ellis challenged any attempt to classify prostitutes as oversexed women and argued that they possessed a fairly average amount of sexual impulse, with variations in both excess and deficiency as well as perversion.[20] Ellis, however, suggested another categorization of prostitutes as pathological. He believed that many of them were "congenital" inverts whose constitutional indifference to intercourse with men probably inclined them to prostitution. Ellis based his concept of the lesbian prostitute on some serious studies of prostitution, particularly by Anna Rüling, who had questioned lesbian prostitutes about why they had turned to prostitution. She reported that more than one such woman replied to her that it was purely a matter of business since no sexual feelings were involved.[21] The studies of Sigmund Freud affirmed this aspect of the prostitute's sexuality although Freud generally ignored the topic himself. But he did state that an overactive sex life in itself was dangerous.[22]

However, since the prostitute was different from other women, something must be wrong with her, and many followers of Freud ignored the temporary or short-lived careers of most prostitutes, and attempted to find psychiatric explanations for why women turned to prostitution. One researcher, Karl Abraham, agreed with Ellis that prostitutes were not necessarily oversexed, but then proceeded to argue, without much evidence, that it was only when a woman could not enjoy the sex act with one partner that she felt compelled to change partners constantly, in other words to become a female Don Juan. In his explanation, the prostitute avenged herself on every male by demonstrating that the sex act, which was so important to him, meant very little to her; she was thus unconsciously or perhaps consciously humiliating all men by having intercourse with any and all customers.[23] Edward Glover argued, primarily from theoretical grounds, that the Oedipus conflict was an important determinant in the development of the prostitute. He felt that even though the prostitute had broken away from her home and love ties with her father, beneath the surface of rebellious independence the prostitute suffered from childish hostilities toward her mother and acute disappointment with her father. Most prostitutes, he concluded, were sexually frigid, had an unconscious hostility toward males, and had homosexual tendencies.[24] Several other investigators accepted the concept of latent homosexuality, although few went as far as Frank Caprio, who argued that prostitution was a defense mechanism against homosexual desires, desires that had forced the prostitute to turn to a pseudo-heterosexuality rather than overt homosexual action.[25]

Most such psychoanalytic studies of prostitution were not based on field work, and even those that did include contact with prostitutes generalized from a pitifully few cases, usually from the chance patient that a psychoanalyst or psychiatrist might have had. For this reason the medical pathology model for prostitution, even in terms of psychoanalytic concepts, has never gained the dominance that it has in other fields of sexual behavior. In fact, medicine seemed as much at a loss in dealing with prostitution as religion or the law. But because prostitution was a matter of medical concern, it was an important boon to research in the field since it enabled serious investigators to look at prostitution as other than a moral problem. The most important of these early investigators was the French physician Alexandre Jean Baptiste Parent-Duchâtelet, who in 1836 put the study of prostitution on a sound scholarly foundation. Parent-Duchâtelet based his studies on registered prostitutes in Paris, of which there were 3,558 at the time he wrote. He agreed with those who felt that prostitution was increasing (at least over those registered in 1814), but he demonstrated that inscribed prostitutes were not increasing more rapidly than the population.[26] Later studies showed that though there were over 4,000 inscribed prostitutes in Paris in 1854, the population of the city had increased proportionately.

Though Parent-Duchâtelet's study excluded the clandestine, part-time, and amateur prostitutes, as well as most of the higher-status prostitutes, it is still invaluable for information on the social background of prostitutes. He found, for example, that the inscribed prostitute was in her late teens or early twenties, illiterate, poor, probably illegitimate or from a broken family, and likely to have regarded herself as a prostitute for only a short time and willing to leave it if something better turned up. Of the 12,607 different women registered as prostitutes between 1816 and 1831, he found that one-third had come from Paris; most of the rest were from other parts of France, usually areas close to Paris. Only 506 of the women had been foreigners or had not indicated the place of their origin.[27] The great majority of the inscribed prostitutes came from domestic or working-class families; four had fathers who were lawyers or physicians, three had teacher fathers, and four had fathers who were architects or builders. Of the 828 fathers about whom he was able to gain information, 113 were unskilled day laborers.[28] One-fourth of the prostitutes born in Paris were illegitimate, a slightly higher ratio than those born outside Paris.[29] More than half the prostitutes were between the ages of 20 and 26, although there was one of 12 and another of 65. Only five of the registered prostitutes were over 58, whereas 229 were 18 or under. One woman had first registered as a prostitute at 62, and two others had become prostitutes when they were 10. A surprising number of prostitutes had been registered for less than a year, while only one had worked as a prostitute for over twenty years. Most of the prostitutes had been plying their trade for less than five years.[30] More than half the prostitutes could not write their names, and many of the others could do so only very badly.[31]

Parent-Duchâtelet also questioned the women in his sample study on why they had become prostitutes; he was aware that his statistics were probably not particularly reliable since the women did not always give the real reasons. Of the 5,138 women he questioned, 1,441 said they had turned to prostitution voluntarily to earn a living; 1,255 others had either been expelled from their homes or deserted by their parents and found prostitution the only way they could support themselves; 60 said they had been forced to turn to prostitution in order to support their parents or other relatives; 280 had arrived in Paris from the country only to find that they were without funds and prostitution was the only work open to them; 404 women said they had been brought to Paris by other people and had turned to prostitution to survive; 289 girls said they had been domestics or servants who had been seduced by their masters and then abandoned, and 1,425 said they had been mistresses or concubines who had been deserted by their lovers.[32] It was obvious from Parent-Duchâtelet's studies that economic, educational, and sociological reasons played a key part in prostitution, whereas in the past, at least in the Judaic-Christian cultures, the prostitute had usually been regarded as a "fallen" woman who had turned to prostitution because of some moral defect in her character, a defect that could be overcome only be reconverting her to religion, a view that in slightly different form was perpetuated by the psychoanalysts in their attempt to establish a medical model for prostitution.

Parent-Duchâtelet furnished a model for others to follow. His work was much admired and widely imitated in the nineteenth century, although most of his successors were not as thorough in their investigations as he was. One of the exceptions was William Tait, a house surgeon in the Edinburgh Lock Hospital, who attempted to do for Edinburgh what Parent-Duchâtelet had done for Paris. His findings were similar in many ways. Tait found that most of the Edinburgh prostitutes, some 60 percent of those he had data on, came from Edinburgh itself. The next largest contingent, 15 percent, came from the neighboring city of Glasgow, with other parts of Scotland and Ireland also contributing.[33] Based on the records of the Lock Hospital, Tait found that of 1,000 women admitted for treatment of venereal disease between 1835 and 1839, more than half were between 15 and 20 years of age, an indication that prostitutes started young. The next largest group, approximately 20 percent, was between 20 and 25 years of age. There were fewer in each succeeding five-year age group. Only six women in his sample were over 40, and forty-two were under 15 years of age. The youngest girl admitted for treatment was 9 years of age.[34] Unlike the Parisian prostitutes, the Edinburgh prostitutes were on the whole literate (only about 14 percent could not read), which showed that better educational opportunities were available in Scotland. The Tait study classed most prostitutes as religious, which was true generally of other nineteenth-century studies. Tait also found that the women in his sample were accustomed to drinking fairly large quantities of alcohol,[35] and he indicated a close correlation between the liquor trade and prostitution. Tait's study also demonstrated the social stratification inherent in prostitution. He identified over 200 premises used as brothels of one kind or another. Three of these he classified as "genteel" houses of assignation, 15 as second-rate houses of assignation, 10 as licensed taverns, 25 as ginger beer shops (i.e., taverns that had lost their liquor license and kept open by selling nonalcoholic beverages), 10 as "genteel" public brothels, 18 as second-rate and 25 as third-rate brothels, plus 97 that he classed as "very low brothels, eating, and lodging houses." The total was 203.[36]

The findings of Tait in Edinburgh were more or less similar to those made by Henry Mayhew and his collaborator Bracebridge Hemyng from London.[37] The difficulty with most of these studies is that they were not comprehensive. Most were based on arrest statistics, and by implication concentrated on the less affluent prostitutes. The London study, for example, was based on a total of 10,000 women arrested for prostitution over an 18-year period, from 1837 to 1854. Parent-Duchâtelet, Tait, and Hemyng, however, were conscious of the limitation of their studies, and tried either to limit their conclusions or to compensate for their skewed sample by including other kinds of data. Hemyng, for example, divided London prostitutes into three classes: those who were kept by men of independent means (and thus were hardly ever arrested), those who lived in apartments and supported themselves "by the produce of their vagrant amours," and those who lived in brothels. He also included many part-time prostitutes, whom he classed as sailors' women, soldiers' women, women of thieves, and other such groups, as well as park women or streetwalkers. All told, Hemyng estimated there were 80,000 prostitutes in London. Though the accuracy of his figures is in doubt, they serve to indicate how inadequate his sample was. Findings similar to the Europeans' were made in New York City by William Sanger in 1855,[38] and by George Kneeland in 1912,[39] the results of which were reported in the last chapter.

As the studies proliferated there was a growing realization that prostitution was far more complicated than it had seemed. It was not just the case of a sinful woman or even a sick woman, but a host of variables, and even the variables had variables. One of the basic causes was undoubtedly economic, but the French investigator A. Desprès, in a detailed demographic study of prostitution in France in 1883, concluded that it was necessary to reverse the belief that "poverty engenders prostitution." Instead he found that prostitution increased with wealth.[40] As Havelock Ellis later pointed out, we have to admit that a

> practicable rise in the rate of wages paid to women in ordinary industries can [not] possibly compete with the wages which fairly attractive women of quite ordinary ability can earn by prostitution, but we have also to realize that a rise in general prosperity—which alone can render a rise of women's wages ... involves a rise in the wages of prostitution, an increase in the number of prostitutes. So that if good wages is to be regarded as the antagonist of prostitution, we can only say that it more than gives back with one hand what it takes with the other.[41]

Obviously there were sociological, psychological, economic, religious, and even historical factors involved.

Because prostitution was so complicated, and involved so many variables, none of the proposed reforms proved effective. Instead the reforms sometimes dealt with symptoms or abuses and not with the basic problem, which was the existence of a double standard and the male view of the functions and duties of the female. Moreover, all the solutions tended to raise as many problems as they solved. As pointed out in an earlier section, reglementation, the favored solution of the military and medical community, did not deal with venereal disease very effectively. And it also gave rise to all sorts of police abuse. Its greatest difficulty, however, was that it put the prostitute into a special class, perpetuating women in an occupation that previously had been a transitional one for most women. The establishment of Magdalen Houses, a traditional religious solution, also raised problems. These houses undoubtedly helped the woman who wanted to leave the life of a prostitute—but only the woman who also wanted to repent and return to religion. Many women might well have wanted to leave "the life," but repentance alone was too thin a diet.

Those who opposed reglementation had no alternative to offer. Though they criticized the system, its advocates argued that it was better than nothing and waited for the reformers to offer something better. The only alternative advocated by many reformers was greater concentration on the redemption of the individual prostitute, a solution advocated since the advent of Christianity, and which had not yet solved the problem. Obviously religious reformers were great advocates of repentance,[42] but so were many secular reformers like Charles Dickens, who perhaps can be taken as representative of the more enlightened reformers.

Dickens publicized in his novels how people in the poorer classes lived. Some of his characters were prostitutes, most notably Nancy in

Oliver Twist. One of his devoted readers and admirers, the Baroness Angela Burdett Coutts, decided, with his assistance, to establish a home for repentant prostitutes. At her insistence the home was called Urania College, though it is evident that Dickens himself would have preferred something less pretentious. The "college" opened its doors for occupancy in 1847 with a strict set of rules and regulations. To recruit prospective residents Dickens wrote a pamphlet to pass out to prostitutes in prisons and on the streets. The pamphlet began:

> You will see, on beginning to read this letter, that it is not addressed to you by name. But I address it to a woman—a very young woman still who was born to be happy, and has lived miserably; who has no prospect before her but sorrow, or behind her but a wasted youth; who if she has ever been a mother, has felt shame instead of pride in her own unhappy child. You are such a person or this letter would not be put into your hands . . .

The pamphlet was simple, moving, and somewhat effective. Some women did come to the college. Many who might have been interested probably never learned of its existence since almost 40 percent of the London prostitutes were unable to read, and most of those who could read did so only with difficulty. Some aspects of the college were questionable. Dickens himself resented the self-righteous superiority of the supervisors. Eventually the home was closed not only because the "inmates" became discontented and rebellious but because the few successful cases of reform did not seem to Miss Coutts and her advisers to justify the time, effort, and money required.[43] After this, Dickens, who never lost interest, concentrated his efforts on reforming individual prostitutes, a practice followed by many other prominent Englishmen of his time, including William Gladstone, who was several times prime minister. Gladstone used to pick up prostitutes on the street, bring them home to have tea and meet his wife, and then together he and his wife tried to persuade them to abandon their life.

Baroness Coutt's scheme failed, though she came to represent a new element in prostitution, namely, women themselves. Part of the difficulty in dealing with prostitution in the past was that prostitution traditionally had been viewed in male terms. Male sexual needs were accepted but female sexual needs were not, and the prostitute was set off from the investigators not only by her occupation but by her sex. Women in the nineteenth century, however, began to assert themselves and in the process became interested in prostitution. Officially their interest was not so much with their prostitute sisters but in preserving the family, although many women also became concerned with the prostitute as a woman.

Though many women continued to regard women as innately pure and men as the aggressive villains, the enemies were no longer men as seducers but males as a group who had kept women down. Inevitably many of the early feminists saw women as victims of male society. As Caroline Dall said: "Lust is a better paymaster than the mill owner or the tailor,"[44] or more simply, prostitution was caused by "the want of bread."[45] Others tended to feel that men should show the same kind of self-control as the majority of women. One commentator wrote: "I am profoundly convinced that the future of civilization hangs upon this pivot point."[46] Emily Blackwell attempted to associate the advancement of women with a decline in prostitution, since women, by their enforced chastity, had remolded their basic sexual instinct, and as they advanced toward equality, would reform men and "licentiousness will inevitably shrink and disappear."[47] Charlotte Gilman said the same thing in slightly different terms. For her, males had been overdeveloped sexually, like stallions, and would in time return to normal.[48] Jane Addams, the founder of Hull House in Chicago, emphasized the need for better economic opportunities for women as a solution for prostitution, but also better education, recreation, and less liquor.[49] Any number of women militants and their allies felt that prostitution was the "direct result of the exclusion of women from public affairs."[50]

Underlying these statements was a growing change in the status and aggressiveness of women. For much of the nineteenth century women were trying to escape from the cage that the emphasis on women as finer creatures had imposed on them. Some of the most extreme statements on this subject appeared in the medical writings of the time. One of the most influential theorists of female weakness was an American physician, Edward H. Clarke. In 1873 he wrote that women were unsuitable for mental activities or for higher education because of the unique period of growth and development that their bodies underwent at puberty. He argued that all females between the ages of 12 and 20 had to concentrate on developing their reproductive systems, and since the bodily systems could not do two things well at the same time, they had to neglect their mental growth. Even after their bodies had ceased to grow, their monthly menstrual flow put such a strain on their psyches that they could never exercise their minds without endangering their mental well-being.[51]

Such opinionizing undermined the faith of women in any medical solution to prostitution. It also inspired some women to question equally any denials of female sexuality. Few, however, went as far as Emma Goldman, who looked forward to a completely free world in which every woman could experience "the rapture of love, the ecstasy of passion, which reaches its culminating expression in the sex embrace."[52] Many women were not so hostile to sexuality as much of the current medical literature would have them,[53] and as the nineteenth century progressed women could come to terms with their own sexuality more easily. This was more likely to be the case if women could avoid pregnancy.

Pregnancy in the past was usually an inevitable consequence of heterosexual intercourse. "This man had his pleasure and the woman had his baby" is a cliché with considerable basis in reality. Although there are variables about age and health to be considered, it is estimated that most women engaging in intercourse with any regularity would become pregnant every other year. This meant that if a women married at eighteen, she might well have thirteen or fourteen pregnancies unless she practiced abstinence or engaged in sex only occasionally. Since the nineteenth century as yet did not know about the process of ovulation, there was really no safe period for intercourse, and the only sure-fire contraceptive was abstinence. On the basis of modern statistics, we estimate that a woman probably had a three percent chance of getting pregnant with any random act of intercourse computed on a statistical average.[54] Thus if a woman could persuade her husband to have sex with her only once a month her pregnancies would likely be further apart than if she had sex weekly or daily. Undoubtedly many women adopted the stance that a good woman felt no sexual urges as a means of avoiding further pregnancy. Many women turned to abortion, which though physically dangerous and regarded as immoral, was not technically illegal until near the end of the nineteenth century.[55] Many also insisted on *coitus interruptus,* which might have led some men to seek out prostitutes. Some women also encouraged their husbands to visit prostitutes, particularly if the men felt unable to adopt the sexual self-control their wives urged on them. Another way of dealing with the problem was for women to marry men much older than themselves, whose sexual urges were no longer as strong as they once had been. This practice also led to prostitution since, denied the companionship of a wife until fairly advanced in life, many men found sexual relief with prostitutes.

Women who did refuse to have intercourse with their husbands were supported by much of the intellectual theorizing of nineteenth-century society, which emphasized that women were not sexual. Indicative of these attitudes is the success of Dr. Thomas Bowdler in literature. Bowdler, a well-to-do physician, who never seriously practiced medicine but did take a great interest in good works of all kinds, was a man of the world who enjoyed reading aloud to his family the great writers of English literature. In the process of his readings he became concerned with the overt sexuality in Shakespeare and the bad effect it might have on the women in his family. This led him in 1818 to edit a ten-volume edition of

Shakespeare that included only that fit to be read "by a gentleman in the company of ladies." *Othello*, however, was too much even for Bowdler's purifying activities and he advised his male readers to transfer this play from the "parlor to the cabinet." Bowdler had been anticipated in his efforts by others, including James Plumptre who in 1805 published an expurgated songbook. Plumptre attempted to remove objectionable ideas and situations for Shakespeare's poetry, including all expressions that were in any way gross or impious, and all romantic love scenes or other activities that might propel young people into unhappy unions. The musician's song in Shakespeare's *Cymbeline:*

> With everything that pretty is
> May lady sweet arise;
> Arise, arise!

was changed to

> With everything that pretty is
> For shame thou sluggard rise.

As the movement gained momentum in the nineteenth century, the English Parliament got into the act by writing new and more stringent codes, with the result that English literature, and to a lesser extent its American counterpart, had to be careful about portraying overt sexuality in order not to offend their "lady" readers. The result was an official cleansing of literature to eliminate sex. One of the first results was the rapid growth of an underground pornography industry that was unofficially tolerated as long as it was not available to women and children, and it is in this new underground literature that the prostitute played a major role.[56]

Somewhat hidden by this attempt to depict women as weak and helpless creatures were real breakthroughs in the field of contraception that ultimately changed the situation of women. The first of the modern contraceptive devices was the sheath or condom. Gabriele Fallopius, a sixteenth-century anatomist who described the clitoris as well as the tubes that bear his name, claimed to have invented the sheath. He wrote that

> as often as a man has intercourse, he should (if possible) wash the genitals, or wipe them with a cloth; afterward he should use a small linen cloth made to the glands, and draw forward the prepuce over the glands; if he can do so, it is well to moisten it with saliva or with a lotion; however, it does not matter; if you fear lest caries [syphilis] be produced [in the midst of] the canal, take the sheath of this linen cloth and place it in the canal; I tried the experiment on eleven hundred men, and I call immortal God to witness that not one of them was infected.[57]

Whether Fallopius invented the condom is debatable. It might well be one of those items that have been invented a number of different times. From the rather crude sheaths described by Fallopius, the condom underwent various improvements. Eventually most of them were made out of animal intestines. There were still difficulties with condoms in terms of contraception. One of the major ones was cost. Until the last quarter of the nineteenth century, when rubber condoms began to appear, they were very expensive, thus not available to all. A second difficulty was the fact that their use was controlled by the male.

One of the contraceptives most favored by women in the first part of the nineteenth century was a sponge moistened with diluted lemon juice and then inserted into the vagina. An equally effective method was used by some German and Hungarian women, who placed disks of melted beeswax against the entrance to the uterus. Most methods were not foolproof, and even if potentially effective as in the case of the two cited above, a lot depended on the accidental fit of the beeswax or the right amounts of citric acid.[58] Most medical writers avoided the subject, which probably served to perpetuate misconceptions about effective methods. One of the first medical writers to advocate the use of a diaphragm, or cervical cap, was a German, Friedrich Adolphe Wilde. In 1838 he urged women to wear a pessary made of elastic resinous material formed from a wax impression of the cervix and designed to completely cover the os. Credit for the invention of the rubber cervical cap, or diaphragm, is claimed by an American, Edward Bliss Foote, but he had difficulty in propagating his ideas because of U.S. government prosecution under the so-called Comstock law of 1873. The most effective of the cervical caps was that developed by Dr. W. P. J. Mensinga at Flensburg in Germany in 1842. He took an ordinary hard rubber ring, such as used for correcting displacements and prolapse of the uterus, and covered it with sheet rubber to form a diaphragm across the vagina. Technically it was not a cervical cap but a diaphragm designed to fit longitudinally in the vagina with the forward end under the pubic bone and back end in the posterior fornix. It proved easier to handle than the cervical cap because it could be made in fewer sizes, and was easier to fit. Its use spread slowly through northern Europe, although widespread knowledge of it did not reach the United States until the twentieth century.[59] Mensinga believed strongly that women should have equal rights with men. He saw no reason why their lives should be made short and painful through bearing too many children. His discussion of birth control was both cautious and enlightening, and his influence as a physician helped persuade other physicians to adopt his recommendations.[60]

At about the same time that mechanical contraceptives began to reach a mass market, chemical ones also appeared. Usually regarded as the first person in the English-speaking world to become active in manufacturing and selling spermicidal suppositories is the English chemist W. J. Rendell, who in about 1880 first put his quinine and cocoa butter pessaries on the market. Cocoa butter, a yellowish hard and brittle vegetable fat obtained from the seeds of the *Theobroma cacao* plant, contains about 30 percent oleic acid, 40 percent stearic acid, and various other fatty acids. It proved to be effective as a spermicidal suppository because of its low melting point, which served to block the cervix with an oily film. The quinine used by Rendell was an effective spermicide since it was a general protoplasmic poison, although in many individuals it probably resulted in a toxic reaction. Other chemical means also began to appear on the market.[61]

While science, sometimes under the table, was applying its talents to the development of contraceptives, the vast majority of women knew little about which devices were effective and which were not. During much of the nineteenth century they continued to buy salves, fluids, powders, tablets, and pessaries indiscriminately, some of which were partly effective, others totally ineffective. The impetus to change came essentially from two contradictory sources: the radicals (incuding some feminists), many of whom saw the continuous burden of childbirth as degrading to women, and who also saw that large families tended to keep individuals mired in poverty; and the eugenicists, most of whom were upper-class people who believed that the world's resources were limited and that unless the poor stopped breeding and the rich increased their birth rate, civilization would fail. This is a somewhat oversimplified synopsis, but the interesting point is that both groups looked back to the Reverend Thomas Robert Malthus and his anonymous *Essay on the Principle of Population* published in 1798. It was only on the second and expanded edition published in 1803 that he put his own name. Malthus believed that human beings were possessed by a sexual urge that led them to multiply faster than their food supply. The result was misery, wars, and vice. Without such checks, the population would increase at a geometrical level of 1, 2, 4, 8, 16, 32, while the food supply would increase only at an arithmetical rate of 1, 2, 3, 4, 5, 6. Human misery was inevitable then, unless the masses could bridle their sexual instinct. Malthus, however, was opposed to any contraceptives; instead he urged his followers to restrain their sex instincts and marry as late as possible. Malthus, in fact, classed all promiscuous intercourse, unnatural passions, violations of the marriage bed, and irregular sexual connections as vice.[62]

It was because of the opposition of Malthus to contraceptives that those who adopted his belief in the necessity for controlling population but advocated the use of contraceptives were known as Neo-Malthusians and not Malthusians. Much of the early information about contraception put out by these groups appeared in the form of throwaway tracts designed to reach the widest possible audience. The modern contraceptive movement in English-speaking countries probably started with the efforts of the English tailor Francis Place. His *Illustrations and Proofs of the Principle of Population,* published in 1822, urged the use of "precautionary means" for married couples but did not go into detail about what these might be.[63] To remedy this, he made up handbills in 1823 addressed to the "married of Both Sexes" describing a way to avoid pregnancy. He advocated the use of a "piece of sponge, about an inch square" which was to be placed "in the vagina previous to coition," and afterwards withdrawn by means of a double-twisted thread or bobbin attached to it. He advised his users to dampen and warm the sponge before insertion.[64]

Place's pamphlets, and similar works by his disciples, such as Richard Carlile, were not subject to any legal interference, probably because the hostility to sex was not yet at the levels it reached in the middle of the century. Place and Carlile, however, were only two individuals with a number of different irons in the fire. Much of their energy was concentrated on a successful effort to repeal the Combination Acts, which prohibited the organization of trade unions. Place also campaigned for a basic reform of the English Parliament. As Place and Carlile diverted their energies to other areas, no one appeared to carry on their work. The next phase of the birth-control movement emerged in America with the appearance of a booklet, *Moral Physiology,* by Robert Dale Owen in 1831. Much of the booklet was devoted to social and eugenic arguments for family limitation. Owen discussed three methods of birth control: coitus interruptus, the vaginal sponge, and the baudruche, or condom. He favored coitus interruptus because in his mind the vaginal sponge was not always successful and the condom was both much too expensive and very disagreeable. He reported that a good condom cost about "a dollar" and could be used only once. He did, however, recognize the effectiveness of the condom in preventing syphilis.[65]

More controversial was the booklet by the Massachusetts physician Charles Knowlton. His *Fruits of Philosophy,* originally published in 1832, was the most influential tract of its kind, although his birth-control methods were not equal to his influence. Knowlton relied chiefly on douching, which consisted of

syringing the vagina, soon after the male emission into it, with some liquid, which will not merely dislodge nearly all the semen, as simple water would do—the female being in the most proper position for the operation—but which will destroy the fecundating property of any portion of semen that may remain.[66]

For a douching solution, he recommended a solution of alum with infusions of almost any astringent vegetables available to the housewife such as white oak or hemlock bark, green tea, or raspberry leaves, although alum itself would do. In some cases, he recommended the use of sulfate of zinc in combination with alum salts. Actually alum as a spermicide would have been fairly effective, although the same cannot be said for zinc sulfate. To be effective, however, it had to be used almost immediately following intercourse, and it is probably doubtful that those who followed his advice were very successful.

Knowlton's work marks the first evidence of difficulty in disseminating contraceptive information. He was fined in 1832 at Taunton, Massachusetts, and in 1833 was jailed at Cambridge for three months for distributing his book. A third attempt to convict him in Greenfield, Massachusetts, led to disagreement between two different juries and the dropping of the case. One of the effects of the attempted censorship was to publicize his book, and by 1839 it had sold over 10,000 copies.

Other works on birth control that appeared after Knowlton's mostly circulated underground until the last two decades of the nineteenth century. The most notable exception, however, was George Drysdale's *Elements of Social Science,* published in 1854 while its author was still a medical student. This is a comprehensive treatise on sex education, only a small part of which is devoted to contraceptive methods, some five and a half pages of the original 449. Drysdale, in fact, was much less interested in contraception per se than in establishing a case for birth limitation. Nevertheless, his was the most comprehensive discussion of the subject up to that time. He discussed five different techniques but preferred the sponge in combination with a douche of tepid water. He felt that coitus interruptus was physically injurious and caused nervous disorders.[67]

Giving a renewed emphasis to birth control in the last part of the nineteenth century was the growth of the eugenics movement. Eugenics defined itself as an applied biological science concerned with increasing from one generation to another the proportion of persons with better than average eugenic endowment. The word was coined by Francis Galton, a cousin of Charles Darwin, in 1883. Galton was a great believer in heredity, but unfortunately he also had many of the prejudices of the upper-class Englishman in regard to social class and race. Carrying some of Galton's hypotheses to a rather extreme conclusion was the first holder of the chair of eugenics that he had endowed at the University of London, Karl Pearson. Pearson believed that the high birth rate of the poor was a threat to civilization. Since this was the case, it became the duty of members of the "higher" races to supplant the "lower," a hypothesis that gave "scientific" support to those who believed in racial and class superiorities. Ultimately his evidence was put to use by such people as Adolf Hitler to justify their "racial" policies. Though the English Eugenics Society eventually opposed Pearson's view, he found widespread support among other groups.[68] One of the results of the eugenics movement was the growth of support for compulsory sterilization of "defective" persons. Many "sterilizers" also became concerned with limiting the fecundity rate of the poor. The "better people" were urged to reproduce and the "lower elements" were propagandized not to produce so much. Though this ultimately worked to the disadvantage of the contraceptive movement, it did raise general interest in population questions.

By the middle of the nineteenth century, however, it was becoming increasingly difficult officially to disseminate contraceptive information since this became classed as pornographic. The first laws against pornography had been passed in 1853 and these had been supplemented in 1857 by Lord Campbell's Act, which gave magistrates the power to order the destruction of books and prints if in their opinion publication would amount to a "misdemeanor proper to be prosecuted as such."[69] The definition as to just what constituted pornography was further extended by the so-called Hicklin decision in 1868, in which Sir Alexander Cockburn stated that the test of obscenity was whether "the tendency of the matter as obscenity is to deprave and corrupt those whose minds are open to such immoral influences and into whose hands a publication of this sort may fall."[70] Almost immediately pamphlets giving contraceptive information came under attack, even those that had long been circulating. The first attack came on Knowlton's *Fruits of Philosophy,* which was seized by a zealous inspector of police in a Bristol bookstore. The court found the bookseller guilty of selling obscene literature. With this decision before them, Charles Bradlaugh and Annie Besant, two English freethinkers who had established the Free Thought Publishing Company, decided to republish the book in London without the illustrations that might, they thought, have prompted the prosecution. Their main purpose was to publicize birth-control information. So, on March 23, 1877, they announced that they would publicly sell the book themselves, an action that more or less invited arrest. The police obliged, and they were tried in court. Sir Alexander Cockburn, the trial judge, held that there never was a more ill-advised or injudicious prosecution because the book had already been sold for more than forty years without interference. He carefully explained the law to the jury, and the jury returned a rather unusual verdict. They found the book was "calculated to corrupt public morals" but exonerated the "defendants from any corrupt motives in publishing it." Cockburn held that this was a verdict of guilty, which caused some consternation among the jury since at least some of them had thought they were acquitting the defendants. Even Cockburn felt ambivalent and had apparently decided to discharge the two without sentence even though they were guilty. This plan went awry when Mrs. Besant addressed a public meeting with Bradlaugh at her side. During her speech she claimed that the judge was on their side and they would continue to publish the book. This unfortunate remark led Cockburn to sentence the two to six months' imprisonment and a fine of 200 pounds each. On appeal the conviction was quashed on the grounds that the indictment itself had been erroneous. The immediate result was a rapid rise in the circulation of the *Fruits of Philosophy*.[71]

Following Mrs. Besant, women entered in force into the fight for birth control and for abolition of prostitution. Mrs. Besant, encouraged by her success, organized the Malthusian League, a militant body that set out to achieve complete freedom of discussion on the subject of contraception. In subsequent decades similar leagues appeared in Holland, Germany, and much of the rest of the Western world. She also published a booklet of her own,[72] in which she gave advice on birth control. In the first edition her favorite method was the sponge, but in later editions she advocated a vaginal suppository, and by 1887 the India rubber pessary (cervical cap).[73] With the Bradlaugh and Besant trial and publicity, the possibility of obtaining information about birth control became apparent to vast numbers of Englishwomen.

In America, however, obstacles still remained. Here censorship had also begun to appear, encouraged by American fears over the growth of the large cities and the gathering together of vast numbers of young people who no longer appeared to have the same values or the common moral code that had bound together an earlier generation. The American movement for censorship and moral purity represented a generation gap. The older generation, the establishment, worried about the rootless young working men and women in the large cities, and about prostitution. To provide moral guidance for these young people, various reformers gathered together in New York City in 1872 to form the New York Society for the Suppression of Vice. Soon afterwards the Boston Watch and Ward Society was organized, followed by similar organizations in most of the larger American cities. The secretary to the New York Society was Anthony Comstock, and his name came to be synonymous to a later generation with the whole movement. One of the first things that the societies succeeded in doing was a tightening of the postal obscenity law in 1873, and Comstock himself was appointed a special postal agent.[74]

The first published American work on birth control to run afoul of Comstock was a pamphlet *Words in Pearl for the Married,* so-called because it was printed in pearl type. Its author was Edward Bliss Foote, a strong advocate of contraception. His discussion of methods of birth control led to his prosecution in 1876 in the U.S. District Court of New York where he was found guilty and fined $3,000. Unfortunately we do not know just what the pamphlet said because no known copy has survived, although it is believed he described the cervical rubber cap.[75] In spite of Foote's prosecution, birth control information continued to circulate surreptitiously, although much of it was undoubtedly inaccurate. This situation was changed drastically by Margaret Sanger, a militant nurse. In 1914 she began to publish a magazine called *The Woman Rebel,* the aim of which was to stimulate working women to think for themselves. In an effort to do so, she announced in the magazine that she would defy the laws pertaining to the dissemination of contraceptive information. In 1914 she proceeded to publish a small pamphlet, *Family Limitation,* for which she was arrested. Though she attended the preliminary hearing, she fled to Europe before her actual trial. During her absence her husband, William Sanger, who had had little to do with his wife's publishing activities, was arrested and convicted after being tricked into giving a copy of the pamphlet to a Comstock agent.

Upset at the infringement of what they considered their right to know, a group of women, the best known of whom was Mary Ware Dennett, organized the National Birth Control League in 1915 to demand a change in the law. In the meantime Mrs. Sanger returned to America, shortly after her husband's conviction, anxious to stand trial if only to publicize birth control. The government, after several delays, refused to prosecute. Undoubtedly one of the reasons for the declining interest of the government in her prosecution was the death of Anthony Comstock. Prominent people from all over the United States had also come to Mrs. Sanger's defense. In the aftermath of the Sanger case, birth control information became more widely disseminated, although Mrs. Sanger felt she was still not reaching the working women, the group about whom she was most concerned. To do more in this direction she, her sister, Ethel Byrne, who was also a nurse, and two social workers, Fania Mindell and Elizabeth Stuyvesant, opened a birth control clinic in the Brownsville section of Brooklyn in October 1916. Since the opening had been publicized, there were long queues of women waiting, along with several vice officers. After some ten days, three women, including Margaret Sanger herself, were arrested. Ethel Byrne was tried first and was sentenced to thirty days in jail, whereupon she promptly went on a hunger strike that attracted national attention. After eleven days she was pardoned by the governor of New York. Fania Mindell was next, but she was only fined $50. By this time the courts were willing to drop charges provided Mrs. Sanger would not reopen the clinic, but she refused such a request. As a result, she was sentenced to thirty days in jail, immediately after which her case went on appeal. The Court of Appeals eventually held that contraceptive information could be disseminated for the "cure and prevention of disease," but did not specify the disease. It was this loophole through which birth control information continued to be disseminated, since the militants regarded pregnancy itself as a disease.[76] New York was just one state, and there were numerous other state laws to overcome. It was not until 1965, when the U.S. Supreme Court removed the last obstacle in the case of *Griswold* v. *Conn.,* that birth control information could be given out freely in all fifty states. At about that time the U.S. government also began to initiate positive programs in this regard as part of a massive program to educate the public. Britain had followed the U.S. lead with the first birth control clinic being opened in 1921 by Dr. Marie Stopes and her husband, H. V. Roe. Others soon followed.[77]

The birth control movement was symbolic of the changing status and leadership role of women,[78] but it had implications for prostitution as well. Women who at one time might have tolerated a husband's turning to a prostitute as the only real alternative to another pregnancy could now assert their own sexuality with little fear of getting pregnant. This correlation between prostitution and avoidance of pregnancy was recognized by many nineteenth-century reformers, although until effective contraceptives were developed there was little they could do. George Drysdale summarized the dilemma:

> It is granted that preventive intercourse is unnatural, but the circumstances of our life leave us no alternative. If we were to obey all the natural impulses, and follow our sexual desires like the inferior animals, which live a natural life, we would be forced to prey upon and check the growth of each other, just as they do. We must of an absolute necessity act unnaturally; and the only choice left us is to take the course from which the smallest amount of physical and moral evil will result. It is not with nature that preventive intercourse is to be compared, but with the other necessary checks to population, sexual abstinence, *prostitution,* and poverty. We have to choose between these checks, not independent of them.[79]

Mrs. Besant made essentially the same point in her trial in 1877:

> I must put it to you that men and women, but more especially men, will not lead a celibate life, whether they are married or unmarried, and that what you have got to deal with is, that which we advocate—early mar-

riage with restraint upon the numbers of the family—or else a simple mass of unlicensed *prostitution,* which is the ruin both of men and women when once they fall into it.[80]

In short, women could justify their reliance on contraceptives in order to save their families and keep their husbands. They need not admit that they had strong sex urges, something that a considerable segment of the intellectual community denied. Though a few militants such as Victoria Woodhull argued that it was essential to recognize the rights of women to sex before they could achieve full equality,[81] she was in a minority.

Though it was not until well past the midpoint of the twentieth century that a majority of women in America used contraceptives, the possibility of their use encouraged leaders of the women's movement, most of whom were the more educated and well-to-do members of society, to demand a change in the laws dealing with prostitution. The campaign that was begun by some of the more militant feminists in the last few decades of the nineteenth century attracted more and more women. These women demanded change in the semiofficial treatment of prostitutes— but for different reasons from those of military leaders and for different reasons from those of medical or religious communities as indicated in the next chapter. Though increasingly secure in their own sexuality, the inhibitions of the past were far too great for women to campaign against prostitution in terms of demanding equal sex rights. Instead they utilized the traditional designated interests of women as their justification, namely preserving the family, protecting the children, and helping other women. The movement began with campaigns against reglementation, moved into the question of involuntary prostitution, and as success came, finally led to a frontal assault on tolerated brothel prostitution. The growth of women's political power in the nineteenth and twentieth centuries can almost be measured by the effectiveness of campaigns to eliminate brothel prostitution. Women, however, were not necessarily alone in their battle against the "degrading" brothel prostitution, and the most effective campaigns were those waged by a coalition of women's groups, medical and scientific groups, and various reform elements.

13   ABOLITION AND THE LAW

This book has attempted to demonstrate that prostitution has historically been looked at from a male point of view, and the prostitute herself often as a base person with perverted sexual instincts. Challenges to this point of view came in the last part of the nineteenth century, and it is no accident that women were important in bringing about changes. Much of the change can be symbolized by the actions of Josephine Elizabeth Grey Butler (1828-1906), one of those powerful women of the nineteenth century who helped bring about a revolution in attitudes. She deserves to be classed with her contemporary Florence Nightingale, with whom she has much in common.[1] Like Nightingale, Mrs. Butler, as she came to be called throughout much of her later life, came from a prominent family. A cousin of her father's, Earl Grey, was prime minister of England in 1832, and her father was a powerful, and for the time, radical politician, who attempted to raise his six daughters to be as informed and independent as his two sons. And also like Florence Nightingale, Mrs. Butler had undergone a religious conversion. Though her sincerity and devotion should not be questioned, it is important to emphasize that religious commitment in the nineteenth century allowed women to enter places and do things that they would not otherwise have been able to do. She believed that God had chosen her to be His chosen instrument, although like Nightingale she was not sure at first in what field she was to be instrumental. There were differences, however, between Nightingale and Butler. The most obvious one was that Mrs. Butler was married, most happily, to George Butler, a dedicated Christian like herself who gave her strong support in all her endeavors. At the time of their marriage, her husband was examiner of schools at Oxford, but his marriage prevented him from rising in the hierarchy there, and the couple left Oxford in 1857, when George Butler became vice principal of Cheltenham College for Boys. Later, in 1866, he became principal of Liverpool College, and it was in Liverpool that Mrs. Butler first became involved with the prostitution issue. Before that, however, she had been active in the antislavery campaign, and the couple in fact had suffered much social isolation in Cheltenham for their support of the Union cause in the American Civil War.

Although Josephine Butler's family supported her and encouraged her, and in fact felt it important that a "lady" make herself socially useful, the immediate incentive for her finding something useful to do came from a series of tragedies. In 1864, her youngest child, her seven-year-old daughter Eva, died from a headfirst fall over a landing railing on the third floor of the family home as she rushed to greet her returning parents. Shortly after this the second of her three sons became ill with diphtheria, and although he eventually recovered, she herself became ill, so ill she thought she was going to die. When she recovered she felt more than ever that God had called her to a special mission. It was shortly after this, in 1866, that the Butler family moved to Liverpool, where her cousin, Charles Birrell, a noted Evangelical reformer, was trying to organize Christian missions to union workhouses. She made the first tentative steps in the work that was to occupy the rest of her life, when at his persistence she visited Brownlow Hill Union, where female and male paupers were housed in strict segregation. On the female side lived some 5,000 women and girls ranging from the incurably sick to the incurably alcoholic, the utterly senile to young children, from the insane to prostitutes. Many destitute prostitutes, reduced by crippling sickness, disfigurement, and winter cold, sought shelter in the prison associated with the union, particularly during the cold winter months.

From these women she came into contact with the facts of prostitution, and some of the girls she met at the union took her on night expeditions to the dockside areas, the Merseyside, where the Maggie Mays, as they were called, plied their trade. Most of these women were the derelicts of prostitution who charged a penny for their services or gave themselves for a piece of bread or a swig of gin. The more she became acquainted with the problem the more she became convinced that many of the girls she encountered were more sinned against than sinning. In her mind the women of the streets were the victims of cruel injustice, suffering from the unequal economic and educational status of women, and the double standards of sex morals imposed on women by society. She began to take home some of the more desperate cases she came across, lodging them in a spare room or in a basement that she had furnished for the purpose. Her husband accepted his wife's newfound mission and gave her his full support. In fact he made a point of meeting each girl she brought home at the door, giving her his arm, no matter how filthy and vermin-ridden she might be, and gently led her to her room as if to imply that she was an honored guest. Though George Butler was only a supporter of his wife in this campaign, he himself was involved in other reform movements, including a campaign to secure better educational opportunities for women.[2]

From her work with prostitutes, Mrs. Butler moved into a leader's role in the fight against the Contagious Diseases Act, which, as mentioned in an earlier chapter, had been enacted in 1864. Her first efforts were hesitant. She had made an indirect attack on the Contagious Diseases Act in a symposium that she edited in 1869 titled *Woman's Work and Woman's Culture*. Emphasizing her own acceptance of the traditional role of women, Mrs. Butler wrote that she sincerely believed that the place of women was in the home, but her acceptance was a two-edged sword. She pointed out that though marriage was the goal of all women, the proportion of married women to unmarried was only three to two, and that society provided no outlet for the gifts and energies of the unmarried, many of whom had much to offer society. As matters stood, this mass of women represented a total waste. She then went on to suggest that many of the social evils of the period were the result of rapid advances in industry, discovery, and science, linked to old-fashioned concepts regarding social conventions and ideals, and it was because of this dichotomy that women, particularly from the artisan and laboring classes, were prevented from obtaining skilled employment. It was this group, suffering from chronic economic insecurity, which formed the armies of prostitutes infesting the great cities. She objected to the attitude that females from such groups should be regarded as an inevitable nuisance in the modern city against which decent people should be protected. She emphasized that any theory that failed to take into account the individuality of females was to be utterly condemned. She stated that she was as eager as anyone to gain the salvation of prostitutes, but added that "by salvation I mean something more than penitentiaries, or sanitary measures for the protection of the Army, Navy, and those to whom it is a present advantage to be able to sin with impunity."[3]

From this hesitant beginning, she gradually entered into full-scale battle against the Contagious Diseases Act. Harriet Martineau, the friend and companion of John Stuart Mill, had sounded the first vocal female protest against the act in a series of letters to the *Daily News*. She had written:

> If the soldier is more immoral than his contemporaries of the working class, it must be because the standard of morality is lower in the army than out of it. Shall we then raise it to what we clearly see it might be, or degrade it further by a practical avowal that vice is in the soldier's case a necessity to be provided for, like his need for food and clothing?

This admission of the necessity of vice is the point on which the whole argument turns, and on which irretrievable consequences depend. Once admitted, the necessity of a long series of fearful evils follows of course. There can be no resistance to seduction, procuration, disease, regulation, when once the original necessity is granted.[4]

Miss Martineau, however, was semi-retired and not in good enough physical condition to lead the battle, so leadership soon fell on the shoulders of Mrs. Butler with results that have already been recounted.

Her ultimate decision to do battle required great courage because she was entering areas not previously regarded as suitable for women. Perhaps typical of some of the initial responses to her efforts was that by a Dr. Preston, who on June 24, 1870, wrote to the *Western Daily Mercury* in Plymouth:

I will pass over Mrs. Josephine Butler's address in public before men . . . because I believe that a very large majority of our sex . . . can only characterize it as the height of indecency to say the least. But it is my opinion that women are ignorant of the subject—but not Mrs. Josephine Butler and Company—they know nothing about it . . . Certainly if such women as Mrs. Butler continue to go about addressing public meetings—they may ultimately do so but at present I venture to say that they are ignorant and long may they remain so. I don't like to see women discuss the matter at all. No men, whomever they may be, admire women who openly show that they know as much on disgusting subjects as they do themselves, much less so those who are so indelicate as to discuss them in public.[5]

Vituperation did not end during her lifetime. A recent historian of prostitution, Bujo Basserman, wrote that though Mrs. Butler may well have felt she was doing good in fighting against the regulation of prostitution, she in fact created far more evil by creating many thousands more syphilitics, who in turn produced syphilitic children. Though Basserman recognized that venereal disease would have existed under any system, he argued it was the unrealistic demands made by the abolitionists that made control of syphilis so difficult.[6]

Basserman's cynical criticism is undeserved, and shows a misunderstanding of what Mrs. Butler was trying to do. Abolitionism in her mind did not mean the elimination of prostitution, only the elimination of reglementation and tolerated houses. Reglementation, at least as practiced in the nineteenth century, was never particularly effective in dealing with venereal disease. His statement also reflects a strong male bias since, if epidemiology was the main concern there were many alternatives to reglementation, such as the inspection of male customers. Nevertheless the arguments of Preston and Basserman can be regarded as typical of the ambivalence that Josephine Butler, both then and now, has evoked.

Ultimately Mrs. Butler and her allies were successful in mounting a campaign against reglementaton, but to do so they had to change an English organization into an international movement, if only because the campaign to institute reglementation had become international. The initiative for international efforts came originally from the medical profession. In 1867, for example, the International Medical Congress meeting in Paris had established a commission to draw up detailed plans for the international control of venereal disease through police measures, i.e., the reglementation system. In 1873 when the commission presented its report to the Congress meeting in Vienna, there were demands to enact international laws regulating the practice of prostitution. To protest this possibility, Mrs. Butler began sending letters to various repeal associations abroad. One of her letters was addressed to a M. Humbert, Neuchâtel, Switzerland, the head of a local repeal association. The letter, however, was delivered to Aimé Humbert, a powerful Neuchâtel politician who was a member of the Swiss Federal Assembly. Upon opening the letter, he immediately responded:

> I accept your communication as providential. I recall the vows and resolutions I made many years ago as to the formation of an International League against the scourge of this government-regulated evil. In my opinion, it is with much tact—I should even say, with a true divination of the mysterious depths of the question—that the English Abolitionists have decided to stretch forth their hands to those persons on the Continent who sympathise with their labours. England alone can take the initiative; but remaining alone, she would not arrive at a successful issue.[7]

As a result of this exchange, Mrs. Butler traveled to the continent at the end of 1874 and 1875. Her visit resulted in the founding of the British and Continental Federation for the Abolition of Government Regulation of Prostitution, of which she served as secretary. Within eighteen months the federation had active branches in most of the European nations. In 1876, largely through a visit of the vice president of the association, Henry Wilson, to the United States, an American group had also joined, many of them former workers in the movement to abolish slavery. Encouraged by the growth of the movement, Mrs. Butler set plans in motion to hold an international congress at Geneva. In September 1877, over 500 delegates assembled in Geneva at just such a conference, representing most of the European states as well as the United States. Almost immediately there was a split in the delegates between those who advocated an outright prohibitionist policy, which would make prostitution an illegal offense subject to severe penalties and those who favored abolition of the reglementation system. Though the prohibitionist policy had strong support from some of the religious groups, particularly the Swiss Calvinists, and would have eased criticism of those who said the abolitionists neglected the problem of venereal disease, Mrs. Butler led the opposition to outright prohibition. She felt that making prostitution a criminal offense would be a direct affront to individual liberty, that it would make rescue work nearly impossible by preventing girls from seeking help, and it would mean the abolition of one set of arbitrary police powers to make way for another.[8] It should be added that this stand of hers had led some to accuse her of being no better than a prostitute herself, but in the long run it enabled the abolition movement to gain a wide variety of supporters since few of those who studied the problem felt it was possible to eliminate prostitution altogether.

By now adept at politics, Mrs. Butler met the threat to her stated position by arbitrarily enlarging the British delegation, i.e., stacking the delegation and recruiting a number of women under the leadership of Mrs. Bright Lucas to pack the legislative and hygienic sections of the congress to oppose prohibition. Her rather ruthless efforts proved successful and the policies adopted by the five sections of the congress coincided with her own views. This is most noticeable in the resolutions advanced by the section on morality, which stated that impurity in males was as reprehensible as it was in women, that regulation of prostitution destroyed the unity of the moral law of sexes, that organized prostitution increased illegitimate births, developed clandestine prostitution, and that compulsory medical regulation of women was an outrage to women, that registration of prostitutes was contrary to the common law and the principles of liberty, that by regulating prostitution the state degraded females, that regulation incited citizens to debauchery, and gave immoral sanction to it. Mrs. Butler, though farseeing, was very much a woman of her time as were the other delegates, since this same section on morality concluded that it was desirable to address an appeal to all authors, editors, printsellers, and booksellers in Europe and America urging them to refuse to lend encouragement to the sale or circulation of pictures or works of a corrupting tendency, or what we would now call pornography. The other sections of the congress included those on hygiene, which contented itself with urging treatment of venereal disease, a section on social economy, which urged more economic opportunities for women, a section on prevention and reformatory work, which included two important solutions, namely, that homes established to reform prostitution "should be as little as possible of a penitential character," and that a system of intercommunication between all countries be established in order to prevent the trading in women and girls for immoral purposes. The section on legislation declared that the state had no right to regulate prostitution, although it did have a right to protect minors and to punish any collective organization of prostitution.[9]

Though the British, Continental and General Federation continued to meet periodically in congresses (its second was in 1879 in Liege), Mrs. Butler as well as many of her co-workers soon became involved in the struggle against child and involuntary prostitution. The question had come up at the first international congress largely through the efforts of Pastor Thomas Borel of Geneva, who had spent much of his ministry in trying to save juveniles from prostitution. He had presided over the section dealing with preventative and reformatory work, and it was at his insistence that this group had adopted a resolution urging a system of communication be set up to prevent trading in women and young girls. Borel had written a book about some of the involuntary prostitution he had observed, and this book was translated into English (1876) by Joseph Edmondson under the title *The White Slavery of Europe*.[10] This work helped popularize the term *white slave* although the term was not technically accurate since the traffic in people included those of all races and colors, and few were actually slaves. The term *white slave,* as eventually used in the treaties between different countries and in various federal and state laws, applied to the procuring and the transferring of girls and women for prostitution.

Clifford G. Roe, an assistant state's attorney in Illinois and a leader in the American fight against involuntary prostitution, was sometimes credited with first using the term in the early 1900s. Roe became involved in a case in which a girl had thrown a written note out the window of a house of prostitution reading: "Help me—I am held captive as a white slave." The incident is possibly true, but as indicated above the term predated Roe's use. The term was used also at an international conference of fifteen European nations that was held in 1905 to discuss the problem of international trade in women and children. Since at an earlier international conference on the Negro slave trade at Vienna in 1815, the French had used the phrase *Traite des Noirs,* trade in Blacks, the term *Traite des Blanches,* trade in Whites, was used at this conference. The British government translated the French term as the "White Slave Traffic or Trade," and this was often abbreviated as *white slavery.*[11]

Involuntary prostitution, as indicated elsewhere in this book, is nothing new, although by the beginning of the nineteenth century most European nations had taken tentative steps to limit the trade in women and girls. The most notable effort in this direction was the promulgation of the Napoleonic Code, which protected the personal rights of a woman until she was twenty-one and made procuration a criminal offense. Paragraph 334 of the code stated that the penalty for the debauching of girls under twenty-one was two years' imprisonment plus a fine of five hundred francs. Great Britain, however, lagged behind the continent in social legislation; under English law in the nineteenth century any child of twelve could legally consent to her own seduction; children under twelve could also be seduced with near impunity since evidence of young children could be accepted in court only if they showed a complete understanding of the nature of the oath. Usually the children were so frightened by court proceedings that they were unable to give satisfactory explanations to the judges so that there was no successful prosecution.[12]

This loophole in the English law made English children particularly vulnerable to involuntary prostitution, and it was precisely children in England who were most in need of protection. This was because Great Britain was the first country to enter the modern mechanized world as a result of the industrial revolution. This revolution uprooted old customs and beliefs, led to mass dislocations of people, and resulted in depressing the conditions of vast numbers. Men, women, and children worked in the newly developing factories from sunup to sundown with few holidays and little relief. Moreover, state intervention in England was slow to come because the factory owners insisted on laissez-faire policies as far as their workers were concerned, but demanded state protection against riots, foreign interference, and piracy. After a series of major campaigns, the British Parliament in the nineteenth century gradually began to enact protective legislation for those unable to protect themselves, or at least those who were believed unable to protect themselves, such as children and women. Instead of easing involuntary prostitution, the effect of the first acts regulating employment of children was to increase the prostitution of young girls since children now became more accessible. There were few alternatives for earning a living except the workhouse, where conditions were often much worse than the alternative of prostitution.

There was a demand for young girls because men were afraid of contracting venereal disease; hence, to lessen the chances of infection, many rich customers insisted that they be furnished disease-free, that is, pure virginal, prostitutes. This was particularly true of the middle- and upper-class males, who tended to set themselves apart from the working classes, the class from which most of these girls came. William Acton in his study of prostitution wrote that:

It cannot be denied by anyone acquainted with rural life that seduction of girls is a sport and habit with vast numbers of men, married . . .

and single, placed above the ranks of labour . . . . Many such rustics of the middle class and men of parallel grades in country towns employ a portion of their spare time in the coarse, deliberate villainy of making prostitutes.[13]

There was also a popular belief that venereal disease would be cured if the diseased person had intercourse with a young virgin.

From the perspective of structural-functional analysis, Victorian poverty served higher social classes in England. It furnished prostitutes and other forms of social amusement so that the men of these wealthier classs could keep their own women chaste. Some of the most detailed description of the exploitation of children from the lower classes comes in the anonymous eleven-volume autobiography, *My Secret Life,* the sexual memoirs of a Victorian gentleman, which was printed in the 1890s. The memoirs are a rather vivid portrayal of prostitution in England, and emphasize that the sale or abduction of young girls was not the figment of the reformers' imagination. Toward the end of his life, the anonymous author wrote about the pleasure he had with young girls, and justified his intercourse with them in sexually explicit terms:

Verily a gentleman had better fuck them for money, than a butcher boy for nothing. It is the fate of such girls to be fucked young, neither laws social or legal can prevent it. Given opportunities—who has them like the children of the poor—and they will copulate. It is the law of nature which nothing can thwart. A man need have no "compunctions of conscience"—as it is termed—about having such girls first, for assuredly he will have done no harm, and has only been an agent in the inevitable. The consequences to the female being the same, whoever she may first have been fucked by . . .[14]

In another volume he wrote that his friend had told him that he had

picked up half a dozen virgins in the streets. That a sovereign, offered to lasses looking in at Linen drapers, will get them a house, and that the sight of gold vanquishes them. He looks out for them quite young, for that turned sixteen they are scarcely ever virgins.[15]

The youngest girl he ever had was ten years old, for which he paid her "aunt" ten pounds. He wrote: "She was the youngest I ever yet have had, or have wished to have" and complained that she could not give the pleasure "that a fully developed woman could." Nevertheless he had several orgasms with her.[16]

It was not only members of the economically depressed groups who were fair game for the procurers and the procuresses but also girls from some of the more well-to-do groups. One reason for this was that the education of the middle-class girls was so prudish and circumscribed that they were often an easy prey for the would-be seducer. Once a girl lost her virginity the social outlook of the time led many of them to believe that they had committed an unforgivable sin and could no longer take their place among proper women. In despair some turned to houses of prostitution as the only means of earning a livelihood. It became a fairly easy matter for a dashing Romeo-type to entrap these girls; after they had been seduced, they were sold to various dealers who placed them in brothels. In fact, English girls supplied many brothels on the continent, and there were a number of procurers attempting to get young girls for the European markets.

There was even a standard pricing system: a healthy working-class girl between fourteen and eighteen years of age was sold for 20 pounds plus expenses; a middle-class girl of the same age group would cost about 100 pounds; and a beautiful child, preferably of the upper classes and under twelve years of age, would sell for 400 pounds, in part because girls of this class often had to be kidnapped. Probably only a small minority of girls were ever actually kidnapped, but few who went voluntarily knew what they were getting involved in.

Many girls volunteered for some sort of job that required them to go abroad, but they did not realize or pretended not to realize that they were in fact entering a brothel. Those who were entirely innocent found themselves stranded on the continent with no way of earning their way back to England. English newspapers connived at this illicit traffic by running advertisements that were ill-disguised appeals for young girls.[17]

Advertisements for "beautiful girls, between 12 and 15," suitable for adoption were not the only means of recruiting girls into prostitution. Railroad stations, public parks, theatrical agencies, and other such places or agencies were usually carefully examined by would-be procurers or procuresses for suitable employees. Obviously such traffic could not exist without considerable public indifference as well as the connivance of various law-enforcement officials. Belgium was a center of the European market because the Brussels police were on the take, perhaps influenced by the example of the King of the Belgians himself, who spent over 1,800 pounds a year importing young British girls from London procuresses.[18] Police of other European countries were not necessarily different although not all had a monarch with the same inclination.

It was the Belgian connection that originally brought the matter to a head. Alfred Dyer, the publisher of many of Josephine Butler's books, as well as of the English translation of Borel's book on white slavery, and a dedicated Quaker, was contacted at one of the weekly meetings of the

Society of Friends by a business acquaintance. The man told how on a business trip to Brussels he had visited a brothel and been assigned a nineteen-year-old English-speaking girl. In the privacy of the room the girl had burst into tears and begged him to help her escape. She told him that she had been in service in London, where she had met a Belgian "gentleman" who appeared to fall in love with her and asked her to come to Belgium and marry her. She agreed, and the couple set out for Belgium, but on arriving at Calais, her husband-to-be discovered that he had left all his money in his London hotel. He requested his future bride to stay with a friend in Calais while he went back to London. The Calais friend then took her on to a hotel in Brussels, which turned out to be a brothel, and the girl alleged she had been a prisoner ever since.

The businessman believed the story, but afraid of compromising himself, had taken no action. On his return to England, however, his conscience had bothered him and led him to confide in Dyer. Dyer investigated, interviewed the girl's parents, visited her previous employers, and came to believe the story he had been told. He set out for Belgium to find her. Josephine Butler, who was then in Belgium in connection with the Second International Congress, introduced Dyer to two Belgians, Pastor Léonard Anet and a lawyer, Alexis Splingard, who undertook to help him locate her. Splingard found her in a hospital being treated for venereal disease and arranged for her to return to England.[19]

During the course of the investigation, Splingard found that the girl was not an isolated case but he was unable to do anything about it. Dyer, after receiving reports of other cases from Splingard and others, joined with Benjamin Scott, chamberlain of the City of London, and Benjamin Waugh, of the National Society for the Prevention of Cruelty to Children, to form a Committee for the Exposure and Suppression of the Traffic of English Girls for Purposes of Continental Prostitution. As a first step the group communicated its findings to several English newspapers. The resulting publicity led to an angry denial from Edward Lenaers, chief of the Brussels Morals Police, who stated that no woman could be admitted to a licensed house of prostitution in Brussels before she had formally declared to the police that she was doing so on her own free will.[20] The British pro consul in Brussels, a certain Thomas Jeffs, also wrote suggesting that Dyer's information was inaccurate.

Dyer, fearful that he might have made a mistake, then went to Brussels, where he spent a week with officials of the Morals Police. Still uncertain, he visited a brothel where he immediately found an English girl who begged him to help her get her release. She reported that she had come to Brussels to work as a domestic servant, but when she arrived she was asked by the *patronne* if she had registered with the police in order to obtain an employment permit, and on replying that she had not, was informed it was essential to do so. Since the girl did not have her birth certificate with her, the *patronne* provided her with a false one that the girl accepted. Since filing a false birth certificate was a criminal offense, the *patronne* then blackmailed her to keep her there. Since she was registered under a false name, the British authorities could not trace her whereabouts. Dyer went to Lenaers's office to report his findings, but the chief was absent and he was referred to his deputy, who behaved, much to Dyer's astonishment, as if Dyer was a rival attempting to steal the girl. When the assistant realized to whom he was talking he left the room, but the incident led Dyer to suspect that the Belgian police were deeply involved. He then returned with Alexis Splingard to the brothel to get the girl but the two were denied entrance and threatened. Thomas Jeffs, the British consular official, refused to intervene. It later turned out he was a personal friend of Lenaers's. To further document his case, Dyer proceeded to visit other brothels in Brussels, where he met several English girls, some of them children, who alleged they were held involuntarily. Armed with their names, he returned to England, where he communicated his information to the press, which proceeded to ignore it. Jeffs in the meantime reported to the Foreign Office that Dyer was making a great deal of fuss over nothing, and hamstrung by official and semiofficial silence, Dyer published a booklet recounting his adventures, *The European Slave Trade of English Girls*.[21]

The Belgian government responded to the charges by inviting British police officers to investigate for themselves. Since the guides for the British police were the very members of the Brussels morals bureau charged with collusion by Dyer, they found nothing. Matters might have ended there, but one of the members of the Brussels morals squad, upset at what he felt was a whitewash of Brussels brothels, journeyed to Paris to visit Josephine Butler and tell her the truth behind the coverup. He made a formal deposition stating that before the arrival of the English police, the Brussels police had gone around to all the brothels and collected all the English children they could find in order to hide them during the investigation. Prostitutes who might have said anything were threatened with punishment, and brothelkeepers were ordered to deny admission to Dyer and Splingard. He added that the assistant chief of the morals squad owned two brothels, and that Lenaers's son was the superintendent-in-chief of immigration, and thus could assure that girls were imported without difficulty. He claimed that both the Lenaers were proprietors of a wine-retailing business and held a monopoly in supplying brothels.[22]

The result was that Mrs. Butler herself entered the campaign against child prostitution. She wrote a pamphlet, *A Letter to the Mothers of*

England,[23] in which she did not merely call attention to what was going on in Belgium but examined the factors that made such abuses possible. As Glen Petrie stated:

> Josephine's frankness in dealing with such matters, her habit of referring to prostitutes as prostitutes and brothels as brothels rather than as "unfortunates" and "certain houses," her attack on Society for its tolerance of these abuses, went much further than Alfred Dyer had done. She dared to point out, and it was the first time anyone had done so, in print, the strange Victorian taste for deflowering virgins, preferably children . . . . She emphasized the twin factors that made the international trade in young girls possible: the Regulationist System controlled by a corrupt police force abroad, and the defective laws regarding the protection of children in England.[24]

Brussels authorities demanded that Mrs. Butler either withdraw her allegations publicly, or under the terms of the extradition treaty with England, require her to make a deposition on oath before a magistrate. This ultimatum left her open to a charge of perjury if she filed a deposition or to libel if she refused. Mrs. Butler, however, had done her homework well. She appeared before the stipendary magistrate of the City of Liverpool to swear her affidavit, submitting case after case, giving names and addresses of Brussels brothelkeepers, and accusing the officials of the Brussels morals bureau of complicity. The magistrate, however, refused to allow her to go into her detailed indictment, fearful that she was incriminating herself. Undaunted, she went home, wrote an extension of her deposition, signed and witnessed it, and sent it with a copy of the Belgian detective's statement to a friend, Sir William Harcourt, the Home Secretary. Another friend of Josephine's, Lord Granville, the Foreign Secretary, unhappy with the earlier investigation by London police of the Brussels situation, had also begun to investigate on his own. The action of her two friends led to a special investigator being sent to Brussels. In the meantime, a copy of Mrs. Butler's deposition was leaked to the Belgian press, where it was reproduced in full by the leading Brussels daily, *Le National*. Lenaers sued the paper for libel and the case broke open.

The investigator sent by the Home Office, Thomas William Snagge, found evidence of a large-scale trade of English girls to Belgium, France, and Holland, and that many girls had been induced by misrepresentation to come to the continent, where they had been detained under duress.[25] On the basis of the detailed evidence submitted by Mrs. Butler and others, as well as a brilliant examination of Lenaers by Splingard, the court convicted Lenaers, his son, his police confederates, and eleven of the proprietors of Brussels brothels. Thirty-four English girls were released from brothels, although Snagge found at least thirty-three other children had also been imported into Europe.

The problem of involuntary prostitution was not confined to the continent, and it was evident that girls were being sold into prostitution in England as well. Benjamin Waugh in his work with children had continually run across cases of young girls who had been raped and tortured in some brothel and then been thrown out on the street to fend for themselves. He had attempted to prosecute their assailants or the brothel-keeper, but the result had been a series of failures, largely because of the court's refusal to admit the child's word as evidence. He, along with other members of the London Committee and Mrs. Butler, decided to move against one of the more fashionable procuresses in London, Mrs. Mary Jeffries. Mrs. Jeffries had started her career as a prostitute in a fashionable Mayfair brothel known as Berthe's, run by Madame Berthe, catering specially to the noble and powerful. As Mrs. Jeffries began to age and her charm began to fade, she turned from prostitute to procuress and accountant for Madame Berthe, and in the process had visited brothels on the continent. She became convinced that Madame Berthe's methods were old-fashioned if only because it had been the house practice to prohibit any of the more exotic sexual practices. With the financial assistance of several wealthy backers, Mrs. Jeffries opened a more "progressive" establishment and soon had several different houses specializing in various types of sexual practices. She had, for example, a flogging house, a house for very young girls, a house for other "perversions," as well as a house that she used as a depot for shipment of girls to the continent.

The only requirement Mrs. Jeffries demanded of her client was that he have a solid front of respectability. Among her patrons were several members of the House of Lords, and members of the royal family including allegedly the Prince of Wales, the very un-Victorian son of Queen Victoria. To keep her houses going, Mrs. Jeffries required a steady stream of new talent, and for this purpose she employed a number of recruiters. Much of her new talent was found at railroad stations where Mrs. Jeffries's assistants made special efforts to meet girls from the country as they first arrived in the city. It was not unusual for her assistant to offer to look after children while their parents bought tickets or saw to their luggage, and when the parents had turned their backs, the children were kidnapped. Her activities were known to the police, but because she had so many distinguished and powerful patrons, she only occasionally got into trouble.[26]

Mrs. Jeffries's establishment had been chosen as a target largely because of the appearance of an ex-police inspector, Jeremiah Minahan, at the publishing offices of Alfred Dyer. Minahan had been forced to resign from the force because he had charged his immediate superiors with giving protection to Mrs. Jeffries's operation. Minahan, who had run into trouble on the force before about allegations against his fellow officers, remained determined to expose the "evils" in the police department and had sent copies of his report to several daily newspapers under the title "How an Inspector of the Metropolitan Police was Punished for Faithfully Performing his Duty to the Public." When the papers ignored his report, he decided to have it privately printed, and went to Alfred Dyer's firm to arrange this. Dyer, who had been awaiting an opportunity to charge Mrs. Jeffries, persuaded the other members of his committee to hire Minahan for two pounds a week to gather evidence against Mrs. Jeffries. Minahan, however, was able to find only one documented case in which Mrs. Jeffries had arranged for the seduction of a child virgin, and this had happened more than a decade before he began his investigation. Nevertheless, he gathered enough evidence for the committee to bring charges against her in 1885 for keeping a disorderly house, which was technically illegal. The trial was a farce. On the day of the trial she arrived in a special coach recently given to her by an earl, and boasted to reporters that "nothing can be done with me, as my clients and patrons are of the highest social order." Evidently some of her patrons became somewhat worried about public exposure, although the judge had forbidden their names to be mentioned in court. Rather than suffer any more publicity, however, Mrs. Jeffries was encouraged to plead guilty to a breach of the peace. She was fined 200 pounds, with another 200 pounds placed on deposit for her good behavior. She paid the fine in cash before leaving court, and a titled Guards officer guaranteed the 200-pound security bond. Her brothels continued to function as before.[27]

The willingness of the establishment to let Mrs. Jeffries off so easily while punishing lesser crimes so severely was a boon to the growing power of the abolitionists. Several newspapers demanded an investigation into charges of police collusion in the vice traffic. The movement to end abuses in prostitution was no longer a fringe movement; it had gained major support. Cardinal Manning, the primate of the Catholic Church of England, insisted that something be done to curb the procurers who waited on London docks to prey on the girls arriving from Dublin. Lord Shaftesbury, president of the Young Women's Christian Association, also called for action. Even the House of Lords had urged action although little had come of it. In 1881 a parliamentary committee from the House of Lords had heard allegations about the traffic in young girls. Its findings were finally made public in 1882, and though the committee suggested that most girls trapped in foreign brothels were probably not averse to the idea of prostituting themselves, only distressed by the conditions they found themselves in, the committee nonetheless recommended that the procuring of English girls for foreign houses be a serious misdemeanor. It also urged that the age of consent be raised to sixteen, that it be unlawful to procure or attempt to procure for unlawful carnal knowledge any woman under twenty-one unless she was a known prostitute, and that it also be illegal for anyone to receive into his home a girl under sixteen for the purpose of having sexual intercourse. To make certain this did not happen, the police were to be empowered to have a search warrant for those houses where they had reason to believe girls under sixteen were being harbored for immoral purposes. The recommendations passed through the House of Lords in 1883, 1884, and in modified form in 1885, but on each of these occasions, died in the House of Commons.[28]

This legislative impasse was broken largely through the efforts of W. T. Stead, editor of the *Pall Mall Gazette,* who had become interested in the problem through the efforts of Dyer, Scott, Waugh, Mrs. Butler, and the Salvation Army. The Salvation Army is particularly important because it had considerable appeal to some of the same groups from which the prostitute seemed to come in the nineteenth century. It had started in the East End of London in 1865 under the direction of William Booth, later General Booth. Booth had resigned from the Methodist ministry because he felt the Methodists were not reaching the churchless masses, especially the underprivileged groups. To help them he founded the Christian Mission in London in 1865, and then in 1878 changed its name to the Salvation Army. The Mission had opened its first shelter for refugees from prostitution and vagrant girls in 1868, and although this project failed for lack of funds, other shelters were soon operating successfully. Bramwell Booth, the son of the General, Florence Booth, Bramwell's wife, and Kate Booth, Bramwell's sister, devoted a good part of their activity to helping prostitutes. They had joined forces with Josephine Butler in 1882, and with other groups concerned with prostitution as well.

When Stead decided to begin investigation of prostitution, Bramwell Booth and Waugh acquainted him with the facts of London prostitution. To point out the abuses, Waugh took Stead to interview some of the children held in the shelters run by the National Society for the Prevention of Cruelty to Children. One seven-year-old told Stead she had been abducted and raped in a fashionable brothel, and Waugh conceded that since no magistrate would accept her statement on oath, nothing could be done. He found another child of four and a half who had been raped twelve times in succession, and whose assailant, despite the efforts of Waugh, had also been acquitted. In order to further document the abuses, Stead assembled a "Secret Commission" on May 25, 1885, really an investigative team, composed of members of his reporting staff, officers of the Salvation Army, Mrs. Butler, and others active in the battle against "white slavery."

Two women, one a member of the *Pall Mall Gazette* staff whose name we do not know, and the other Jenny Turner, a Salvation Army officer, undertook to enter brothels as prostitutes bound for the continental market. Jenny Turner managed to have herself decoyed into one of Mrs. Jeffries's clearinghouses, where she took notes, and then with the help of her fiancé escaped with her virginity intact. The other woman also lived in a brothel for some ten days without selling her services. Stead and his collaborators, pretending to be customers, visited brothels. Stead became nauseated when he saw young children, three to five, being chloroformed before they were violated by adult men.

As conclusive proof of what he saw, Stead felt he had to show that a child could actually be bought in England for immoral purposes, then spirited away to the continent without any official protest. To do this he turned to Rebecca Jarrett, who before being converted to the Salvation Army had been both a prostitute and a brothelkeeper. Reluctantly she agreed to find him a "pure child," although the first two attempts to do so were unsuccessful because the procuresses she contacted were suspicious. Ultimately she decided to act as a procuress herself, a mistake in strategy. She purchased Eliza Armstrong from her mother, nominally for domestic service, although Rebecca Jarrett insisted that she made it clear to the girl's mother that she was to be used for prostitution. An intermediary was paid two pounds for calling attention to the girl, and promised more if the girl proved to be a virgin. The mother was given a pound. Stead had the girl examined by a midwife who specialized in certifying virgins for various London brothels. The midwife also sold Stead some chloroform so the girl would not suffer too much pain. He took her to an accomodation house that he knew was often used to deflower young virgins, took rooms there, and after the girl had retired, he entered her room, locking the door behind him. Here he enacted a mock seduction. Stead was careful to have the girl examined afterward by a physician to emphasize that the girl was still a virgin, whereupon she was spirited away to the continent under the protection of Salvation Army officers.

Stead set the stage for his exposé by forewarning his "squeamish" readers on July 4, 1885, to be prepared for a series of articles on the traffic in women and girls. Then on Monday, July 6, he started his series with a six-page account of the seamy side of London's sex life under the title "The Maiden Tribute of Modern Babylon." His main target was the rich:

In all the annals of crime can there be found a more shameful abuse of power of wealth than that by which in this nineteenth century of Christian civilization, princes and dukes and ministers and judges and the rich of all classes are purchasing for damnation . . . the as yet uncorrupted daughters of the poor?

The public reaction to the story was instantaneous. So great was the demand of readers that by the end of the day the paper was selling for a shilling a copy, twelve times its usual price. Some people, however, were upset by the topic. When one of the biggest chains of news agents refused to handle distribution, the Salvation Army undertook to help. For the five days the series continued, public reaction mounted. Officials were upset enough to consider prosecuting Stead for publishing material with prurient content, but no action was taken because they feared to do so would give the appearance of sheltering "depravity of the rich at the expense of the poor."

As word of the series spread beyond London, other papers picked it up. Copies were telegraphed across the Atlantic for syndication in America. It was also published in book form and rapidly translated into Danish, German, Russian, Polish, and French. Stead's articles, moreover, did not run in isolation. Big rallies were staged in London demanding the enactment of the long-stalled legislation. By July 29 a petition signed by 393,000 people was presented to the Houses of Parliament by a corps of hundreds of Salvation Army soldiers who marched from East London to Trafalgar Square accompanied by a carriage drawn by four white horses bearing the petition. By August 1885, Parliament had passed a bill raising the age of consent to sixteen, putting some teeth into the prohibition of the traffic in women and children.

Stead, however, had enemies, and his series gave them a chance to get at him, since he, certain that he had saved Eliza Armstrong from a life of prostitution, refused to allow her to return to her parents. This refusal enabled the parents not only to sue to get her back but to charge him and Rebecca Jarrett with abducting the child. Found guilty in a publicized trial, Stead had to serve three months in prison for his part in the abduction, and Rebecca Jarrett was sentenced to six months. Stead's press rivals also accused him of manufacturing evidence; and, even if his tactics in the Armstrong case were questionable, the reaction of the press to his conviction was unjustified. Some of his rival editors attempted to dismiss all the evidence out of hand. But this reaction was only temporary, and the Criminal Law Amendment Act was eventually adopted. Unfortunately the new law did more than raise the legal seduction age of young girls. It also outlawed homosexual acts between consenting adults in private; provided that boys who had sexual intercourse with girls under sixteen should be thrashed even when they were younger than their partners. This extension of a law designed for one purpose but also dealing with another kind of sex activity was typical of the whole abolitionist campaign. Though prostitution was the main concern of the abolitionists, many were concerned with pornography, homosexuality, and prohibiting the sale of contraceptives. If the opportunity presented itself, some lobbyists took advantage to push their own private crusades. In the long run the excesses of some abolitionists weakened the whole abolitionist movement. Stead in a sense was typical, since on his release from prison he traveled and lectured, becoming an international propagandist not only for abolitionism but for general moral reform. Two of his books, for example, dealt with vice and crime in Chicago and New York and helped launch clean-up campaigns in these cities. Stead drowned when the *Titanic* went down in 1912.[29]

An early result of Stead's efforts was the formation of the British Vigilance Society under the direction of W. A. Coote, who traveled throughout Europe and America organizing similar societies. Another result was the International Congress on the White Slave Traffic in London in 1899. This was followed in 1902 by an invitation of the French government to sixteen different nations to assemble in Paris to draft an international treaty to protect women and girls from the white-slave traffic. On May 18, 1904, after a two-year recess, thirteen nations ratified an agreement to collect more information regarding the traffic and to coordinate all information regarding the traffic and to coordinate all information relative to the procurement of women or girls for immoral purposes abroad. Later the United States agreed to join up with these countries.[30]

In the United States several moral reform movements came into existence after the Civil War. At first some of these were concerned primarily with prostitution, but soon they extended their efforts to purifying all society, not only by abolishing evil institutions such as the brothel and the saloon but by eliminating pornography, and raising children to live clean lives. Much of the early efforts of these groups were concentrated on raising the legal age of consent.[31] American movements were also fertilized by contact with European ones, and both Stead and Coote had visited this country, as did some of the followers of Mrs. Booth. A New York Committee, the Committee of Fifteen, had reported on prostitution in that city in 1905, and the publication of this book may be taken as symbolic of a renewed attack on the problem in the United States.[32] Other commttees and individuals began investigating prostitution in various cities,[33] and even on a national scale. The most important of these early investigations was one by George Kibbe Turner,[34] who emphasized that though poverty itself might have been a causal factor, there was a close tie-in with urban politics. An increasing number of muckraking articles emphasized the tie-in with political corruption, but the most successful campaign was that associated with white slavery. Though some progressives, such as Brand Whitlock, the mayor of Toledo, doubted the existence of white slavery, it seems clear in retrospect that there was child prostitution in America just as in England, and that in many brothel districts there were women who would have preferred to leave. Many Chinese prostitutes were held in virtual slavery, for example. Whitlock, however, had a right to doubt since the popular press was full of lurid tales of abduction, many of them fictional. As mayor of Toledo, he decided to verify one such tale by a young social worker who had told of rescuing a young "white slave" kidnapped from a prominent local family. Whitlock found out there was not the "slightest ground for the silly tale," and this experience led him to question all such unsubstantiated stories. Rather than resorting to sensationalism, however, Whitlock wanted to attack what he felt was the basic cause, the low wages paid to working women.[35] And prostitution itself increasingly became a subject for legislative concern.

One of the earliest attempts to deal with prostitution on a national level was made during the administration of Ulysses S. Grant. In 1874 Grant had asked Congress to take action on the importation of Chinese women for prostitution, but Congress went further and in 1875 prohibited the importation of any "women for the purposes of prostitution." Anyone found guilty of importing or causing the importation of such women was guilty of a felony and subject to a $5,000 fine and five years' imprisonment.[36] When the intention of the law was challenged in 1881, the U.S. Supreme Court agreed that the law was to exclude the importation of prostitutes from any country and was now a federal responsibility.[37] This was the effective beginning of federal action. As agitation over white slavery mounted, efforts also mounted to extend federal intervention. In 1903 the act was amended to deny entry to prostitutes and procurers,[38] and in 1907 the language was further modified to prohibit the importation of "any alien woman or girl" for the purposes of prostitution or "any other immoral purpose," either "for hire or without hire." The 1907 change also provided that any alien woman or girl found engaged in prostitution within three years after she entered the country would be deported. In addition, the statute provided for the establishment of a special commission to study the problem of white slavery and immigration.[39]

This 1907 law was soon challenged. In the case of *United States* v. *Bitty* a man was charged with importing an Englishwoman in order that she might live with him as his concubine, not as a prostitute per se. The U.S. Supreme Court in a decision by Justice John Marshall Harlan declared that concubines fell within the intent of the law and were included by the wording "or for any other immoral purpose."[40] The question of enforcement became further complicated in 1909 with the decision in *Keller* v. *United States*. This case dealt with a woman who voluntarily entered a house of prostitution in Chicago after her entry into this country from the Austro-Hungarian Empire. Justice David Brewer held that since the woman had not been a prostitute when she entered but only later had become one, to deport her would violate her protections under the Tenth Amendment.[41]

Though the United States had agreed to comply with the 1904 International Treaty on white slavery in 1908,[42] Justice Brewer in his decision said there was nothing in the records to indicate that the legislation could be supported under the treaty power since the United States and the Austro-Hungarian Empire had no specific treaty dealing with the subject. The result of the decision was an extensive legislative investigation. A study by the Commission on Immigration and Naturalization held that there was little international traffic in innocent women. Rather, most of those imported for prostitution to the United States were experienced women or mistresses and that there were so many of these in Europe that there was no need "to seduce and debauch" innocents to assure the needed supply in the United States.[43] A special Senate Committee on Immigration after an investigation of prostitution in several cities concluded that few women immigrants in prostitution were innocents but in fact were experienced European ones.[44]

In spite of such reports, the legislators preferred to act otherwise. The House Committee on Immigration drew up a bill that became law in 1910, amending the 1907 ban on alien prostitutes by dropping the three-year limitation and excluding all persons who were "supported by the proceeds of prostitution."[45] At the same time Representative James R. Mann (R. Ill.), the chairman of the House Committee on Interstate Commerce, introduced a bill to deal with interstate commerce in prostitution. The bill was an effort to supplement various state laws aimed at white slavery, the first of which had been passed in Mann's home state of Illinois in 1908, largely through the efforts of Clifford G. Roe.[46] The Mann Act was in fact largely the work of Roe. As passed in 1910, the act provided for heavy penalties for the transporting or in any way aiding, abetting, or causing the transporting of a woman from one state to another for "immoral" purposes.[47]

The first test case involved a New Orleans madam who had been convicted under the new law of persuading, inducing, and enticing a woman to travel to Beaumont, Texas, for purposes of practicing prostitution. She appealed her conviction on the grounds that the Mann Act violated the privileges and immunities clause of Article VI of the Constitution and was contrary to the intent of the Ninth and Tenth Amendments. The U.S. Supreme Court in upholding her conviction also extended the federal power to regulate interstate commerce of any kind.[48] On the same day the Court rendered a decision in the New Orleans case it ruled on a Florida case involving a Tampa theater owner who had been convicted under the provisions of the act of enticing a girl from Suwanee, Georgia, to come to work for him. The girl claimed that when she arrived in Tampa the theater owner attempted to seduce her and that the job was merely one of entertaining young men whose immoral advances she had to fight off. Though no seduction had taken place, the conviction of the theater owner was upheld on the grounds that it had been his intent to entice the girl into debauchery and that preparation to commit debauchery was included within the provisions of the act.[49] In 1917 the provisions of the law were further extended by the decision in *Caminetti* v. *United States* to include even noncommercial sex. In this case, two married Californians who were having marital difficulties took their girl friends (whom incidentally they had promised to marry when they received their divorces) to Reno, Nevada. Later they were convicted of violations of the Mann Act, and their convictions were upheld by the U.S. Supreme Court in a 6 to 3 decision.[50] The result of such decisions was to change a law that had been designed to prevent white slavery to one designed to enforce morals, even declaring private amorous pleasure trips that crossed state lines to be illegal.[51] It was this broad interpretation that upset some of the originators of the law, including Clifford Roe, since he believed it now encouraged blackmail and other evils almost as bad as the excesses of prostitution it had been designed to remedy.[52]

It was not until 1944 that the first reversal of this trend took place. In that year the conviction of two owners of a Nebraska brothel who had taken two of their prostitutes on a vacation trip to Yellowstone National Park in Wyoming was overturned by a margin of 5 to 3 by the U.S. Supreme Court. The Court held that the expedition had been a pleasure trip, and that no amorous activity had been intended.[53] Even prostitutes had the right to take a vacation. Though this seemed to be a watershed decision, the ambivalence of the Court toward sexual activities was evident in 1946, when the conviction of a polygamous Mormon under the Mann Act was upheld; in the opinion of the Court polygamous practices were included in the Mann Act prohibition of "other immoral purposes."[54]

The tendency of the U.S. Supreme Court for a time to include all sexual activity under the categories prohibited by the Mann Act undoubtedly reflected what was taking place in the United States. What had been intended to be an abolition movement had become a prohibition movement, far removed from the original intent of Mrs. Butler and her co-workers. The United States advanced further toward prohibition than any other country. The attack on illicit sex coincided with the movement to ban alcoholic beverages and just as the temperance drive became a prohibition movement so did the movement against reglementation become prohibitionist. One of the key figures in the transformation was the New York physician Prince A. Morrow, a specialist in venereal disease. Morrow was a leader in publicizing the dangers of venereal disease, particularly of third-stage syphilis, not only to the victim himself or herself but to innocent spouses and children. To carry on more effective educational campaigns against the dangers of venereal disease, he organized the American Society of Sanitary and Moral Prophylaxis in 1905. Though he at first believed prostitution inevitable and was concerned primarily with better sex education, he eventually came to the conclusion that the only solution to the problem of venereal disease was to eliminate prostitution itself. The various purity organizations, too, which had originally campaigned against immorality and white slavery, began to realize the need for effective education about sex. In 1911 two of the main purity organizations, the American Purity Alliance and the American Vigilance Committee, elected the same officers, and the next year the two consolidated to form the American Vigilance Association dedicated to fighting prostitution and educating the young about the dangers of immorality. In the meantime many of the medically oriented groups that had followed Morrow's lead met and elected him president of a new national organization, the American Federation for Sex Hygiene. After Morrow's death in 1913, the two forces, medical and moral, merged formally and symbolically to form the American Social Hygiene Association, dedicated to eliminating prostitution and educating the young about the dangers of venereal disease. Though Morrow and his allies helped change the sex-is-unclean ideology of some of the purity ,associations, and emphasized the mutual obligations of the sex act for men and women, they accepted the purity movement's emphasis on marriage, and agreed that those who had sexual intercourse outside of marriage should be warned of the dangers. In a series of graphic "exhibits" the horrors of fornication were shown; they were aimed at frightening people with bad thoughts and wicked tendencies into refraining from sexual activity except in marriage. The movement also gained converts from the women's groups, who enlisted as part of their struggle against the double standard and an effort to raise men "up to the higher standards" of the female. One of the results of such alliances was the elimination of most tolerated red-light districts. Along with this was a growing consciousness in women of their own sexuality and what to do about it. H. L. Mencken's description of the sophisticated flapper, for example, records this new awareness.

Life, indeed, is almost empty of surprises, mysteries, horrors to this Flapper of 1915 . . . She knows exactly what the Wasserman reaction is, and has made up her mind that she will never marry a man who can't show an unmistakable negative. . . . She has read Christabel Pankhurst and Ellen Key, and is inclined to think that there must be something in this new doctrine of free motherhood. She is opposed to the double standard of morality, and favors a law prohibiting it.[55]

In return for some public discussion of sexuality, and for growing success in the effort to emphasize the dangers of venereal disease, concessions had to be made; namely, moral idealism had to accompany any kind of sex education. The result was an emphasis on continence and middle-class morals, and since education did not take place in a vacuum, inevitably there was a spate of laws on the books outlawing all aspects of prostitution. The result of these laws, however, was not the successful elimination of prostitution but rather the establishment of a new kind of double standard in which the prostitute was punished but her customers were allowed to go free. Another result was the institutionalization of class bias in enforcement of laws against prostitution. What before, at least among some segments of American culture, had been regarded as normal male-female relationships could now be classed as prostitution since this is what promiscuity was considered by many of the middle-class enforcers. There was also a class bias in enforcement since it was the lower-class prostitute who was most often picked up and arrested while the discreet but well-established mistress was rarely touched. This was not necessarily the fault of the police. In the burst of reform almost all the states enacted laws against enticing, procuring, importing and transporting women for purposes of prostitution, harboring minors for such purposes, accepting the earnings of and aiding or abetting prostitution, associating with a prostitute, frequenting a house of prostitution, pandering, placing a wife in or consenting to her remaining in a house of prostitution, inducing a woman to leave her home and go to another state for an immoral purpose. Even fornication was made a crime in many states. In 1920, for example, some twenty states regarded habitual fornication as a punishable act, and in sixteen states a single act was enough to bring conviction. Such widespread legal measures against all aspects of sexual activity, however, made enforcement impossible. Most juries proved unwilling to convict for illegal fornication; moreover, the Supreme Court soon recognized that prostitutes had the same rights as other citizens and could be charged with or convicted of only a specific offense. Thus, simply police suspicion that a woman was a prostitute was not enough to have her arrested. Similarly, attempts of municipalities to enact ordinances that prohibited men from talking to suspected prostitutes on streets or sidewalks, or that stated they could not walk along the sidewalk with prostitutes, have been ruled unconstitutional. As far as individual prostitutes were concerned, this meant that conviction could come only through the activities of vice officers, who had to encourage a woman to solicit them to engage in sexual intercourse. In many jurisdictions, simple solicitation itself was not enough; to obtain a conviction the transaction had to be carried almost to the point of consummation. Since to be "propositioned," a police officer had to indicate that he wanted to be propositioned or was available, and since prostitutes became adept at recognizing many vice officer tricks, the vice officers increasingly had to resort to dubious tactics to get a prostitute to commit herself; in the process he often crossed the thin line of entrapment. Inevitably, such tactics were most successful against the streetwalker and other comparatively poorly paid prostitutes, cases in which the public was willing to tolerate such dubious legal actions. Rarely was it used against the high-priced call girl or more sophisticated upper-income prostitute. Another difficulty with this kind of enforcement was that it was open to wide-scale bribery. An officer could appear to be unaware of prostitution taking place on his beat unless there was considerable public pressure for him to respond, and not infrequently this looking the other way by the police officer was something that could be and has been bought.

Brothels, too, could be ignored by the police officer, even though they are the most readily located and the easiest form of prostitution to eliminate. They came under the so-called injunction and abatement laws, the first of which was passed by Iowa in 1909 and subsequently by every state. They were enacted to allow the states to rid themselves of disorderly houses without appeal to the criminal courts, and allowed individuals in any community to obtain injunctions against any houses of lewdness or prostitution on the grounds that they were public nuisances. Most important, the individual citizen did not have to prove that he or she suffered damages. If the judge was satisfied that a nuisance existed he could grant a temporary injunction, and if a trial established the existence of a nuisance, the court would issue a permanent injunction. The court could also issue an abatement order under which the personal property used in the house could be sold and the premises closed for one year. These injunction and abatement laws were difficult to enforce since they required proof that the owner of the property knew what was going on. To make them more effective a clause was added that held the landlord legally responsible for the use of his premises, even if he claimed not to know what the use was. Nine states went further by stipulating that law-enforcement officials *must* (rather than *may*) initiate actions to enjoin and abate prostitution. Although the laws have been challenged, generally the courts have upheld them, at least in the past.[56] Since brothels or call houses continue to operate, at least in some areas, they obviously do so with the connivance of law-enforcement officials.

Perhaps the most obvious example of this is the state of Nevada, where in a 1949 Nevada Supreme Court decision, *Cunningham* v. *Washoe County,* it was held that a house of prostitution was a common-law nuisance and could be abated by appropriate legal action. The key word was *could,* since Nevada already had more than enough laws on its books to enable law-enforcement officials to close down the brothels existing in that state. In fact, at the time of the court decision, fifteen of Nevada's seventeen counties allowed houses of prostitution to be maintained, and they did not change their policy after the decision. Obviously district attorneys in these fifteen counties did not regard prostitution as a nuisance, but by implication they could regard it as a nuisance any time the brothels got out of line. Brothels in most of the counties are rather isolated, open from 4 p.m. to 5 a.m. Police drive by every half hour in case any customer becomes rowdy.[57] Prostitution technically, as of this writing, is still illegal in Washoe and Clark counties, the site of Reno and Las Vegas respectively, but this only means that these cities lack brothels. Brothels in small towns are one thing (and Nevada small towns are very small) and quite another thing in larger cities. Regulating brothels in a city the size of Las Vegas would impose great difficulties.

One lightly populated Nevada county went a step further in 1971, when Storey County, the site of perhaps the state's most famous brothel operator, Joe Conforte and his Mustang Ranch, persuaded the Storey County commissioners to pass an ordinance legalizing and licensing prostitution. The commissioners then issued a license to Joe Conforte, the largest taxpayer in the county. Soon afterwards a former madam, Mrs. Irene York, also applied for a license to operate, but the Storey County commissioners, under Conforte's influence, refused to issue her one. She sued, lost in the lower court, and in 1973 the Nevada Supreme Court upheld the refusal of the county commissioners in denying her a license. In the process of the litigation it became quite clear that a Nevada county could legalize prostitution and it could also restrict its licenses. Thus legal, as distinct from tolerated prostitution, is now a county option in Nevada.

For a time both Reno and Las Vegas were hostile to prostitution, fearful that prostitution would detract from gambling; at the least, prostitution was not particularly conspicuous. As the two communities boomed, however, and as the convention business increased, so did prostitution. In 1977 the office of Sheriff Ralph Lamb of Clark County had compiled dossiers on some 7,000 prostitutes, and it was estimated that about 3,000 were plying their trade every day. The observant visitor can see prostitutes in nearly every casino bar, some placed in the most conspicuous public areas available, since as one casino operator stated, "They're good for business." If the prostitute is good looking, well dressed, and discreet, she usually has no problem. Every casino has its own security guards who make sure that the prostitutes tolerated on their floors do not become too obvious. Periodically the sheriff's office launches massive sweeps picking up known and suspected prostitutes off the streets, sometimes as many as 300 or 400 a night to "keep Las Vegas clean." Indications are that the sweeps focus on the "outlaws," those prostitutes who do not have the sanction of the hotels and casinos that work closely with the police. Most women picked up are charged with vagrancy or disorderly conduct and only rarely with solicitation. Few of those arrested, however, are ever convicted.

In other areas of the country, particularly in the larger cities, prostitution is probably no less open than it is in Las Vegas, although few cities also have the private police forces that exist in Las Vegas. The Hollywood area of Los Angeles and the Times Square area of New York contain numerous streetwalkers, and the police mount sweeps similar to those taking place in Las Vegas. Few cities, however, would allow their chiefs of police the power that Lamb had in Las Vegas. Boston, in 1974, tried to confine its pornographic shops, its X-rated movies, its massage parlors, and other associated activities, including prostitution, in the Liberty Tree Neighborhood. The area was soon nicknamed the Combat Zone, and one police superintendent reported that "you could get anything you wanted" in the area. Police, however, soon found themselves in a difficult situation because in effect the city fathers had said it was all right to do in the Combat Zone what was illegal to do in the rest of the city. Since almost anything went, citizens soon hesitated to enter the area because it was so dangerous, and as of this writing the Boston zone plan is a failing experiment. Its failure could have been predicted, for unless basic laws are changed legalizing some of the illicit activity, such an area is impossible to regulate. To be effective also, such areas need to be fairly large, such as the Strip in Las Vegas, accessible, and heavily policed. It also helps to have ingress and egress from the area controlled, a regulation most Americans would find a violation of their constitutional right to come and go as they please. Detroit has offered a more effective counterplan through zoning several areas to permit various kinds of "adult" entertainment and then limiting the number of establishments in any one zone.

Whatever plans are proposed, it seems clear that prostitution survives. Our present policies rest on unrealistic concepts of sexual behavior. The frequency of divorce and the alteration of family life have undermined the foundations on which Mrs. Butler and her allies wished to build. Rather than face up to the problems, however, we pretend they do not exist.

An excellent example of casting a bind eye is the behavior of officials in the U.S. armed forces. Obviously the mobilizing of millions of men into military service, and then isolating them from women at an age in life when their sexual urges are at their peak, poses problems. One must keep in mind that the most significant cause of absenteeism from military duty traditionally has been venereal disease. Rather than establish regulated houses of prostitution as the military officials had been accustomed to do in earlier wars, there was an attempt in World War I to close brothels. This left the field to the free-lance prostitute. To deal with the problems of disease that might result, the military eventually turned from inspecting prostitutes to inspecting troops, and in Europe provided prophylactic measures, educated the soldiers about venereal disease, and gave medical care to those infected. Though there was punishment for those who did become infected, in that they were not permitted to go on leave or furlough, emphasis was on rehabilitation rather than punishment. Within the continental U.S., military officials also worked to eliminate brothel prostitution, and military commanders could declare brothels off limits. The same program was adopted in World War II, with even more effective results in curtailing venereal disease. Officially the army discouraged prostitution but unofficially emphasized prophylactic devices and the necessity of treatment.[58] Though the effectiveness of such programs cannot be denied, it depended on more or less official hypocrisy, occasional persecution of prostitutes, and effective dissemination of condoms to the troops.

The legal statutes with their emphasis on punishing the prostitute, not the client who employed her, encouraged hypocrisy. Though a small number of states did enact statutes specifying punishment for the customer of the prostitute or making participation in illicit intercourse a crime by the male as well as the female, restrictive prosecution and court interpretations have usually led to the exoneration of the males involved.[59] In the past, enforcement was difficult because it was in the hands of the police, and few police forces were willing to hire policewomen to deal with the problems of "indecent proposals," also an illegal act since without the proposal there could be no prostitution. But even when the police raid the brothels they rarely arrest the customers, and the reason for this, probably, is that police see nothing wrong with men wanting sex, only with women charging for it (and this is true even if the men are willing to pay). It is part of the double standard infecting not only police but legislative efforts to deal with prostitution, and it is this attitude that most upsets feminists today.

The trend toward absolute prohibition of prostitution in the United

States did not spread internationally, and most countries limited their activities to the abolition of the white slave traffic. In 1910 a document was signed by thirteen nations participating in yet another International Convention for the Suppression of the White Slave Traffic. This convention held that it was a criminal act to procure a girl under twenty years of age even with her consent. It also declared that traffic in women over twenty years of age was a criminal act if it involved fraud or violence.[60] Before much progress could be made, however, World War I intervened, and in the aftermath of the war the campaign against white slavery was carried out under the auspices of the League of Nations. An article in the League's constitution entrusted it "with the general supervision over the execution of agreements with regard to traffic in women and children," and the first official step in this direction was the adoption of a new international convention in 1921. In this convention the age of consent was raised to twenty-one, and a system for licensing and supervision of international employment agencies was introduced. The League also appointed a body of experts to make a thorough investigation of the white slave traffic, the reports of which continued on into the Second World War. The effectiveness of the League in this respect is established in that, by 1938, forty-eight countries and a large number of dependent territories had adhered to the 1921 convention.[61] In 1933 the League moved to strengthen the convention by making traffic in adult women for the purposes of prostitution, even with their consent, a criminal offense. By 1938 this also had been ratified or acceded to by twenty-eight countries and signed by eleven others. The result was a decrease in the traffic in prostitutes, particularly in Europe, but also between Europe and South America. Encouraged by these successes, the League prepared to move against licensed brothels, and in 1937 a draft convention to outlaw licensed houses was drawn up. But World War II intervened before an international conference could agree to it.[62]

Following World War II the United Nations continued the work started by the League. In 1949 a Convention for the Suppression of the Traffic in Persons and the Exploitation of the Prostitution of Others was adopted by the United Nations General Assembly. The resolution was to take effect on July 23, 1951, and, among other things, prohibited the exploitation of others whether or not the person had passed the age of consent, prohibited regulation of prostitution by government authorities, and urged governments to cooperate to prevent prostitution and to work toward the reintegration into society of prostitutes. As of 1968 six nations had formally ratified it, while forty-one others had acceded to it without going through the process of ratification. The United States was not one of the signatories. The United Nations also continued with mixed success to work for suppression of licensed houses as well as the prevention and treatment of venereal disease. Aiding the UN program are several volunteer agencies including the International Bureau of the Suppression of Traffic in Persons, which was founded in 1899 in London. Even older is the International Abolitionist Federation founded in 1875, which has headquarters in Geneva. Also important is the International Union Against the Venereal Diseases and the Treponematoses established in 1923 with headquarters in Paris. Both the federation and the union have consultative status with the United Nations.[63]

The adoption of a convention by the League and agreement to it by a signatory power, however, does not necessarily mean that the provisions of the agreement are enforced. France, for example, agreed to punish all traffic in women under the age of twenty-one, yet the League of Nations Report in 1927 found that almost one-third of the registered prostitutes in that country were under twenty-one. Several countries that have agreed to prohibit regulation of prostitution by government authorities continue to regulate it. They regard the UN program as an ideal toward which they can work rather than a reality. The difficulty here is that the UN programs dealing with prostitution tend to reflect a Western orientation and bias, and are not always in accord with the reality of the situation in many other parts of the world. Some of these different views were recounted earlier in this book.

What is true of policies adopted by the United Nations as regards various parts of the world is also true of policies adopted by other countries as far as the United States is concerned. For example, the Soviet Union, realizing that female prostitutes simply could not exist without male customers, ultimately decided to move against male customers as well. The Soviets have claimed at various periods in the postrevolutionary period to have eliminated prostitution as a result of the total social liberation of women, new forms of marriage, economic opportunities for women, and so forth, but in spite of such claims prostitution as defined in the West still exists. Nonetheless, the Soviets' intention is not to have the war against prostitution degenerate into a war against the prostitute herself. To emphasize this, their antiprostitution campaign decreed that

whenever officers raided a place of vice—whether it was a house, a tavern, or simply a dark street—they were to take down the names, addresses, and places of employment of all men found there. The customers were not to be arrested, but on the following day would have their names and identifying information posted in a public place, under the heading "Buyers of the Bodies of Women." These lists were to be prominently displayed outside public buildings or on factory bulletin boards.[64]

What the Soviet law illuminates is the discriminatory enforcement in American law, discrimination still present in the Model Penal Code proposed by the American Law Institute in 1962.[65] What is basically needed is a rethinking of the whole subject of prostitution and the law. Obviously involuntary prostitution should be eliminated, children and young people should be protected, but when the question is asked whether the current American system is workable the answer must be in the negative. The ephemeral results of the various attempts to outlaw prostitution can easily be illustrated by the New York City experience, since New York has had more privately organized groups of citizens attempting to deal with prostitution than any other city. Despite the efforts of such groups an investigator in 1932 concluded that prostitution was rampant and that the only way to lessen prostitution was for the public to be continually vigilant and for volunteer societies to keep public opinion aroused.[66]

But the New York experience offers no testimonial either for the effectiveness of vigilante groups or for the morals of vice squads. The Seabury investigation in New York in 1930-31 revealed that a blackmailing ring of stool pigeons, corrupt policemen, crooked judges, bondsmen and lawyers was extorting money from women accused of prostitution whether guilty or not. The investigation also found that the Committee of Fourteen, the successor to the Committee of Fifteen organized in 1901, had helped contribute to the problem by widely publicizing its effectiveness through arrest statistics. Since the statistics mostly recorded arrests of novices, girls just starting in the profession, it became readily apparent that the committee, undoubtedly unconsciously, had been aiding and abetting the blackmail operations of the vice and morals squad. As a result of the Seabury investigation, the Committee of Fourteen disbanded, feeling that it had been discredited. Though the committee was not particularly effective in lessening prostitution in New York, the Seabury investigation in the long run was not any more effective. Though many houses of prostitution temporarily closed, and some prostitutes left the city for a time, within a short time prostitution was again functioning as strong as ever, and again it was with the connivance of law-enforcement officials.[67] The whole system in fact encourages police corruption.

The abolition movement eliminated many of the more obvious abuses associated with prostitution, but in spite of these efforts prostitution did not come close to being eliminated. Many, such as Mrs. Butler, never intended that it should be. In America, where abolition turned to prohibition, the prohibitionists of prostitution ran into the same difficulty that the prohibitionists of alcoholic beverages did. Both prohibition groups misjudged their public, went beyond what the public was willing to tolerate, and the result was a widespread disobedience of the law.

Though prohibition of alcohol was eliminated in 1933 by constitutional amendment, prohibition of prostitution was simply ignored, and only occasionally was there public agitation for effective law enforcement. Obviously it is time we examined our laws again. Laws are not made for eternity and conditions and attitudes change. Women are now recognized to be as sexual as men and yet our prostitution laws made a distinction between the "good" asexual woman and the "bad" sexual woman. Moreover, prostitution could not exist without the male customer, and yet we regard it more less as inevitable that men have the right to seek sex and stil deny that right to women. There has been a cultural lag in changing the laws based on erroneous assumptions by a significant proportion of the population. The reasons for the change and the form the new laws should take are detailed in the next chapter.

14   THE CHANGING
DOUBLE STANDARD

Though accurate statistics about prostitution in the past are nonexistent, we do know that proportionately fewer males are visiting prostitutes now than in the past and are doing so less frequently. The alternatives to prostitution explain the change. Premarital sex relations among young women, for example, are approaching the same rate as among young men. Opportunities for employment have become more numerous and varied for women. Contraceptives have made women more willing to tolerate the sexual advances of their spouses instead of denying them sex and urging them to go to a prostitute. The new studies on female sexuality have encouraged women to accept the fact that they are sexual beings. Divorce is more frequent and couples who are sexually incompatible no longer need find sexual relief in prostitution or adultery. There are swinging bars for singles, and group sex parties for interested couples. People can live together without taking marriage vows, and contraceptives are sold at drugstore counters. The list of reasons that prostitution is declining could be further amplified, but even though quantitatively prostitution is declining it still exists, and there is probably no city or town of any size in the United States or in the world at large where there is not a prostitute functioning in some way or another. The nature of prostitution, however, is changing, and based on the preceding chapters it is possible to make some generalizations about its existence and to offer some tentative conclusions about social policy.

The most obvious generalization that can be made is that in all societies and periods that have been examined, institutionalized prostitution has been aimed at a male clientele and the overwhelming majority of prostitutes have been women. Though male prostitutes have existed in many societies, they have primarily served other males whose sexual preference was males or who turned to fellow males in special circumstances where there was a lack of contact with women. Only occasionally has the male prostitute who serviced a female clientele been mentioned in literature; to document the existence of such individuals on any scale has been impossible.

Since women have a potential for sex enjoyment that is at least equal to that of man,[1] we have to conclude that either male prostitution is physiologically impossible or its absence is tied to other norms, values, and power systems in society. Although it is a physiological fact that the need for male tumescence creates problems for multiple intercourse, the refractory period is relatively short in young males and has not proved to be an impossible barrier to the development of male homosexual prostitution. Societal factors must be involved. Witness the smaller incidence of male gigolos and kept men, as compared to the number of mistresses and kept women. By implication the focus of prostitution seems related to the traditional dominance of men over women. The various expressions of that dominance include the conceptualization of women as property, the double standard, and the belief that the sexual needs of the male were the only sexual desires that needed to be given serious consideration.

If this hypothesis is accepted, then prostitution can be seen as a symptom of the victimization and subordination of women, or, in the case of the male homosexual prostitutes, the victimization of the surrogates who take the role of women. At the same time prostitution becomes an outstanding example of the perverse resilience of human beings, since women, including prostitutes, have turned their sexual subordination into a weapon that allows them in turn to victimize men. This very successful counter play has been built on the culturally supported myth that men enjoy, want, and need sex more than women. That this myth was not built on a physiological basis has not deterred its acceptance; a social reality can be much more powerful than a contradictory physiological fact. Each generation of girls, at least in much of Western culture, has been socialized to believe this myth and has learned to abstain from sexual activity, or to participate only under certain circumstances.

To perpetuate the myth, elaborate systems of reward and punishment have been developed emphasizing the shortage, or at least giving an illusion of a shortage, of willing female sex partners. In those periods when some traditional barriers broke down, contemporary male writers seemed perfectly willing to label every woman who was in the least promiscuous as a prostitute. Women, on the other hand, by preserving their chastity, have forced men to bargain for sex either through contractual arrangements such as marriage or concubinage, or on a direct fee-for-service basis as in the case of prostitutes. Since the common prostitute was the most removed from the other rewards of security and respectability in these bargaining arrangements, traditionally she has felt the most entitled to victimize her customers, to seize all the direct rewards she could openly or surreptitiously obtain. In fact most of the regulation of prostitution has been established not to protect the prostitute but her customers. In the process of losing status in society, i.e., selling a status loss, prostitutes could obtain sufficient rewards to maintain themselves.

If this line of reasoning is accepted, it suggests that the two essential conditions for supporting prostitution in the forms in which it traditionally has existed are dominant males and a shortage of willing female sex partners. These two conditions have also, to a greater or lesser extent, supported the marriage contract. The fewer restrictions that society has placed on sexual activities for women, the less institutionalized prostitution there has been. Most of the nonrestrictive societies before the present time were the more primitive ones, although some non-Western *cultures* were also much less restrictive. Having a positive attitude toward sex was not enough, however, and many societies that recognized female sexuality also had a different standard for the sexual conduct of men than they did for women. In the double-standard societies women were expected to remain virgins until marriage and were punished variously for failure to do so. These punishments could include being censured, banishment, or death. Respectable women were conceptualized as property; their value was enhanced by monopoly ownership by one man. Besides protecting female virtue and prohibiting premarital or extramarital sex for women, these societies allowed or at least did not punish extramarital and premarital sex activities for males. To prohibit such activity led to greater dangers for society, even in the minds of the celibate-oriented Christian Church Fathers. Since each man protected the virtue of the women he controlled, other men's wives and daughters were not available for sex activity outside of marriage; inevitably there was a market price on the services of women who were willing to accept a position outside the respectable structure in order to fill the needs of a large group of men who sought extramarital sex. Most double-standard societies have had different gradations for the women engaged in prostitution. At the top were those who had something more to sell than their bodies: the geisha, the hetaira, the courtesan, and the cocotte; at the bottom were the slaves, members of minority populations, or women otherwise unacceptable to society. In many African tribes widows were pushed into this life since there was no other position for them; this was true also in parts of India, and historically even in much of the Western world. In some societies the role of the respectable wife and mother implied so much repression that the alternative of prostitution seemed more attractive to many; in others, where the life of the prostitute was not particularly attractive, recruitment was more or less forced. Regardless of the source of recruits, prostitution in all double-standard societies was visible and operated on a large scale, and the declassed group was fairly stable.

Although the double standard has been and continues to be the structural basis for the institution of prostitution, other factors have also contributed to it, including a long- or short-term shortage of women. Generally, throughout history until recent times adult men have probably outnumbered adult women as they still do in many undeveloped countries of the world.[2] Though there were areas and periods when special factors temporarily changed this disproportion, the sex balance began to change only in the nineteenth century as advances in medicine helped lower the death rate of women in childbirth. Progress was made in the treatment of childbed fevers, and the development of sterile ligatures and anesthesia made survival after Cesarean section possible. In many areas the sex disparity was accentuated because of concubinage and polygamy, and by barriers designed to make it more difficult to marry. Men unable to marry either because of a shortage of marriageable women—or an actual shortage of women—were eager for and willing to pay all they could afford for the company of a woman, even if society regarded her as a prostitute, and even if she would serve only as a temporary companion. In fact, it was to serve such groups that society often justified its tolerance of prostitution.

The segregation of men, for example, for schooling or punishment, also helped increased the desire for feminine companionship, but the segregation often cut off access to women, so men were pushed into service as surrogates in greater numbers than would be the case in a population where women were available. Thus homosexuality was most common in prisons, boys' schools, and military bases, where women were not allowed. Not all the homosexual contacts in these settings are necessarily of a prostitute nature, and much of the time sexual activities were collegial, but not infrequently some kind of a barter or other exchange system developed.[3]

The market for prostitution has also been enhanced by the cultivation of exotic sexual desires. Men satiated with or not aroused by ordinary sexual activities have looked for variety. With wives (if they have wives) who were usually sexually conservative, these variety-seekers found it difficult to satisfy their sexual needs at home and turned to the fee-for-service system of satisfaction. Sometimes wives, even if they had the desire to do so, could not have satisfied their spouses' sexual desires as evidenced by the nineteenth-century taste of many upper-class Englishmen for deflowering young virgins. Brothels specializing in whipping and other sadomasochistic pleasures are well documented, as are brothels that catered to transvestites, featured anal intercourse, and many other varieties of sexual expression. Many of these still exist.

The good wife or devoted lover has also often consciously or unconsciously created a market for prostitutes. There is evidence of this in the late nineteenth and early twentieth centuries in the United States when values were switching from the pronatalism of the agricultural society to the antinatalism of the urban industrial society.[4] Since this change occurred before the technology of birth control was fully developed, many women were attracted to abstinence as a method of controlling family size. Abstinence undoubtedly proved a natural approach for women who had grown up believing that they could not and would not enjoy sex; moreover, the hasty act they experienced with their husbands all too often proved to them that their childhood socialization had been correct. The rhetoric of the feminist movement in the late nineteenth century was evidence that many women practiced abstinence. It was fueled by women who as yet lacked the ability to relax and freely enjoy the sex act or the security to demand better performance from their husbands, but these women did have enough power to nag, cajole, or freeze their husbands out of the house into the brothel or an extralegal liaison.

Prostitution, like many other professional human service industries, is primarily an urban phenomenon. Inevitably there are fewer hospitals, social workers, psychiatrists, or even prostitutes in the rural than in the urban areas. This does not mean that no rural prostitutes were to be found, only that they were fewer and tended to locate in areas where there were more customers. A classic description of one such prostitute appeared in the story "Hatrack" by Herbert Asbury, in the *American Mercury*. Hatrack was the nickname of a small-town prostitute with a beanpole figure, who each Sunday tried unsuccessfully for a saving forgiveness and acceptance in one of the two churches, and after being rebuffed, plied her trade in the local cemetery.[5]

Prostitution, it should be emphasized, fulfilled a social need. It served to protect the good women; it stabilized marriage against the disintegrative force of promiscuous male sexuality. This was its justification in much of Western history. But in functional sociological terms, it also served other needs. Sociologist Robert Merton, for example, has analyzed the function of the much maligned urban political machine and argued that it persisted in spite of reform rhetoric. It performed important tasks, providing a central authority toward which the ordinary person could turn, and at the same time humanizing the political process by making it accessible.[6] Sociologist Herbert Gans similarly analyzed the functions of poverty, pointing out that poverty provides a pool of workers, who must of necessity accept low wages for dirty, unpleasant, and often dangerous work. Poverty also furnishes employment for police, judges, social workers, and public health nurses, as well as numerous other individuals. Gans concluded that poverty persists partly because alternative solutions to those problems would be difficult for the society to accept or its more affluent members to find.[7] Similarly prostitution must have important functions in society to have persisted through so many centuries and in such a variety of settings. It should be emphasized, as Gans also pointed out, that institutions or social arrangements are seldom if ever functional to all elements of society; they tend to function positively for one group in the society and negatively for another. Thus the primary function of prostitution has been to uphold the double standard, since without prostitution the double standard could have been preserved only through slavery, homosexuality, and rape. Prostitution was regarded by society as a better alternative than these, and since the establishment, as represented by the church, the government, and the intellectual community, has adhered rather consistently to the double standard, prostitution has persisted.

Prostitution, moreover, is a market institution and as such necessarily is influenced by the supply of recruits. In some societies all women who fell outside the traditional marriage system were candidates for prostitution because there were either few or no other viable occupational choices. Widows without children or relatives, orphans, women without dowries, women who had lost their virginity, and poor women without any other means of support became prostitutes as a way of supporting themselves. The ranks of prostitution were also temporarily swollen by great national tragedies such as famines or by the derangements that followed defeat in wars, as was the case in post-World War II Germany, Japan, and Italy, Immigrant, minority, and peonage populations have always furnished more recruits than the more advantaged segments of society, and the availability of such recruits supported prostitution as an institution particularly when there was also a flourishing advantaged segment of male buyers. Prostitution tends to be symptomatic of economic inequality rather than uniform poverty in a society.

This is important to emphasize because, in the Marxist tradition, many reformers have suggested that capitalism itself has been a base cause of prostitution, and that prostitution would be abolished if the salaries of working girls were raised. As Havelock Ellis pointed out over fifty years ago, and as Kinsley Davis later affirmed, this answer is much too simplistic. They reasoned that as soon as the salaries of working girls were raised, the supply of prostitutes might temporarily diminish, but the resulting scarcity of prostitutes would raise the price, and working girls with higher salaries would then enter the life.[8] Moreover, prostitution in the Soviet Union has never really been eliminated although the prostitute operates under considerable handicap, not the least of which is the shortage of housing in many of the major Russian cities.[9]

Undoubtedly poor living conditions, unhealthy neighborhoods and neglected homes, inadequate education, low levels of intelligence, ignorance of sexual matters or too-early sex experience, and a whole combination of personal and environmental factors are found in the backgrounds of a great many prostitutes.[10] The remarkable factor is not that women with such backgrounds become prostitutes but that so many from the same background do not.

Moreover, in spite of the continued economic inequality in this country and in much of the Western world, prostitution is declining. In 1947 Alfred C. Kinsey and his associates reported that 69 percent of the men in his sample of white males had some experience with prostitutes, although only 15 percent visited prostitutes on anything like a regular basis and contacts with prostitutes represented only 3.5 to 4 percent of their total sexual outlet. The largest proportion of the regular users were bachelors, divorcees, and widowers. Significantly, however, Kinsey reported that there was a generational difference in contacts with prostitutes, and the young male at the time he was writing made only two-thirds or half as many contacts as the older generation did at the same period in their lives.[11] Other studies tend to verify this generational difference, and the explanation for this is not difficult: Kinsey attributed it to an increase in intercourse with girls who were not prostitutes.

Kinsey's findings emphasize what in our opinion are the two most significant factors relating to the decline in prostitution, namely, the development of effective contraception and the current sexual revolution, both of which have seriously undermined the double standard. Because of these changes, women, particularly some of the younger ones, have become more willing to participate freely in sexual activities, with the result that the demand for the services of professionals is diminishing. Though many of the early twentieth-century advocates of women's liberation hoped to raise men to what they regarded as the women's higher standards of celibacy, what has in fact happened is that neither women or men are putting quite so much emphasis on female chastity as was once the case.

The development and dissemination of effective contraceptives gave women a feeling of more power over their own fate, and though the loss of a hymen is still an emotionally charged subject for many people, women need no longer become pregnant if they do not want to. If perchance there is a contraceptive failure, the woman can now obtain a legal abortion. A woman can choose motherhood, a career, or both, and if she does decide to have children she can space them so that they will offer the least interference to her career. Effective contraceptives have allowed women to have many of the social freedoms of men, and to recognize and cultivate their own sexuality without quite the fear of penalty that once existed. Aiding this has been the growth of the women's liberation movement, which has created a climate of openness about female sexuality. Inevitably some women have selected lesbianism as their sexual outlet, and others have chosen to engage in sexual activities without the extrinsic rewards of marriage or cash. These changes in the attitudes and behavior of women are still in a period of transition, but they are already having a revolutionary impact on all sex-related institutions including marriage and prostitution. Closely allied with these changes has been the growth of greater economic independence of women, with the result that sex for money has for many women become a decision to be made willingly rather than unwillingly.

Concomitantly a publicity revolution has also taken place in which sexual activities are more open; an increasing amount of scientific research and more literature are available, and the media feature open expressions of sexuality. Pioneer sexual researchers, including Sigmund Freud, Havelock Ellis, Alfred Kinsey, Harry Benjamin, William Masters, Virginia Johnson, and others, deserve credit for this trend, although other factors in society may be equally or more important. Among these are the overall developments in science, the decline in the efficacy of religion's restrictions, the development of effective contraceptives, and the legal emancipation of women. Kinsey deserves credit for making Americans aware of their own sexual nature, but once the taboos about sexuality began to fall, others cleared new ground. Masters and Johnson, for example, helped dispel some of the myths about the lack of sexual response in women, and more recently have moved on to experiment with therapy for sexual dysfunction. In this they have paid equal attention to the prematurely ejaculative male and to the nonorgasmic woman, both classified as sexually dysfunctional persons.[12] Just how radical such an approach is can be seen only when it is realized that the basis of the old double standard was the belief that respectable women should be nonorgasmic. Thus premature ejaculation simply was not a problem since it could be defined only as such in relation to the pleasure of the female sexual partner. The sexual revolution has made the pleasure of intercourse and other types of erotic stimulation more of a two-way street and increased the probability that more women, married or unmarried, would be willing to participate without payment.

From the point of view of some males, the egalitarian approach to sexuality poses problems. Many men do not know how or do not want to learn how to participate in what they consider foolish foreplay or do not want to spend their time trying to satisfy their partner. Sex paid for in cash may seem to some of them a better bargain than sex paid for in social interaction. This at least might be concluded from an empirical study by Martha L. Stein of the clients who visit call girls. Stein observed the encounters of 1,230 men with call girls. Using this data, she categorized nine types of clients: opportunists, fraternizers, promoters, adventurers, lovers, friends, slaves, guardians, and juveniles. Regardless of type, however, she found that all wanted their sex needs met conveniently, professionally, and without obligations other than the monetary one, although some enjoyed the temporary illusion of ove or friendly involvement.[13]

That many males fear the new sexual egalitarianism is evidenced on college campuses, where staffs of student health services have reported that some men are beginning to worry about impotence brought on by what are called "castrating women." Socialized to expect subordinate women whose only sexual ambition would be to please men, many men cannot accept assertive partners who think of themselves as full participants in the sex act. Some of these young men seek the company of prostitutes, who do not impose reciprocal demands or who fake satisfaction. Some of this reporting is suspect simply because student health services in the past did not deal with such questions.

Stein's study emphasizes the fact that the encounter with the prostitute is completely client centered, and that every effort is made to fill his needs. Perhaps for this reason, Edward Glover, an early researcher into the psychology of the male customer, felt that many men were able to enjoy the sex act only with people that they did not hold in high esteem. He believed that these men separated love into sacred and profane, and classed their wives, female friends, and mothers as worthy only of sacred love while they equated the prostitute with the profane. Thus the low status of the prostitute became a necessary part of the forbidden pleasure they they associated with sexuality.[14] Since Glover did no broader research to test his hypothesis other than talking to his patients, the number of men who fit his description is difficult to estimate. Whatever their number, those males probably could not find pleasure with the egalitarian members of the women's liberation movement. Thus, although increased sexual freedom might be lessening the need for prostitutes, there are still some persons who feel their needs can be met only by "market" sex.

Most autobiographies, biographies, case studies, and clinical investigations of the modern prostitute show that she is sought out by large numbers of males who have fetishist tendencies.[15] There are also any number of males who feel unable to attract a woman to serve their sexual needs other than through purchase. Many men with physical disabilities

who feel unable to marry but still want sex turn to prostitutes. Quadru-
plegics and other severely disabled men have reported that a prostitute is
often the only source of sexual contact for them. One disabled person
stated that since he had to have help in removing a catheter, in being put
into position for intercourse, and assisted in any number of other aspects
of sex, it was very difficult to approach non-prostitutes. To avoid the
embarrassment of rejection and the inherent difficulties involved, he, and
others like him, relied on prostitutes to serve their sexual needs.[16]

Some marriage counselors, as well as others concerned with sexual
dysfunction, have utilized sexual surrogates to assist in treatment. Often
in the past prostitutes served a similar function. The increase in the
numbers of surrogates and the attempt to distinguish them from prostitutes may eventually result in the replacement of prostitutes in this capacity, at least at the upper-income levels of society since surrogates, as
professional therapists, are not inexpensive. Nevertheless, the helping and
teaching function of prostitutes in the past cannot be ignored and provides a different view of the prostitute from that held by many people.

The sexual revolution and the women's movement are inducing
changes in the relations between the sexes seemingly so fast that many
people suffer from a sense of sexual anomie, if a sociological term such as
anomie can be extended to apply. Anomie, as defined by Emile Durkheim
in the late nineteenth century, was a condition of confusion, even to the
point of depression or suicide, brought on by social change that took
place too fast for easy adjustment. Durkheim described the anomie of
people who had been caught up in the rapid changes caused by industrialization. They were forced out of the stability of the village social
system and the support of family, friends, and tradition, forced to cope
with new complex urban environments. In this situation the old rules lost
their salience, but not enough time had elapsed for new norms and traditions to develop. Symptomatic of their feelings of being adrift without
support were the high suicide rates in rapidly industrialized societies.[17]
Obviously, such a conceptualization helps explain prostitution in the
eighteenth and nineteenth centuries. But amended, it would also apply
today. The norm of sexuality is, in a period of change, comparable to
that which took place earlier in the economic and industrial sphere. Symptomatic of this sexual anomie are some of the excesses of our time: the
frantic search for new varieties of sexual behavior; the vending of pornographic literature, devices, massages; the seeking of anonymous pleasure
that ends in depression. Probably as time passes and the Western world is
able to establish new sexual norms, some of this will prove transitional,
and as pressure to perform lessens, people will feel more relaxed about
sex. If this is the case, then there might be still further decline in prosti-

tution since the sexual anxieties that today encourage some men to seek nondemanding partners will also disappear.

One recent study has emphasized the importance of better law enforcement in lessening the amount of prostitution,[18] but though the police and the law have played a role in changing the form and scope of prostitution, they have never had much effect in lessening prostitution. This is important to emphasize because many people put great faith in the law and the police to eliminate or lessen prostitution without paying attention to the underlying causes for its existence. Obviously the police can supervise prostitution, and the courts can punish those who are caught, but prostitution has not been and cannot be eliminated by more effective laws. Moreover, the laws usually have been unequally enforced, with the burden falling on the lower economic levels of prostitution. The inevitable result was a cynicism about law enforcement by the public, a willingness to turn the other way by police officials, and political manipulation of the laws by those in power to suit their convenience.

A good example of how the law worked was revealed in 1919, when *Madeleine,* one of the first autobiographies of an American prostitute, was published. The anonymous autobiography carried an introduction by Denver's famous Judge Ben B. Lindsey, with an appeal that society change its attitude toward prostitutes. The author was particularly hard on some of the "hypocrites who called themselves reformers," and although the book, to at least one reviewer, seemed to make prostitution so distasteful that it resembled "a report of the Comstock Society" it became a political football. The publisher was Harper & Brothers, whose president, Harry T. Brainard, was a secretary of a grand jury investigating municipal corruption in New York City during the administration of Mayor John F. Hylan. Hylan enjoyed the support of William Randolph Hearst, a scion of yellow journalism and a not too respectable self-appointed guardian of public morals. When Hearst (or his agents) learned that Harper was publishing *Madeleine,* he leaped to the attack implying that Hylan was being persecuted by a corrupter of youth, a man who sold autobiographies of prostitutes. Brainard agreed to withdraw all copies of the book and destroy the plates, but the Hearst press hammered so hard that the prosecutor would not allow it. Brainard was convicted in December 1919, and fined $1,000, although on appeal the sentence was reversed. The judge in the higher court added that "no one can read this book and truthfully say that it contains a single word or picture which tends to excite lustful or lecherous desire." During World War II another biography of a prostitute, *Call House Madam: The Story of the Career of Beverly Davis,* by Serge J. Wolsey, ran into difficulty with the U.S. Post Office and was banned from the mails for a time. In England a similar fate awaited the autobiography of a prostitute who called herself Sheila Cousins. Her story, *To Beg I Am Ashamed,* was withdrawn from circulation in 1938 by her English publishers, although an American edition was kept in print. Sheila Cousins and Serge Wolsey both experienced publishing difficulties partly because they painted prostitution in fairly realistic terms. Wolsey's book also documented police connivance and bribery as did several later books about prostitution. What seems evident in retrospect is the misuse of police power to cover up police and political abuse.

Police corruption, however, is no more responsible for the continued existence of prostitution than effective enforcement is responsible for its elimination. Prostitution would obviously end overnight if there were no customers, and as emphasized in the last chapter, enforcement has been primarily directed at the prostitute rather than the clients who keep her in business. One of the main arguments against enforcement of the customer laws is that police, who use entrapment as a means of arresting prostitutes, would be found guilty every time they made an arrest since they offer money in exchange for sexual access.[19] In short, our enforcement procedures against prostitution are of dubious constitutionality, and the police find themselves in an untenable position if only because prostitution, by legal definition, is a victimless crime—that is, those who violate the law by going to a prostitute are most unlikely to denounce her. Since the only possible direct enforcement procedure is entrapment, police of necessity turn to doubtful tactics, and often end up blackmailing the prostitute or engaging in indiscriminate sweeps.

The American system, though corrupt, is probably not the worst one. Wholesale licensing and regulation as practiced in West Germany and the Netherlands (although abandoned in most other Western countries) seem worse because the official police lists can be used for blackmail and to restrict social mobility. Parent-Duchâtelet made a point of this over one hundred and fifty years ago but it is still ignored by the German officials. The essence of prostitution remains eternally the same, but it is just as important for the prostitute to keep up with the times as it is for any other person in business. In Germany the computer age gave birth to the Eros Center, a brothel that first opened its doors in 1967 in the Reeperbahn section of Hamburg. The original Eros Center (a copyrighted name) was a four-story drive-in motel with accommodations for 130 prostitutes who worked in rooms identical to each other from furniture to wallpaper to curtains to wall safe. Each room also had an alarm button connecting it to the nearby police station. For convenience of customers there is an underground garage that gives access to an infrared heated courtyard (Hamburg is cold in winter), where the women await their customers. The building complex is divided into nine parts around the open courtyard with each complex containing twelve to fifteen rooms. Each part has a resident male custodian to maintain order and otherwise be helpful. Heading the establishment is a male director, who when the center first opened was referred to as the "Kaiser of St. Pauli." Since there is a federal German law prohibiting individuals from living off the "immoral earnings" of another, the prostitutes who use the facilities are simply regarded as tenants, a euphemism that allows the public prosecutor to look the other way, and the owners and managers to reap a tidy profit.[20]

The Eros Center has been criticized by some as being too clinical, but Hamburg offers a variety of houses for every possible taste, all paying taxes to the city. Technically, Germany originally tolerated and regulated prostitution because it was argued that government control would decrease prostitution and cut down venereal disease, neither of which claim can be documented.[21] In fact, Italy and France, long the bastions of regulated prostitution, abandoned their regulated systems after World War II, not only because of organized efforts by women to abolish it but because the claims of regulated prostitution to cut down on venereal disease were not valid, at least when compared with other alternatives. The United States, for example, attacked the problem during World War II by inspecting male soldiers and tracing the sexual contacts of those infected. Probably the most effective way to deal with venereal disease is through a vaccination program and there is now a bright prospect that a vaccination against gonorrhea will be effective. In Germany, on the other hand, women have dealt with the system by establishing their own brothels, and in 1972 Hamburg opened a special "Yellow House" for female customers, access to which was through a beauty parlor. When the new brothel initially advertised for staff, some 1,600 males volunteered. Probably the main reason many German states still regulate prostitution is that it can be made to pay, although when it is concentrated into narrow city districts such as the Reeperbahn, police expenses mount enormously.

The most rational legal approach is that used in Great Britain. Concern over prostitution (and homosexuality) in the period after World War II led to a parliamentary investigation and report,[22] some of whose recommendations were enacted into law. The Street Offenses Act of 1959 made soliciting on the streets a crime, but left enforcement to uniformed police so the whole entrapment game was avoided. At the same time, prostitution itself was decriminalized; that is, prostitution per se was no longer against the law. The British prostitute had to adopt a more discreet approach to her customers in order to avoid charges of solicitation but at the same time she had to remain visible for any would-be customers. Though there were complaints that Parliament, by tolerating less open forms of prostitution, was merely "sweeping the dirt under the carpet," most Britons agreed with the member of the House of Lords who stated that hidden dirt was more healthy and less unsightly than dirt on the floor. In essence, what the Parliamentary report concluded was that control of prostitution was not possible simply through law enforcement,[23] which is what most Americans have failed to perceive.

Police scrutiny of prostitution has declined, especially the association of prostitution with organized crime. Thomas E. Dewey rose to national prominence in the thirties by pointing out the tie-in between the numbers racket, narcotics, and prostitution; in the process he sent Salvatore "Lucky" Luciano to a 30- to 50-year prison term. Probably the greatest prosperity of the so-called vice syndicates came during the Prohibition era, when bootlegging supplemented by prostitution was a principal source of profit. William Hale Thompson was returned to office as mayor of Chicago in 1927 with the help of a fund (allegedly $5 million) contributed by organized vice. The following year 2,000 vice establishments were reported to be paying $100 to $750 a week in return for police protection, and those that did not pay were raided and closed.[24] In 1936 when "Motzie" de Nicola, overlord of a chain of Connecticut vice resorts, was sentenced to the Lewisburg Federal Penitentiary, his control of prostitution was said to be yielding approximately $2 million annually.[25] What was true in these cities was true in Los Angeles, Buffalo, Phenix City, Alabama, Galveston, Texas, Newport, Kentucky, and elsewhere, but the changing sexual mores have made organized prostitution much less lucrative. The absence of tolerated districts, either official or unofficial, makes it extremely difficult for organized crime to control prostitution unless there is widespread police corruption. Moreover, the greater availability of sexual services by women who are not necessarily prostitutes makes it almost impossible to control the distribution of sex services. The most that organized crime can do is control segments. The fact that organized crime is not greatly involved in prostitution at this time, however, does not mean that there is not a strong criminal element.

By making prostitution a crime, American laws have forced the prostitute to associate with other groups of outcasts, namely the criminal. In those cities where organized prostitution functions on a large scale, organized crime at some level will be involved. Prostitution functioning on that scale under existing laws implies police and political connivance, something that can take place only through bribery and intimidation. Generally, however, criminal groups do not take a great interest in prostitution because it doesn't pay enough, there are too many amateurs in it, and there are more lucrative fields in which to operate. For the petty criminal, however, prostitution remains one of the chief sources of income.[26]

Decriminalizing prostitution would probably eliminate much of this connection, but it would do little to curb the traditional venereal diseases that in the 1970s were again reaching serious proportions. Medical research has also shown that other diseases such as hepatitis can also be transmitted venereally. There are several reasons for the increase in venereal disease, but the chief reason is simply that the venereal disease is no longer feared as much as it was before the advance of antibiotics. This has changed the nature of the problem, and accentuated the fact that venereal disease is a public health rather than a police problem. During World War II the United States, with federal government sponsorship, had an effective VD control program involving the tracing of carriers, but this was dropped when more effective cures appeared, and the problem was then more or less ignored until venereal disease, particularly gonorrhea, again reached what officials called epidemic proportions. Some strains of gonorrhea also developed that proved immune to penicillin, further accentuating the problem. It is not at all clear, however, that prostitutes are the chief source of contamination as much as the changing pattern of sexual relations among the young, and the increasing abandonment of the condom, the use of which was an effective prophylactic as well as a less effective contraceptive. The emergence of AIDS in epidemic form, however, has again accentuated the problem. Though the female prostitute can still be a carrier of venereal disease, in some of the larger cities such as Los Angeles, the male homosexual prostitute is far more infectious, at least as of this writing. Yet few advocates of regulation propose the establishment of male homosexual brothels, emphasizing the double standard inherent in the reglementation system.

In the last few decades, many observers have looked on the prostitute as if her occupational choice was an illness. The reasons for this attitude have been examined in earlier chapters, but for the most part the simple medical model of disease, involving treatment and cure, was not adopted until the advent of modern psychiatry. The early theories of Karl Abraham and Edward Glover on the subject have already been mentioned, but their studies should also be added to this context. Karl Abraham theorized that it was only when a woman could not enjoy the sex act with one partner that she felt compelled to change partners in the Don Juan fashion. Taking pay for the sex act by such women demonstrated their own hostility to men; they took revenge on men by emphasizing that the sex act, which men held important, meant nothing to the prostitute.[27] Edward Glover, whose work has been called the outstanding psychiatric contribution to the study of prostitution,[28] interpreted prostitution as evidence of an unresolved Oedipus conflict; the woman still hated her mother and was disappointed with her father. Glover agreed with other psychoanalytic writers that the prostitute was sexually frigid, hostile to men, and had homosexual tendencies. He also argued that many customers of prostitutes were able to enjoy the sex act only with people they held in low esteem.[29]

The theme of latent or open homosexuality runs through both of these analyses, but was most strongly advocated by Frank Caprio. In 1953 Caprio toured the world visiting brothels in most of the major cities. In his interviews with prostitutes, he found two or more lesbians in every brothel he visited who reported that they engaged in homosexual activities between customers for their own gratification, or at other times for exhibitions for the customers. Using this data, Caprio argued that prostitution was a behavior deviation that appealed primarily to women with strong homosexual tendencies; their activities with their customers were a pseudoheterosexual defense against their true desires for lesbian love; eventually, however, many of them lost their inhibitions and turned to open homosexuality. He stated that prostitutes were emotionally sick people whose activities were manifestations of their illness.[30]

Taking a different tack was Tibor Agoston, who maintained that the prostitute developed a pseudopersonality to ecsape her feelings of guilt. By denying her true identity and offering a pseudopersonality for hire, the prostitute was able to proceed to complete infantile regression with her rented pseudopersonality.[31] This emphasis on the identity problem of the prostitute was accepted by Helene Deutsch, but she saw the problem in a different way. For her the prostitute suffered from disconnected identities. Identification was with the masochistic mother, and the deriding of social institutions, law, morality, as well as the men who imposed such authority, since all represented a focus of paternally directed hostility. Another type of prostitute, however, she believed, renounced tenderness and feminine gratification in favor of the aggressive masculinity they imitate. This idea is similar to Caprio's idea of the lesbian prostitute.[32] H. Lichtenstein identified prostitution as representing symbiosis with the original love object, the mother, and the prostitute achieved a symbolic phallus by permitting "castrated" men sexual use of her body as a prostitute,[33] which is another version of the secret lesbian.

J. Lampi de Groot also saw prostitution as a manifestation of homosexuality. He hypothesized that in the Oedipal struggle the prostitute turned to the man out of revenge on the mother, not with an attitude of feminine surrender but masculine assertiveness and activity, making the client the "feminine" partner in the sexual act.[34] Marc H. Hollender saw prostitution and hypochondriasis as closely related, in that both were one step removed from a totally objectless state. Bodily and sexual contacts became the regressive substitutes for interpersonal relationships, and the male, after achieving orgasm, was felt to be powerless and castrated, thus gratifying sadomasochistic and hostile dependent wishes.[35] The objectless state was further amplified by Thomas Szasz, who implied that prostitution was a mechanism by which a woman, by indiscriminately participating in sexual intercourse, could give up parts of her body (the genitals) and experience these as nonexistent.[36] F. Wengraf emphasized the latent homosexuality of the prostitute,[37] as did P. L. Gotoin.[38]

Maryse Choisey, a French psychoanalyst, wrote that the union of the prostitute with her client was one of debasement in which both partners expressed their aggression and hostility in a sadomasochistic relationship. The women were seeking revenge against their fathers and the men against their mothers; the money that changed hands was a symbol of the mutual contempt they felt for each other.[39] Her source of data included interviews with patients as well as firsthand experience working as a waitress in a brothel for one month while she collected material for a newspaper series.[40] There are other explanations, to a large extent dependent on the investigator's view or school of thought.

The overall impression left by the review of these psychiatric studies is not a favorable one; quite frankly, most of the studies lack scientific validity. The analysts place diagnostic labels on everyone they see, regard them as sick persons, and generalize from patient population to the population at large. Since most conclusions were on the basis of patients undergoing therapy these are undoubtedly natural, but is a patient undergoing therapy representative of all prostitutes not undergoing therapy? When the question is put this way, it becomes obvious why the studies permit such great distortion.[41]

The psychoanalytic-oriented investigators have also lumped all prostitutes into the same category without looking at the social conditions that led them to prostitution: this might well have given them different outlooks from that of the upper-middle-class-analysts. Moreover, the prostitute was usually examined without reference to her customer, and if the prostitute by psychiatric definition is sick, then by implication her client might also be so labeled. Yet only one part of what could be a mutual sickness ordinarily has been examined. Another problem in studying the prostitute is the primitive research methodologies used. The best psychoanalytic study in this respect is that by Harold Greenwald. His initial sample of prostitutes numbered twenty, and he is generally very cautious in specifying his course of data, but even he failed to use any control group. Greenwald found that the primary predisposing factor to prostitution was a history of severe maternal deprivation. This loss of mother love caused the child to turn increasingly to her father for affection, but usually the father failed to give the necessary emotional support; this led the girls to turn to self-abasement in an attempt to hurt their mothers. Prostitution represented a way to search for security, warmth, and love that the adult woman had not received as a child.[42]

Although some of the arguments of the psychoanalytic school about the psychopathology of the personalities of prostitutes contain elements of truth, inevitably they leave unanswered more questions than they answer. It is still impossible to know whether prostitutes dislike men more than nonprostitutes do or whether prostitutes are more likely to be lesbians than a group of teachers or nurses or any other occupational group dominated by women.

Even if prostitutes are shown to be lesbian in orientation beyond other groups of women, it is not certain whether this is a cause or a consequence of their occupation. Women who continually have to fake orgasm with men might well turn to other women for satisfaction. In short, it would seem to be a distortion of the evidence to conclude that prostitution is a mental illness. It would also be in contradiction to the historical data that suggests, if it does not prove, that the position of the individual in the social stucture is a significant variable in the person's choice of occupation and particularly significant in distinguishing between the common prostitute and the higher-status courtesan.

Psychiatric-oriented investigators might be able to explain why a particular woman turned to prostitution, but their research is far too incomplete to tell us generally why women become prostitutes. Incontestably, the prostitute is often a troubled woman, evidenced by the high rate of drug addiction and alcoholism. But whether drug addiction results from prostitution or prostitution is a result of drug addiction is debatable, since prostitution is often the easiest way for a drug addict to support her habit.

There are statistical studies of prostitutes that are somewhat more rigorous than the psychiatric. Most of this solid research, comparable to that in other areas of social science, is of relatively recent origin. One of the more significant studies in this respect was a 1955 English study titled *Women of the Streets,* which included statistical studies of 150 prostitutes with in-depth interviews of a portion of the sample. The author, who chose to remain anonymous, indicated that there were many different personality types as well as outlooks among the streetwalkers, and she described a type of alienation that she called a state of not belonging. She also reported that the women in her sample worked hard, transferring any guilt feelings (which the author apparently felt they should have) to their customers; they felt that they were honest, hard-working women but that their customers were men who cheated on their wives or acted in other dishonest ways. There were also social-class differences among the group. The richer streetwalkers who worked in affluent neighborhoods seemed charming, educated, and sympathetic; those who worked in poorer neighborhoods were more embittered and more obviously out to get the best of their customers.[43]

The Kinsey group also gathered information about prostitution, although much of the data has never been published. Wardell Pomeroy in 1965, however, reported some of the findings based on a sample of 175 prostitutes. (The sample may be somewhat skewed since 154 of the subjects were in prison when they were interviewed.) Significantly, and in contrast to the assumptions in the psychiatric literature, these women were not frigid. In fact, they were more sexually responsive than the women interviewed for the major Kinsey study on female sexual behavior.[44] Ninety percent of the prostitute group reported that they had orgasms in their nonprofessional contacts; even in sexual contacts with clients approximately 80 percent reported having orgasms at least occasionally. Nearly two-thirds of the group reported that they felt no regrets about their choice of occupation, although the prison inmates did regret being in jail. The women reported that they chose prostitution as work because it offered a good income, an opportunity to meet interesting people, was comparatively easy, was fun, and gave sexual pleasure. Pomeroy emphasized that these were only the conscious factors entering into their selection.[45] Nevertheless, his data would seem to challenge much of the psychiatric view of prostitution.

Prostitution is difficult to research partly because it is a temporary occupation for many women who leave it if something better turns up. This temporary nature of the work was emphasized by a British study of some four hundred wayward girls, many of whom turned to prostitution usually on a temporary basis as they attempted to find an adjustment to life. Those girls who did become prostitutes had normal intelligence and superficially little more emotional difficulties than those who did not.[46] Other studies have shown that though the general social values have some impact on the isolated prostitute, she rationalizes her rejection of those values. These justifications include her financial success and her ability unselfishly to assume the financial burdens of people dependent on her.[47]

Another way of examining prostitution is through the biographies and autobiographies of the more literate prostitutes. Many of these prostitute authors reported suffering feelings of degradation that made them the willing victims of dope salesmen, pimps who beat them, sadistic clients, and even of suicide. What comes through strongest in these accounts, however, is that prostitution is hard work, and though some girls demand extremely high fees, very few have managed to hold onto the money they earned. The call girl has to see the same shows night after night and yet act enchanted and delighted with her sponsor, and the lowly streetwalker has to snag a customer in order to pay for food. The girl who works in a brothel has her life carefully circumscribed; in fact she is more carefully supervised than a girl in a dormitory in a strict religious college. Most autobiographies of prostitutes fail to fit the psychoanalytic model (a system of examining the client based on the work of Sigmund Freud. It involves probing the mental life, conscious and unconscious, with emphasis on the unconscious, of individual patients. In this context, it makes generalizations about prostitutes, which are not supported by the wealth of other data available). Though most of those women who are writing about themselves are concerned with some sort of self-justification and might not tell the truth even if they know it, a surprising number reportedly found pleasure in prostitution.[48]

The work of the creative writer offers another view of prostitution, and many twentieth-century writers have found the prostitute an interesting and challenging heroine. For a time American and English writers were reluctant to deal with the prostitute in any realistic way, although even in prudish times, Charles Dickens, Rebecca Harding Davis, Stephen Crane, and Theodore Dreiser in their novels vividly described prostitutes. And as mentioned in an earlier chapter, the French novelists Honoré de Balzac and Alexandre Dumas fils also wrote stories about prostitute heroines. Another Frenchman, Emile Zola, wrote *Nana,* first published in 1880, about a streetwalker turned actress. Nana was a vulgar, greedy, cruel, and beautiful woman who made her living as an actress, although she lacked real acting ability. Her face, figure, and reputation allowed her to live a luxurious life, disgracing, ruining, or hurting her various lovers until she finally died of smallpox. Zola's novel, because of its naturalistic portrayal, aroused considerable antagonism. It was put on the Catholic *Index of Forbidden Books* and was also denounced by Anatole France. France later himself dealt with a prostitute in *Thaïs* (1890), a historical re-creation of the adventures of the beautiful Alexandrian courtesan who converted to Christianity. Jules Massenet's opera *Thaïs* (1894) was also based on romance. Other French writers dealing with prostitution in this period included J. K. Huysmans (*Marthe*), Gustave Flaubert (*November*), and Guy de Maupassant, who wrote several stories on the subject. The writers were not all of the same mind.

Leo Tolstoy, for example, was rather ambivalent about the topic. In *Resurrection* (1899) he has his prostitute heroine Katsushna Maslova in one instance call prostitution a life of "hell," and in another he has her expressing satisfaction and pride in her occupation. Katushna comments that everyone must make her own occupation seem important and good regardless of her position in life, an attitude adopted by many prostitutes in their own autobiographies. Tolstoy's fellow Russian, Feodor Dostoevski, also portrayed prostitutes in many of his works, most notably *The*

Brothers Karamazov and *Crime and Punishment.* In the latter novel, the heroine, Sonya, turns to prostitution in order to save her family from starving. Eventually she becomes a saintly figure at a prison camp in Siberia, where she is known as Little Mother Sonia, and helps Raskalnikov begin his regeneration. Arthur Schnitzler, Gerhart Hauptmann, Stefan Zweig all wrote novels in German dealing with prostitution. The most famous of the German works was Hermann Sudermann's *Das Hohe Lied* (1908), which was translated into English as *The Song of Songs.* The heroine, Lily Czepanek, was a successful prostitute.

Playwrights also put the subject of prostitutes and prostitution on the stage. In the United States, after a period of repression against dramatic portrayals of prostitution, the issue came to a head with George Bernard Shaw's play *Mrs. Warren's Profession,* produced in 1905. The play deals with the reactions of a rather haughty girl who has been kept in comfort and refinement by her mother's prostitution. When the daughter finally discovers how her mother has supported her, she turns contemptuous and angry instead of being grateful. Shaw had been refused a license to produce the play in England in the 1890s, and although it was performed privately in 1902, no public performance was allowed in England until 1925. The first public performance took place in the United States, where, in spite of the efforts of Anthony Comstock to ban it, the courts allowed it to run. The newspaper critics, however, were far less tolerant; one critic called it a "tainted drama," and another, perhaps fearful of using the word *prostitution,* reported that the play had an "unspeakable theme."

From such controversial beginnings the prostitute moved into the center of American dramatic consciousness, so much so that a 1960s survey of the dozen best performances by Broadway actresses over the past half century reported that half of them were portrayals of prostitutes. Obviously, Americans had considerable ambivalence about the fallen women. Among the most notable roles singled out for attention was that of Jeanne Eagels in *Rain,* a 1923 play by John Colton and Clemence Randolph based on the Somerset Maugham short story "Miss Thompson." The play recounted the arrival of the prostitute Sadie Thompson on a South Sea island, where she was frightened into confessing her past sins to the Reverend Mr. Davidson, but who returned to a defiant cynicism after he revealed his lust for her. Prostitutes might well be sinners, but they are not alone in this respect. Also picked for special attention was another play by Colton, *Shanghai Gesture* (1926), which starred Florence Reed. This depicted the subtle vengeance of the madam (Miss Reed) of a Chinese brothel on an Englishman who betrayed her, namely, by placing his two daughters in the establishment. Many other plays have also dealt with prostitution. Included in the list would be many of the waterfront plays of Eugene O'Neill; Zoë Akins, *The Varying Shore* (1921), Sidney Howard, *Morals* (1925), Robert Sherwood, *Waterloo Bridge* (1930), Jack Kirkland and John Steinbeck, *Tortilla Flat* (1938), Marc Blitzstein, *The Cradle Will Rock* (1938), William Saroyan, *The Time of Your Life* (1940), Tennessee Williams, *A Streetcar Named Desire* (1947), Arthur Miller, *Death of a Salesman* (1949); *I Am a Camera* (1955), based on stories by Chistopher Isherwood, and any number of others. The point to emphasize is that the role of prostitute is an attractive, even glamorous, one for actresses. Prostitutes are not always portrayed as the lost, forlorn lesbians that psychiatric literature claims they are. These stage and screen portrayals serve, incidentally, as a reinforcement to those prostitutes who feel they do not fit the psychoanalytic model.

American writers as diverse as James T. Farrell, Henry Miller, William Faulkner, John O'Hara, Nelson Algren, Norman Mailer, and Alexander Woollcott have written extensively about prostitutes. Though the literary merits of some fictional accounts, especially those written for the paperback market, might be debated, the public is provided an opportunity to see the prostitute in more dimensioned portrayals. Few readers of James Jones's *From Here to Eternity,* for example, will fail to come away without considerable understanding and sympathy for the prostitute Lorene, and readers of William Bradford Huie's *Revolt of Mamie Stover* can only admire the prostitute's single-minded determination to achieve her goal. Her brothel advertised $3 for 3 minutes as her price, and she herself could handle four beds almost at once, slipping from one to another after each serviceman client had been appropriately prepared by an assistant. By the end of her career she was earning $20,000 a month. When she left the island of Hawaii, she did so in triumph This protrayal is quite different from that in medical literature about prostitution.[49]

What is true of the stage, the novel, and the short story has also become increasingly true of the cinema. The prostitute is no longer a stereotype. In the movie version of *Rain* made in 1932, Joan Crawford portrayed a rather sympathetic Sadie, a character that became much more flamboyant in the 1953 remake *Miss Sadie Thompson,* in which Rita Hayworth sang and danced to "The Heat Is On." In the 1964 film *Irma La Douce* the police inspector is a client of the prositute. Sometimes there were attempts to reform the prostitute as in *The World of Suzie Wong* (1960), but the prostitute was also pictured as a complex, well-adjusted woman in the movie *Never on Sunday* (1961), which brought Melina Mercouri to American attention. These characterizations imply that the personality of a prostitute differs from country to country, from period to period, and even from woman to woman[50]—a rather radical change from conceptualizations of the past.

The changes the movies have brought about over the years have been accelerated by television, and a superficial analysis of 1976 TV shows indicates that prostitution formed a significant subtheme in a number of police shows, and prostitutes have become accepted characters, even in some so-called family shows. Prostitutes were significant characters in *Gunsmoke*, in *Hot l Baltimore*, and in individual episodes of such shows as *Laverne and Shirley, All in the Family, M.A.S.H., Laugh-In*, and others.

Probably the ultimate framework for viewing prostitution is an occupational one. *Occupation*, as defined by American sociologists Stewart and Cantor, is "a social role performed by the adult members of society that directly or indirectly yields social and financial consequences."[51] Prostitution is clearly an occupation, it has filled a social need, and it offers financial reward to its participants. Though it is a deviant or stigmatized occupation, the stigma attached to it depends on who is plying the trade. It varies significantly from the high-paid courtesan or call girl to the low-level prostitute, and generally the higher the fee the less the stigma. Both prostitution and marriage have the same basic objectives of filling the sexual and social needs of men, but marriage also has other goals. The occupational explanation is not inconsistent with modern sociological theory, which accepts the fact that both deviant and accepted behaviors and conditions can be built on the same social structures and values.[52]

Most contemporary recruits probably drift into the occupation, at least in countries like the United States. Usually they experiment hesitantly with accepting payment and then ultimately decide to become professional. Though they go through a process of working into their new identities, the crucial factors in their coming to think of themselves as prostitutes are reactions of society toward them and the labels that others attach to their work.[53] A good historical example of this is those nineteenth-century upper-class women who became addicted to paregoric or laudanum and when the narcotics legislation was passed at the beginning of the twentieth century found themselves classed as addicts. Their behavior remained the same but now their addict label carried with it a cluster of negative connotations. Though the prostitute identity is not sought and can be painful at first, eventually it can also be supportive as the subculture provides an explicatory world view to the prostitute, which defines her work as significant and allows her to develop friends "in the life." She realizes she fills a need in the lives of her clients, who need affection or physical release. These clients express their thanks in words, gifts, and money. Many prostitutes feel their occupation serves an important public service, more useful than many other occupational groups. But since it is an occupation in which the mobility tends to be downward as the woman ages, most women tend to seek other roles. If the legal or other barriers are not too rigid, ultimately they leave the life for marriage or other work, and this is as true today as it was in the past. A large subculture of males regards prostitutes as desirable wives because their wives selected them over all other males, but many prostitutes probably fail to tell their husbands of their past life. If the prostitute does not leave "the life" voluntarily, ultimately she will face a difficult time because there are fewer customers for the older prostitute and her price declines. Legalized or highly organized prostitution such as exists in Germany and other countries acts as a barrier to mobility out of the profession, and for this reason, if not any other, we feel prostitution should not be regulated. An arrest for lewd vagrancy cannot compare in terms of trauma to being labeled a registered prostitute.

The exploitation of women for prostitution is still a significant factor, and unfortunately even today there is the apparent willingness and ability of some of the more developed countries to exploit the underdeveloped ones. Cuba, until the Castro revolution, for example, was one of the chief centers of brothel prostitution, catering primarily to the American tourist. Tiajuana in Baja California serves a similar function for much of Southern California in spite of periodic efforts of the Mexican authorities to prevent this from happening. And the movement to eliminate white slavery has tended to cut down the trade in women for which Buenos Aires was once notorious,[54] but there are still women who are more or less forced into prostitution in much of Latin America as well as in many other parts of the world.

In the Near East and Far East, where cultures with different ideals and sexual attitudes exist, prostitution has been going through some of the same changes that it has in the West. Japan, the home of the geisha, has gone through a period of rapid social change since World War II and though husbands and wives now do more entertaining and socializing together, some of the old ways remain. A Japanese businessman is still likely to conduct business in a special house where the geisha, trained in the arts of pleasing men, entertains him and his guests,[55] but this old system has come under increasing attack by the younger wives.

Prostitution still exists in China, and as indicated at the beginning of this book, "roadside chickens" solicit customers in Canton and other cities.[56] To cut down on prostitution, China is distributing contraceptives and publishing pamphlets indicating that the sex urge is normal among young people and encouraging them to have sex with one another rather than with professionals. As the status of women in China improves, and the economic level of society rises, many of the abuses associated with the old system disappear. In Taiwan the old notion that a daughter could be bought or sold like a commodity is on the decline,[57] although it persists among the uneducated people, and the longtime use of Taiwan, Thailand, and other areas by American troops for recreation and rehabilitation served to provide a ready market for many of the prostitutes.[58] In India a 1957 estimate gave the number of prostitutes in Bombay as 40,000; though the accuracy of such figures might be doubted, the large numbers of men without women in Bombay, Calcutta, and other large cities certainly creates a demand for them. In 1956 the Indian government moved against the operators of brothels, but prostitution was not made illegal; rather the prostitute was merely prevented from practicing her trade in close proximity to certain public places.[59] Since social security benefits are still inadequate in India, a woman who loses her family through death or disaster often can turn only to prostitution.[60] In fact, in large parts of the world poverty still remains a major factor in prostitution.

Egypt has also forbidden organized prostitution by law, but less overt forms have mushroomed, with prostitutes employed as cabaret artists, dancers, and entertainers of various kinds.[61] Lebanon still has a reglementation system, and it is in such a system that the prostitute feels the most helpless and alienated from society. A study of the Lebanese prostitute by Samir Khalif found that over 80 percent would leave the profession if they could, and another 18.5 percent found their chances for abandoning the occupation as hopeless. Most of those who wanted to leave hoped to find a husband or to save enough money to go into business for themselves as a beautician or in a similar commercial enterprise.[62] The Arab world is still plagued by white slavery, and it is still possible in parts of the oil-rich but socially backward Middle East to buy women. This is true in other places (parts of Africa, India, and the Philippines) as well, although the buyers are not potentially so rich.[63]

Regardless of where in the world prostitution exists, the reasons are not hard to find. It will normally be found in its most rampant form in those situations where large groups of men are concentrated away from wives and families for long periods of time; this has usually been the case with large armies, with merchant caravans and traveling salesmen, or, without quite the same justification, at the modern American convention. Prostitution is also highly evident in those societies with a severe double standard, where great freedom is allowed to the male, and the female is rigidly circumscribed. When "proper" women do not dance, sing, write poetry, or engage in other types of social or intellectual activities, then the male usually turns to women who do, women often looked upon as prostitutes by the society.

When there are obstacles to marriage such as dowries, achievement, age, or other barriers, then prostitution is more likely to exist than when such barriers are lacking; too many qualifications prevent many would-be candidates from getting married. Conversely, where divorce is difficult, prostitution and concubinage are widespread. For example among Western nations, Spain, Italy, Brazil, and Portugal have the highest per capita illegitimacy ratio, and it is no accident that divorce in these countries has not been permitted, although Italy and Spain have recently made a change. Prostitution then becomes the safeguard for marriage. In societies where there is little or no provision for women to earn a living, single women (whether unmarried, widowed, divorced, or abandoned) are often driven to prostitution. In many cases economic pressures are all important, but it also seems clear that in societies where women are socially acceptable only as wives and mothers, many women rebel against the legal bondage that marriage entails. Some societies and cultures, as we have already mentioned, permitted women of beauty, intelligence, or other attributes to advance to positions of influence and affluence by prostitution; often this was the only way a woman could advance, emphasizing again the importance of the double standard. In spite of statements to the contrary, prostitution historically has been less likely to exist when divorce is easy and women have alternatives to marriage.

Prostitutes, however, fulfill other functions than that of a partner in sexual intercourse; in the United States at the present time the expensive prostitute is often a symbol of conspicuous consumption, and a man who cannot achieve status in other ways can signify his achievement by escorting such a woman to public places. It should also be emphasized that the prostitute has become one of the chief means for the male to gratify unusual sexual desires. The fact that the prostitute serves so many functions ensures that the profession will not easily die away. In fact, prostitution will continue to exist as long as there is a demand for the services of prostitutes, and there will be a demand as long as there is greater sexual freedom for the male and a more circumscribed life for the female. One of the more obvious comments that can be made about youthful prostitution in the United States is that prostitution serves a function. It is difficult if not impossible for young people under eighteen to get jobs. We insist that such people be in school, yet many do not go to school. We also insist that they live at home, but many, including many from well-to-do families, move out of their homes. Hollywood and New York City and other large cities are inundated with young women and young men, seeking their fortunes in the movies, on the stage, or simply fleeing what they regard as the boredom of their home towns or the tyranny of their parents. Once they arrive in the cities they find there is little they can do, and inevitably many turn to prostitution. Undoubtedly some are forced into it by a pimp or panderer, but the main reason is that there is no alternative for them. To the uninitiated, prostitution seems an easy way of earning a living, of becoming a glamorous adult. These young prostitutes become a major social problem, one that society easily could deal with by creating occupational alternatives. Society, however, prefers to assume that all young people attend school until they are eighteen, after which they either go on to college or get an honest job. This is simply not realistic.

Laws have not ended prostitution, although they have directed it into new forms. Pouring more money into law enforcement will not end prostitution either, although it might increase the likelihood that the street-walker will be harassed, and it might make prostitution less noticeable (which some equate with the elimination of prostitution). One hopes that the development of a new sex ethic that emphasizes mutual enjoyment and emotional involvement as well as physical need will lessen the demand for prostitution, but even if this does happen, there undoubtedly will be men who can find no other way to satisfy their sexual needs than through the service of a prostitute.

Though societies have come to terms with prostitution in many different ways, it is not at all clear that those societies that have severely condemned all forms of prostitution have been any more effective in dealing with the problems raised than those that have demonstrated a more tolerant attitude. Since this is the case, what policy should be adopted by a state to deal with prostitution? Social critics complain that it is not enough for scholars and scientists to examine a problem; they must also suggest solutions. To this end, let us examine such recommendations and the difficulties inherent in them.

1. Perhaps the most extreme recommendation that could be made would be to outlaw prostitution entirely, to throw all the resources of the state into a legal campaign to eliminate prostitution totally. Of course prostitution has often been outlawed in the past, with no great effectiveness. But, in our opinion, such a policy would be doomed to failure, if only because it would be impossible to enforce unless police powers, using all the efforts of the state, were brought to bear on every act of sexual intercourse. This policy would be much worse than any problems it purported to solve. It would not only go contrary to all historical insights but would violate privacy, and ignore the biological needs or drives of men and women. It would also ignore the economic and social realities of everyday living and could be possible only in the kind of absolute police state imagined by George Orwell in *1984*.

Elizabeth L. Ray, the employee of former Congressman Wayne Hays, who called herself the "Washington fringe benefit,"[64] could have been prevented from operating in Washington only in a system that absolutely prohibited any male from having sex with a female other than his wife. Enforcing such a policy would require vast numbers of policemen and policewomen, and then the new problem would be to control the activities of the law-enforcement officials. Undoubtedly what would happen is that only certain kinds of behavior would be identified as critical to law enforcement, and much of what could be called prostitution would continue to exist. The problem in effect would be solved by redefining what prostitution is.

2. In a sense this is existing policy. Many jurisdictions outlaw some aspects of behavior associated with prostitution, primarily solicitation, but almost immediately difficulties appear in what constitutes solicitation. Almost every female has been solicited at least sometime in her life, and though female solicitation of males is less blatant and less obvious, most women have to give signals that they would like to know a man better for him to approach her.[65] The whole concept of romantic love is based upon the assumption that males and females have some kind of attraction for each other. To get around this problem we have sometimes attempted to make illegal only overt "solicitation," but what is overt to one person might not be to another. Courts in wrestling with this problem have insisted that solicitation specifically be a solicitation to commit a sexual act for money. This has led to further difficulties in enforcement because male vice officers then have to hold off arrest until such an offer is made, and a streetwise prostitute is reluctant to name money until the officer himself does. The end result is entrapment, and a basic perversion of the law. But if we are going to arrest prostitutes for solicitation, should not her customers be arrested for making offers to solicit? Probably yes, but the same difficulty exists here, since in order to arrest soliciting customers, a vice officer has to act the part of a prostitute and encourage her would-be client to offer money. The result is the same danger of entrapment that led to the arrest of Congressman Alan Howe in Salt Lake City in 1976. If either the female prostitute or the male client denies the allegations in court, the court in the overwhelming majority of cases takes the word of the vice officer, even against a congressman. This puts the vice officer in the position of exercising great power over the prostitute (and her client) and opens a Pandora's box of police extortion. The effect of such a policy is to put the policeman in a more powerful position than we are usually willing to give even our elective officials. Moreover, the difficulty with an arrest for solicitation is that only the more obvious prostitutes are arrested, primarily the streetwalkers, and the more discreet call girls or high-class party girls are untouched. The result is a class bias in law enforcement that mocks equal justice under law.

3. Recognizing the difficulty of outlawing prostitution, some states in

the past, as well as the present, have attempted to legalize and control it, usually on the grounds of preventing the spread of venereal disease. Medical inspection of prostitutes is not a particularly effective way to control venereal disease, since to be effective every client of a prostitute would have to undergo examination before being given access to her, and the examination would have to be more than superficial. As indicated earlier, a far better way of controlling venereal disease is to treat those who have been diagnosed and trace their sexual contacts, a policy that proved very effective in the United States during World War II. Reglementation not only is a failure in controlling disease, it raises other problems. The reglementation system makes prostitution a career choice for many who might otherwise have been involved only temporarily. Individual histories of prostitutes in times when prostitutes were not slaves and stigmatized forever, indicate that prostitution was a passing phase in their lives; they engaged in it until something better showed up. However, once a woman was listed as a prostitute by authorities she was forever labeled as such, even though she had not even been arrested for soliciting.

Reglementation also implied that certain districts be set apart for prostitution, and entry to these districts be policed. Theoretically this limited vice to certain neighborhoods, but what happened if a prostitute plied her trade in another area? If caught, she was arrested and transported to the official district; so to prevent this from happening the police were forced not only to patrol the official vice district but the unofficial ones as well. Reglementation was also justified on the grounds that minors would thereby be excluded; but not registering them as prostitutes did not mean that they did not practice, albeit illegally. By concentrating vice in one area it was believed police could better control crime, but in reality the concentration of prostitution creates special problems because allied services such as pornography, petty crime, and other establishments also concentrate in these areas. This raises not only special police problems but special problems for the neighborhood. One of the complaints mentioned at the beginning of this book was that of the merchants in Times Square and other areas where prostitutes concentrate. In the small Nevada towns where prostitution is regulated, it is not difficult to isolate a house of prostitution in the boondocks, a few blocks from the center of town, but in New York City or San Francisco or Chicago or Miami or Philadelphia, the obvious place to locate such a district is where the tourists and transients are most likely to go. If the legal district is far from the focus of activity, the prostitute will move to that location and the police then would have to arrest people for doing in one part of the city what would be legal in another. Moreover, no neighborhood wants to be labeled as the center of vice. Still another difficulty with reglementation is that it deals only with the more blatant forms of prostitution and seldom touches the high-priced prostitute. The Elizabeth Rays would be no more effectively curtailed by this system than by the existing one.

4. To us the obvious solution is the decriminalization of sexual activities between consenting adults whether or not money changes hands. The merit of such a system is that it would free the majority of the members of the urban vice squads for other tasks, specifically for crimes involving victims. Prostitutes could be encouraged to be discreet, advertising their services in the so-called underground press, establishing telephone-answering services, recruiting customers in parlors emphasizing erotic massages, in adult bookstores, through special escort services, the establishment of erotic night clubs. Those who wanted prostitutes would find them, and those who did not could avoid them.

We do not believe that such a system would radically increase the number of prostitutes and would become less violative of individual privacy and property rights than the present system. If citizens become concerned that solicitation in their neighborhood is a serious infringement on their privacy, they can adopt the London system of establishing a patrol of uniformed police officers to encourage both the clients and the prostitutes to be more discreet. We believe, however, that once decriminalization has taken place, and there are easy ways for the interested parties to come together, this will not be a serious problem.

We strongly believe that the law should protect young girls from being enticed into prostitution, but the laws on statutory rape and age of consent already deal with this. The strong prohibitions against involuntary prostitution should also remain on the books. As we have emphasized, Western society, in spite of all its apparent condemnations, has actually condoned prostitution. It has indicated its ambivalence by making the prostitute subject to legal harassment, imprisonment, fines, and other penalties, but then enforced these penalties only sporadically and mainly directed their enforcement at the poorer prostitutes who could least afford to be prosecuted. Though there are probably deep psychological factors that have encouraged some women to enter into a life of prostitution, it is not at all clear that the prostitute should be regarded as a sick person; rather she should be treated as sick only when she herself feels the need for help and treatment. Ultimately, and hopefully, society will eliminate the double standard of sexuality that remains the bulwark of prostitution in all societies. It might also work to eliminate the poverty, the drug addiction, and other social evils that serve as recruiting grounds for prostitution. Until we reach these utopian solutions, however, we have to deal wth prostitution as it exists, but to throw the burden of enforcement on the police as we do today is to admit almost total failure. Sex is here to stay, and though mores are changing rapidly, prostitution is not going to disappear in the foreseeable future. Though we think prostitution will continue to decline as a percentage of the population's total sexual contacts, we can predict that there will be a demand for the prostitute for the rest of our lifetime and for many lifetimes thereafter. We need to deal with prostitution realistically and not brush aside the problems associated with it as we do today.

BIBLIOGRAPHY

Since scholars in general have neglected the study of prostitution, most of the studies in the past made little pretension to scholarship, and the few that did are almost impossible to locate in American libraries. The researcher who wants to pursue the topic is encouraged to follow the footnotes in this book. Those who investigate will soon find that most studies are at a very low level, not particularly sophisticated or analytical, and often aimed more at arousing an erotic response in male readers than in trying to explain the phenomenon. A valuable guide is the bibliography that we, along with others, have compiled. See Vern L. Bullough, Barrett Elcano, Margaret Deacon, and Bonnie Bullough, *A Bibliography of Prostitution* (New York: Garland Publishing, 1977).

Basic research into the subject of prostitution began in the nineteenth century. One of the first serious studies was that by A. J. B. Parent-Duchatelet, *De la prostitution dans la ville de Paris* (2 vols., Paris: J. B. Baillière, 1836). Parent-Duchatelet treated prostitution as a social problem, one of the first persons to do so, and his work is more sociological and statistical than historical. Still he included a great deal of historical information. The work is still valuable and has often been translated and reprinted, sometimes under different titles. Following this pioneering study was the work of F. F. A. Béraud and A. M. [Albert Montemont]: *Les filles publiques de Paris, et la police qui les régit; précédé d'une notice historique sur la prostitution chez les divers peuples de la terre* (2 vols., Paris: Chez Desforge et Compagnie, 1839). This work, as the title indicated, included a précis of the history of prostitution. An English version was published in New York in 1849. Augustin-Philippe Edouard Rabataux, *De la prostitution en Europe depuis l'antiquité jusqu'à la fin du XVIe siècle* (Paris: Séré, 1851) was a work that went through several editions. It included a bibliography by Paul La Croix, who under the pseudonym of Pierre Dufour, soon followed with his own *Histoire de la prostitution chez tous les peuples du monde depuis l'antiquité la plus reculée jusqu'à nos jours* (6 vols., Paris: Séré, 1851-53, and Brussels: Librairie Encyclopedique de Perichon, 1851-54). It later appeared in a seven-volume edition from Brussels in 1861. La Croix's account is primarily anecdotal but at the same time is full of moralizing statements. It was translated into English under the title *History of Prostitution, Among All the Peoples of the World, from the Most Remote Antiquity to the Present Day* by Samuel Putnam (3 vols., Chicago: Pascal Covici, 1926; and 2 vols., revised, New York: Covici Friede, 1932). Though the three-volume edition is the edition that was most widely distributed, Putnam himself felt that he could not recommend this edition because it was full of typographical and other errors.

Michael Ryan, in *Prostitution in London with a Comparative View of Paris and New York* (London: H. Baillière, 1838) attempted to do for London what Parent-Duchâtelet had done for Paris, but Ryan's research and statistical sampling were not as accurate. One of the first attempts at scholarly investigation in English was William W. Sanger's *History of Prostitution* (New York: Harper & Brothers, 1858). Since it was first published, Sanger's work has been kept in print almost continuously by one publishing house or another. A so-called new edition appeared in 1897 after the death of Sanger, but this new edition was different from the original only in the inclusion of an appendix recounting some developments after 1858. No other additions have been made to the book in spite of its frequent republication. Sanger made his study in order to justify the legalization of prostitution, and it was regarded as an official report to the Board of Almshouse Governors of the City of New York. Henry Mayhew included a long section on prostitution in his *London Labour and the London Poor* (4 vols., London: Griffin, Bohn & Company, 1861-62), but the author was not Mayhew himself. Instead it was written by Bracebridge Hemyng, who based many of his statistics on those collected by Ryan and these are not always to be trusted.

One of the earliest histories in German was that by Franz Seraph Hügel, *Zur Geschichte, Statistik und Regelung der Prostitution* (Vienna: Typographisch-literaisch-artistische Anstalt, 1865). Many histories of prostitution turn out on examination to be condensations of others, often including long verbatim sections without attribution. Th. F. Debray, in *Histoire de la prostitution et de la débauche chez les peuples du globe depuis l'antiquité la plus reculée jusqu'à nos jours* (Paris: Lambert et Cie, 1880), and Dr. Caufeynon [Jean Fauconney], in *La Prostitution* (Paris: Charles Offenstadt, 1902), rely heavily on La Croix; in fact, Caufeynon, except for the material on the nineteenth century, is almost entirely a rephrasing of La Croix. There are many others. Honoré Antoine Frégier, in *Des classes dangereuses de la population dans les grandes villes et des moyens de les rendre meilleures* (Paris: J. B. Baillière, 1840), goes over much the same ground as Parent-Duchâtelet but not so comprehensively. More specialized histories and accounts include Edmond Dupouy's *La prostitution dans l'antiquité* (Paris: Librairie Meruillon, 1887), and François Louis Fiaux's *La prostitution réglementée et les pouvoirs publics dans les principaux états des deux mondes* (Paris: F. Alcan, 1902).

Perhaps the most ambitious history was that undertaken by Iwan Bloch, but it was never completed. The first volume, by Bloch himself, *Die Prostitution* (Berlin: L. Marcus, 1912), was followed by an incomplete second volume with Georg Loewenstein as coauthor (Berlin: Louis Marcus Verlagsbuchhandlung, 1925), some thirteen years later. Bloch included a tremendous amount of information, much of which is difficult to verify. His footnotes are often inaccurate and do not convey the information for which they are cited and some of his references have proved impossible to find. This means that his work must be used with caution. W. Harriet's *Geschichte der Prostitution aller Völker* (Berlin: Schöneberg, Jacobstahl, 1912) was published at the same time as Bloch's first volume but is not nearly as comprehensive. Other German works include Wolfgang Sorge's *Geschichte der Prostitution* (Berlin: Potlhof & Company [1919]) and Wilhelm Fischer's *Die Prostitution* (Leipzig: Verlag von Hans Hedwig's Nachfolger Curt Ronninger, 1920). Marius-Noël Boiron's study *La prostitution dans l'histoire devant le droit-devant l'opinion* (Nancy: Berger-Levrault, 1926) is an early attempt to relate the issue of prostitution to public opinion; Boiron also discussed the question of state regulation versus abolition. Ernest Armand's *Libertinage et prostitution* (Paris: Editions Prima, 1932) is primarily an anecdotal work. George Ryley Scott's *History of Prostitution* (London: T. Werner Laurie, 1936; reprinted, New York: Medical Press, 1954) is not really a history in spite of its title, but instead a plea for an adequate history; Scott includes a few selected essays on some aspects of prostitution. A slightly more detailed account is by Willi Bauer, *Geschichte und Wesen der Prostitution* (Stuttgart: Weltspiegel Verlag, 1956). The most ambitious undertaking in recent years was Fernando Henriques's *Prostitution and Society* (3 vols., London: MacGibbon, 1962-1968). The third volume in the series is sometimes regarded as a separate book because it was titled *Modern Sexuality,* although the subtitle remained *Prostitution and Society.* Henriques often includes long extracts of the pertinent materials, but his work is not so much a history as an attempt to formulate a hypothesis regarding the place of prostitution and the prostitute in society. Also important was an earlier work by one of the authors of this book, Vern L. Bullough's *History of Prostitution* (New Hyde Park, New York: University Books, 1964). Though this volume includes much that was in the earlier study, they are two quite different books. See also Lujo Basserman's *The Oldest Profession; the History of Prostitution* (New York: Stein and Day, 1968).

Studies of prostitution that are concerned with one city, country, or even period are the closest existing approach to monographs available on the subject. See, for example, F. J. Behrend's *Die Prostitution in Berlin* (Erlangen: Palm & Enke, 1850); William Acton's *Prostitution, considered in its moral, social, and sanitary aspects, in London and other Large Cities. With Proposals for the mitigation and Prevention of Its Attendant Evils* (London: J. Churchill, 1857); Carlo Calza's *Documenti inediti sulla prostituzione, tratti dagli archivi della Repubblica Veneta* (Milan: Società cooperativo, 1869); Julien François Jeannel's *De la prostitution dans les grandes aux dix-neuvième siècle et de l'extinction des maladies veneriennes* (Paris: J. B. Baillière, 1874). This last is just one of the many books dealing with prostitution and venereal disease; in fact much of the literature about prostitution is concerned with this issue.

Other works include Gustave Schlegel's *Histoire de la prostitution en Chine,* translated from the Dutch by C. S. of Brussels (Rouen: Lemonnyer, 1881); Yves Guyot's *Études de physiologie sociale: La Prostitution* (Paris: Charpentier et Cie, 1882); *La prostituzione in Perugia nei secoli XIV e XV; documenti inediti* (Turin: dell-Editore, 1885) and *La prostituzione nei secoli XIV, XV, e XVI; documenti inediti* (Turin: dell-Editore, 1890), edited by Arodante Fabratti; Emile Richard's *La Prostitution à Paris* (Paris: J. B. Baillière, 1890); and Julius Kühn's *Die Prostitution im 19 Jahrhundert* (Leipzig: H. Barsdorf, 1892). François Louis Fiaux did several area studies on prostitution, including *La prostitution en Belgique* (Paris: F. Alcan, 1892).

See also Alfred Blaschko's *Syphilis und Prostitution* (Berlin: S. Karger, 1893); Oscar Commenge's *Hygiene sociale: La prostitution clandestines à Paris* (Paris: Schlicher frères, 1897); Joseph Schrank's *Die amtlichen Vorchriften betreffend die Prostitution in Wien* (Vienna: J. Safar, 1899); Alfred Blaschko's *Die Prostitution im 19 Jahrhundert* in vol. 12, *Anfang des Jahrhunderts* (Berlin: Verlag die Socialist. Monatschifte, 1902); J. E. De Becker's *The Nightless City: or the History of Yoshiwara Yuwau* (numerous editions under slightly varied titles). We consulted the revised fourth edition (London: Probsthain & Company, 1905). See also Louis Le Pileur's *La Prostitution du XIIIe aux XVIIIe siècle. Documents tirés des archives d'Avignon, du comtat Venaissin de la Principauté d'Orange et de la ville libre impériale de Besançon* (Paris: H. Champion, 1908); "Doctor" Amdel's *La Prostitución en España* (Madrid, 1934); A. Navarro Fernandez's *La Prostitucion en la villa de la Madrid* (Madrid: 1909); Francisco Ignacio dos Santo Cruz's *De prostituicao na cidade de Lisboa* (Lisbon, 1841); Robert Hessen's *Die Prostitution in*

Deutschland (Munich: Albert Langen, 1910); Anton Otto Neher's *Die geheime und öffentlich Prostitution in Stuttgart, Karlsruhe und München, mit Berucksichtingung des Prostitutionsgewerbes in Augsburg und Ulm sowie die übrigen grösseren Stadten Wurtembergs* (Paderborn: F. Schöning, 1912); Stephan Leonhard's *Die Prostitution* (Munich: E. Reinhardt, 1912); E. Rodriques-Solis's *Historia de la Prostitución en España y America* (Madrid: 1921); Saturnino Sepulveda Nino's *La Prostitucion en Colombia* (Bogota: Editorial Andes, 1970). Many others are listed in Bullough, Elcano, et al., the bibliography cited on page 322.

American investigation into prostitution began in earnest at the beginning of the twentieth century with studies by committees, many of which were similar to committees specifically established in New York City to deal with prostitution. Almost every major city in the United States, as well as many lesser ones, had such committees. Setting the example was the New York Committee of Fifteen's *Social Evil* (New York: G. P. Putnam's Sons, 1902). There was also a New York Committee of Fourteen's *Social Evil in New York City* (New York: Andrew H. Kellogg, 1912). Each committee issued several reports. Chicago had a Committee of Fifteen as well as a special vice commission. The latter group published *Social Evil in Chicago* (Chicago: Municipal Reference Library, 1911). The Bureau of Social Hygiene under the influence of John D. Rockefeller, Jr., initiated a whole series of studies into prostitution. These included Abraham Flexner's *Prostitution in Europe* (New York: Century Company, 1914); George J. Kneeland's *Commercialized Prostitution in New York City* (New York: Century Company, 1913), and Howard B. Woolston's *Prostitution in the United States* (New York: Appleton-Century-Crofts, 1921). Little serious study was done after the Woolston study for some twenty or thirty years, but in recent years another generation of studies has appeared. David Pivar, in *Purity Crusade: Sexual Morality and Social Control 1868-1900* (Westport, Conn.: Greenwood Press, 1973), recounts the background for the numerous studies at the turn of the century. Other recent studies include Charles Winick and Paul M. Kinsie's *The Lively Commerce: Prostitution in the United States* (Chicago: Quadrangle, 1971); Gabriel R. Viglotti's *The Girls of Nevada* (Secaucus, N.J.: Citadel Press, 1975); Martha Stein's *Lovers, Friends and Slaves* (New York: Berkley Medallion Books, 1974); and *The Politics of Prostitution* by Jennifer James et al. (Seattle, Washington: Sociological Research Associates, 1975).

Among the more valuable books published in the past few years (many with a feminist orientation) are: Leah Lydia Otis, *Prostitution in Medieval Society* (Chicago: University of Chicago Press, 1985); Anne M. Butler, *Daughters of Joy, Sisters of Mercy in the American West 1865-90*

(Urbana: University of Illinois, 1985); Frances Finnegan, *Poverty and Prostitution* (New York: Cambridge University Press, 1979); Marion S. Goldman, *Gold Diggers and Silver Miners* (Ann Arbor: University of Michigan Press, 1981); Sue Gronewold, *Beautiful Merchandise: Prostitution in China, 1860-1936* (New York: Institution for Research in History and Haworth Press, 1982); Jill Harsin, *Policing Prostitution in Nineteenth Century Paris* (Princeton: Princeton University Press, 1985); Paul Mc-Hugh, *Prostitution and Victorian Social Reform* (London: Croom Helm, 1980); Ruth Rosen, *The Lost Sisterhood* (Baltimore: Johns Hopkins University Press, 1982); Judith R. Walkowitz, *Prostitution and Victorian Society* (New York: Cambridge University, 1980); somewhat more narrow is Edward J. Bristow, *Prostitution and Prejudice: The Jewish Fight Against White Slavery* (New York: Schocken, 1983), and covering prostitution only indirectly but still valuable is Allan M. Brandt, *No Magic Bullet: A Social History of Venereal Disease in the United States Since 1880* (New York: Oxford University Press, 1985). The fact that so many of the recent studies have been published by university presses is indicative of the growing scholarly concern.

No historical listing would be complete without some reference to the studies undertaken by the League of Nations between the two world wars. From the first session of the Advisory Commission for the Protection and Welfare of Children and Young People held at Lausanne in 1922 (M.265,1922.IV) to the last meeting of the Advisory Committee on Social Questions in 1943 (C.26.M.26.1943,IV), the League surveyed all aspects of prostitution. The United Nations has continued to issue reports.

More recent historically oriented studies are often listed in the *Bibliography of the History of Medicine* issued annually since 1964 by the National Library of Medicine and published by the U.S. Government Printing Office. Periodically the annual reviews are combined into a more comprehensive bibliography encompassing four- or five-year periods. Also helpful is the *Current Work in the History of Medicine* published by the Wellcome Institute for the History of Medicine in London. Some materials, which might not be included in these bibliographies, can be found in *Sociological Abstracts, Psychological Abstracts,* or in the more general guides to periodical literature. There is also a growing legal literature about prostitution, the American aspects of which are summed up in the *Sexual Law Reporter.* T. E. James's *Prostitution and the Law* (London: William Heinemann, 1951) provides good background material to the current legal issues.

Prostitution is closely correlated with other aspects of sexual behavior. A good general survey of scholarly work into sexuality is Flora C. Seruya, Susan Losher, and Albert Ellis's *Sex and Sex Education: A*

Bibliography (New York: R. R. Bowker, 1972). Such scholarly journals as the *Journal of Sex Research, Archives of Sexual Behavior,* and the *Journal of Homosexuality* reflect updated views.

The above is quite obviously not an exhaustive listing of the histories or of the sources we used in writing this study of prostitution. Other sources are given in the footnotes. Not included in the bibliography are the occasional references to prostitution that still need to be ferreted out in the documents. Tracing their incorporation into specialized monographs and the more general works will then give the reader more acute insights. We hope that this book and this brief bibliographical essay will prove a helpful beginning.

NOTES

Introduction

1. *Oxford English Dictionary*, edited by James A. H. Murray, Henry Bradley, W. A. Craigie, C. T. Onions (Oxford: Clarendon Press, 1933), entry on "prostitution."

2. Havelock Ellis, "Sex in Relation to Society," in *Studies in the Psychology of Sex*, 2 vols. (New York: Random House, 1936), II, part 3, pp. 225-26.

3. Johannes Teutonicus, *Glossa ordinaria* to the *Decretum* in the version revised by Barthlomaeus Brixiensis (d. 1258) (Venice: Apud Iuntas, 1605), D. 34 c. 16 v. *quae multorum* and D. 45 c. 9. v. *paucorum*.

4. Thomas of Chobham, *Summa confessorum* 7.2.6.1, edited by F. Broomfield, *Analecta mediaevalia Namuricensia*, vol. 25 (Louvain: Editions Nauwelaerts, 1968), pp. 346-47.

5. Accursius, *Glossa ordinaria* to the *Digestum seu Pandekta*, in *Corpus iris civilis*, ed. T. Mommsen et al., 3 vols., Berlin, 1872), 3.2.4 v. *quaestuaria*.

6. A. J. B. Parent-Duchâtelet, *De la prostitution dans la ville de Paris*, 2 vols. (Paris: J. B. Baillière, 1836), I, pp. 26-27.

7. Some evidence for this can be found in Alfred C. Kinsey, W. B. Pomeroy et al., *Sexual Behavior in the Human Female* (Philadelphia: W. B. Saunders, 1953), pp. 356 ff.

8. See William Acton, *The Functions and Disorders of the Reproductive Organs in Childhood, Youth, Adult Age, and Advanced Life Considered in Their Physiological, Social and Moral Relations*, 5th ed. (London: J. A. Churchill, 1871).

9. Iwan Bloch, *Die Prostitution*, 2 vols. (Berlin: L. Marcus, 1912), 1, p. 38.

10. Vern L. Bullough, *The Subordinate Sex: A History of Attitudes Toward Women* (Urbana: University of Illinois Press, 1973).

Chapter 1

1. Henry W. Nissen, "Social Behavior in Primates," in *Comparative Psychology*, ed. Calvin P. Stone (New York: Prentice Hall, 1951), pp. 423-57. See also Wolfgang Wickler, *The Sexual Code: The Social Behavior of Animals and Men* (Garden City, N.Y.: Doubleday, 1972), pp. 217-18.

2. Sir Henry Maine, *Ancient Law* (London: Murray, 1861), p. 122.

3. J. J. Bachofen, "Mother Right," in *Myth, Religion, and Mother Right*, selected writings of Bachofen, translated by Ralph Manheim, Bollingen series, no. 84 (Princeton: Princeton University Press, 1967), passim; the quoted phrases are from p. 86.

4. See L. H. Morgan, *The League of the Iroquois* (Rochester, N.Y., 1851) and *Ancient Society* (1871; reprinted, New York: World Publishing Company, 1963), passim and p. 511.

5. See, for example, John McLennon, *The Patriarchal Theory* (London: Macmillan, 1885).

6. Friedrich Engels, *The Origins of the Family, Private Property and the State*, 4th ed. (reprinted, New York: International Publishers, 1942), p. 49.

7. Ibid., p. 50.

8. Ibid., p. 59.

9. Ibid., p. 67.

10. August Bebel, *Woman under Socialism,* translated from the 33rd German edtion by Daniel de Leon (New York: New York Labor News, 1904), p. 5.

11. Ibid., p. 146, and passim chap. III, pp. 146-66.

12. Robert Briffault, *The Mothers: A Study of the Origins of Sentiments and Institutions,* 3 vols. (New York: Macmillan, 1927).

13. Ibid., III, pp. 210-13.

14. Ibid., III, pp. 215-16.

15. Edward Westermarck, *The History of Human Marriage,* 5th ed., 3 vols. (London: Macmillan, 1922).

16. Ibid., I, pp. 138, 207-35.

17. Ernest Crawley, *The Mystic Rose,* revised and enlarged by Theodore Besterman. 2 vols. in 1 (reprinted, New York: Meridian Books, 1960), I, pp. 25-58; the quotation is from p. 259.

18. Theodore Besterman, *Men Against Women: A Study of Sexual Relations* (London: Methuen, 1924), p. 1.

19. Ibid., passim, especially pp. 223-32.

20. Ibid., pp. 87-89.

21. Sigmund Freud, *A General Introduction to Psychoanalysis,* translated by Joan Riviere (New York: Garden City Publishing Company, 1943), pp. 23-24. See also Freud, *Civilization and Its Discontents* (London: Hogarth Press, 1930).

22. See, for example, Sigmund Freud, "Notes Upon a Case of Obsessional Neurosis," in *Collected Papers,* translated and edited by Joan Riviere, James Strachey et al., 5 vols. (New York: Basic Books, 1959), III, pp. 293-383; "Contributions to the Psychology of Love. A Special Type of Object Choice in Men," IV, pp. 192-202. There are other papers that also bear on prostitution.

23. Ann Bedford Ulanov, *The Feminine in Jungian Psychology and on Christian Theology* (Evanston, Ill.: Northwestern University Press, 1971).

24. Erich Neumann, *The Great Mother: An Analysis of the Archetype,* translated by Ralph Manheim, Bollingen series, no. 47 (New York: Pantheon Books, 1955), pp. 43, 96 n.

25. J. D. Unwin, *Sexual Regulations and Human Behavior* (London: Williams and Norgate, 1933), p. ix-x, 85, 87, 108, and Unwin, *Sex and Culture* (London: Oxford University Press, 1934), passim.

26. Havelock Ellis, "Sex in Relation to Society," in *The Psychology of Sex,* 2 vols. (New York: Random House, 1936), II, part 3, pp. 224, 228.

27. For the existence of prostitution and its cultural setting, see Kenneth L. Little, *The Mende of Sierra Leone* (London: Routledge and Kegan Paul, 1951), p. 167; M. E. C. Pumphrey, "The Shilluk Tribe," *Sudan Notes and Records,* XXIV (1941), 34, 44; Louis S. B. Leakey, *Mau Mau and the Kikuyu* (London: Methuen and Company, 1952), pp. 75-76; Lucien de Reinach, *Le Laos* (Paris: A. Charles, 1901), p. 150; Virginia Thompson, *French Indo-China* (New York: Macmillan, 1937) p. 361; John E. DeYoung, *Village Life in Modern Thailand* (Berkeley: University of California, 1955), p. 62; Roy F. Barton, *The Half-Way Sun: Life Among the Headhunters of the Philippines* (New York: Brewer and Warren, 1930), p. 52; Edward Conzemius, *Ethnographical Survey of the Miskito and Sumum Indians of Honduras and Nicaragua,* Bureau of American Ethnology, Bulletin No. 106 (1932), p. 149; Vincenzo Petrullo, *The Yaruros of the Capangaparo River, Venezuela,* Bureau of American Ethnology, Bulletin No. 106 (1932), p. 149; Aurel Krause, *The Tlingit Indians,* translated from the German by Erna Gunther (Seattle: University of Washington, 1956), p. 155; Richard Van Valkenburgh, "Navaho Common Law: Etiquette-Hospitality, Justice," Museum of Northern Arizona, *Notes,* X (1938), 44; J. Allan Burgesse, "The Woman and Child Among the Lac-St. Jean Montagnais," *Primitive Man,* XVII (1944), p. 13. An index to references to prostitution and some extracts of the material can be found in the Human Relations Area Files in New Haven as well as various depositories across the United States. See also Fernando Henriques, *Prostitution and Society* (London: MacGibbon & Kee, 1962), vol. I, pp. 371-425.

28. Prince Peter of Greece, "Tibetan, Toda, and Tiya Polyandry: A Report on Field Investigations," New York Academy of Sciences, *Transactions,* series 2, X (1948), p. 217.

29. Geoffrey Gorer, *Himalayan Village: An Account of the Lepchas of Sikkim* (London: Michael Joseph, Ltd., 1938), p. 331.

30. William O. Douglas, *Beyond the High Himalayas* (Garden City, N.Y.: Doubleday, 1953), pp. 183, 226.

31. Ho-t'ien Ma, *Chinese Agent in Mongolia,* translated by John De Frances (Baltimore: Johns Hopkins Press, 1949), pp. 128-29.

32. Robert Briffault, op. cit., II, 76-78.

33. Ibid., II, 76-77.

34. Gladys A. Reichard, *Navaho Religion* (New York: Bollingen Foundation, 1950), p. 384.

35. Ruth Murray Underhill, *Papago Indian Religion* (New York: Columbia University Press, 1946), p. 64.

36. John R. Swanton, *Social Organization and Social Usages of the Indians of the Creek Confederacy,* Bureau of American Ethnology, *Forty-Second Annual Report* (1924-25), p. 384.

37. Alice C. Fletcher and Francis LaFlesche, *The Omaha Tribe,* Bureau of American Ethnology, *Twenty-seventh Annual Report* (1905-6), p. 325.

38. Wendell C. Bennett and Robert M. Zing, *The Tarahumara: An Indian Tribe of North Mexico* (Chicago: University of Chicago Press, 1935), p. 230.

39. Ralph L. Beals, *Chéran: A Sierra Tarascan Village,* Smithsonian Institution, Institute of Social Anthropology, *Publications,* II (1946), p. 177.

40. Kalvero Oberg, "Crime and Punishment in Tlingit Society," *American Anthropologist,* XXXVI (1934), p. 148.

41. Briffault, op. cit., pp. 73-74.

42. John J. Honigman, *Culture and Ethos of Kaska Society* (New Haven: Yale University Press, 1949), pp. 163-65.

43. See Briffault, op. cit., II, 609, note 2 for a bibliographical discussion of this, and also pp. 631ff; see also Vladimir Germanovich Bogaraz-Tan (Waldemar Bogoras), "The Chukchee," American Museum of Natural History, *Memoirs,* XI (in 3 parts, 1904-1909), p. 607, and Gawrila Sarytschew, *Account of a Voyage of Discovery to the Northeast of Siberia* (London: Richard Phillips, 1806), II, 76-77.

44. See Philip Drucker, *The Northern and Central Nootkan Tribes,* Bureau of American Ethnology, *Bulletin* no. 144 (1953), p. 309.

45. Siegfried F. Nadel, *A Black Byzantium: The Kingdom of Nupe in Nigeria* (London: Oxford University Press, 1942), pp. 42-43.

46. A. A. D. Delobsom, *L'empire du Mongho-Naba, coutoumes des Mossi de la Haute-Volta* (Paris: Domat-Montchrestien, 1932), pp. 176-77.

47. Günter Tessman, *Die Pangwe: Völkerkindliche Monographie eines West Africanischen Negerstammes* (Berlin: Ernst Wasmuth, 1913), I, 108.

48. Lucy P. Mair, *Native Marriage in Buganda,* International Institute of African Languages and Cultures, *Memorandum,* XIX (1940), p. 25.

49. Louis S. B. Leakey, op. cit., p. 75.

50. Gustave Hulstaert, *Le mariage des Nkundö,* Institut de Royal Colonia Belge, *Mémoires,* I (1838), 44, 64-69.

51. Jan Czekanowski, *Forschungen im Nil-Kongo-Zwischengebiet,* I, *Ethnographie; Zwischenseengebiet Mpororo: Ruanda,* in vol. VI, *Wissenschaftliche Ergebnisse der Deutschen Zentral-Afrika-Expedition 1907-08* (Leipzig: Klinhardt und Bierman, 1917), p. 137.

52. Georges Balandier, *Sociologie Actuelle de l'Afrique Noire: Changements Sociaux au Gabon et au Congo* (Paris: Presses Universitaires de France, 1955), p. 60.

53. Hulstaert, op. cit., I, 308.

54. Bronislaw Malinowski, *The Sexual Life of Savages in Northwestern Melanesia,* 2 vols. (New York: Horace Liveright, 1929), II, 323.

55. Clellan S. Ford and Frank A. Beach, *Patterns of Sexual Behavior* (New York: Harper and Brothers, 1951), pp. 98-99, 127-128. See also Henriques, op. cit, I, 371-425.

56. Wilhelm Reich in *The Sexual Revolution,* translated from the German by Theodore P. Wolfe, 4th ed. (New York: Noonday Press, 1962), wrote on this at great length.

Chapter 2

1. Samuel Noah Kramer, *Sumerian Mythology,* rev. (New York: Harper, 1961), gives a good account of the myths dealing with Inana (Ishtar).

2. Alexander Heidel, *The Gilgamesh Epic and Old Testament Parallels,* 2nd ed. (Chicago: University of Chicago Press, 1949), tablet 1, col. iv., p. 22. Heidel did not translate all this portion of the poem into English but instead put it into Latin. In translating from the Latin, I followed basically the forms set by H. W. F. Saggs, *The Greatness That Was Babylon* (New York: New American Library, 1968), pp. 332-35.

3. For more details, see the various law codes. The standard collection in English is that edited by G. R. Driver and John C. Miles, *The Assyrian Laws* (Oxford: Clarendon Press, 1955). There are also translations of some of the codes by Albrecht Goetz and Theophile J. Meek, in *The Ancient Near East,* edited by James B. Pritchard (Princeton: Princeton University Press, 1965), pp. 85-86. Reuven Yaron, *The Laws of Eshnunna* (Jerusalem: Hebrew University, 1969), discusses these particular laws. There are several other editions of the various laws, most notably those of Hammurabi.

4. Richard Lewinsohn, *A History of Sexual Customs* (New York: Harper & Brothers, 1958), p. 26.

5. Saggs, op. cit., pp. 332-35.

6. E. O. James, *Myth and Ritual in the Ancient Near East* (New York: Frederick A. Praeger, 1958), pp. 113-43, and B. Z. Goldberg, *The Sacred Fire* (New York: University Books, 1958).

7. Herodotus, *Persian Wars,* I, 181-82, edited and translated by A. D. Godley (London: William Heinemann, 1921). Wherever possible, I have used the translations in the Loeb Classical Library for classical authors. They have the merit of also including the Greek or Latin text on the facing page.

8. Socrates Scholasticus, *Ecclesiastical History,* I, 18 (London: G. Bell, 1904), and Eusebius, *Life of Constantine,* III, 55, translated by Ernest Cushing Richardson, in vol. I, *Nicene and Post-Nicene Fathers* (reprinted, Grand Rapids: Wm. B. Eerdmans, 1952).

9. Herodotus, I, 199.

10. See, for example, Robert Briffault, *The Mothers,* 3 vols. (New York: Macmillan, 1927), III, 209; James G. Frazer, *The Golden Bough,* 12 vols. (New York: Macmillan, 1935), V, *Adonis, Attis, Osiris,* pp. 50-52, 57-61.

11. L. Delaporte, *La Mesopotamie* (Paris: La Renaissance du livre, 1932), pp. 93-96.

12. Lewinsohn, op. cit., pp. 27-28.

13. Herodotus, I, 196.

14. Robert D. Biggs, *SA.ZI.Ga.: Ancient Mesopotamian Potency Incantations,* in *Texts from Cuneiform Sources* II (1967), passim.

15. Pritchard, op. cit., sec. 185-93.

16. See, for example, A. T. Olmstead, *History of Assyria* (New York: Charles Scribner, 1923), pp. 549-50.

17. Ibid., p. 553.

18. E. Neufield, *The Hittite Laws,* edited and translated into English (London: Luzac & Company, 1951), pp. 54-56, 121.

19. Samuel Noah Kramer, *History Begins at Sumer* (Garden City: Doubleday, 1959), pp. 99-100. Prostitution is listed among the *me* (25).

20. James H. Breasted, *A History of Egypt,* 2d ed. (reprinted, New York: Charles Scribner's Sons, 1951), p. 85.

21. William C. Hayes, *The Scepter of Egypt,* 2 vols. (Cambridge: Harvard University Press, 1953-59), I, 219.

22. Ibid., I, 219-20.

23. Gaston Maspero, *Popular Stories of Ancient Egypt,* translated by A. S. Johns (reprinted, New Hyde Park, N.Y.: University Books, 1967), pp. xlvii, 14, 24, 185 ff.

24. Vern L. Bullough, "Homosexuality as Submissive Behavior; Example from Mythology," *The Journal of Sex Research,* IX (1973), 283-88.

25. Maspero, op. cit., pp. 136-40.

26. Adolf Erman, *The Ancient Egyptians: A Sourcebook of Their Writings,* translated by Aylward M. Blackman (reprinted, New York: Harper Torchbooks, 1966), p. 190. From *Exhortations and Warnings to Schoolboys.*

27. Ibid., p. 236. This is from the *Wisdom of Anii.*

28. Joseph Kaster, translator and editor, *Wings of the Falcon: Life and Thought of Ancient Egypt* (New York: Holt, Rinehart and Winston, 1968), p. 170. From the Instructions of Ptah Hotep.

29. Ibid., pp. 225-26 (Love Lyrics).
30. Ibid., pp. 169-70, Ptah Hotep.
31. James Henry Breasted, *Ancient Records of Egypt,* 5 vols. (Chicago: University of Chicago Press, 1907), IV, 75.
32. Abd El-Mohsen Bakir, *Slavery in Pharaonic Egypt* (Cairo: Imprimerie de l'institut Français d'archéologie Orientale, 1952), p. 83.
33. Herodotus, I, 182, II, 60, 64, and Strabo, *Geography,* translated by Horace Leonard Jones, XVII, 1, 31, 46-47, 8 vols. (reprinted, London: William Heinemann, 1959-1960).
34. Herodotus, II, 64, see also II, 219-20.
35. Herodotus, II, 126.
36. Herodotus, II, 121.
37. Herodotus, II, 135.
38. Herodotus, II, 135.
39. See, for example, W. M. Flinders Petrie, *Social Life in Ancient Egypt* (New York: Houghton Mifflin, 1923), pp. 109-120. There are qualifications to this description that now seem overdrawn. See, for example, John A. Wilson, *The Culture of Ancient Egypt* (Chicago: University of Chicago Press, 1951), pp. 94-98, 201-03, 213-14, 303.
40. Leviticus 19:29.
41. Exodus 21:7.
42. Leviticus 21:7, 9.
43. I Samuel 2:22.
44. I Kings 14:24.
45. II Kings 23:7. For earlier attempts see I Kings 15:11, 22:47.
46. Deuteronomy 23:18.
47. Genesis 38.
48. Deuteronomy 23:19.
49. Louis M. Epstein, *Sex Laws and Customs in Judaism* (New York: Ktav Publishing House, 1948), p. 155.
50. Ibid., pp. 158-59.
51. Joshua 2:1 ff.
52. Joshua 6:25.
53. Isaiah, 23:15-16.
54. Judges 11:2.
55. Judges 16:1.
56. I Kings 3:16-28.
57. Epstein, op. cit., p. 159.
58. Isaiah 23:16.
59. Ezekiel 16:24-25; Proverbs 7:12.
60. Proverbs 9:14-15.
61. Proverbs 7:10.
62. Proverbs 5:8.
63. Jeremiah 5:6-7.
64. See, for example, Jeremiah 3:3; Proverbs 2:16; 5:3; 6:24-25, and 7:5-11 and the Pseudo Epigrapha, Ecclesiasticus 9:3-9; 19:2, and 26:9.
65. Tobit 4:12.
66. Leviticus 19:29, 21:9.
67. Deuteronomy 22:20-21.
68. Proverbs 7:9-23. For this quotation I have used the King James Authorized Translation because of its poetic qualities.
69. David Mace, *Hebrew Marriage* (London: Epworth Press, 1953), pp. 210-11.
70. Judges 8:30.
71. Leviticus 20:10.
72. Genesis 39:7-18.
73. Genesis 30:1-24.
74. Judges 16:4-20.
75. II Samuel 11:2-27.
76. I Kings 11:4.
77. I Kings 16:31-33; 18:13; 19; 19:1, 2; 21:5-25; II Kings 9:7, 10, 22, 30, 36-37.

78. Proverbs 6:24-35; 7:10-27, et passim.
79. See, for example, I Samuel, 2:22-24; Numbers, 25:1-9; Deuteronomy, 23:18-19; II Chronicles 1, 14:3, 17:6, I Kings 15:12, and II Kings 23:7, among others.

Chapter 3

1. For a listing of some of these terms, see Hans Licht, *Sexual Life in Ancient Greece,* translated by J. H. Freese (London: Routledge & Kegan Paul, 1932), pp. 329-32.
2. For a discussion of the status of women in Greece, see Vern L. Bullough, *The Subordinate Sex* (Urbana: University of Illinois Press, 1973), pp. 50-76.
3. See Plutarch, "Solon," 22-23 in *Lives,* edited and translated by Bernadotte Perrin, 11 vols. (London: William Heinemann, 1959-61); Athenaeus, *The Deipnosophists,* XIII, 569d, 568e, edited and translated by C. B. Gulick, 7 vols. (reprinted, London: William Heinemann, 1957-63); Lucian, *Dialogues of Courtesans,* passim, edited and translated by M. D. MacLeod in vol. VII, *Lucian* (London: William Heinemann, 1961), and Diogenes Laertius, *Lives of Eminent Philosophers,* VI, 4, edited and translated by R. D. Hicks (London: William Heinemann, 1959).
4. Demosthenes, *Contra Naeream,* 30, in vol. VI of *Orations,* translated by A. T. Murray (London: William Heinemann, 1957). This is a court case involving a famous courtesan. See also Aeschines, *Against Timarchus,* 119, 188, edited and translated by Charles Darwin Adams (London: William Heinemann, 1948); Pollux of Naucratis, *Onomasticon,* IX, 29, edited by Eric Bethe (Leipzig: Teubner, 1900-1937). See also Herodes, II, *The Brothel Keeper,* edited and translated by J. M. Edmonds (London: William Heinemann, 1953).
5. *Greek Anthology,* translated by W. R. Paton (London: William Heinemann, 1960), V, 46 (Philodemus).
6. Ibid., V, 101 (Anonymous).
7. Licht, op. cit., p. 338.
8. *Greek Anthology,* V, 158 (Asclepiades)
9. Lucian, *Dialogues of Courtesans,* passim.
10. Theophrastus, *Characters,* VI, edited and translated by J. M. Edmonds (London: William Heinemann, 1953).
11. Plato, *Laws,* XI, 918 D-E, edited and translated by R. G. Bury (London: William Heinemann, 1952).
12. Strabo, *Geography,* XII, viii, 17 (578), edited and translated by H. L. Jones, 8 vols. (reprinted, London: William Heinemann, 1960-61).
13. Plutarch, "Demetrius," 26, in *Lives.* Plutarch reported that because Demetrius had made the Parthenon his headquarters the people sang a song stating that he had made the Acropolis his hotel and brought hetairae into the temple.
14. Athenaeus, XIII, 608b.
15. Ibid., IV, 129 a-b.
16. Ibid., XIII, 607 c-d.
17. Ibid., XIII, 607 d-e.
18. Ibid., XIII, 576 f.
19. Ibid., XIII, 557 d-f.
20. Athenaeus, XIII, 573 c-e.
21. Strabo, VIII, vi, 20 (378).
22. Athenaeus, XIII, 573 f.
23. Strabo, VI, ii, 6 (272) Diodorus Siculus, *History* IV, 83, edited and translated by C. H. Oldfather, Russell M. Geer, F. R. Walton (London: William Heinemann, 1935-1967).
24. Pindar, *Eulogies,* "For Xenophon of Corinth," Fragments 122 (87) in Pindar, *Odes,* edited and translated by John Sandys (London: William Heinemann, 1946), pp. 580-83.
25. There are numerous references to this. See, for example, Lucian, *Dialogues of Courtesans,* 11th dialogue, Tryphena and Charmides.
26. Lucian, *Dialogues of Courtesans,* 6th dialogue, Crobyle and Corinna.
27. Diodorus Siculus, *History,* XVII, 72, and Plutarch, "Alexander," 38.
28. Athenaeus, XIII, 577c.
29. Ibid., XIII, 574d.
30. Ibid., XIII, passim.

31. Ibid., XIII, 579-85.

32. Ibid., XIII, 584c.

33. Ibid., XIII, 588e.

34. Ibid., XIII, 588 e-f.

35. See Paul La Croix (Pierre Dufour), *History of Prostitution,* translated by Samuel Putnam, 3 vols. (New York: Covici-Friede, 1931), I, 178-83.

36. Athenaeus, XIII, 590e.

37. Ibid., XIII, 590f.

38. Ibid., XIII, 591d.

39. Aristophanes, *The Acharnians,* 524 ff. Edited and translated by Benjamin Bickley Rogers (London: William Heinemann, 1950).

40. Plutarch, "Pericles," 24, 32, *Lives;* Athenaeus, XIII, 570 a.

41. Licht, op. cit., pp. 354-56; The stories of many of these were compiled by C. Hayward, *The Courtesan* (London: Casanova Society, 1926), a book that was reprinted under the title *Dictionary of Courtesans* (New Hyde Park, N.Y.: University Books, 1962).

42. Alciphron, *Letters of Courtesans,* no. 15, edited and translated by Allen Rogers Benner and Frances H. Fobes (London: William Heinemann, 1962).

43. Plutarch, "Pericles," 24; Xenophon, *Oeconomicus,* III, 14-15, edited and translated by E. C. Marchant (London: William Heinemann, 1953).

44. Diogenes Laertius, 6: 96-97.

45. Athenaeus, 13:594 b-c; Alciphron, *Letters of Courtesans,* no. 3.

46. Robert Briffault, *The Mothers,* 3 vols. (London: George Allen & Unwin, 1952), II, p. 342.

47. Demosthenes, *Contra Naeream,* 122 (1386).

48. See Philip E. Slater, *The Glory of Hera: Greek Mythology and the Greek Family* (Boston: Beacon Press, 1868), pp. 7-12. I have criticized this at some length in Bullough, op. cit., pp. 50-55.

49. See, for example, Jane Harrison, *Prolegomena to the Study of Greek Religion* (reprinted, New York: Meridian Books, 1955), chaps. IX, X, XI. There has been considerable research into the Orphic mysteries since Professor Harrison first wrote her book, but her work still serves as a starting point for the source materials on Orphism, even though her specific interpretations have been challenged.

50. See Plato, *Cratyllus* 400C, translated by H. N. Fowler (London: William Heinemann, 1953).

51. Aristotle, *Metaphysics,* Book I, v, 3-7 (986A), edited and translated by Hugh Tredennick (London: William Heinemann, 1936).

52. Plato, *Symposium* (211B), edited and translated by W. R. M. Lamb (London: William Heinemann, 1953).

53. Plato, *Phaedrus,* 246-57, edited and translated by Harold North Fowler (London: William Heinemann, 1953).

54. Diogenes Laertius, Book X, 118, 132.

55. A good explanation appears in Epictetus, *Discourses,* edited and translated by W. A. Oldfather, 2 vols (London: William Heinemann, 1956, 1959).

56. Vern Bullough has developed these ideas at greater length in *Sexual Variance in Society and History* (New York: Wyley Interscience, 1976).

Chapter 4

1. Propertius, *Elegies,* IV, 11, edited and translated by H. F. Butler (reprinted, London: William Heinemann, 1962).

2. Ibid., IV, 5.

3. Ovid, *Amores,* I, viii, edited and translated by Grant Showerman (reprinted, London: William Heinemann, 1958).

4. Suetonius, "Gaius Caligula," *Lives of the Caesars,* XL, edited and translated by J. C. Rolfe, 2 vols. (London: William Heinemann, 1950-1951); and Pauly-Wissowa, *Real-Encyclopaedie, der classischen Altertumwissenschaft* (Stuttgart: J. B. Metzler, 1914-1961), XV, 1022.

5. Livy, *History,* X, 31, edited and translated by B. O. Foster, Evan T. Sage, F. G. Moore, 14 vols. (London: William Heinemann, 1935-1959).

6. Juvenal, *Satire*, IX, 24, 27. "Nam quo non prostat femina templo?" edited and translated by G. J. Ramsay (reprinted, London: William Heinemann, 1940).

7. Martial, II, 63, III, 82, XI, 61, etc., edited and translated by C. A. Ker, 8 vols. (reprinted, London: William Heinemann, 1961); Propertius, II, xxiii, 15; Juvenal, II, 65. See also Otto Kiefer, *Sexual Life in Ancient Rome* (London: Routledge & Kegan Paul, 1934), p. 61.

8. Seneca (Lucius) *Controversiae*, I, 2, edited by A. Kiesling (Leipzig: Teubner, 1872); Juvenal, VI, 132.

9. Juvenal, VI, 122, 128; Martial, *Epigrams*, XI, 45.

10. Martial, *Epigrams*, XI, 45; Seneca, *Controversiae*, XI, 45.

11. Martial, *Epigrams*, XIV, xxxix-xlii, c, LVIII, cii.

12. Plautus, *Asinaria*, IV, i, 11, 756-60; edited and translated by Paul Nixon (reprinted, London: William Heinemann, 1961).

13. Martial, *Epigrams*, I, xxxiv, XI, xlv.

14. Some of these were reproduced in Jean Marcadé, *Roma Amor* (Geneva: Nagel Publishers, 1965), pp. 71, 116-23, 129.

15. Pauly-Wissowa, op. cit., XII, 1942 f, XV, 1023-25.

16. See Julius Rosenbaum, *The Plague of Lust: Being a History of Venereal Disease in Classical Antiquity* (Paris: Charles Carrington, 1901), pp. 111 ff.

17. Kiefer, op. cit., p. 61.

18. Catullus, *Carmina*, xxxvii, edited and translated by F. W. Cornish (revised and reprinted, London: William Heinemann, 1962); Horace, *Epistles*, I, 21, edited and translated by H. Rushton Fairclough (reprinted, London: William Heinemann, 1961), and Rosenbaum, op. cit., p. 91.

19. Plautus, *Poenulus*, IV, 1, edited and translated by Paul Nixon (reprinted, London: William Heinemann, 1957).

20. Pauly-Wissowa, op. cit., XV, 1025.

21. Propertius, II, xxiii, 21.

22. Seneca, *Controversiae*, I, 2, 3.

23. Martial, *Epigrams*, VI, lxvi.

24. *Scriptores Historia Augustae*, "Hadrian," xviii, 8, edited and translated by David Magie, 3 vols. (reprinted, London: William Heinemann, 1953-54).

25. Plautus, *Poenulus*, IV, 826.

26. Horace, *Satires*, I, ii, 29; edited and translated by H. Rushton Fairclough (reprinted, London: William Heinemann, 1966); Petronius, *Satyricon*, VIII, translated by William Arrowsmith (Ann Arbor: University of Michigan Press, 1959), p. 95, and Rosenbaum, op. cit., p. 103.

27. Translated by J. P. V. D. Balsdon: *Roman Women* (London: The Bodley Head, 1962), p. 226.

28. Martial, *Epigrams*, I, xxxiv; and Kiefer, op. cit., p. 62.

29. Ovid, *Amores,* passim, and Rosenbaum, op. cit., p. 103.

30. Petronius, op. cit., IV (p. 23).

31. Ibid., IV (p. 24).

32. See Lucius Apuleius, *The Golden Ass*, translated by William Adlington (London: Abbey Library, n.d.), X, xlvi.

33. Horace, *Satires* I, ii, 120 ff.

34. Balsdon, op. cit., pp. 230-34.

35. Plautus, *Mostellaria*, edited and translated by Paul Nixon (reprinted, London: William Heinemann, 1963).

36. A. M. Duff, *Freedmen in the Early Roman Empire* (reprinted, Cambridge: W. Heffer & Sons, 1958), pp. 33, 61-62.

37. Ovid, *Fasti*, V, 331 ff., edited and translated by Sir James Frazer (reprinted, London: William Heinemann, 1959).

38. Martial, *Epigrams*, I, intro.

39. Seneca, *Ad Lucilium Epistulae Morales*, 97, edited and translated by Richard M. Gummere (London: Wiliam Heinemann, 1953).

40. Plautus, *Asinaria*, IV, i, 11. 746 ff.

41. Tacitus, *Annals*, II, 85; edited and translated by John Jackson (London: William Heinemann, 1956); Suetonius, "Tiberius," XXXV, 2. Suetonius implies the legislation dated from the reign of Tiberius.

42. Livy, XXV, ii.

43. Pauly-Wissowa, XII, 1942 f, XV, 1023-25.

44. Aulus Gellius, *Attic Nights*, IV, iii, edited and translated by John C. Rolfe, 3 vols. (reprinted, London: William Heinemann, 1952-1960).

45. Horace, *Satires*, I, ii, 63, 82; Edmond Dupouy, *La prostitution dans l'antiquité* (Paris: Librairie Meuillon, 1887), p. 144.

46. Suetonius, "Domitian," viii.

47. Carl G. Bruns, *Fontes Juris Romani*, 7th ed., edited by Otto Gradenwitz (Tubingen: I. C. B. Mohrii, 1909), 18, 123; 23, 1. See also Kiefer, op. cit., p. 63.

48. *Scriptores Historiae Augustae*, "Severus Alexander," XXIV, 3.

49. Juvenal, *Satires*, VI, 216 ff.

50. Aulus Gellius, *Attic Nights*, IV, xiv.

51. Horace, *Satires*, I, ii, 32-37.

52. Licht, op. cit., p. 337.

53. Cicero, *Pro Caelio*, XX, 48, edited and translated by R. Gardner (revised, London: William Heinemann, 1965).

54. *Oratorum Romanorum Fragmenta*, edited by Enrica Malcovati (2nd ed., Aug. Taurinorum: Paraval et Sociorum, 1955), 7, 133 ff.

55. See Catullus, Propertius and Tibulus, *Elegies*, edited and translated by J. P. Postgate (revised, London: William Heinemann, 1962), III, 894-99.

56. Lucretius, *De Rerum Natura*, edited and translated by W. H. D. Rouse (London: William Heinemann, 1924).

57. Juvenal, *Satires*, VI, 114-29.

58. Livy, intro., 9.

59. Livy, I, 4, 11-13; Dionysius of Halicarnasus, *Roman Antiquities*, I, 76-79; II, 25, 30, 38-46, edited and translated by Ernest Cary (London: William Heinemann, 1950).

60. *Livy*, 1: 57-60.

61. Ludwig Friedlander, *Roman Life and Manners under the Early Empire*, translated by Leonard Magnus, 7th ed. (London: George Routledge and Sons, 1940), pp. 232-34.

62. Tacitus, *Annals*, III, 33 f.

63. Plautus, *Poenulus*, iv, 831 ff.

64. A. C. Van Geytenbeck, *Musonius Rufus and Greek Diatribe*, translated by B. L. Hijamans, Jr. (Assen, the Netherlands: Van Gorcum & Company, 1963), pp. 71-77.

65. Seneca, *Fragments*, in vol. III of *Opera*, edited by Frederich G. Haase (Leipzig: Teubner, 1853), no. 85. The passage is found in Saint Jerome, *Against Jovinian* (1:30), and Haase claims the passage came from a lost treatise on marriage, *De Matrimonio*.

66. Celsus, *De Medicina*, edited and translated by W. G. Spencer (London: William Heinemann, 1935-38), I, 1.4.

67. Soranus, *Gynecology*, edited and translated by O. W. Temkin (Baltimore: Johns Hopkins Press, 1956), I, vii (32).

68. Philo, *On the Special Laws* [*De Specialibus Legibus*], edited and translated by F. H. Colson (London: William Heinemann, 1958), III, 113.

69. Ibid., III, 34-36.

70. Plotinus, *The Enneads*, edited and translated by Stephen MacKenna, revised by B. S. Page (London: Faber and Faber, 1956), V, 3: par 1-9; I, 6: par 9.

71. Ibid., I, 4: par 1.

72. Ibid., I, 3: par 1; V, 9; par 1.

73. Porphyry, *Abstinence from Animal Food*, translated from the Greek by Thomas Taylor (London: Thomas Rodd, 1823), I, 45, IV, 8, 20. There are many other references.

Chapter 5

1. Athanasius, *In passionem et crucem Domini*, XXX, in J. P. Migne, *Patrologiae cursuscompletus, Series Graeco-Latina*, vol. XXVIII (Paris: Garnier, 1887). The attribution of this work to Athanasius is probably erroneous.

2. Ambrose, *Commentaria in Epistolam B. Pauli ad Corinthos Primam*, cap v, in Migne, *Patrologia Latina*, XVII (Paris: 1879).

3. Tertullian, *Apology*, L, 12, translated by Sister Emily Joseph Daly, in vol. 10, *The Fathers of the Church* (New York: Catholic University of America, 1950), p. 125.

4. Eusebius, *Ecclesiastical History*, VI, 8, translated by Roy J. Deferrari, in vols. 19 and 29, *Fathers of the Church.*

5. Justin Martyr, *The First Apology*, chap. 29, edited and translated by Thomas B. Falls in vol. 6, *Fathers of the Church;* Origen, *Commentari in evangeliums secundum Matthaeum* XV, 1 (651), Migne, *Patrologiae Graeco-Latina*, XIII; and Tertullian, *De Monogamia*, cap. III, in Migne, *Patrologia Latina*, II.

6. St. Luke 7:37.

7. St. Matthew 21:31.

8. St. Matthew 5:28.

9. St. John 8:7.

10. I Corinthians 6:12-20.

11. See Derrick Sherwin Bailey, *Sexual Relations in Christian Thought* (New York: Harper, 1959), p. 10.

12. I Corinthians 7:7, 26, 29, 32-34.

13. St. Matthew 19:12.

14. I Corinthians 7:7, 9, 17.

15. I Corinthians 7:3-6.

16. Ephesians 5:22-23.

17. I Corinthians 7:9.

18. Revelation 14:4.

19. I Corinthians 11:8-9.

20. I Timothy 2:14.

21. See the discussion in A. Vööbus, *Celibacy: A Requirement for Admission to Baptism in the Early Syrian Church* (Stockholm: Estonian Theological Society in Exile, 1951).

22. See Jean Doresse, *The Secret Books of the Egyptian Gnostics*, translated by Philip Mairet (London: Hollis and Carter, 1960), pp. 13-14, and Clement, *Stromata*, III, i (3), ii (5-8), iv (25-30), in vol. II, *The Ante Nicene Fathers*, edited and translated by Alexander Roberts and James Donaldson; American editor A. Clement Coxe (reprinted, Grand Rapids: Eerdmans Publishing, 1961). Parts of this section are left in Latin; for an English translation of the third book, see John E. L. Oulton and Henry Chadwick, *Alexandrian Christianity* (Philadelphia: Westminster Press, 1954).

23. Bailey, op. cit., p. 33, and St. Jerome, *Ad Eustochium*, XXII, 14, in *Lettres*, edited and translated into French by Jerome Labourt, 6 vol. (Paris: Société d'edition, "Les Belles Lettres," 1949-58), and Cyprian, *Epistolae*, LXII, 2-3, Migne, *Patrologia Latina*, IV.

24. See also Basil, *Letters*, LV, translated by Sister Agnes Clare Way, in vols. XIII and XXVIII, *Fathers of the Church;* Gregory of Nyssa, *De Virginitate*, XXIII, in Migne, *Patrologiae Graeco-Latina*, XXV. There are other references in St. John Chrysostom, Cyprian, et al.

25. Jerome, *Vita Pauli*, in Migne, *Patrologia Latina*, XXIII.

26. Ambrose, *De Virginibus*, II, 4, in Migne, *Patrologia Latina*, XVI.

27. See his life by Gregory of Nyssa.

28. The story is rather delightfully translated by Helen Waddell, *The Desert Fathers* (reprinted, Ann Arbor: University of Michigan, 1957), pp. 190-201.

29. *Butler's Lives of the Saints*, edited, revised, and supplemented by Herbert Thurston, and Donald Attwater, 4 vols. (London: Burns and Oates, 1956), II, 14-15. See also C. Hayward, *The Courtesan* (London: Casanova Society, 1926), pp. 28-83.

30. Ibid., pp. 6-7, and *Butler's Lives of the Saints*, III, 267-68.

31. Waddell, op. cit., pp. 177-88.

32. *Butler's Lives of the Saints*, IV, 267-68, and Hayward, op. cit., pp. 426-28.

33. Ibid., pp. 441-42, and *Butler's Lives of the Saints*, III, 681-82.

34. James Brundage, "Prostitution in the Medieval Canon Law," paper given at the Medieval Conference. Western Michigan University, Kalamazoo, Mich., 1972 and published and signed II (1976-77). See also Gratian, *Decretum*, Distincto 34, Canon 16, in *Corpus Juris Canonici*, edited by Emil Friedberg, 2 vols. (Leipzig: B. Tauschnitz, 1879, reprinted Graz: Akademische Oruck-und Verlags anstalt, 1959). The original citation is St. Jerome, *Epistolae* LXIV, 7 in Migne, *Patrologia Latina* XXII.

35. St. Augustine, *Confessions*, VII, vi, 17, edited and translated by Albert C. Outler, *Library of Christian Classics* VII (London: SCM Press, 1955). This volume is part of a Protestant series of translations of the Church Fathers. There are many other English translations of Augustine.

36. Ibid., IV, ii, 2: VI, xii, 20-22, xv, 25; VIII, i, 2.

37. St. Augustine, *Concerning the Nature of Good*, xviii, translated by A. H. Newman in *Basic Writings of St. Augustine*, edited by Whitney J. Oates (New York: Random House, 1948), p. 455.

38. St. Augustine, *Soliloquies*, 17, translated by Thomas F. Gilligan, in vol. I, *Fathers of the Church* (New York: Fathers of the Church, 1948), p. 10.

39. St. Augustine, *De Ordine*, II, iv, 12, in Migne, *Patrologia Latina*, XXXII.

40. *Constitutiones Apostolicae*, II, xxvi, in Migne, *Patrologiae Graeco-Latina*, I.

41. St. Basil, *Letters*, CXCIX, 21; CLXXXVIII, 9: CCXVII, 58, 59, 77.

42. Koran, IV, *An Nisâ* [Women], 34. Officially the Koran cannot be translated since Arabic is the language of God. Actually there are several English versions that might be consulted, including one by Mohammed Marmaduke Pickthall issued as a Mentor Paperback (New York: New American Library, 1953).

43. Reuben Levy, *The Social Structure of Islam* (Cambridge: University Press, 1957), p. 94, and W. Robertson Smith, *Kinship and Marriage in Early Arabia* (Cambridge: University Press, 1885), pp. 71-75.

44. H. R. P. Dickson, *The Arab of the Desert: A Glimpse into Bedouin Life in Kuwait and Sau'di Arabia* (London: George Allen and Unwin, Ltd., 1951), pp. 162-63.

45. Koran, IV, *An Nisâ* [Women], 3. The passage in question deals primarily with captives but it has been interpreted to include other marriages.

46. Koran, LXX, *Al-Ma'ârij* [The Ascending Stairways], 29-31; XXIII, *Al Mu'minûn* [The Believers], 5-7; IV, An Nisâ [Women], 3, 24 f.

47. For a discussion of this, see Hamilton Gibb and Harold Bowen, *Islamic Society and the West* (Oxford: University Press, 1957), I, part 1, 73-88.

48. There are several translations of this. The most complete is that by Richard Burton, but also adequate are those by Edward Lane and John Payne.

49. There are a whole series of passages in the Koran dealing with divorce. See especially II, *Al Baqarah* [The Cow], 226-32, 241; IV, *An Nisâ* [Women], 25; XXXIII, Al-Ahzâb [The Clans], 4, 49; LVIII, Al-Mujâdilah [She That Disputeth], 203; LXV, *At Talâq* [Divorce], 1-6.

50. Levy, op cit., pp. 121-24.

51. Koran, IV, *An Nisâ* [Women], 24.

52. Levy, op. cit., pp. 115-17.

53. Robert Surieu, *Saru-é naz: An Essay on Love and Representation of Erotic Themes in Ancient Iran*, translated by James Hogarth (Geneva: Nagel Publishers, 1967), p. 146.

54. W. Heffening, "Mut'a," in *Shorter Encylopaedia of Islam*, edited by H. A. R. Gibb and J. H. Kramers (Leiden: E. J. Brill, 1961), pp. 418-20.

55. Simon David Messing, *The Highland-Plateau Amhara of Ethiopia* (unpublished dissertation, University of Pennsylvania, 1957), pp. 540-41.

56. Koran, IV, *An Nisâ* [Women], 22-23.

57. J. Schacht, "Umm al-Walad," in *Shorter Encyclopaedia of Islam*, pp. 601-03.

58. Koran, XXIV, *An Nûr* [Light], 33.

59. Levy, op. cit., p. 118.

60. Koran, IV, *An Nisâ* [Women], 15.

61. Koran, XXIV, *An Nûr* [Light], 4. For an account of the incident that led to this surah, see Nabia Abbott, *Aishah: The Beloved of Mohammed* (Chicago: University of Chicago Press, 1942), pp. 29-38.

62. J. Schacht, "Zina," in *Shorter Encyclopaedia of Islam*, pp. 658-59.

63. Koran, XVII, *Bani Isrâîl* [Children of Israel], 32; XXV, *Al-Furqàn* [The Criterion], 68; XXXIII, *Al-Ahzâb* [The Clans], 30.

64. Levy, op. cit., pp. 118-19.

65. Raphael Patai, *Sex and Family in the Bible* (New York: Doubleday, 1959), p. 147.

66. Koran, XXIV, *An Nûr* [Light], 30.

67. Alû ibn Abu Bakr, Burhan al-Din, al-Marghinani, *The Hedaya or Guide: a Commentary on the Mussulman Laws*, translated by Charles Hamilton and edited, with a preface and index, by Standish Grove Grady, 4 vols. in 1 (reprinted, Lahore: Premier Books House, 1957), IV, 598-99, or Book xliv, sec. 4.

68. Surieu, op. cit., p. 65.

69. Ibid., p. 150.

70. Dickson, op. cit., p. 244.

71. Ibid.; Messing, op. cit., p. 479; J. B. Glubb, *The Sulubba and Other Ignoble Tribes of Southwestern Asia* (Menasha, Wis.: George Banta Publishing Company, 1943), p. 3.

72. Glubb, op. cit., p. 29, and Walter Clines, *Notes on the People of Siwah and El Garah in the Libyan Desert* (Menasha, Wis.; George Banta Publishing Company, 1936), p. 106.

73. Many baths were illustrated with erotic paintings. See Philip Rawson, *Erotic Art of the East* (New York: G. P. Putnam's Sons, 1968), p. 206.

74. See Abbas Hamdani, "The Huhtasib as Guardian of Public Morality," unpublished paper given at the Western Michigan Medieval Conference at Kalamazoo, Michigan, 1972.

Chapter 6

1. S. C. Sarkar, *Some Aspects of the Earliest Social History of India* (London: Oxford University Press, 1928), pp. 92-94.

2. Benjamin Walker, *The Hindu World,* 2 vols. (New York: Praeger, 1968), II, 242-43.

3. Strabo, *Geography* XV, i, 62 (C714), edited and translated by H. L. Jones, 8 vols. (London: William Heinemann, 1930).

4. See Johann Jakob Meyer, *Sexual Life in Ancient India* (New York: Barnes and Noble, 1953), p. 6. This account is primarily based on the two Indian epics, the *Ramayana* and the *Mahabharata,* and includes long extracts from them.

5. *Laws of Manu,* III, 55-58, edited and translated by G. Bühler in vol. XV, *Sacred Books of the East* (reprinted, Delhi: Motilala Banarasidass, 1964).

6. Meyer, op. cit., p. 496.

7. *Laws of Manu,* II, 213-15, IX, 17-18; Meyer, op. cit., pp. 496-500.

8. A. S. Altekar, *The Position of Women in Hindu Civilization* (Banaras: Motilala Banarasidass, 1956), pp. 5-6; Vern L. Bullough, *The Subordinate Sex* (Urbana: University of Illinois Press, 1973), pp. 230-34.

9. Meyer, op. cit., p. 346, n. 1.

10. Quoted by Francis Leeson, *Kama Shilpa: A Study of Indian Sculptures Depicting Love in Action* (Bombay: D. B. Taraporevala Sons, 1962), p. 30.

11. Ibid., p. 30. The missionary in question was Ferdinand de Wilton Ward.

12. In addition to Leeson, op. cit., see Mulk Raj Anand, *Kama Kala* (Geneva: Nagel Publishers, 1963); P. Thomas, *Kama Kalpa* (Bombay: D. B. Taraporevala Sons, 1959), and any number of other collections of photographs of erotic sculpture.

13. Meyer, op. cit., pp. 376-80.

14. Ibid., p. 380 n. 2.

15. E. Crook, "Prostitution," *Encyclopedia of Religion and Ethics,* 12 vols. (New York: Charles Scribner, 1928), X, 406.

16. Meyer, op. cit., pp. 125-26.

17. Altekar, op cit., pp. 33, 55-61.

18. Ibid., pp. 180-82, and J. A. Dubois, *Hindu Manners, Customs and Ceremonies* (Oxford: Clarendon Press, 1906), p. 337, and P. Thomas, op. cit., pp. 140-41.

19. Dubois, op. cit.

20. Walker, op. cit., II, 247, and N. M. Penzer, "Sacred Prostitution," in *Poison Damsels and Other Essays* (London: Charles J. Sawyer, 1952).

21. J. N. Farquhar, *Modern Religious Movements in India* (London: Macmillan and Company, 1929), pp. 408-10; Sir George MacMunn, *The Religions and Hidden Cults of India* (London: Sampson Low, Martson and Company, 1932), pp. 176-78. For a sympathetic fictionalized re-creation of a temple prostitute, see A. Mardann, *Deva-Dasi* (New York: Macaulay, 1959).

22. Vatsyayana, *Kama Sutra,* translated by Richard F. Burton (New York: E. P. Dutton & Company, 1962), Part VI, pp. 205-37. The quotation is from the third chapter of Part VI, p. 220.

23. Ibid., VI, chap. VI, p. 237. A greater amplification of the sketchy summation in this particular translation can be found in Thomas, op. cit., pp. 103-04.

24. Meyer, op. cit., p. 275.

25. Damodaragupta, *Kuttanimatam* [Lessons of a Bawd], translated into English by E. Powys Mathers, in *Eastern Love,* vol. I (London: John Rodker, 1927).

26. Kshemendra, *Samayamatrika* [Harlot's Breviary], translated by E. Powys Mathers, in vol. II, *Eastern Love.* The quotes are from the *Epilogue,* pp. 99-100.

27. Thomas, op. cit., p. 105.

28. Meyer, op. cit., pp. 266-71.

29. Pratap Chandra Chunder, *Kautilya on Love and Morals* (Calcutta: Jayanti, 1970), chap. X, pp. 98-113.

30. Walker, op. cit., II, 248.

31. Meyer, op. cit., pp. 274-75.

32. Altekar, op. cit., p. 163, and M. N. Srivinas, *Marriage and Family in Mysore* (Bombay: New Book Company, 1942), p. 75.

33. Chunder, op. cit., pp. 112-13.

34. Altekar, op. cit., pp. 104-12.

35. Ibid., pp. 312-16, and John D. Mayne, *Treatise on Hindu Law and Usage,* 11th ed. (Madras: Higgensbotham, 1953), p. 104.

36. *Laws of Manu,* IV, 209, 211, 216, IX, 259.

37. This was still often the results in the twentieth century. See Alberto C. Germano S. Correia, *Prostituçao e Profilaxia Anti-venérea India Portuguesa* (Tipografia Rangel Bastorica India Portuguesa, 1938), p. 36.

38. Altekar, op. cit., pp. 180-82.

39. Giuseppe Tucci, *Tibetan Painted Scrolls,* 3 vols. (Rome: Libreria dell Stato, 1949), I, 242.

40. R. H. Van Gulik, *Sexual Life in Ancient China* (Leiden: E. J. Brill, 1961), pp. 341-42.

41. B. Bhattacharyya, *Introduction to Guhyasamaja,* viii, quoted in Chou-Yi-Ling, "Tantrism in China," *Harvard Journal of Asiatic Studies,* VIII (1944-45), Appendix E, p. 313.

42. See Giuseppe Tucci, *Rati Lílà: An Interpretation of the Tantric Imagery of the Temples of Nepal,* translated into English by James Hogarth (Geneva: Nagel Publishers 1966); also Tucci, *Tibetan Painted Scrolls,* and Tucci, *The Theory and Practice of the Mandala,* translated by Alan Houghton Brodrick (London: Rider & Company, 1969); H. V. Guenther, *Yuganaddha: The Tantric View of Life* (Varanasi, India: The Chokhambra Sanskrit Series Studies, vol. III, 2d ed. 1969); *Hevajra Tantra,* translated by D. L. Snellgrove, 2 vols. (London: Oxford University Press, 1959); D. N. Bose, *Tantras: Their Philosophy and Occult Secrets,* 3rd ed. (Calcutta: Oriental Publishing Company, 1956). Much valuable work on the subject was done by Sir John Woodroof who wrote under the name of A. Avalon. The difficulty with many of his editions and translations is that he was the subject of rather violent and unscholarly criticism and this sometimes tended to force him to adopt the role of an apologist and elevate the philosophical aspects of the system he was dealing with while glossing over some of the more material aspects.

43. Van Gulik, op. cit., p. 5.

44. *The Sayings of Confucius,* translated by James R. Ware (New York: New American Library, 1955), XVII, 23.

45. L. Weiger, *Moral Tenets and Customs in China,* translated by L. Davrout (Hokien-fu, Catholic Mission Press, 1913), p. 25.

46. R. H. Van Gulik, op. cit., pp. 44-45. See also Florence Ayscough, *Chinese Women Yesterday and Today* (Boston: Houghton Company, 1937), pp. 14-16.

47. Van Gulik, op. cit., pp. 42-43.

48. Eloise Talcott Hibbert, *Embroidered Gauze* (New York: E. P. Dutton, n.d.), pp. 15-29; see also Ayscough, op. cit., passim, and Albert R. O'Hara, *Position of Women in Early China* (Washington, D.C.: The Catholic University of America, 1945), passim. O'Hara's work includes a translation of the *Lieh Nü Chuan,* or biographies of eminent Chinese women, compiled very early in Chinese literary history.

49. Van Gulik, op. cit., p. 114.

50. In addition to the works cited in footnote 48, see P. S. Tseng, "The Chinese Woman, Past and Present," in *Symposium on Chinese Culture,* edited by Sophia H. Chen Zen (Shanghai: China Institute of Pacific Relations, 1931), pp. 285-86.

51. *I Ching,* LXIII, translated by James Legge in vol. XVI, *The Sacred Books of the East,* edited by F. Max Müller.

52. Joseph Needham, assisted by Wang Ling, *Science and Civilization in China,* vol. II (Cambridge: Cambridge University Press, 1956), pp. 149-50, and Van Gulik, op. cit., pp. 70-71. See also Heinrich Wallnöfer and Anna von Rottauscher, *Chinese Folk Medicine,* translated by Marion Palmedo (New York: Crown Publishers, 1965).

53. Van Gulik, op. cit., pp. 70-71.

54. One has been translated into English by Akira Ishihara and Howard S. Levy under the title of *The Tao of Sex* (Yokohoma: Shibundö, 1968). Translations of other fragments can be found in Van Gulik, op. cit., pp. 122-34.

55. Van Gulik, op. cit., p. 17.

56. Weiger, op. cit., p. 301.

57. Van Gulik, op. cit., p. 17.

58. Ibid., p. 65 n. 2.

59. Ibid., p. 171.

60. Hibbert, op. cit., pp. 21-41. See the collection of stories, *The Courtesan's Jewel Box,* edited and translated by Yang Hsien-Yi and Gladys Yang (Peking: Foreign Language Press, 1957), for several literary accounts of the prostitute. The stories are taken from the sixteenth-century collection of Feng Meng-lung and Ling Meng-chu.

61. Van Gulik, op. cit., p. 174.

62. Van Gulik, op. cit., pp. 176-77.

63. A translation of the story can be found in Arthur Waley, *Translations from the Chinese* (New York: Alfred A. Knopf, 1941), "The Story of Miss Li," pp. 275-96.

64. Waley, op. cit., p. 49.

65. Van Gulik, op. cit., p. 181.

66. See the story "The Oil Vendor and the Courtesan" in the collection *The Courtesan's Jewel Box.* Some indication of the unhappy condition of many courtesans is demonstrated in the folksong printed by Ayscough, op. cit., pp. 95-99.

67. The sale and pawning of women by relatives and even kidnappers is an ancient custom in China, one that proved difficult to stamp out. See M. H. Van der Valk, *Conservatism in Modern Chinese Family Law* (Leiden: E. J. Brill, 1956), pp. 60-61.

68. Van Gulik, op. cit., pp. 181-84, 230-35.

69. Ayscough, op. cit., p. 93.

70. Marco Polo, *Travels,* edited by George R. Parks (New York: Book League of America, 1929), II, 22.

71. Ibid., III, 77.

72. Van Gulik, op. cit., pp. 189-90.

73. Ibid., pp. 78-79. For other views see Michel Beurdeley, Kristofer Schipper, Ch'ng Fu-Jui, Jacques Pimpaneau, *Chinese Erotic Art* (Rutland, Vermont: Charles E. Tuttle, 1969), which includes many art objects as well as a documented text.

Chapter 7

1. *The Theodosian Code,* Book XV, titulus 8, *"De Lenonibus"* [Procurers], translated with commentary by Clyde Pharr in collaboration with Theresa S. Davidson and Mary B. Pharr (Princeton: Princeton University Press, 1952), p. 435.

2. Ibid., *Novella,* "De Lenonibus," titulus 18, p. 504.

3. *Digest,* Lib. XII, titulus v in *Corpus Juris Civilis,* edited by Rudolf Shoell and Juilelem Kroll, 3 vols. (Berlin: Weidmann, 1959).

4. *Novella,* XIV, Collatio III, titulus i, *"DeLenonibus,"* in *Corpus Juris Civilis.*

5. *Digest,* XXV, v, 1, 3, 4; XXXIX, ix, 16; L, xvi, 144; *Codes* V, xxvi, and *Novella,* LXXXIX, xii, 4-5.

6. *Novella,* XIV, *"Proemium,"* and Joannes Malalas, *Chronographia,* XVII, 5-6, edited by Ludwig Dindorf (Bonn: Impensis Ed. Weberi, 1831), pp. 440-41. This particular portion has been translated by Matthew Spinka (Chicago: University of Chicago, 1940).

7. Procopius, *Anecdota,* translated by H. B. Dewing (London: William Heinemann, 1935), and Procopius, *Buildings,* I, 9, edited and translated by H. B. Dewing and Glanville Downey (London: William Heinemann, 1954).

8. See A. A. Vasiliev, *Justin the First* (Cambridge: Harvard University Press, 1950), pp. 393-4.

9. Procopius, *Anecdota*, Books IX-X, describes the alleged career of Theodora.

10. Ibid., Book I.

11. William Gordon Holmes, *The Age of Justinian and Theodora* (London: G. Bell and Sons, 1912), I, 107-08.

12. For a discussion of these institutions, see Demetrios J. Consantelos, *Byzantine Philanthropy and Social Welfare* (New Brunswick, N.J.: Rutgers University Press, 1968), pp. 185-221, especially p. 221.

13. Ibid., p. 233.

14. Ibid., p. 196.

15. Michael Psellus, *Chronographia*, translated by E. R. A. Sewter (New Haven: Yale University Press, 1953), Book IV, "Michael IV," 36 (pp. 73-74).

16. The most complete account of Byzantine prostitution is in P. Koukoules, *The Private Life of the Byzantines* (in Greek), 8 vols., (Athens, 1947-57), II, 2, 117-62.

17. *Leges Alamannorum*, edited by Karl Lehmann in *Monumenta Germaniae historica, Leges nationum Germanicarum*, vol. V, part 1 (Hanover: Hahn, 1888), p. 115.

18. *Lex Ribuaria*, edited by Rudolph Sohm, *Monumenta Germaniae historica, Legum*, vol. V (Hanover: Hahn, 1875-79), pp. 216, 231.

19. P. D. King, *Law and Society in the Visigothic Kingdom* (Cambridge: Cambridge University Press, 1972), p. 118.

20. Ibid., p. 202 n. 5.

21. Ibid., p. 241.

22. *The Lombard Laws*, translated with an introduction by Katherine Fischer Drew (Philadelphia: University of Pennsylvania Press, 1973), "Rothair's Edict," 198, p. 90.

23. *The Burgundian Code*, XXXIII, translated by Katherine Fischer Drew (Philadelphia: University of Pennsylvania Press, 1972), p. 45.

24. Ibid., XLVII (p. 54). This states that the wife was to be deprived of her liberty and sentenced to servitude. In some cases such servitude was prostitution.

25. Gregory of Tours, *The History of the Franks*, translated with an introduction by O. M. Dalton, 2 vols. (Oxford: Clarendon Press, 1927), I, 397-402.

26. Ibid., Book IV, 18 (25), 19 (26).

27. Ibid., X, 16.

28. See the account in Einhard, *Life of Charlemagne*, translated by William Glaister (London: G. Bell and Sons, 1877).

29. See, for example, *Capitulare Missorum Generale*, translated by Dana Carleton Munro in University of Pennsylvania, *Translations and Reprints from the Original Sources of European History*, VI, no. 5, pp. 16ff. For other regulations of Charles, see the *Capitula Regum Francorum*, edited by Alfred Boretius, *Monumenta Germaniae Historica, Leges*, II, 44ff.

30. See John T. McNeill and Helena M. Gamer, editors and translators, *Medieval Handbooks of Penance* (New York: Columbia University Press, 1938) for a collection of several examples of medieval penitentials. The collection attributed to St. Patrick is not technically penitential but canon. See nos. 14, 19, pp. 78-79, and no. 26 (2nd Synod), p. 85.

31. *The Penitential of Finnian*, nos. 39-49, ibid., p. 95.

32. Ibid., pp. 302-04 (Roman Penitential).

33. Burchard of Worms, *Decretum Libri XX*, IX, v, vols. 957-60, 966-69, in col. CXL, J. P. Migne, *Patrologia Latina* (Paris: Garnier, 1887), nos. 182-94. This section was not translated by McNeil and Gamer, op. cit.

34. Hostiensis (Henricus de Segusio), *In quinque Decretalium libri commentaria*, 5 vols. in 2 (Venice: Apud Luntas, 1851; reprinted, Turin: Bottega d'Erasmo, 1965), *Lectura to X* 4.13.11, no. 1 (vol. VI, fol. 27ra).

35. For a treatment of some of the quandaries involved in this, see James Brundage, "The Crusader's Wife: A Canonistic Quandary," *Studia Gratiana* XII (1967), 425-42. Brundage has written rather extensively on the whole subject of canon law and prostitution.

36. Hostiensis, *Lectura to X* 4.13.11, no. 2 (in op. cit., IV, fol. 27ra).

37. *The Summa Parisiensis on the Decretum Gratiani*, c. 32, q. 5, c. 1 ad. v. tolerabilius, edited by Terence P. McLaughlin (Toronto: Pontifical Institute of Medieval Studies, 1952).

38. Hostiensis, *Lectura to X* 3.30.23, no. 3 (op. cit., III, vol. 100vb) and 4.1.20, no. 5 (IV, fol. 6^{nb}).

39. Thomas Aquinas, *Summa Theologica*, II-II, Q. X, Art. II and II-II, Q. lx, 2 and 5, II-II, LXXXVII, 2, ad 2, and II-II, CXVIII, 8, ad. 4 in the edition translated by the English Dominicans, 22 vols. (Burns, Oates & Washburne, 1922).

40. Edward Gibbon, *The Decline and Fall of the Roman Empire*, edited J. B. Bury, 3 vols. (reprinted, New York: Heritage Press, 1946), pp. 1707-08.

41. George F. Fort, *History of Medical Economy During the Middle Ages* (New York: J. W. Bouton, 1883), p. 340.

42. William E. H. Lacky, *History of European Morals*, 2 vols. (reprinted, New York: George Braziller, 1955), II, 152.

43. John of Joinville, *The Life of St. Louis*, translated by René Hague (New York: Sheed and Ward, 1955), XXXVI, par. 170-71.

44. Hostiensis, *Summa aurea* (Lyons: Joannes de Lambray, 1537; reprinted, Aalen: Scientia Verlag, 1962), lib 3, no. 11 (fol. 117rb).

45. Hroswitha, "Paphnutius" *The Plays of Hroswitha*, translated by Christopher St. John (London: Chatto and Windus, 1923), pp. 75-100.

46. Paul La Croix, *History of Prostitution*, translated by Samuel Putnam, 2 vols. (New York: Covici-Friede, 1931), I, 728-29.

47. The ordinance is given in Joinville, op. cit., CXL, par. 702. See also *Ordonnances de rois de France*, edited by Eusébe Jacob de Lauriére, Denis François Secousse, et al. (Paris: 1728-1849), I, 74, 104.

48. Ibid., XX, 180.

49. *Monumenta Germaniae historica, Legum,* sec. 4, const. 1 (p. 240).

50. Iwan Bloch, *Die Prostitution,* 2 vols. (Berlin: Louis Marcus, 1912), I, 676, 722.

51. G. T. Salisbury, *Street Life in Medieval England* (Oxford: Pen-In Hand, 1948), pp. 148-55.

52. Ibid.

53. Fort, op. cit., p. 339.

54. For a survey of some of this legislation, see Robert Ulysse, *Les signes d'infamie au moyen âge* (Paris: Honoré Champion, 1891), pp. 176-89.

55. Jacques de Vitry, *Historia occidentalis,* c. 7., ed. Hinnebusch, p. 91.

56. Ralph B. Pugh, *Imprisonment in Medieval England* (Cambridge: Cambridge University Press, 1968), p. 51.

57. *Ordonnances*, VII, 127.

58. Fernando Henriques, *Prostitution in Europe and the New World,* vol. 2 of 3 vols. (London: MacGibbon & Kee, 1963), pp. 48-49.

59. G. G. Coulton, *Five Centuries of Religion* (Cambridge: Cambridge University Press, 1927), II, 566.

60. Ibid., II, 585.

61. Jean Gerson, *Compendious Declaration of the Defects of Ecclesiastics,* I, col. 206-10 quoted in Coulton, op. cit., II, 642.

62. Quoted in Coulton, op. cit., II, 642.

63. The Avignon regulations, because of the provision for medical inspection, have been much examined, and for this same reason are thought not to be genuine. See P. Pansier, "Histoire des prétendus statuts de la reine Jeanne," *Janus,* VII (1902).

64. Louis M. Epstein, *Sex Laws and Customs in Judaism* (reprinted, New York: Ktav Publishing House, 1967), pp. 172-73.

65. For discussion, see Iwan Bloch, op. cit., I, 670, 767-70. The historian has to be careful in using Bloch. Though he has a lot of invaluable information it is not always easy to trace his sources, even when they are cited, because of his carelessness.

66. G. C. Coulton, *Medieval Panorama* (Cambridge: Cambridge University Press, 1949), p. 172.

67. Fort, op. cit., pp. 336-47.

68. Gratian, *Decretum,* Distincto 81, c. 28, *glos, ord.* ad v. *omino, Causa* 24, quaestio 1 canon 24 *glos. ord.* ad v. *balneas* in *Corpus Juris Canonici,* edited by Emil Friedberg, 2 vols. (Leipzig: B. Tauschnitz, 1879; reprinted, Graz: Akademische Druck-und Verlags-anstalt, 1959). See also Rufinus, *Die Summa Magistri zum Decretum Gratiani* to D. 81, c. 20, edited by Heinrich Singer (reprinted, Aalen: Scientia Verlag, 1963).

69. John Stow, *The Survey of London* (1598) edited by Henry Wheatley (London: J. M. Dent & Co., 1912), pp. 360-61.

70. A. P. E. Rabutaux, *De la Prostitution en Europe depuis l'antiquité jusqu'à la fin du XVI siècle* (Paris: Lebigre-Duquesne Frères, 1851), p. 54; Mayhew, op. cit., pp. 187-88; Bloch, op. cit., I, 814-15.

71. Mayhew, op. cit., pp. 183-84.

72. Ulrich Richental, *Chronicle of the Council of Florence*, in *The Council of Constance*, translated by Louise Rope Loomis, edited and annotated by John Hine Mundy and Kennerly M. Woody (New York: Columbia University Press, 1961), *Summary*, p. 190. He said there were others he could not count. The prostitutes were among the 72,460 persons he estimated to have come to Constance.

73. Jacques de Vitry, *Historia occidentalis*, c. 8, pp. 99-100; Milton R. Gutsch, "A Twelfth-Century Preacher—Fulk of Neuilly," *The Crusades and Other Essays in Honor of Dana C. Munro* (New York: Appleton-Century-Crofts, 1928), pp. 190-91.

74. Max Heimbucher, *Die Orden und Kongregationen der Katholischen Kirche*, 2 vols., 3d ed. (Munich: F. Schöningh, 1965), I, 646-48.

75. Bernard Guillemain, *La cour pontifical d'Avignon, 1309—1376; étude d'une société* (Paris: E. De Boccard, 1966), p. 485-86.

76. Joinville, *Life of St. Louis*, CXLII, 725.

77. Richard Lewinsohn, *A History of Sexual Customs*, translated by Alexander Mayce (New York: Harper & Brothers, 1958), pp. 147-48.

78. Gratian, *Decretum*, Causa 32, quaestio 1, canon 1, and C. 33, q. 2. C.11-12.

79. *Decretalis D. Gregorii papae IX suae integrati una cum glossi*, Liber 4, Titulus 1, canon 20 in *Corpus Juris Canonici*.

80. Fort, op. cit., p. 344.

81. Coulton, *Medieval Panorama*, p. 172.

82. Fort, op. cit., p. 341.

83. For a detailed listing see Bloch, op. cit., I, 747-50.

84. Ibid., I, 740-45. His lists for other countries are not so complete. For France, see pp. 745-46; for Italy, p. 747.

85. Sidney Painter, *French Chivalry* (Baltimore: Johns Hopkins Press, 1957), pp. 111-12.

86. Andreas Capellanus, *The Art of Courtly Love*, translated by J. J. Parry (New York: Columbia University Press, 1941), Book 1, chaps. 1-4, and final section.

87. For two conflicting views on this see Denis de Rougement, *Love in the Western World*, translated by Montgomery Belgion, rev. ed. (New York: Pantheon, 1956), pp. 275 ff, and Morton M. Hunt, *The Natural History of Love* (New York: Alfred A. Knopf, 1959), pp. 171 ff.

88. John Charles Nelson, *Renaissance Theory of Love* (New York: Columbia University Press, 1958), p. 78.

89. C. S. Lewis, *Allegory of Love* (reprinted, Oxford, England: Galaxy Books, 1958), and Nelson, op. cit., passim.

90. Nina Epton, *Love and the French* (London: Cassell, 1959), p. 114.

91. There are numerous editions of Brantôme's work. I have utilized the translation by A. R. Allinson, *Lives of Fair and Gallant Ladies* (New York: Liveright, 1933), Book VI, chap. 2 (p. 313).

92. Ibid., Book VI, chap. 2 (p. 315).

93. Ibid., Book I, chap. 4 (pp. 336-37).

94. Epton, op. cit., pp. 93-95.

95. Brantôme, op. cit., Book I, chap. 5 (pp. 35-36).

96. Ibid., Book I, chap. 12 (p. 97).

97. Ibid., Book I, chap. 12 (p. 96).

98. Andreas Capellanus, op. cit., Book I, chap. 11.

99. Ibid., Book I, chap. 12.

100. Baldassare Castiglioni, *The Courtier*, translated by Thomas Hoby (New York: National Alumni, 1907), Book IV, chap. 61. There are many editions.

101. There are many translations of Villon. See D. B. Wyndham Lewis, *François Villon* (New York: Literary Guild, 1928), pp. 276-77 for a survey of his life and translations of many of his poems. See also François Villon, *The Complete Works*, translated by Anthony Bonner (New York: David McKay Company, 1960), pp. 51 ff. and Norman Cameron, *Poems of François Villon* (London: Jonathan Cape, 1952). Other translations are by John Payne, H. de

Vere Stackpoole, J. Heron Lepper, and separate poems have been translated by Rossetti, Swinburne, Wilfred Thorley, and many others.
102. The French version of these are given by Lewis, op. cit., pp. 324-25. Not all scholars attribute the poem to Villon.
103. Villon (Anthony Bonner), op. cit., pp. 106-09.
104. Jean Hervez, *Ruffians at Ribaudes au moyen âge* (Paris: Bibliothèque des Curieux, 1913), pp. 112-113. Other visitors were greatly impressed by the number of prostitutes.
105. As quoted in Maurice Valency, *In Praise of Love: An Introduction to the Love Poetry of the Renaissance* (New York: Macmillan, 1956), p. 3.

Chapter 8

1. Martin Luther, *Works,* edited by Jaroslav Pelikan and Helmut Lehmann (Philadelphia and St. Louis: Muhlenberg and Concordia, 1955 ff), XLVIII, 278.
2. John Calvin, *Institutes of the Christian Religion,* IV, xiii, 18, translated by Ford Lewis Battles in vols. 20 and 21, *Library of Christian Classics,* edited by John T. McNeill (Philadelphia: Westminster Press, 1960).
3. Luther, *Works,* XLIV, 1-8.
4. John Calvin, *Epist. I ad Cor.,* vii, 5-6, in *Opera,* edited by G. Baum, E. Cunitz et al., (Brunswick and Berlin: C. A. Schwetschke, 1863-1900), VII, 150, and *Quattuor Reliq. Lib. Mos.,* Deuteronomy, xxiv, 5, Leviticus, xx, 18, in *Opera,* I, 515, 518.
5. This is developed further in Vern L. Bullough, *The Subordinate Sex* (Urbana, Ill.: University of Illinois Press, 1974), p. 195-229.
6. Calvin, in Genesis, ii, 18, in *Opera,* I, 14.
7. Derrick Sherwin Bailey, *Sexual Relation in Christian Thought* (New York: Harper & Brothers, 1959), p. 206.
8. Martin Luther, *Table Talk,* V, 297 in *Werke: Kritische Gesamtsgabe* (Weimar: Böhlau, 1883ff). Much of *Table Talk,* but not all, is translated in the Pelikan and Lehmann edition; hence the German reference.
9. Luther, *Works,* XLIV, 214.
10. Martin Luther, *Letters of Spiritual Counsel,* edited and translated by Theodore G. Tappert (Philadelphia: Westminster Press, 1955), p. 293.
11. Ibid.
12. Luther, *Works,* LIV, 382.
13. Luther, *Werke, Correspondence,* IV, 140.
14. Preserved Smith, *The Age of the Reformation* (New York: Henry Holt, 1920), p. 174.
15. Nina Epton, *Love and the English* (London: Cassell, 1960), pp. 68, 91.
16. Quoted in Ruth Kelso, *Doctrine for the Lady of the Renaissance* (Urbana: University of Illinois Press, 1956).
17. Ludovico Ariosto, *Orlando Furioso,* translated with notes by Allan Gilbert, 2 vols. (New York: S. F. Vanni), I, 55.
18. Edward Fuchs, *Illustrierte Sittengeschichte* (vol. I, "Renaissance," Munich: Albert Langen Verlag für Literatur und Kunst, 1909), pp. 381-82.
19. Jakob Burckhardt, *The Civilization of the Renaissance in Italy* (reprinted, New York: Modern Library, 1954), pp. 295-96.
20. Fuchs, op. cit., p. 415.
21. Ibid., p. 399.
22. Bloch, op. cit., I, p. 97.
23. Ibid., II, 189-90.
24. Ibid., I, 88.
25. Pietro Aretino, *Dialogues,* translated by Raymond Rosenthal (New York: Stein and Day, 1971). This is primarily a discussion of prostitution, although *Dialogue I* deals with various types of women, and concludes with Antonia advising Nanna to make a whore of her daughter Pippa, since nuns betray their vows and the married women violate the bonds of matrimony. See pp. 105-59 for a discussion of courtesans, as compared to other life-styles for women.
26. Antonii Panormitae, *Hermaphroditus* (Frider. Carol. Forbergius-Cobugri Sumtibus Meuseliorum, 1824), p. 138.

27. Aretino, op. cit., Part II, first day, pp. 161-237.

28. Ibid., Part II, first day, pp. 195-96.

29. Preserved Smith, op. cit., pp. 506-07.

30. Centro di Documentazione, *Conciliorum Oecumenicorum Decreta* (Freiburg im Breisgau: Verlag Herder, 1962), Session XXV of Council of Trent.

31. J. Donovan, editor and translator, *Catechism of the Council of Trent* (Dublin: James Duffy & Company, 1908), pp. 317-18.

32. R. H. Van Gulik, *Sexual Life in Ancient China* (Leiden: E. J. Brill, 1961), p. 182.

33. See Julius Rosenbaum, *The Plague of Lust* (reprinted, New York: Frederick Publications, 1955), Book II, 187-223. This is a classic work.

34. Desiderius Erasmus, *The Colloquies*, translated by Craig R. Thompson (Chicago: University of Chicago Press, 1965), pp. 401, 405.

35. Ulrich von Hutton, *Of the Wood Called Guaiacum*, translated by Thomas Paynel (London: Thomas Bertheleti, 1539), p. 1.

36. Ruy Diaz de Isla, *Tractado llamado fructo de todos los sanctos: Contra el mal Serpentino* (Seville: 1542), iii, passage reprinted in Iwan Bloch, *Der Ursprung der Syphilis*, 2 vols. (Jena: Gustav Fischer, 1901-11), pp. 306-07.

37. There is a vast literature on venereal disease dating from the late fifteenth century. Karl Sudhoff collected ten tracts written between 1495 and 1498 in a work that was reedited and in part translated by Charles Singer, *The Earliest Printed Literature on Syphilis* (Florence: R. Lier & Company, 1925). Most modern accounts start with the famous work of Jean Astruc, *De Morbus Venereis* (Paris: 1736), translated into English under the title *A Treatise of Venereal Diseases* (London: W. Innys, J. Richardson, C. Davis, J. Clarke, R. Manby, and H. S. Cox, 1754). Astruc, motivated mostly by national pride, argued for the American origin of the disease. Since Astruc's time the most important work arguing for an American origin is Iwan Bloch, *Der Ursprung der Syphilis* cited above. Until recently the leading opponent of the American origin was Karl Sudhoff, *Der Ursprung der Syphilis* (Leipzig: F. C. W. Vogel, 1913).

38. William Allen Pusey, *The History and Epidemiology of Syphilis* (Springfield, Ill.: Charles C. Thomas, 1933), p. 5. See also E. Jeanselme, *Histoire de la Syphilis* (Paris: G. Doin, 1931).

39. Gonzalo Fernández Oviedo y Valdés, *Historia General y Natural de las Indias*, 4 vols. (Madrid: Imprenta de la Real Academia de la Historia, 1851-55), I, 55. This has been translated into English by Sterling A. Stoudemire, under the title *Natural History of the West Indies* (Chapel Hill: University of North Carolina Press, 1959), pp. xi, xii, 88-90.

40. Bartolome de las Casas, *Historia de las Indias*, 5 vols. (Madrid: Imprenta de Miguel Ginestra, 1876).

41. Ruy Diaz de Isla, op. cit., iii. See also Richmond C. Holcomb, "Ruiz Díaz de Isla and the Haitian Myth of European Syphilis," *Medical Life*, XLIII (July, August, September, November, 1936), 270-316, 318-64, 415-70, 487-514.

42. For a long listing of the various names see Bloch, op. cit., I, 297-305. For a work in English that gives some of them, see J. R. Whitwell, *Syphilis in Earlier Days* (London: H. K. Lewis & Company, 1940), pp. 8-12.

43. There is an anonymous English prose translation of the poem *Syphilis* (St. Louis: Philmar Company, 1911). There are many others. See selections from a translation by S. C. Martin reprinted in Logan Clendening, editor, *Source Book of Medical History* (New York: Dover, 1960).

44. Fracastor, *Contagion*, translated by W. C. Wright (New York: G. P. Putnam's Sons, 1930).

45. Dennie, op. cit., p. 30, and Robert S. Munger, "Guaiacum, the Holy Wood from the New World," *Journal of History of Medicine and Allied Sciences*, IV (1949), 196-229.

46. For an evaluation of the evidence, see Samuel Eliot Morison, *Admiral of the Ocean Sea*, 2 vols. (Boston: Little, Brown, 1942), II, 193-218.

47. Ferdinand Columbus, *The Life of Admiral Christopher Columbus by His Son Ferdinand*, translated by Benjamin Keene (New Brunswick, N.J.: Rutgers University Press, 1959), pp. 155, 191.

48. Frederick F. Cartwright, with Michael D. Biddiss, *Disease and History* (New York: Thomas Y. Crowell, 1972), p. 60.

49. See E. H. Hudson, "Treponematosis and African Slavery," *British Journal of Venereal Diseases,* XL (March 1964), 43-52; "Treponematosis and Man's Social Evolution," *American Anthropologist,* LXVII (August, 1965), 885-901; "Treponematosis in Perspective," *Bulletin of the World Health Organization* 32 (1965), 735-48, and *Treponematosis* (New York: Oxford University Press, 1946). See also C. J. Hackett, "On the Origin of Human Treponematoses," *Bulletin of the World Health Organization,* XXIX (1963), 7-41. For two recent studies, see Theodor Rosebury, *Microbes and Morals* (New York: The Viking Press, 1971), and Alfred W. Crosby, Jr., *The Columbia Exchange: Biological and Cultural Consequences of 1492* (Westport, Conn., Greenwood Publishing Company, 1972). This last is particularly valuable.

50. Astruc, op. cit., Book I, chap. xiii, pp. 95-101, and chap. xiv, pp. 103-10.

51. Richard Waldegg and Werner Heinz, *Geschichte und Wesen der Prostitution* (Stuttgart: Weltspiegel Verlag, 1956), p. 95.

52. Bloch, op. cit., II, 261-62.

53. Waldegg und Heinz, op. cit., p. 97.

54. Smith, op. cit., p. 506.

55. Paul La Croix, *History of Prostitution,* translated by Samuel Putnam, revised English edition, 2 vols. (New York: Covici-Friede, 1932), II, 1174-78.

56. Ibid., II, 839.

57. Theodore Haupe, *Crime and Punishment in Germany* (New York: E. P. Dutton, 1926), p. 85.

58. Ibid., p. 86.

59. Bloch, op. cit., I, 75.

60. See Ruth Pike, *Aristocrats and Traders: Sevillian Society in the Sixteenth Century* (Ithaca: Cornell University Press, 1972), pp. 204-11.

61. Christian Bürckstümmer, *Geschichte der Reformation und Gegenreformation in der ehemaligen freien Ruchsstadt Dinkelstühl (1524-1648)* (Leipzig: Im Kommissionverlag con Rudolf Haupt, 1914), p. 84.

62. Michel de Montaigne, *The Essays of Montaigne,* translated by John Florio (New York: Modern Library, n.d.), Book II, chap. V, p. 783. There are many other editions of Montaigne; Florio's translation is a classic one, but it is not always true to the original.

Chapter 9

1. Lord Acton, *Essays on Freedom and Power* (reprinted, Boston: Beacon Press, 1948), p. 364.

2. Irene Mahoney, *Royal Cousin* (Garden City, N.Y.: Doubleday, 1970); Henry, Lord Russell, *Henry of Navarre* (New York: Praeger, 1969); Desmond Seward, *The First Bourbon* (Boston: Gambit, 1971) and Marcelle Vioux, *Henry of Navarre,* translated by J. Lewis May (New York: E. P. Dutton, 1937).

3. There are several accounts of the reign of Louis XIV. A popular yet scholarly account is W. H. Lewis, *The Splendid Century* (New York: William Sloane, 1953). For a biography of Louise de la Vallière, see Joan Sanders, *La Petite: The Life of Louise de la Vallière* (Boston: Houghton Mifflin, 1959). Madame Montespan allegedly wrote her own account, *Memoirs of Madame la Marquise de Montespan,* translated by P. E. P., 2 vols. (London: Grover Society [1904]). Actually *Memoirs* was written by G. L. Lafont D'Aussonne.

4. Two other literary works were also dedicated to her: *The Spanish Rogue* by Thomas Duffet, and a book by Robert Whitcomb. See Peter Cunningham, *The Story of Nell Gwyn* (reprinted, Edinburgh: John Grant, 1908), pp. 132, 203-05.

5. See the work by Cunningham cited above, which originally appeared as a serial in the *Gentleman's Magazine* in 1851, and though it should be used with caution it is still valuable. There is another reprint of this work in the Little Blue Book series of reprints (Girard, Kansas: Haldeman-Julius, n.d.). There are many other biographies, probably the best of which is by John Harold Wilson, *Nell Gwyn: Royal Mistress* (New York: Pellegrini & Cudahy, 1952). Wilson also did an account of the place of the actress during this period under the title *All the King's Ladies: Actresses of the Restoration* (Chicago: University of Chicago Press, 1958). An account of the Duchess of Cleveland can be found in Maurice Petherick, *Restoration Rogues* (London: Hollis Carter, 1951), and in more detail in Allen Edwardes, *The Royal Whore* (New York: Chilton Books, 1970). See also H. Noel Williams, *Rival Sultanas: Nell Gwyn and*

Louise de Kéroualle (London: Hutchinson & Co., 1915), Henri Forneron, *Louise de Kéroualle: Duchess of Portsmouth* (London: Sonnenschein, 1887).

6. For the court of Louis XV, see Iain D. B. Pilkington, *The King's Pleasure* (London: Jarrolds, 1957); Nancy Mitford, *Madame de Pompadour* (London: Reprint Society, 1954); H. Noel Williams, *Memoirs of Madame du Barry* (New York: Collier, 1910), and more recently Stanley Loomis, *Du Barry* (Philadelphia: J. B. Lippincott, 1959).

7. A. J. B. Parent-Duchâtelet, *De la prostitution dans la ville de Paris,* 2 vols. (Paris: J. B. Baillière, 1837), II, 466-71.

8. Quoted by Loomis, op. cit., pp. 42-43.

9. Iwan Bloch, *Marquis de Sade: His Life and Works,* translated by James Bruce (reprinted, New York: Brittany Press, 1948), pp. 65-68.

10. Iwan Bloch, *120 Days of Sodom and the Sex Life of the French Age of Debauchery,* translated and edited by Raymond Sabatier (New York: Falstaff Press, 1934), pp. 80-83.

11. Casanova, *Memoirs,* translated by Arthur Machen (New York: George Putnam's Sons, n.d.), Book II, chap. VII, pp. 140-42.

12. Bloch, *120 Days of Sodom,* pp. 84-87.

13. Ibid., pp. 89-90 and Bloch, *Marquis de Sade: His Life and Works,* p. 72.

14. Bloch, *120 Days of Sodom,* p. 67.

15. Ibid., pp. 91-92.

16. Ibid., p. 68.

17. Ibid., pp. 75-78.

18. Friedrich Schulz, *Ueber Paris und die Pariser* (Berlin, n.p. 1791) I, 451-55, 467-74, 501. Only one volume was published.

19. Bloch, *120 Days of Sodom,* pp. 92-96.

20. Casanova, op. cit., Book II, chap. VI, pp. 112-14.

21. Bloch, *120 Days of Sodom,* p. 65.

22. Abbé Prévost, *Manon Lescaut* (New York: Modern Library, [1920]). The work was made into an opera by Massenet and by Puccini.

23. Bloch, *120 Days of Sodom,* pp. 98-101.

24. Casanova, op. cit., Book II, Chap. VI, pp. 125-26.

25. Parent-Duchâtelet, op. cit., II, 472-78.

26. Richard Head, *The English Rogue* (London: 1665; reprinted, London: G. Routledge & Sons, 1928). This is from the chapter titled "How he frequented bawdy houses; what exploits he committed in them; the character of a bawd, a whore, a pimp, and a trapan; their manner of living; with detection of their wicked lives and conversations."

27. Robert Burton, *The Anatomy of Melancholy,* edited by Floyd Dell and Paul Jordan-Smith (New York: Tudor Publishing Company, 1927), par 3, sec. 2, member 2, subsection 5 (p. 716).

28. Thomas Heywood, *Nine Books of Various History Concerning Women* (London: 1624), and quoted in Nina Epton, *Love and the English* (Cleveland: World Publishing, 1960), p. 128.

29. Epton, op. cit., p. 90.

30. Walter Besant, *London in the Time of the Stuarts* (London: Adam and Charles Black, 1903), pp. 318-19.

31. Ibid., pp. 356-57.

32. *The Whores Rhetorick, Calculated to the Meridian of London and Conformed to the Rules of Art in Two Dialogues* (London: Printed for George Shell, 1683). Though the English work is anonymous it is a translation with little change of Ferrante Pallavicino's work by the same name in Italian, which in turn was based on Aretino and other similar works. It was reprinted as Ferrante Pallavicino, *The Whore's Rhetorick* (New York: Ivan Obolensky, 1961), pp. 67-73.

33. *The London-Bawd with Her Character and Life Discovering the Various Subtile Intrigues of Lewd Women,* 4th ed. (London: Printed for John William, 1711). The copy in the British Museum is incomplete.

34. *The Prostitutes of Quality or Adultery a-la-mode. Being Authentic and General Memoirs of Several Persons of the Highest Quality,* (London: Printed for J. Cook and J. Coote, 1757).

35. Martin Madan, *An Account of the Triumphant Death of F. S.: A Converted Prostitute Who Died April 1763, aged 26* (London: Reprinted for Z. Fowle, n.d.). This is an 8-page pamphlet in the British Museum.

36. *List of the Sporting Ladies*/[London? c. 1770], a single sheet of 36 × 18 printed on one side. It is reprinted in *Venus Unmasked*, compiled by Leonard de Vries and Peter Fryer (New York: Stein and Day, 1967), pp. 31-32.

37. *Harris's list of Covent garden ladies; or, man of pleasure's kalendar, for the year, 1788: containing the histories and some curious anecdotes of the most celebrated ladies now on the Town, or in keeping, and also many of their keepers.* (London, for H. Ranger, 1788). The title page indicates that directories for other years are still available. There is an extract of this in de Vries and Fryer, op. cit., pp. 186-89.

38. James Boswell, *London Journal: 1762-1763*, edited by Frederick A. Pottle (New York: McGraw-Hill, 1950), pp. 49-50.

39. Ibid., December 14, 1762, pp. 83-84.

40. Ibid., January 12, 1763, pp. 138-39.

41. Ibid., January 18, 1763, p. 149, and January 20, 1763, pp. 155-62. The quote is from pp. 155-56.

42. Ibid., February 12, 1763, p. 187.

43. Daniel Defoe, *Moll Flanders*. There are many editions of this work.

44. Daniel Defoe, *Roxana*. There are also many editions of this work.

45. Cleland's novel was not as readily available to the reading public as Defoe's works until fairly recently. For a time buyers had to purchase the book in Paris to import into the United States. One of the editions first generally available was an Olympia Press edition dating from 1962 or a Putnam one of 1963. Since then it has often been published both in this country and in England.

46. Both Richardson novels have been published in several editions.

47. Jean Jacques Rousseau, *The Confessions* (New York: Modern Library, n.d.), Book VII, p. 325.

48. Ibid., p. 326.

49. Ibid., p. 327.

50. Ibid., pp. 331-32.

51. Much evidence for this has been summed up in a series of articles by Edward Shorter. See his "Illegitimacy, Sexual Revolution and Social Change in Europe, 1750-1900," *Journal of Interdisciplinary History* 2 (1971), 237-72, and "Female Emancipation, Birth Control and Fertility in European History," *American Historical Review*, 78 (June, 1973), 605-40.

52. Some research has been carried out on this subject, although not in this time period. See William J. Goode, "Illegitimacy, Anomie, and Cultural Penetration," *American Sociological Review* 26 (1961), 910-25. Sydney H. Croog, "Aspects of the Cultural Background of Premarital Pregnancies in Denmark," *Social Forces*, 30 (1951-52), 215-19, and Hyman Rodman, "Illegitimacy in the Caribbean Social Structure: A Reconsideration," *American Sociological Review* 31 (1966), 673-83.

53. For some early discussions of it see *Die Moralstatistik in ihrer Bedeutung für eine Socialethik*, 3rd ed. (Erlangen: A Deichert, 1882), pp. 289-346; Georg von Mayr, *Sosialstatistik*, vol. 3 of *Statistik und Gesellschaftslehre* (Tübingen: J. C. B. Mohr, 1909), pp. 127-50, and Louis Chevalier, *Classes laborieuses et classes dangereuses à Paris pendant la première moitié au XIXᵉ siècle* (Paris: Plon, 1958), p. 380-97. More recently Senator Daniel Patrick Moynihan made these assumptions. See Lee Rainwater and William L. Yancey, *The Moynihan Report and the Politics of Controversy* (Cambridge, Mass.: MIT Press, 1967), pp. 39-124.

54. See Friedrich Engels, *The Condition of the Working-Class in England in 1844* (London: Allen and Unwin, 1892), p. 128.

55. See Ernst Fabri, *Der Notstand unserer Zeit und seine Hebung* (Erlangen, 1850), and for a survey of some of the writings in Germany, see Edward Shorter, "Middle-Class Anxiety in the German Revolution of 1848," *Journal of Social History*, 2 (1969), 189-215.

56. Shorter, "Illegitimacy, Sexual Revolution and Social Change."

57. [Bernard Mandeville], *A Modest Defence of Public Stews; or An Essay Upon Whoring, as It Is Now Practis'd in These Kingdoms* (London: A. Moore, 1724), pp. 1-10. One edition in the British Museum (there are eight different ones) bears the date 1624, but I think it is a misprint.

58. Ibid., pp. 12-26, 31 ff.

59. Ibid., pp. 64-73.

60. [Nicholas Edmé Restif de la Brentonne], *Le pornographie; ou, Idées d'un honnête-homme sur un projet de réglement pour les prostitutées propre à prevenir les malheurs qu'occasionne le publicisme des femmes* (Londres: J. Nourse; la Haie: Gosse junior & Pinet, 1770).

61. [Martin Madan], *Thelypthora: or a Treatise on Female Ruin, in its Causes, Effects, Consequences, Prevention, and Remedy; Considered on the Basis of the Divine Law*, 3 vols., 2d ed. (London: Printed for J. Dodsley, 1781), I, xxi-xxii.

62. See, for example, *Martin's Hobby Houghed and Pounded or Letters on Thelyphthora* (London: Printed for J. Buckland, 1781); James Penn, *Remarks on Thelyphthora* (London: Printed for the author, 1781), and *Remarks controverting Martin Madan's Thelyphthora* (n.p. 178-?). The first work is in the British Museum. The last two are in the Newberry Library, Chicago.

63. Richard Hill, *The Blessings of Polygamy Displayed* (London: J. Mathews, 1781), pp. 38-39.

64. For biographies of many of the more famous courtesans, see Horace Bleackley, *Ladies Fair and Frail: Sketches of the Demi-Monde During the Eighteenth Century* (London: John Lane: The Bodley Head, 1909). Several of these women had their portraits painted by such artists as Joshua Reynolds, Thomas Gainsborough, and other lesser-known figures.

65. The full title of the tract is *Pretty Doings in a Protestant Nation: Being a View of the Present State of Fornication, Whorecraft, and Adultery, in Great Britain, and Territories and Dependencies thereunto belonging. Inscrib'd to the Bona-Roba's in the several Hundreds, Chaces, Parks, and Warrens, North, East, West, and South of Covent-Gardens; and to the Band of Petticoat Pensioners, etc.* ([London]: Printed for J. Roberts, 1734), p. 18.

66. M. Ludovicus [John Campbell], *A Particular but Melancholy Account of the Great Hardships, Difficulties, and Miseries, That Those Unhappy and Much-To-Be-pitied Creatures, The Common Women of the Town, Are plung'd into at this juncture. The Causes of their Misfortunes fully laid down; and the bad Effects that too much Rigour against them will produce* (London: Printed for the author, 1752), pp. 6-16.

67. Ibid., p. 27.

68. *Thought on the Plan for a Magdalen House* (London: James Waugh, 1758).

69. John Fielding, *An Account of the Origin and Effects of a Police Set on Foot by His Grace the Duke of Newcastle in the Year 1753, upon a plan presented to His Grace by the late Henry Fielding, Esq.; To which is added a Plan for preserving those deserted Girls in this Town, who become Prostitutes from Necessity* (London: A. Millar, 1758), p. 32.

70. Ibid., p. 49.

71. Ibid., pp. 51-53.

72. Saunders Welch, *A Proposal to Render Effectual a Plan To Remove the Nuisance of Common Prostitutes from the Streets of this Metropolis; To prevent the Innocent from being seduced; To provide a Decent and Comfortable Maintenance for those whom Necessity or Vice Hath already forced into that famous Course of Life, And to Maintain and Educate Those Children of the Poor, who are either Orphans, or are deserted by wicked Parents, To which is annexed, A Letter Upon the Subject, wrote in the Year 1753* (London: C. Henderson, 1758), passim.

73. Ibid., p. 25.

74. [Jonas Hanway], *Letter V. To Robert Dingley, Esq.; Being a Proposal for the Relief and Employment of Friendless Girls and Repenting Prostitutes* (London: R. and J. Dodsley, 1758).

75. Ibid., pp. 16-23.

76. J[onas] Hanway, *Letters Written occasionally on the Customs of foreign nations in regards to Harlots: The lawless commerce of the sexes: The repentance of Prostitutes: The great humanity and beneficial effects of the Magdalene Charity in London: and the Absurd Notions of the Methodists* (London: John Rivington, 1761), p. 13.

77. Casanova, *Memoirs*, V (London and Moscow), 513-16.

352 NOTES

Chapter 10

1. Quoted in Burton Stevenson, editor, *The Macmillan Book of Proverbs, Maxims, and Famous Phrases* (New York: Macmillan, 1948), p. 2490, #8.
2. A. J. B. Parent-Duchâtelet, *De la prostitution dans la ville de Paris,* 2 vols. (Paris: J. B. Baillière, 1836), II, 462-64.
3. Ibid., II, 196-236.
4. Ibid., I, 492-531.
5. See A. J. B. Parent-Duchâtelet, *La Syphilis et les autres maladies veneriennes chez les prostituées de Paris* (Paris: Pierre Fort, 1900), p. 249ff. This work is an extract of the work by Parent-Duchâtelet cited above, although this particular one is from a later edition and therefore has some additional information. See also the Committee of Fifteen, *The Social Evil with Special Reference to Conditions Existing in the City of New York* (New York: G. P. Putnam's Sons, 1902), pp. 29-34; William L. Sanger, *The History of Prostitution* (new edition reprinted, New York: Eugenics Publishing Company, 1937), pp. 120-281; Abraham Flexner, *Prostitution in Europe* (New York: The Century Company, 1914), pp. 138-39.
6. For a discussion of some of these ideas see Phillip Ricord, *Letters on Syphilis,* translated by W. P. Lattimore (Philadelphia: Blanchard and Lea, 1854). In this 1854 book the introduction still speaks of the difficulty some physicians have in tossing aside the concepts of John Hunter.
7. Benjamin Scott, *A State Iniquity: Its Rise, Extension and Overthrow* (London: Kegan Paul, Trench, Trubner & Company, 1890; reprinted, New York: Augustus M. Kelley, 1968), p. 6.
8. Willi Bauer, *Geschichte und Wesen der Prostitution* (Stuttgart: Weltspiegel, 1956), pp. 98-101; Committee of Fifteen, op cit., pp. 40-42.
9. The figures are given in Henry Mayhew, *London Labour and the London Poor,* 4 vols. (London: Griffin, Bohn, and Company, 1861-62; reprinted, New York: Dover Publications, 1968), IV, 199. A section of volume IV is devoted to the study of prostitution throughout Europe and the rest of the world. It includes much valuable information, but is less valuable than it might have been because of Mayhew's tendency (and that of his coauthor Bracebridge Hemyng) to label individuals and cultural groups as barbarous or semicivilized (China, for example) and to put all kinds of moral judgments in their work.
10. Flexner, op. cit., pp. 123-29.
11. Ibid., pp. 130-36. Flexner in a series of appendixes includes the actual regulations, many of them dating from early in the nineteenth century, of Paris, Berlin, Hamburg, Vienna, ibid., pp. 405-44. A summary of earlier regulations is included in Mayhew, op. cit., pp. 181-210.
12. See Emile Richard, *La prostitution à Paris* (Paris: J. B. Baillière, 1890), pp. 120-21, 141; Flexner, op. cit., pp. 204-64.
13. Flexner, op. cit., p. 227.
14. *Statement Respecting the Prevalence of Certain Immoral Practices in His Majesty's Navy* (London: Ellertson and Henderson, 1821), pp. 1-3.
15. Scott, op. cit., pp. 11-56.
16. Ibid., pp. 82-83. See also Berkeley Hill, "Should the Principle of the Contagious Diseases Act be applied to the Civil Population?" *Transactions of the National Association for the Promotion of Social Science,* 1869, pp. 428-38. The association went on record against extension.
17. Scott, op. cit., passim.
18. [William Rathbone Greg], "The Great Sin of Great Cities," *Lancet,* January 20, 1855. The article was also published as a pamphlet.
19. James Miller, *Prostitution Considered in Relation to Its Cause and Cure* (Edinburgh, 1859), a pamphlet in the British Museum.
20. William Edward Hartpole Lecky, *History of European Morals,* 2 vols. in 1 (reprinted, New York: George Braziller, 1955), II, 283. The work was originally published in 1869.
21. Michael Ryan, M.D., *Prostitution in London with a Comparative View of That of Paris and New York* (London: H. Baillière, 1839), pp. 168-69. Ryan based his estimate on the researches of a Mr. Talbot, secretary of the London Society for the Prevention of Juvenile Prostitution. He at the same time ignored a much lower estimate by a Mr. Mayne, a metropolitan police commissioner.

22. The skeptical reader was Mayne, the above-mentioned police commissioner, whose remarks were quoted with little sympathy by the Rev. Ralph Wardlaw, *Lectures on Magdalenism: Its Nature, Extent, Effects, Guilt, Causes and Remedy* (reprinted, New York: J. S. Redfield, 1843), pp. 41-43.

23. Ryan, op. cit., pp. 170-71.

24. This is the testimony of William Watts, M.D., resident medical officer of the Nottingham Poor Law Union, *Parliamentary Papers*, 1843, vol. XIV, p. 58, and reprinted in Royston Pike, *Hard Times* (New York: Praeger, 1966), p. 294.

25. William Osburn, *Parliamentary Papers*, 1831-32, vol. XV, p. 467, and Pike, op. cit., p. 294.

26. Mayhew, op. cit., IV, 201.

27. Hemyng in Mayhew, op. cit., IV, 259-60.

28. William Acton, *Prostitution, Considered in Its Moral, Social, & Sanitary Aspects* (London: John Churchill, 1857), pp. v-vi.

29. Patrick Colquhoun, *A Treatise on the Police of Metropolis*, 6th ed. (London: Joseph Mawman, 1800), p. 340-41.

30. Benjamin Bradshaw, cloth dresser of Holbeck Moor in evidence, *Parliamentary Papers*, 1831-32, XV, p. 159, and in Pike, op. cit., p. 298.

31. Richard Carlile, "What is Love," *The Republican*, XI (1825), pp. 562-64. Part of this is reprinted in Pike, op. cit., pp. 301-03.

32. See Anita Leslie, *Mrs. Fitzherbert* (New York: Charles Scribner's Sons, 1960); Queen Caroline, for her part, was accused of adultery. See Roger Fulford, *The Trial of Queen Caroline* (New York: Stein and Day, 1968).

33. See Lesley Blanch, editor, *The Game of Hearts: Harriette Wilson's Memoirs Interspersed with Excerpts from the Confessions of Julia Johnstone, Her Rival* (New York: Simon and Schuster, 1955), p. 128.

34. Ibid., p. 230.

35. Ellen Moers, *The Dandy* (New York: Viking, 1960), pp. 32-33.

36. Blanch, op. cit., pp. 39-49.

37. Ibid., p. 56.

38. Ibid., pp. 63-67.

39. Ibid., p. 37.

40. Ibid., pp. 58, 68-69.

41. Ibid., pp. 46-50.

42. See Walter Sichel, *Emma Lady Hamilton* (New York: Dodd Mead and Company, 1907), for an earlier account, and Mollie Hardwick, *Emma, Lady Hamilton* (New York: Holt, Rinehart and Winston, 1969), for a more recent one.

43. Cyril Pearl, *The Girl with the Swansdown Seat* (Indianapolis: Bobbs-Merrill, 1955), pp. 143-45.

44. For brief accounts of some of them, along with illustrations, see Claude Blanchard, *Dames de Coeur* (Paris: Editions du Pré aux clercs, 1946).

45. Pearl, op. cit., p. 147.

46. Ibid., pp. 147-52.

47. See Simone André Maurois, *Miss Howard and the Emperor* (New York: Alfred A. Knopf, 1957).

48. Roger L. Williams, *Gaslight and Shadow: The World of Napoleon III* (New York: Macmillan, 1957), pp. 140-61.

49. Pearl, op. cit., pp. 126-40.

50. Much has been written about Lola Montez, not all of it accurate. See Isaac Goldberg, *Queen of Hearts* (New York: John Day Company, 1936); Helen Holdredge, *The Woman in Black* (New York: G. P. Putnam's Sons, 1955); Doris Foley, *The Divine Eccentric: Lola Montez and the Newspapers* (Los Angeles: Westerlore Press, 1969).

51. See Gustave Flaubert, *Madame Bovary* (New York: International Collectors Library, 1949); Enid Starkie, *Flaubert: The Making of the Master* (London: Weidenfield and Nicolson, 1967); and especially Francis Steegmuller, *Flaubert and Madame Bovary: A Double Portrait* (London: Collins, 1947).

52. Alexandre Dumas, *Camille* (New York: Modern Library, n.d.); Jean Prasteau, *The Lady of the Camellias*, translated by Stella Rodway (London: Hutchinson, 1965).

53. See Joanna Richardson, *The Courtesans: The Demi-Monde in 19th-Century France* (Cleveland: World Publishing, 1967).

Chapter 11

1. Edmund S. Morgan, *The Puritan Family*, new edition revised and enlarged (New York: Harper & Row, 1966), p. 115.

2. Ibid., pp. 127-32. See also Edmund S. Morgan, "The Puritans and Sex," *The New England Quarterly*, XV (1942); Emil Oberholzer, *Delinquent Saints* (New York: Columbia University Press, 1956).

3. *Records of the Colony of New Plymouth in New England, 1631-1691*, edited by Nathaniel B. Shurtleff, David Pulsifier (Massachusetts, Published by Order of the General Court, William White, Printer to the Commonwealth, 1855-1861), IV, 106 (1665).

4. *Records of the Suffolk County Court, 1671-1680*, published as vols. 29 and 30 of *Collections of the Colonial Society of Massachusetts*, introduction by Zechariah Chafee, Jr. (Boston, 1933), XXIX, 82-83 (1672).

5. Quoted in Edwin Powers, *Crime and Punishment in Early Massachusetts* (Boston: Beacon Press, 1966), pp. 179-80.

6. For a discussion of this, see David H. Flaherty, *Privacy in Colonial New England* (Charlottesville: University Press of Virginia, 1972), pp. 212-13.

7. See, for example, Arthur W. Calhoun, *A Social History of the American Family*, 3 vols. in 1 (reprinted, New York: Barnes and Noble, 1945), I, 312-29.

8. The eminent historian John Fiske, *The Dutch and Quaker Colonies in America*, 2 vols. (Boston: Houghton Mifflin, 1899), II, 65, says the lane was so named because women did their washing there. This explanation seems to be more of an attempt by a historian to ignore sex than face reality.

9. Alexander Hamilton, *Gentleman's Progress: The Itinerarium of Dr. Alexander Hamilton, 1744* (Chapel Hill: University of North Carolina Press, 1948), pp. 46, 151.

10. Flaherty, op. cit., p. 180.

11. There are many editions of Franklin's *Autobiography*. The original manuscript is in the Huntington Library, San Marino, California. A facsimile copy of this, edited by Max Farrand, was published by the University of California Press, 1949. Franklin's advice on choosing a mistress is also available in many editions, but can easily be found in Benjamin Franklin, *Satires and Bagatelles*, edited by Paul McPharlin (Detroit: Fine Book Circle, 1937).

12. Médérick Louis Élie Moreau de St. Méry, *Moreau de St. Méry's American Journey, 1793-1798*, edited and translated by Kenneth Roberts and Anna Roberts (New York: Doubleday, 1947), pp. 287-88.

13. Calhoun, op. cit., I, 333-36.

14. Richard Henry Dana, *Two Years Before the Mast* (reprinted, Cleveland: World Publishing, 1946), chap. 21, p. 194.

15. Calhoun, op. cit., II, 171-99.

16. Marcus L. Hansen, *The Immigrant in American History* (Cambridge, Mass.: Harvard University Press, 1940), p. 114.

17. See Robert E. Riegel, "Changing American Attitudes Toward Prostitution," *Journal of the History of Ideas*, XXIX (1968), 437-38. The article is most helpful.

18. *New York Morning Courier*, June 3, 4, 6, 7, 8, 10, 1836, and Riegel, op. cit., p. 439.

19. *The Ladies' Garland* (Philadelphia), April 18, 1837, 1:3.

20. *The American Museum* (Philadelphia) August, 1787, 2:206.

21. *Advocate of Moral Reform*, August 15, 1870, XXVI, 248, and June 1, 1869, XXXV, 123-28.

22. Earnest E. Calkins, *They Broke the Prairie* (New York: Charles Scribner's Sons, 1937), p. 167.

23. Riegel, op. cit., p. 443.

24. Philip D. Jordan, *The People's Health* (St. Paul, Minnesota, Historical Society, 1948), p. 246.

25. See Curt Gentry, *The Madams of San Francisco* (New York: Doubleday, 1964), pp. 30-31.

26. Quoted in ibid., p. 41. See also Sarah Royce, *A Frontier Lady's Recollections of the Gold Rush and Early California,* edited by Ralph Henry Gabriel (New Haven, Conn.: Yale University Press, 1932), passim.

27. Bret Harte, *Selected Stories of Bret Harte* (Chicago: Puritan Publishing Company, n.d.). There are many editions.

28. See, for example, Max Miller, *Holladay Street* (New York: Signet Books, 1962), which deals with prostitutes in Colorado; Ronald Dean Miller, *Shady Ladies of the West* (Los Angeles: Westerlore Press, 1964); Joseph W. Snell, *Painted ladies of the Cowtown Frontier* (New York: Dodd, Mead, 1969); Zeke Daniels, *The Life and Death of Julia C. Bulette* (Virginia City: Lamp Post, 1958); Duncan Aikman, *Calamity Jane and the Lady Wildcats* (New York: Henry Holt, 1927); Herbert Asbury, *The Barbary Coast* (New York: Alfred A. Knopf, 1933); Dee Brown, *The Gentle Tamers: Women of the Old West* (New York: G. P. Putnam's Sons, 1958); Ella M. Cain, *The Story of Bodie* (San Francisco: Fearon Publishers, 1956); Helen Holdredge, *Mammy Pleasant* (New York: G. P. Putnam's Sons, 1953); James D. Horan, *Desperate Women* (New York: G. P. Putnam's Sons, 1953); John Willard Horner, *Silver Town* (Caldwell, Idaho: Caxton Printers, 1950); E. Hueston, *Calamity Jane of Deadwood Gulch* (Indianapolis: Bobbs-Merrill, 1937); Nancy Wilson Ross, *Westward the Women* (New York: Alfred A. Knopf, 1944); Stanley Vestal, *Queen of Cowtowns, Dodge City* (New York: Harper & Brothers, 1952); Benjamin Lloyd, *Lights and Shades of San Francisco* (San Francisco: A. L. Bancroft, 1876). There are many others.

29. See, for example, *San Francisco Call,* November 28, 1869; *San Francisco Chronicle,* December 5, 1869, and the various books cited above. Research on Western prostitution was done by Laurie Rosenfeld, a student in one of my classes.

30. The census of 1870 is quoted in Snell, op. cit., p. 14.

31. For a description of some of the brass checks, see Fred and Jo Mazzulla, *Brass Checks and Red Lights* (Denver, privately printed, 1966).

32. William L. Sanger, *The History of Prostitution* (New York: Harper & Brothers, 1858), p. 460. The book has often been reprinted, A copy of the first edition can be found in the Newberry Library in Chicago, among other places.

33. George J. Kneeland, *Commercialized Prostitution in New York City* (New York: The Century Company, 1913), p. 251.

34. Asbury, op. cit., pp. 164-97.

35. *San Francisco Chronicle,* December 5, 1869.

36. Sanger, op. cit., p. 20.

37. For statements in favor of reglementation, see the *Nation,* February 21, 1867, IV, 153-54; *California Medical Gazette,* I (1869), 171.

38. Howard B. Woolston, *Prostitution in the United States* (New York: The Century Company, 1921), pp. 26-29. This work is listed as volume 1, but no second volume was ever published.

39. See John C. Burnham, "Medical Inspection of Prostitutes in America in the Nineteenth Century: The St. Louis Experiment and Its Sequel," *Bulletin of the History of Medicine,* XLV (1971), 203-18. See also the appendix in the revised edition of Sanger, *The History of Prostitution* (new edition reprinted, New York: Eugenics Publishing Company, 1937), pp. 694-97.

40. S. D. Gross, "Syphilis in Its Relation to the National Health," American Medical Association, *Transactions,* XXV (1874), 249-92. See also Burnham, op. cit., p. 210.

41. J. Marion Sims, "Address of J. Marion Sims, M.D., President of the Association," American Medical Association, *Transactions,* XXVII (1876), 100-111.

42. Woolston, op. cit., p. 30.

43. Logan, op. cit., pp. 243-65, summarizes activites in Minneapolis and St. Paul, although not quite in such terms.

44. Ibid., pp. 119-20.

45. Ibid., p. 104.

46. Ibid., pp. 104-05.

47. Sanger, op. cit., pp. 549-74 (posthumous edition).

48. For this, see Charles Washburn, *Come Into My Parlor* (New York: Knickerbocker Publishing Co., 1934); Herbert Asbury, *Gem of the Prairie* (New York: Alfred A. Knopf, 1960).

356 NOTES

49. The *"Blue Book"—A Bibliographical Attempt to Describe the Guide Books to the Houses of Ill Fame in New Orleans* by *"Semper Idem"* (Heartman's Historical Series, n. 50, 1936), passim. The Chicago Historical Society has a directory for Chicago, *The Sporting and Club House Directory, Chicago: Containing a Full and Complete List of All Strictly First Class Club and Sporting Houses* (Chicago: Ross & St. Clair, 1889). Many other cities have similar books.
50. The Los Angeles directory was reprinted in a booklet by W. W. Robinson, *Tarnished Angels*, printed for members of the Roxburghe Club and the Zamorano Club, September, 1964, by the Ward Ritchie Press.
51. Nell Kimball, *Nell Kimball: Her Life as an American Madam*, with introduction by Stephen Longstreet (New York: Macmillan, 1970), p. 219.
52. Washburne, op. cit., passim. The Chicago Historical Society has a brochure put out by the sisters in 1902, titled *The Everleigh Club*.
53. Chicago Vice Commission, *The Social Evil in Chicago* (Chicago: Gunthrop-Warren Printing Company, 1911).
54. An example of a city commission is the Committee of Eighteen, *The Social Evil in Syracuse* (Syracuse, New York: Moral Survey Committee, 1913), and of a state one, *Report and Recommendations of the Wisconsin Legislative Committee to Investigate the White Slave Traffic and Kindred Subjects* (Madison, Wis.: Democrat Printing Company, 1914).
55. Woolston, op. cit., pp. 132-33. For a semischolarly account of some of them, see Craig Scott, *The Houses They Lived In* (North Hollywood, Calif.: Brandon House Books, 1963).
56. Washburn, op. cit., passim.
57. Holdredge, op. cit., passim.
58. Nell Kimball, op. cit., passim. Dreiser's brother spelled his name Dresser.
59. Theodore Dreiser, *Sister Carrie*.
60. Drago, op. cit., pp. 208-22.
61. For a discussion of some of these writers, see Mary Noel, *Villains Galore* (New York: Macmillan, 1954). One of Buntline's more famous creations was Buffalo Bill, thinly based on the life of W. F. Cody. Buntline wrote more than 400 novels. His novels of New York include *The Mysteries and Miseries of New York* (New York: Belford & Company, 1848), and *The Wheel of Fortune* (New York: Garrett & Company, 1853).
62. Rebecca Harding Davis, *Margaret Howth* (Boston: Ticknor and Fields, 1862).
63. Edgar Fawcett, *The Evil That Men Do* (New York: Belford Company [1889]).
64. Stephen Crane, *Maggie* (Gainesville, Florida: Scholars' Facsimiles and Reprints, 1966).

Chapter 12

1. See Lester S. King, *The Medical World of the Eighteenth Century* (Chicago: University of Chicago Press, 1958).
2. See Joseph Needham, *A History of Embryology* (New York: Abelard-Schuman, 1959), and Clifford Dobell, *Antony van Leeuwenhoek and His "Little Animals"* (New York: Russell and Russell, 1958).
3. Hermann Boerhaave, *Institutiones medicae*, in *Opera Medica Universa* (Geneva: Fratres de Tournes, 1728).
4. John Brown, *The Elements of Medicine*, revised by Thomas Beddoes, 2 vols. in 1 (Portsmouth, N.H.: William and Daniel Treadwell, 1803), and King, op. cit., pp. 143-49.
5. See S. A. D. Tissot, *Dissertatio de Febribus Biliosis . . . Tentamen de Morbis ex Manustupratione* (Lausanne: Marci-Mic Bousequet, 1758). The work was translated into various languages and usually much amplified by the translator. An early edition in English was entitled *Onanism; or, A Treatise Upon the Disorders of Masturbation*, translated by A. Hume (London: J. Pridden, 1766).
6. Michael Ryan, *Prostitution in London, with a Comparative View of That of Paris and New York* (London: H. Baillière, 1839).
7. Sylvester Graham, *Lecture to Young Men* (Providence, R.I.: Weeden and Cory, 1834; reprinted, New York: Arno Press, 1974), pp. 32-33.
8. Ibid., p. 35.

9. Claude-François Lallemand, *On Involuntary Seminal Discharges*, translated by William Wood (Philadelphia: A. Waldie, 1839).

10. J. H. Kellogg, *Plain Facts for Old and Young* (Burlington, Iowa, 1882; reprinted, Buffalo, New York, Heritage Press, 1974), pp. 400-401.

11. E. P. Miller, *A Treatise on the Cause of Exhausted Vitality; or, Abuses of the Sexual Function* (New York: John A. Gray and Green, 1867), p. 77.

12. William Acton, *The Functions and Disorders of the Reproductive Organs in Childhood, Youth, Adult Age, and Advanced Life Considered in Their Physiological, Social, and Moral Relations*, 5th ed. (London: J. & A. Churchill, 1871).

13. William Acton, *Prostitution, Considered in Its Moral, Social & Sanitary Aspects* (London: John Churchill, 1857), p. 15.

14. Ibid., p. 20.

15. Ibid., chap. IX, pp. 161-89.

16. Caesar Lombroso and William Ferrero, *Female Offender* (reprinted, New York: Philosophical Library, 1958), passim.

17. Charles Samson Féré, *Sexual Degeneration in Mankind and in Animals*, translated by Ulrich Van Der Horst, (reprinted, New York: Anthropological Press, 1932), pp. 284-85.

18. For a discussion of some of these concepts, see Erich Wulffen, *Woman as a Sexual Criminal*, translated by David Berger (New York: American Ethnological Press, 1934), pp. 493-522, and Havelock Ellis, *Sex in Relation to Society* in *Studies in the Psychology of Sex*, 2 vols. (reprinted, New York: Random House, 1936), II, part 3, 266-80. The discussion by Ellis is under the general description of biology of prostitution.

19. Richard von Krafft-Ebing, *Psychopathia Sexualis*, translated by Charles Gilbert Chaddock (Philadelphia: F. A. Davis, 1894), pp. 13-14. The book was first published in 1886.

20. Ellis, op. cit., pp. 268-70.

21. Ibid., p. 273, and *Jahrbuch für Sexuell Zwischenstufen, Jahrgang* VII, (1905), 148.

22. See, for example, Sigmund Freud, *Collected Papers*, translated under the direction of Joan Riviere et al., 5 vols. (New York: Basic Books, 1959). Pertinent papers include "The Defense of Neuro-Psychoses," I, 66; "Sexuality and the Aetiology of the Neuroses," I, 220-48, and "Female Sexuality," V, 252-72; Sigmund Freud, *The Standard Edition of the Complete Psychological Works of Sigmund Freud* (London: Hogarth Press, 1971), I, 180; III, 150; see also William Graham Cole, *Sex in Christianity and Psychoanalysis* (New York: Oxford University Press, 1955), pp. 199-236.

23. Karl Abraham, *Selected Papers*, translated by Douglas Bryan and Alix Strachey (London: Hogarth Press, 1942), chap. XXII, "Manifestations of the Female Castration Complex," p. 361. This paper was written in 1920.

24. Edward Glover, *The Psycho-pathology of Prostitution* (London: Institute for the Scientific Treatment of Delinquency, 1945), p. 4. This paper was also reprinted in Glover, *The Roots of Crime* (New York: International Universities Press, 1960), pp. 244-67.

25. Frank Caprio and Donald Brenner, *Sexual Behavior: Psycho-Legal Aspects* (New York: Citadel Press, 1961), p. 249-52.

26. A. J. B. Parent-Duchâtelet, *De la prostitution dans la ville de Paris*, 2 vols. (Paris, J. B. Baillière, 1836), I, 28-38.

27. Ibid., I, 38-55.

28. Ibid., I, 55-63.

29. Ibid., I, 65-70.

30. Ibid., I, 83-89.

31. Ibid., I, 76-83.

32. Ibid., I, 89-102. Some of the figures include the same person more than once.

33. William Tait, *Magdalenism, An Inquiry into the Extent, Causes, and Consequences of Prostitution in Edinburgh* (Edinburgh: 1840), p. 25.

34. Ibid., p. 24.

35. Ibid., pp. 26, 29-31, 36-37.

36. Ibid., p. 22.

37. Bracebridge Hemyng, "Prostitution in London," in Henry Mayhew, *London Labour and the London Poor*, 4 vols. (reprinted, New York: Dover Books, 1968), IV, 210-72. The original work was published in 1861.

38. William L. Sanger, *The History of Prostitution* (new edition reprinted, New York: Eugenics Publishing Company, 1897).

39. George J. Kneeland, *Commercialized Prostitution in New York City* (New York: The Century Co., 1913), p. 251.

40. A. Desprès, *La prostitution en France* (Paris: J. B. Baillière et fils, 1883).

41. Ellis, op. cit., II, part iii, 263-64.

42. See Ralph Wardlaw, *Lectures on Magdalenism: Its Nature, Extent, Effects, Guilt, Causes and Remedy* (reprinted, New York: J. S. Redfield, 1843), p. 166; John Blackmore, *The London by Moonlight Mission* (London: Robson and Avery, 1860), and various other accounts, particularly by religious reformers.

43. Edward F. Payne and Henry H. Harper, *The Charity of Charles Dickens, His Interest in the Home for Fallen Women and a History of the Strange Case of Caroline Maynard Thompson* (Boston: Printed for Members of the Bibliophile Society, 1929), passim.

44. Caroline H. Dall, *The College, The Market, and the Court* (Boston: Lee and Shepard, 1867), p. 135.

45. Caroline Wells Healey Dall, *Woman's Right to Labor* (Boston: Walker, Wise & Co., 1860), p. 15.

46. For the source of this quotation and a more extended discussion, see Robert E. Riegel, "Changing American Attitudes Toward Prostitution," *Journal of the History of Ideas,* XIX (1968), 437-52.

47. Emily Blackwell writing in *Woman's Journal,* 41 (February 5, 1910), 23.

48. Charlotte Gilman, "The Oldest Profession in the World," *The Forerunner,* IV (March, 1913), 65.

49. See Jane Addams, *A New Conscience and an Ancient Evil* (New York: Macmillan Company, 1913), passim.

50. H. B. Blackwell in *Woman's Journal,* XXVI (December 21, 1895), p. 402.

51. Edward H. Clarke, *Sex in Education; or A Fair Chance for Girls* (Boston: James R. Osgood & Company, 1874), pp. 37-41. For a more complete discussion of this, see Vern Bullough and Martha Voght, "Women, Menstruation, and Nineteenth Century Medicine," *Bulletin of the History of Medicine,* XLVII (1973), 66-82.

52. Emma Goldman, *Mother Earth,* VIII (1913), 211.

53. Some evidence for this assumption can be found in the surveys made by Clelia Duel Mosher (1863-1940). Extracts of the papers, the originals of which are in the Stanford University Archives, were published in Carl N. Degler, "What Ought to Be and What Was: Women's Sexuality in the Nineteenth Century," *American Historical Review,* LXXIX (December, 1974), 1467-90.

54. For some probability samples, see Mindel C. Sheps and Jane A. Menken, *Mathematical Models of Conception and Birth* (Chicago: University of Chicago Press, 1973).

55. Abortion before quickening was not considered an abortion in most states until the last part of the nineteenth century. See Lawrence Ladder, *Abortion* (Indianapolis: Bobbs-Merrill, 1966), pp. 75-93.

56. See, for example, Steven Marcus, *The Other Victorians* (New York: Basic Books, 1966).

57. Quoted and translated by Norman Himes, *Medical History of Contraception* (reprinted, New York: Schocken Books, 1970), p. 190.

58. Ibid., pp. 182-83.

59. Ibid., pp. 321-22. For a discussion of the various devices as they existed in the 1920s, see, James F. Cooper, *Technique of Contraception* (New York: Day-Nichols, 1928).

60. See W. P. J. Mensinga, *Über facultative sterilität I. Beleuchet von prophylactischen und hygenischen standpunkte für practische aerzte. II. Das pessarium occulsium und dessen applikation* (Neuwid und Leipzig, 1885). This is not the first edition.

61. A good discussion of the chemical contraceptives from the viewpoint of the 1930s can be found in Cecil I. B. Voge, *The Chemistry and Physics of Contraceptives* (London: Jonathan Cape, 1933).

62. Thomas Robert Malthus, *An Essay on the Principle of Population* (London: 1803), p. 11. This is the second edition.

63. Francis Place, *Illustrations and Proofs of the Principle of Population,* with an introduction, critical notes, and unpublished letters, edited by Norman E. Himes (London: George Allen & Unwin, 1930).

64. For further discussion, see Peter Fryer, *The Birth Controllers* (London: Secker & Warburg, 1965), pp. 43-57, 72-74; a reproduction of his handbill is published in Himes, op. cit., pp. 216-17.

65. Fryer, op. cit., pp. 92-93; Himes, op. cit., pp. 224-25. The booklet went through several editions and had sold approximately 60,000 copies up to 1874.

66. The quotation is from Charles Knowlton, *Fruits of Philosophy*, annotated and with comments by Norman E. Himes and Robert Latou Dickinson (Mount Vernon, N.Y.: Peter Pauper Press, 1937), p. 60. Himes and Dickinson based their edition on the tenth edition of Knowlton. Many of the pirated editions added other methods, although none of these can be traced to Knowlton.

67. [George Drysdale], *The Elements of Social Science: or Physical, Sexual and Natural Religion*, 3rd edition enlarged (London: Trulove, 1860).

68. For some of these works, see Lothrop Stoddard, *The Rising Tide of Color* (New York: Charles Scribner's Sons, 1922), and *The Revolt Against Civilization* (New York: Charles Schribner's Sons, 1923), or Alfred P. Schultz, *Race or Mongrel* (Boston: L. C. Page & Company, 1908). For a continuation of such views in somewhat more gentlemanly form, see Carleton Putnam, *Race and Reason* (Washington, D.C.: Public Affairs Press, 1961).

69. Norman St. John-Stevas, *Obscenity and the Law* (London: Secker & Warburg, 1956), pp. 66-67.

70. Ibid., pp. 70, 126-27.

71. Ibid., pp. 70-74.

72. Annie Besant, *Law of Population* (London: Freethought Publishing Company, 1879).

73. Himes, op. cit., pp. 243-50.

74. For a good discussion of the reasons for the American censorship movements, see Paul S. Boyer, *Purity in Print* (New York: Charles Scribner's Sons, 1968).

75. Edward B. Foote, *Plain Home Talk* (New York: Murray Hill Publishing Company, 1887), has a passing reference to his difficulties with the law. Foote wrote that he could not advise his readers of the effective ways of contraception and that he had to withdraw *Words in Pearl* from circulation. (Ibid., p. 880).

76. For a discussion of Mrs. Sanger's work, see her own autobiography written in 1938, published under the title *Margaret Sanger: An Autobiography* (republished, New York: Dover Books, 1971). There are several other biographies of her that we have relied on rather heavily, including Lawrence Lader, *The Margaret Sanger Story* (New York: Doubleday, 1955).

77. In addition to Fryer, op. cit., see Clive Wood and Beryl Suitters, *The Fight for Acceptance* (Aylesbury, England: Medical and Technical Publishing Company, 1970), for discussion of the English situation.

78. For more detail, see Vern L. Bullough, *The Subordinate Sex* (Urbana, Ill.: University of Illinois Press, 1973), and the references therein.

79. Drysdale, op. cit., p. 351. Italics ours.

80. Quoted by J. A. and Olive Banks, *Feminism and Family Planning in Victorian England* (New York: Schocken Books, 1964), p. 116. Italics ours.

81. Victoria C. Woodhull, *The Elixir of Life* (New York: Woodhull & Claflin, 1873).

Chapter 13

1. We have dealt with the reforming efforts of Miss Nightingale in Vern and Bonnie Bullough, *The Emergence of Modern Nursing* (New York: Macmillan, 1964; revised edition, 1969).

2. For the background, see Glen Petrie, *A Singular Iniquity* (New York: Viking Press, 1971), pp. 5-68, which is an account of Josephine Butler's campaigns. See her own autobiography, *Personal Reminiscences of a Great Crusade* (London: Horace Marshall & Sons, 1896), as well as A. S. G. Butler, *Portrait of Josephine Butler* (London: Faber and Faber Ltd., 1954), E. M. Turner, *Josephine Butler: An Appreciation* (London: The Association for Moral and Social Hygiene, 1928), and Millicent Fawcett, *Josephine Butler* (London: The Association for Moral and Social Hygiene, 1927).

3. Josephine E. Butler in her introduction to *Woman's Work and Woman's Culture*, (London: Macmillan, 1869).

4. Quoted by Josephine Butler, *Personal Reminiscences of a Great Crusade*, p. 9.

5. Quoted by E. M. Sigsworth and T. J. Wyke, "A Study of Victorian Prostitution and Venereal Disease," in Martha Vicinus, *Suffer and Be Still* (Bloomington, Ind.: University of Indiana Press, 1972), p. 97.

6. Lujo Basserman, *The Oldest Profession,* translated by James Cleugh (New York: Stein and Day, 1967), p. 244. For a realistic survey of reglementation in England, see Judith Walkowitz, *The Making of an Outcast Group: Prostitutes and Working Women in 19th Century Plymouth and Southampton,* "In a Widening Sphere," *Changing Roles of Victorian Women,* edited by Martha Vicinus (Bloomington, Ind.: University of Indiana Press, 1977).

7. Josephine Butler, *Recollections of George Butler* (Bristol: Arrowsmith, 1892), p. 282.

8. Petrie, op. cit., p. 195.

9. Butler, *Personal Reminiscences of a Great Crusade,* pp. 294-300.

10. Thomas Borel, *The White Slavery of Europe,* translated by Joseph Edmondson (London: Dyer Brothers, n.d. [1876]); a second English edition appeared in 1880. The original French edition, however, was entitled *Un Question sociale* (Neuchâtel, 1876). This would make the publisher Dyer the popularizer of the term *white slave.*

11. Even earlier, on March 20, 1870, Victor Hugo in a letter to Josephine Butler in 1870 had written that "the slavery of black women is abolished in America, but the slavery of white women continues in Europe," Butler, *Personal Reminiscences of a Great Crusade,* p. 36. Still earlier the term had been applied to factory workers in England. Probably it was one of those terms that several people hit upon at the same time. See also Adolph F. Niemoeller, *Sexual Slavery in America* (New York: Panurge Press, 1935), pp. 121-23, and Howard B. Woolston, *Prostitution in the United States* (New York: The Century Company, 1921), p. 159.

12. Charles Terrot, *Traffic in Innocents* (New York: E. P. Dutton, 1960), pp. 13-21.

13. William Acton, *Prostitution, Considered in Its Moral, Social & Sanitary Aspects* (London: John Churchill, 1857), p. 175.

14. *My Secret Life,* introduction by G. Legman, eleven vols. (reprinted, New York: Grove Press, 1966) XI, 2191-92.

15. Ibid., V, 1035-36.

16. Ibid., II, 206.

17. Terrot, op. cit., pp. 22-40.

18. Ibid., p. 44.

19. Petrie, op. cit., p. 210.

20. Alfred Dyer, *Six Years' Labour and Sorrow: The Fourth Report of the London Committee for Suppressing the Traffic in British Girls for the Purposes of Continental Prostitution* (London: Dyer Brothers, 1885), p. 2.

21. Alfred Dyer, *The European Slave Trade in English Girls* (London: Dyer Brothers, 1880).

22. Petrie, op. cit., pp. 216-17.

23. Josephine Butler, *A Letter to the Mothers of England* (Liverpool: Brakell, 1881).

24. Petrie, op. cit., p. 217.

25. Pearson, op. cit., pp. 109-12; Terrot, op. cit., pp. 90-96.

26. This account is essentially based on the account in Terrot, op. cit., pp. 117-31, and some parts of Mrs. Jeffries' background cannot be documented except through him, although her activities are reported in many other sources. Terrot's source for much of the information was Rosa Lewis, onetime mistress of Edward VII when he was prince of Wales. See Michael Pearson, *The 5 Virgins* (New York: Saturday Review Press, 1972), p. 106.

27. Petrie, op. cit., pp. 240-41; Pearson, op. cit., pp. 109-11.

28. See *Select Committee of the House of Lords, to enquire into the law relating to the protection of young girls* (1881-82), and Petrie, op. cit., p. 227; Terrot, op. cit., pp. 117-31.

29. Perhaps the best and most even-handed account of Stead's campaign is that by Michael Pearson cited above. See also the *Pall Mall Gazette* for the period under discussion, and the account by Terrot, op. cit., passim. The two works by Stead dealing with America are *If Christ Came to Chicago* (Chicago: Laird and Lee, 1894), and *Satan's Invisible World Displayed* (New York: R. F. Fenno, 1897).

30. The original countries were France, Germany, Great Britain, Italy, Russia, Sweden, Denmark, Belgium, Holland, Spain, Portugal, Norway, and Switzerland. Later Austria-Hungary, Brazil, and the United States adhered to the terms. The treaty is reprinted in the House of Representatives, 59 Cong., 1 Sess., *Foreign Relations,* 1905, Document No. 729, pp. 462-64, and *Statutes at Large,* XXXV, 1979-84.

31. David Pivar, *Purity Crusade, Sexual Morality, and Social Control, 1868-1900* (Westport, Conn.: Greenwood Press, 1973). Pivar's book is an excellent survey of much of the background.

32. Committee of Fifteen, *The Social Evil* (New York: G. P. Putnam's Sons, 1902). Harold U. Faulkner, *The Quest for Social Justice* (New York: Macmillan, 1931), p. 159, called this the first serious attack on the problem in the United States, but this is simply not the case. A similar misconception was perpetuated by Louis Filler, *Crusaders for American Liberalism* (New York: Collier's, 1961), p. 266, who notes that Alvin J. Johnson, who prepared the section on the history of prostitution for the committee, "had to use foreign authorities exclusively, there being no reliable American sources." This is to ignore the work of William Sanger and other reformers of an earlier generation.

33. See, for example, Lincoln Steffens, "Pittsburgh: A City Ashamed," *McClure's*, XXI (May, 1903), 24-39; George Kibbe Turner, "The City of Chicago," ibid., XXVIII (April, 1907), 575-92. There were also reports on what was taking place in Europe, in addition to the Stead appearances in such publications as the *Contemporary Review*. See, for example, "The White Slave Trade," *Contemporary Review*, LXXXII (November, 1902), 735-40. See Filler, op. cit., pp. 267-69.

34. George Kibbe Turner, "The Daughters of the Poor," *McClure's*, XXIV (November, 1909), pp. 45-61.

35. Brand Whitlock, "The White Slave," *Forum*, LI (February, 1914), 193-216.

36. James D. Richardson, compiler *Messages and Papers of the Presidents* (Washington, D.C.: 1913), VI, 4242. *Statutes at Large*, XVIII, 477-78.

37. United States v. Johnson, 7 Fed. (1881), 453.

38. *Statutes at Large*, XXII, 1213.

39. Ibid., XXIV, 898.

40. United States v. Bitty, 208 U.S. 393 (1908).

41. Keller v. United States, 213 U.S. 138 (1909).

42. U.S. Senate, 61 Cong., 2 Sess. *Reports*, No. 886 (Serial 5584), 15-18.

43. "Suppression of the White Slave Traffic," Senate Document No. 214 (Serial 5657). The committee noted that 143 prostitutes and 43 procurers had been barred in 1908, and 323 prostitutes and 181 procurers the next year.

44. "Importation and Harboring of Women for Immoral Purposes," U.S. Senate, 61 Cong., 2 Sess., *Documents*, No. 196 (Serial 5662).

45. *Statutes at Large*, XXXVI, 263.

46. See Clifford G. Roe, *The Great War on White Slavery* (n. p., 1911).

47. *Statutes at Large*, XXXVI, 825.

48. United States v. Hoke, 227 U.S. 308 (1913). For a discussion, see Edward S. Corwin, *The Commerce Power versus States Rights* (Princeton: Princeton University Press, 1936), pp. 103-05, 166.

49. Athanasaw v. United States, 227 U.S. 326 (1913).

50. Caminetti, v. United States, 242 U.S. 470 (1917).

51. For some articles dealing with this, see Martin J. McManus, "Comments," *Southern California Law Review*, XIX (March 1946), 250-56; "Interstate Immorality: The Mann Act and the Supreme Court," *Yale Law Journal*, LVI (April, 1947), 718-30; Lewis C. Nelson, "A Re-examination of the Purpose of the White Slave Traffic Act," *George Washington Law Review*, XV (February, 1947), 214-15. There are many others.

52. Niemoeller, op. cit., p. 195. For a discussion of blackmailing that allegedly resulted from the operation of the Mann Act, see Mark Sullivan, *Our Times*, 6 vols. (New York: Charles Scribner's 1926-35), IV, 135, as well as Berkely Davids, "Application of Mann Act to Non-Commercial Vice," *Law Notes*, XX (1916), 144-46.

53. Martensen v. United States, 322 U.S. 369 (1944).

54. Cleveland v. United States, 329 U.S. 14 (1946).

55. Quoted by John C. Burnham, "The Progressive Era Revolution in American Attitudes Toward Sex," *Journal of American History*, LIX (March 1973), 885-908; the quote is from p. 504. We are indebted to Burnham for some of the ideas in this section.

56. For a discussion of some of these laws, see T. E. James, *Prostitution and the Law* (London: William Heinemann, 1951), Appendix C; Morris Ploscowe, *Sex and the Law*, rev. ed. (New York: Ace Books, 1962), pp. 225-51; Leon Kanowitz, *Sex Roles in Law and Society* (Albuquerque: University of New Mexico Press, 1973), pp. 89-97.

57. Ploscowe, op. cit., p. 237. See also Charles Winick and Paul M. Kinsie, *The Lively Commerce; Prostitution in the United States* (Chicago: Quadrangle Books, 1971), pp. 221-23.

58. For a discussion of the army in World War II, see U.S. Army Medical Department, *Preventive Medicine in World War II*, vol. V, *Communicable Diseases* (Washington: Office of the Surgeon General, 1960).

59. Kanowitz, op. cit., pp. 94-95.

60. League of Nations, Advisory Committee on Social Questions, *Prevention of Prostitution* (Geneva, 1943), Document C. 26. M. 26. 1943. IV, pp. 10-11.

61. Ibid., pp. 22-23.

62. The history of the efforts of the League to deal with prostitution has not yet been written. From the first session of the Advisory Commission for the Protection and Welfare of Children and Young People held at Lausanne in 1922 (M. 265.1922.IV) to the last meeting of the Advisory Committee on Social Questions in 1943 (C. 26. M. 26. 1943. IV) the League surveyed all aspects of prostitution. Reports covered such topics as "abolition of licensed houses," "prevention of prostitution," "traffic in women and children," "rehabilitation of prostitutes," "suppression of the exploitation of prostitution of others," all of which included some historical information.

63. See United Nations, *Study on Traffic in Persons and Prostitution* (New York: 1959), No. 59. IV. 5. See also S. Barclay, *Bondage: The Slave Traffic in Women Today* (New York: Funk and Wagnalls, 1968).

64. Quoted in Kanovitz, op. cit., p. 95. See also James, op. cit., pp. 91-108.

65. American Law Institute, *Model Penal Code: Proposed Official Draft 1962* (Philadelphia: American Law Institute, 1962), Section 251.2, pp. 233-36.

66. Willoughby C. Waterman, *Prostitution and Its Repression in New York City* (New York: Columbia University Press, 1932), pp. 117-59.

67. See Polly Adler, *A House Is Not a Home* (New York: Rinehart, 1953).

Chapter 14

1. For some data on this, see William H. Masters and Virginia E. Johnson, *Human Sexual Response* (Boston: Little, Brown, 1966).

2. For a discussion of this and some statistics, see Gy. Acsadi and J. Nemeskeri, *History of Human Life Span and Mortality* (Budapest: Akademia Kiado, 1970), pp. 182-86. See also Marcel R. Reinhard, André Armengaud, Jacques Dupaquier, *Histoire Génerale de la Population Mondiale* (Paris: Editions Montchrestien, 1968).

3. This has been developed at greater length in Vern Bullough, *Sexual Variance in Society and Culture* (New York: Wiley Interscience, 1976).

4. Ansley J. Coale and Melvin Zeinik, *New Estimates of Fertility and Population in the United States* (Princeton: Princeton University Press, 1963).

5. Herbert Asbury, "Hatrack," *The American Mercury*, VII (April, 1926), p. 479-83.

6. R. K. Merton, "Manifest and Latent Functions," in *Social Theory and Social Structure* (Glencoe, Ill.: Free Press, 1949).

7. Herbert J. Gans, "The Positive Functions of Poverty," *American Journal of Sociology*, LXXVIII (1972), 275-89.

8. Kingsley Davis, "The Sociology of Prostitution," *American Sociological Review*, II (1937), 744-55, and "Prostitution," in *Contemporary Social Problems*, edited by Robert K. Merton and Robert A. Nisbet (New York: Harcourt, Brace & World, 1961).

9. See, for example, V. Bronner, *La lutte contre la prostitution en USSR* (Moscow: 1936); Dyson Carter, *Sin and Society* (New York: Heck Cattell, 1946), passim, especially pp. 208-13; John Gunther, *Inside Russia Today* (New York: Harper and Brothers, 1957), p. 331, or the various dispatches of Harrison Salisbury to the *New York Times*, an example of which appeared on September 10, 1959. One of the difficulties the observer has is in recognizing the new forms of Soviet prostitution. For example, the Leningrad-to-Moscow train is used for prostitution, with prostitutes riding both ways, taking customers into their compartments, which they share, but the observer has to know what to look for. The interested reader will have to examine various accounts by newspaper reporters. For a survey of Russian laws on the subject, see T. E. James, *Prostitution and the Law* (London: William Heinemann, 1961), pp. 91-108. See also Yuri Brokhin, *Hustling on Gorky Street* (New York: Dial Press, 1975).

10. A whole list of such factors is given by Howard B. Woolston, *Prostitution in the United States* (New York: The Century Company, 1921), pp. 300-301, a work that is one of the pioneering sociological studies. See also Maude E. Miner, *Slavery of Prostitution* (New York: Macmillan Company, 1916), pp. 53-87; for another list, see the League of Nations, *Prevention of Prostitution*, Document No. C.26M.26.1943.IV, pp. 25-32. See also Mamoru Iga, "Sociocultural Factors in Japanese Prostitution and the 'Prostitution Prevention Law,'" *Journal of Sex Research*, IV (May 1968), 127-46.

11. Alfred C. Kinsey, Wardell B. Pomeroy, Clyde E. Martin, *Sexual Behavior in the Human Male* (Philadelphia: W. B. Saunders Company, 1948), pp. 596-609; especially p. 603.

12. William H. Masters and Virginia E. Johnson, *Human Sexual Inadequacy* (Boston: Little, Brown, 1970).

13. Martha L. Stein, *Lovers, Friends, Slaves: Nine Male Sexual Types: Their Psycho-Sexual Transactions with Call Girls* (New York: Berkley Publishing Corporation and G. P. Putnam's Sons, 1974).

14. Edward Glover, *The Psycho-pathology of Prostitution* (London: Institute for the Scientific Treatment of Delinquency, 1945); the paper was also reprinted in Glover, *The Roots of Crime* (New York: International Universities Press, 1960), pp. 244-67.

15. Among nonfictional biographies and autobiographies are the following: *Madeleine: An Autobiography* (New York: Harper, 1919); Sheila Cousins, *To Beg I Am Ashamed* (New York: Vanguard Press, 1938), which was reprinted under the title *Prostitute* (New York: Lancer Books, 1962); Serge G. Wolsey, *Call House Madam* (San Francisco: The Martin Tudordale Corporation, 1942); Polly Adler, *A House Is Not a Home* (New York: Rinehart Books, 1953); O. W. [Marjorie Smith], *God Have Mercy on Me* (New York: Sheridan House, 1931), as well as *No Bed of Roses* (New York: Macaulay, 1930) and *With My Eyes Wide Open* (New York: Sheridan House, 1949) by the same author; Nancy Dean with Jack Powers, *Twenty Years Behind Red Curtains* (Chicago: Newsstand Library, 1959); Carol Erwin with Floyd Miller, *The Orderly Disorderly House* (New York: Doubleday, 1960); Ben L. Reitman, *Sister of the Road: The Autobiography of Box Car Bertha* (New York: Sheridan House, 1937); Susan Kale, *The Fire Escape* (New York: Doubleday, 1960); Sara Harris, *Nobody Cries for Me* (New York: Signet Library, 1959); Virginia McManus, *Not for Love* (New York: G. P. Putnam's Sons, 1960); Anonymous, *Street Walker* (London: Bodley Head, 1959); Martha Watts, *The Men in My Life* (New York: Lyle Stuart, 1960); Madame Sherry [Ruth Barnes] with S. Robert Tralins, *Pleasure Was My Business* (New York: Lyle Stuart, 1961); Helen Cromwell, with Robert Dougherty, *Dirty Helen* (Los Angeles: Sherbourne Press, 1966); Sally Stanford, *The Lady of the House* (New York: G. P. Putnam's Sons, 1966); Iolana Mitsuko, *Honolulu Madam* (Los Angeles: Holloway House Publishing Company, 1969); Helen "Rocking Chair" McGowan, *Big City Madam* (New York: Lancer Books, 1965); Pauline Tabor, *Pauline's* (New York: Fawcett Crest Book, 1973); Xaviera Hollander, with Robin Moore and Yvonne Dunleavy, *The Happy Hooker* (New York: Dell Publishing Co., 1972); Ms. Hollander made herself into an industry, and there are several additional volumes in her series; Terry Randall, *Hooker* (New York: Award Books, 1969); Kristin Anderson with Linda DuBreuil, *The Wholesome Hooker* (New York: Norton Publications, 1973); there are many others in our collection from the United States and elsewhere.

16. Jim Smith and Bonnie Bullough, "Sexuality and the Severely Disabled Person," *American Journal of Nursing* 75 (December 1975), pp. 2194-97.

17. Emile Durkheim, *Suicide: A Study in Sociology*, translated by John A. Spaulding and George Simpson (Glencoe, Ill.: The Free Press, 1951). The original French edition was published in 1897.

18. Charles Winick and Paul M. Kinzie, *Prostitution in the United States* (Chicago: Quadrangle Books, 1971), p. 225.

19. Isabel Drummond, *The Sex Paradox* (New York: G. P. Putnam's Sons, 1953) and John Roeburt, *Sex Life and the Criminal Law* (New York: Belmont Books, 1963), pp. 33-39.

20. A good guide to prostitution in the Europe of the early seventies is Allan H. Mankhoff, *Mankhoff's Lusty Europe* (New York: Viking, 1972).

21. C. Arnelunxen, "Moderne Erscheinungs formen der Zühälterei," *Neue Polizei* XXI (1967), 12-16, and Winick and Kinzie, op. cit., p. 288.

22. *Report of the Committee on Homosexual Offences and Prostitution* (London: Her Majesty's Stationery Office, 1957). The report is often called the Wolfenden Report after its chairman, Sir John Wolfenden.

23. James, op. cit., pp. 28-56.

24. Walter C. Reckless, *Vice in Chicago* (Chicago: University of Chicago Press, 1933), chap. 3.

25. *New York Times,* November 11, 1936.

26. See, for example, Christina and Richard Milner, *Black Players* (Boston: Little, Brown and Company, 1972); Susan Hall, *Gentleman of Leisure* (New York: New American Library, 1972); Sara Harris, *They Sell Sex* (Greenwich, Conn.: Fawcett Publications, 1960); Monroe Fry, *Sex, Vice and Business* (New York: Ballantine Books, 1959); and Ed Reid, *The Mistress and the Mafia: The Virginia Hill Story* (New York: Bantam Books, 1972).

27. Karl Abraham, *Selected Papers,* translated by Douglas Bryan and Alix Strachey (London: Hogarth Press, 1942), chap. XXII, "Manifestations of the Female Castration Complex," p. 361. This paper was written in 1920.

28. Arnold S. Maerov, "Prostitution: A Survey and Review of 20 Cases," *Psychiatric Quarterly,* XXXIX (1965), 675-701, especially p. 680. His survey was helpful.

29. Glover, op. cit., passim.

30. Frank Caprio and Donald Brenner, *Sexual Behavior: Psycho-Legal Aspects* (New York: Citadel Press, 1961), pp. 249-52.

31. Tigor Agoston, "Some Psychological Aspects of Prostitution—the Pseudo-Personality," *International Journal of Psycho-Analysis,* XXVI (1945), 62-67.

32. Helene Deutsch, "The Genesis of Agoraphobia," *International Journal of Psycho-Analysis,* X (1929), 51-69, and vol. I of *The Psychology of Women* (New York: Grune & Stratton, 1944).

33. H. Lichtenstein, "Identity and Sexuality," *Journal of the American Psychoanalytic Association,* IX (April, 1961), 179-260.

34. J. Lampi de Groot, "The Evolution of the Oedipus Complex in Women," *International Journal of Psychoanalysis,* IX (1928), 322.

35. Marc H. Hollender, "Prostitution, the Body and Human Relatedness," *International Journal of Psycho-Analysis,* XLII (1961), 404-13.

36. Thomas S. Szasz, *Pain and Pleasure—A Study of Body Feelings* (New York: Basic Books, 1957).

37. F. Wengraf, "Fragment of an Analysis of a Prostitute," *Journal of Criminal Psychopathology,* V (October, 1943), 247-53.

38. P. L. Gotoin, "The Potential Prostitute," *Journal of Criminal Psychopathology,* III (January, 1942), 359-67.

39. Maryse Choisy, *Psychoanalysis of the Prostitute* (New York: Philosophical Library, 1961).

40. Maryse Choisy, *A Month Among the Girls,* translated by Lawrence G. Blochman (New York: Pyramid Books, 1960). The book was first published in 1928.

41. See, for example, Sandor Fereczi, *Contributions to Psychoanalysis* (Boston: Richard C. Badger, 1916), p. 269; Sandor Rado, *Psychoanalysis of Behavior* (New York: Grune and Stratton, 1956), p. 116; Eustace Chesser, *Live and Let Live* (New York: Philosophical Library, 1958), and Siegfried Borelli and Willy Starck, *Die Prostitution als Psychologischen Problem* (Berlin: Springer-Verlag, 1957).

42. Harold Greenwald, *The Call Girl: A Social and Psychoanalytic Study* (New York: Ballantine Books, 1958), passim; a revised edition of this was published under the title *The Elegant Prostitute* (New York: Walker, 1970).

43. Anonymous, *Women of the Streets,* edited by C. H. Rolph (London: Secker and Warburg, 1955), pp. 46-50.

44. Alfred C. Kinsey, Wardell B. Pomeroy, Clyde E. Martin, Paul H. Gebhard, *Sexual Behavior in the Human Female* (Philadelphia: W. B. Saunders, 1953).

45. Wardell B. Pomeroy, "Some Aspects of Prostitution," *The Journal of Sex Research* I (November, 1965), 177-87.

46. T. C. N. Gibbons, "Juvenile Prostitution," *The British Journal of Delinquency,* VIII (July, 1957), 3-12.

47. Norman R. Jackman, Richard O'Toole, and Gilbert Geis, "The Self-Image of the Prostitute," *The Sociological Quarterly,* IV (1963), 150-61.

48. See the list of biographies and autobiographies in footnote 15 above.

49. For some accounts of these works as well as guides to others, see Harold Greenwald and Aron Krich, *The Prostitute in Literature* (New York: Ballantine Books, 1960); Martin

ACKNOWLEDGMENTS

This book, we hope, will encourage further investigations into the subject of prostitution, a field that until recently has been neglected or ignored by scholars and scientists. Research for this book was in part supported by the Erickson Educational Foundation. Our attitudes toward the prostitute and prostitution have changed somewhat over the years since we first began writing about it in the late 1950s and early 1960s, and this change has come about in part from our research and in part from our acquaintance with prostitutes themselves. To gather material for our book we have traveled extensively throughout the world and interviewed, observed, and researched wherever we have gone. In the process we built up a major research library dealing with prostitution, part of which is now in the university library at California State University, Northridge, and part in our own personal library. We owe a great debt to librarians in the many countries we have visited. Several typists helped prepare versions of this manuscript including Joy Thornbury, Debra Heisler, Patricia Messinger, and Diane Mann. This edition of the book would not have been possible without the encouragement of Paul Kurtz, Doris Doyle, and Victor Gulotta. Special thanks is also due to Elizabeth Darhansoff for her help in getting permission to reprint it.

INDEX

INDEX